PERSPECTIVES ON
HUMAN COMMUNICATION

Perspectives on Human Communication

B. AUBREY FISHER

Professor of Communication, University of Utah

MACMILLAN PUBLISHING CO., INC.
NEW YORK

COLLIER MACMILLAN PUBLISHERS
LONDON

Macmillan Publishing Co., Inc.
866 Third Avenue, New York, New York 10022

Collier Macmillan Canada, Ltd.

Library of Congress Cataloging in Publication Data

Fisher, B   Aubrey, (date)
  Perspectives on human communication.

  Includes bibliographical references and index.
  1. Interpersonal communication.   I. Title.
BF637.C45F57   301.14   77–1144
ISBN 0–02–337990–1

Printing: 4 5 6 7 8   Year: 1 2 3 4

— Preface —

During the process of writing this book, I was continually asked what "new theory" I was presenting. When I explained that I was not presenting a "new theory," the response was typically one of absolute bewilderment. People would ask, implicitly or explicitly, "Then why are you writing a book?" There were certainly times when I pondered that same question myself.

This book attempts to provide no "new" theory or reconceptualization of communication. I am not even sure that a new theory of communication is possible, although I am convinced that one is not desirable at this stage of theoretical development. This book provides no whither-are-we-going analysis, either; that is, I do not attempt a stock-taking synthesis directed at some rose-colored view of the future of communication theory. Such analyses invariably turn out to be a "first affirmative" for the author's pet biases and, consequently, provide only a myopic view of theoretical development. My purpose in writing this book is fundamentally different.

The story is told of the city slicker who was lost on a back-country road. He drove aimlessly for hours until he chanced upon a farmer leaning against a fence near the road. He immediately stopped his shiny new car and inquired, "Could you tell me the directions to the nearest town?" The farmer replied, "Nope." The city slicker was surprised but persistent. "Well, then, could you show me how to get back to the main highway?" Again the farmer responded, "Nope." Now thoroughly exasperated, the city slicker screamed, "Don't you know anything?" The reply: "Nope. But I ain't lost neither!"

There are three basic questions in the process of any serious inquiry—the road to understanding and knowledge. Where am I going? How do I get there? Where am I now? We in communication have placed too much emphasis, perhaps, on the first two questions. The result has been a continual internal squabbling over whose approach to the study of communication is better, which techniques are more "scientific," which "theory" is better—in short, quibbling and nitpicking with no results other than shortened tempers. It seems to me that the fundamental question is the third—where are we now? The present analysis of competing perspectives characterizing the field of communication addresses this where-are-we-now question. Implicitly, the competition of the perspectives within the scientific community reflects, as well, the absence of any dominant theoretical approach to the study of human communication.

I have discussed the ideas included in this book with a number of colleagues and acquaintances. Some have accused me of being too relativistic; others have called me too rigid. Some have characterized me as a data-crunching experimentalist; others have called me a bleeding-heart humanist. A few have even intimated that they might actually agree with me. Frankly, I enjoy a good argument and hope that this volume does stir some controversy. Nothing is more damaging to one's ego than being ignored!

Whereas the credit for many of the ideas in this book must go to many people and many influences, I don't wish any of them to share the blame for my own idiosyncrasies. Nevertheless, I do feel some need to acknowledge and express my appreciation, however inadequately: to Lloyd Chilton, whose patience is apparently inexhaustible; to students, past and present, who will probably never realize that I was the real student; to colleagues and friends, with whom insults and arguments have become signs of close personal friendship and abiding respect; to Lee, Terry, and Tracy, who provide for me the ultimate argument against birth control; and to Irene, with whom I would look forward to growing old if the present were not so downright enjoyable!

B. A. F.

— Contents —

Part Two   The Perspectives

Part Three   Conceptual Implications

— PART ONE —

THE STUDY OF HUMAN COMMUNICATION

—1—

Orientation to Human Communication

Donald Lang is deaf—totally, irrevocably deaf. His story is true. It is simply too incredible to be fiction. In 1965, at the age of twenty, Donald Lang was accused of murder, a charge finally dismissed in 1971 after a series of bizarre legal battles unprecedented in legal history. Less than a year later under even more bizarre circumstances, Donald Lang was again charged with murder. The legalistic catch-22s, courtroom battles, and unbelievable twists of fate are the subject matter of *Dummy*, a best seller by Ernest Tidyman. Were it not for the criminal charges brought against Donald, his story might never have been known outside Chicago.

To call Donald Lang "dummy" is probably an error. In the sense that *dummy* implies substandard intelligence, psychologists and psychiatrists who examined Donald after his first murder charge disagreed vehemently as to his intellectual capacity. Whereas some considered him a virtual moron, others believed him to be above average in intelligence. They did agree on one factor of his IQ—the virtually insurmountable difficulty in measuring it. True, Donald's deafness was due to aphasia owing to brain damage of undetermined origin. But his intellectual capacity was apparently not affected by his aphasia.

In the sense that "dummy" refers to an inability to utter any sound, Donald Lang was not necessarily a dummy. Although his utterances were not intelligible, Donald was physiologically, at least, not dumb. Nevertheless, for all practical purposes, Donald Lang was a deaf-mute.

3

What distinguishes Donald Lang from the mainstream of society and provides the basis for his social and legal problems is not his deafness but his capability for human communication. In one strict sense Donald could "communicate" in that he could convey simple needs or wants through his own primitive sign language. But in a more important sense Donald could not communicate at all. He was undoubtedly never aware that he was ever on trial for a crime. Indeed, he could not even conceptualize the meaning of "crime," let alone a courtroom or a trial. For in the true tradition of anthropocentrism, Donald Lang was subhuman! He could communicate little better than a primate, an ape, a dolphin, a rat, a bee. Compared with a primate, Donald was utilizing a relatively sophisticated communication system. But in the sense of *human* communication, Donald Lang was subhuman.

Donald possessed no symptom of symbolic capacity—no knowledge of a language or an alphabet. He was unable to develop any human relationship. For example, his relationships with women were purely physical. He learned about prostitutes and would point to his genitals and offer money to signify his sexual desire. He would fulfill his desire for sex just as he fulfilled his desire for food. The notion of a more intimate social relationship with a woman, such as love, was beyond his ability to conceptualize.

Donald did develop some semblance of a relationship with some laborers unloading trucks and worked with them as something of a friend. He proved to be a good worker—strong, physically coordinated, eager, and to a great extent reliable. He learned to support himself with his own wages and learned the value of money. But the notion of striking for more pay and fringe benefits was not within his capacity to understand.

Most of us who learned at an early age the story of Helen Keller find the story of *Dummy* incomprehensible. After all, we say, Helen Keller was blind, too; yet she lived a productive life. For that matter, Donald's lawyer, Lowell Myers, was also totally deaf. And despite this handicap, Myers proceeded to earn his law degree and become a trial lawyer. Furthermore, he practiced law, in the sense of communicating, very "normally." Myers learned to speak—forcefully and with emphasis and inflection—even though he could not hear what he himself was saying. He memorized the appropriate way to make sounds with his larynx and mouth, lips, tongue, teeth, and so on. And he even memorized the appropriate patterns of pitch, inflection, volume. He was extremely adept at lipreading and using the sign language for the deaf. Helen Keller learned an equivalent sign language even though she could not see. What was wrong with Donald Lang? Truly, he must be a dummy.

The biggest difference between Donald Lang and Helen Keller or Lowell Myers was probably not ability but opportunity. Donald had no Anne Sullivan—no "miracle worker," no well-to-do parents to provide such specialized training or encouragement to continue the frustrating task of learning. Donald Lang is a product of the slums of Chicago— poor, orphaned, and black. As a child he had no opportunity to learn, for example, the concept of a language—letters, words, sentences. The public school system and private agencies refused to accept him as a student. As an adult, he was, emotionally perhaps, unable to learn. In fact, no educational system—public, private, or mental—was ever capable of adapting itself to fit his needs. His compassionate and ultimately helpless lawyer endured insufferable frustrations, sacrifices, and hardships. He, too, failed. Donald Lang became a sociological and psychological misfit.

In the end, society proved to be as unable to cope with Donald Lang as he was ill-equipped to cope with society. He is now destined to live out the remainder of his life in Cook County Jail, his final legal appeal exhausted, with little legal, rational, or moral assurance that he is guilty of any criminal act. The story of Donald Lang is, in every respect, a tragedy. It is a tragedy traceable at all levels to that phenomenal ability we all take for granted—the ability of human communication.

COMMUNICATION—THE PHLOGISTON OF SOCIETY

For centuries physicists and chemists explained the process of combustion, fire, through the presumed existence of phlogiston—a vitalistic substance that was allegedly contained in any combustible matter. Substances that burned readily, such as coal, were considered rich in phlogiston whereas other substances, such as metals, were thought to contain only a small amount of phlogiston. About the time of the American Revolution in the now classic experiments of Karl Scheele, Joseph Priestley, and Antoine Lavoisier, scientists rejected the phlogistic explanation of combustion in favor of an explanation based on a chemical union with the newly discovered gas that Lavoisier named oxygen. Now, two hundred years later, phlogiston is often employed as an analogy to describe an explanation fallaciously attributed to an imaginary cause.

In many respects communication is the phlogiston of society. What social problem exists that has not at one time or another been attributed to some problem of communication? For that matter, what social problem exists for which a proposed solution has not at one time or another involved "more" or "better" communication? At least one political scientist has depicted wars between nations as a problem of cultural misunderstanding that could be alleviated through international political communication. One of the oft-repeated premises underlying the United Nations begins something like this: "If only nations could just sit down and talk with each other. . . ." As for myself, one of the most memorable lines from Hollywood is that uttered by the prison warden who keeps telling *Cool Hand Luke*, "What we've got here is a failure to communicate!" That statement in that context epitomizes the utter absurdity of the too prevalent belief that communication is or contains some phlogistonlike quality that explains nearly every aspect of social life. Yet someone somewhere sometime will persist in considering communication as the cause and/or the solution of racial strife, labor-management tension, the generation gap, corruption in government, ad infinitum. The tragedy of Donald Lang may indeed lie in his capacity, or lack of capacity, for human communication. That is what makes his story so extraordinary.

One of the words that has recently gained prominence through sheer repetition in the research literature describing communication is *ubiquitous*. I must plead guilty to using the word myself. But it is true. Communication is, if nothing else, ubiquitous. Everyone communicates. Communicative phenomena are everywhere. One certainly natural consequence of this ubiquity is that we are all too familiar with communication, so that every person considers himself or herself to be something of an "expert" on communication—problems and solutions. It seems strange that if our television set goes on the blink, we may test a few tubes at the corner discount store's tube-tester, but we ultimately call a television repairman if the problem is at all serious. If our wiring shorts out, we immediately call an electrician. When our plumbing goes, most of us call in a plumber. When we feel sick, we seek out a medical specialist. Yet when we have a communication problem, we are typically do-it-yourselfers.

A person who claims to be a specialist in communication is a relatively recent phenomenon. New acquaintances will often ask me just what it is that I do. The typical man or woman on the street understands a person who specializes in repairing television sets or even giving public speeches. But, overall, communication is simply ubiquitous. The result is a proliferation of conventional wisdom in our society about communication along with a frightening lack of understanding. The primary purpose of the present volume is to emphasize the latter and, correspondingly, to de-emphasize the former. To paraphrase an old cliché, an ounce of understanding is worth a pound of knowledge. If it is true that the most dangerous animal in the world is the person with one semester of psychology, the reason must be attributed to the possession of too much "knowledge" and too little "understanding." I fervently hope that this distinction becomes clear upon further reading.

DEFINING COMMUNICATION

If communication is ubiquitous, it is equally equivocal. Go to any convention of the International Communication Association or the Speech Communication Association—communication specialists all—and trip ten persons in the hall at random. Ask each of them to define his or her specialty, that is, communication. The chances are excellent that you will receive ten differing definitions. Granted, many of the definitions will possess overlapping properties, but probably none will be common to all definitions.

Although definitions of communication certainly differ, one can discern certain properties of communication that seem to receive greatest emphasis in typical definitions. For example, Berelson and Steiner (1964) focus on the "transmission" property when they define communication as "the transmission of information, ideas, emotions, skills, etc., by the use of symbols—words, pictures, figures, graphs, etc." The property of transmission is probably the most prevalent property of communication in the definitions of communication typically encountered. So, too, is the use of symbols in the transmission process.

The famous team of Shannon and Weaver (1949) also accept the transmission property but add another inherent property as they define communication "to include all of the procedures by which one mind may affect another." Similarly, Schachter (1951) writes that "communication is the mechanism by which power is exerted." Such definitions impute to communication the property of social control in which one person affects or seeks to affect the behavior, beliefs, attitudes, and so on, of another person in a social setting.

Dance (1967) defines communication within the broad framework of behavioristic psychology by defining human communication as "the eliciting of a response through verbal symbols" in which "verbal symbols" act as the stimuli for the elicited response. Gray and Wise (1959) concur with this behavioristic conceptualization of communication as "the presenting of stimuli" as well as "a response, real or imagined, as it comes into the awareness of the initiator of the process." Without dwelling on the assets and liabilities of behaviorism, one can safely assume that viewing communication in terms of stimuli-response phenomena reflects the influence of, broadly speaking, Skinnerian or behavioristic psychology along with its attendant revisions and refinements of recent years.

Yet another property of communication might have been the result of a desire to distinguish good or effective communication from bad or ineffective communication. Fotheringham (1966) indicates that the pervasive purpose of communication is highly pragmatic—"to help a receiver perceive a meaning similar to that in the mind of the communicator." Gode (1959) implies a similar property, typically called "shared meaning," when he defines communication to be "a process that makes common to two or several what was the monopoly of one or some." Without putting words in the mouths of Fotheringham and Gode, we take but a small logical step to infer that communication might be considered good or effective to the extent that the ideas, information, and so on, are shared by or common to those people involved in the communicative act.

It is not my purpose at this point to exhaust all classes of definitions of communication but rather to survey only a few basic properties that have been frequently suggested as the functional bases for defining the phenomenon of communication. One final property in this admittedly incomplete survey of definitional statements appears in the definition of communication advanced by Colin Cherry (1964): "the establishment of a social unit from individuals by the use of language or signs. The sharing of common sets of rules, for various goal-seeking activities." Harnack and Fest (1964), writing on group decision making, understandably utilize a similar definition of communication: "the process by which people interact for the purpose of interpersonal and intrapersonal integration." Edwin Newman (1948) also defines communication as "the process by which an aggregation of men is changed into a functioning group." Thus, the property of communication upon which these definitions are based appears to be that of social integration. Where communication exists, one might say that a social unit exists, and vice versa.

This brief survey of representative definitions should lead us to several conclusions. First, communication as a phenomenon is certainly equivocal. This is not to say that even the definitions surveyed above are necessarily inconsistent with each other. It would be more just to conclude that although those who define communication don't always agree with each other, they don't necessarily disagree. As a whole, these definitions indicate that two persons may possess knowledge of a phenomenon that might be equivalent, but their understanding of that phenomenon might be quite equivocal.

A second conclusion drawn from this survey is, perhaps, a corollary of the first. The distinction between knowledge and understanding might become clearer if we were to ask ourselves whether we are able to identify a specific phenomenon as communication when we confront it. Every student new to the study of human communication becomes engrossed, at some time or another, with such quasi-philosophical questions as, "Can a person engage in communication when he is absolutely alone?" Coupled with such tree-falling-in-the-forest issues is a question such as, "Is one engaged in communication when he stubs his toe on a rock?" Laying these angels-on-the-head-of-a-pin trivialities aside momentarily, nearly all of us will agree that we can and do recognize communication as communication when we see it in the real world. We see two people talking with one another, and we will invariably label it communication. We watch television and agree that we are engaged in communication. In other words, few people disagree, broadly speaking, on the identity of the phenomenon called communication. But many will disagree on the crucial properties that constitute that phenomenon.

An analogy might aid in clarifying further this distinction between knowledge and understanding. Consider a physical object such as an automobile. An auto mechanic observing the automobile sees a finely tuned mechanism consisting of an internal combustion engine, a transmission, steering linkages, brakes, and so on. A commuter observes a mode of transportation that is expensive and difficult to park but convenient. An avid environmentalist sees a pollution-generating monster created and sustained by a technological society. An antique buff sees the classic styling and engineering of a nonduplicated era in auto manufacturing.

Our list could continue indefinitely, but the point should be clear. Regardless of the reasons for these differing "definitions" of the automobile, the significant factor is that not one of these definitions is "wrong" in any sense of the term. Although the definitions are in disagreement, not one of the definitions presumes that another definition is in error. Knowledge, in general, incorporates all these definitions. But understanding requires that one of the definitions be selected and used.

A completely thorough understanding, of course, would involve all the definitions being employed—one at a time or in combinations. And conclusions drawn from those understandings might differ. For example, the environmentalist might conclude with a negative evaluation of the automobile whereas the antique buff might infer a highly positive evaluation of the same automobile. The point remains. Neither is wrong. Both may have precisely the same knowledge, but their understanding of that knowledge is in conflict.

If any truism is universally applicable to the whole of communication (or for the social sciences, for that matter), it is simply this: *The phenomenon of communication is a constant. It does not change. Only our understanding of it changes.* That is, communication, the phenomenon itself, is not problematic. Only human understanding of communication is problematic.

Only a few years ago I was disturbed that the field that I had chosen for my academic specialty, namely, communication, suffered from an identity crisis. We who are actively involved in its study could not even come close to agreeing even on its definition. None of my sociologist or psychologist friends alleviated my concern when they informed me that their own specialties suffered from a highly similar identity crisis. I vainly sought to provide a definition of communication for the students in my classes (and for myself) that would incorporate all the equivocality of existing definitions. Such a task I now believe to be not only impossible but distinctly trivial.

I came late to the conclusion that definitions of communication aren't really that important after all. In fact, defining communication is incredibly simple. But understanding communication is considerably more complex. It is infinitely more important to understand what the definition does or does not imply, what the definition considers to be or not to be the crucial properties. In other words, anyone with one semester (or less) of communication study can define communication. It is the advanced student of communication who finds definitions more difficult and less fruitful. In fact, definitions probably evolve as the result of advanced study of the phenomena of communication rather than as a preliminary step in its initial stages.

Some of you will probably find the preceding discussion quite unsatisfying. You will demand that any book with the word *communication* in its title must be capable of defining its principal phenomenon. I fear these readers will remain frustrated. I can only respond to the request for a definition of communication with the most pervasive of all qualifications —it all depends on your perspective. A definition of communication ensues from the perspective employed to understand it; it does not provide the basis for the perspective. But perspectives are the focus of Part Two of this book. Any further discussion of definitions from perspectives is premature in this initial chapter.

To alleviate perhaps some of the potential frustrations, I can assure such readers what this book is *not* about. For one thing, this book is concerned with *human* communication and avoids overgeneralizing the phenomenon of communication beyond that of humans. As such, this volume will not consider the study of a computer, for example, "talking" to another computer. Nor will it concern itself with the physiological/biological similarities between humans and nonhumans. (See, for example, Marler, 1961.) Nor will our discussion of communication as human allow for including the study of behavioral similarities or dissimilarities between humans and (take your pick) rats, primates, fish, apes, rhesus monkeys, bees, Galápagos turtles, ravens, and so on. (See Bertalanffy's [1967] discussion of the "zoomorphic fallacy.") When the word *communication* occurs in the pages following, the reader can read "human communication"—a process uniquely and exclusively human.

Although the book deals with human communication, it is also not interested in differentiating what makes human communication unique. Stuart Altmann (1965) provides a succinct statement for justifying the separation of human and primate communication for those interested in pursuing this matter. For example, Altmann focuses on the nature of symbols and linguistic variability as the basis for his distinction. Few will need further justification for eliminating nonhuman communication from our discussion; but for those who do, I direct you to Altmann's discussion.

This book is also not concerned with a physiological explication of communication. I am aware, for example, of the vast quantity of such research, typically involved in language usage specifically, which pinpoints the areas of the brain most actively involved in communication. Although the posterior-superior portion of the temporal lobe and the area in front of the cortical representation should be most important for communication students, this communication student is more concerned with nonphysiological perspectives of the communicative process—behavioral, perceptual, and so on. Consequently, this body of research, though potentially relevant, is excluded from the present discussion.

COMMUNICATION—AN HISTORICAL VIEW

The identity crisis of communication suggests the obvious question as to whether such diverse perspectives are identifiable within the single umbrella of a unified discipline of study; that is, is communication a phenomenon of human activity (albeit very important) that is only a variable of interest to a variety of disciplines, or is communication identifiable as a discipline of study on its own merits? The fact that I am a degree holder from a university department of communication and presently a faculty member of a university department of communication should suggest that this question is rhetorical at best and that the answer to it is obvious. And, of course, it is. I have addressed this introspection before (1974) for another purpose and with a slightly different conclusion. Nevertheless, the question is a valid one and not worthy of early dismissal.

The fact that many disciplines involve themselves directly and indirectly in the study of communication suggests that communication is highly eclectic. But other phenomena are also the province of numerous disciplines—for example, personality, attitudes, human values, perception, groups, culture, and so on. But a university department of, say, perception simply does not seem credible. Certainly, eclecticism can be a vice as well as a virtue. Whereas the dialogue across disciplinary boundaries should lead to fresh insights and innovative ideas, it can just as easily lead to misunderstanding, noncollaboration, and polemics. The late Malcolm MacLean (1969, p. 205) has warned that scholars in the field of communication "engage in too much borrowing and imitating and too little creating and inventing."

Despite the obvious misunderstandings and noninteraction prevalent among those involved in the study of communication, it is important to an understanding of perspectives on human communication that the eclectic nature of communication study be clearly understood. Historically, the study of communication numbers among the two or three oldest identifiable disciplines existing today. But the evolution of communication study over the centuries has at once broadened and narrowed the study until it has achieved its present form (or, more accurately, forms).

The Rhetorical Tradition

If the ancient Greeks had a synonym for communication, that word would be *rhetoric,* a word that persists in our contemporary English language with considerable modification in its meaning. Today we use the term *rhetoric* (often with the antecedent *mere*) to signify emptiness of discourse, generally artificial, and typically at the expense of truth or thoughtfulness. Two thousand years ago, however, the term referred to a field of study considered absolutely indispensable and extremely valuable for success in ancient Greek society.

Some evidence suggests that the study of rhetoric predates Greece and existed in the ancient Egyptian culture with such rhetoricians as Kagemni and Ptah-Hotep. Nevertheless, the earliest extant systematization of rhetoric is that of Aristotle—logician, philosopher, and sophist (that is, teacher of rhetoric). Aristotle's systematization serves as the bench mark against which other treatments of rhetoric are compared. As late as 1965, Ed Black used Aristotle as the keystone for his treatment of a neo-Aristotelian school of rhetorical criticism (that is, the scholarly analysis and evaluation of discourse through application of criteria). Much of the contemporary research in persuasion and mass communication exhibits the influence of Aristotle although many of the researchers do not always acknowledge their heritage.

To understand the underpinnings of communication in the Greco-

Roman study of rhetoric requires an understanding of the culture contemporaneous with ancient Greece and, later, Rome. Theirs was an oral tradition. Information and news spread by word of mouth—no radio, television, or newspaper. Whereas Aristotle considered rhetoric to include written as well as oral discourse, success in the culture was pragmatically the province of oral eloquence—not written. In politics it was the speaker whom people voted for or against. Lawyers did not exist. Each citizen was required to argue his own case in court. Success in life was clearly attributable to one's skill in the art of rhetoric.

Artistotle viewed rhetoric as inherently persuasive. He considered rhetoric the counterpart of dialectic (broadly defined as seeking truth through dialogue) and believed it inherently involved advocating truth. In situations in which the truth is not obvious, rhetoric was essential to persuade the audience of the truth. Aristotle classified those situations as deliberative (exhorting an audience to a course of action typically in the context of the legislative assembly), forensic (dealing with justice and defense typically in the context of the courts), and epideictic (bestowing of praise or blame typically in the context of some special occasion or ceremony).

Aristotle defined rhetoric to include all the available means of persuasion and went on to schematize those means under the broad rubrics of ethos, pathos, and logos. Ethos is equivalent to the contemporary concept of communicator or source credibility. Pathos might refer to nonlogical proofs and has often been oversimplified as appeals to underlying or implicit emotional premises. Logos includes the appeals of logical argument, the formal basis for which Aristotle considered to be the rhetorical enthymeme rather than the logical syllogism (developed in Aristotle's exposition of a logical system in the *Organon*).

Aristotle was one of the earliest psychologists as well. Although his knowledge of psychology was understandably primitive, he strongly espoused the speaker's adaptation to the situation and to the audience. He clearly foresaw that adaptation required selecting strategies from among the available means of persuasion in order to achieve the persuasive effect desired by the rhetor. Aristotle, together with the Roman orator Cicero, canonized rhetoric into five basic elements: invention (lines of argument), disposition (organization or arrangement of ideas), elocution (the linguistic style or choice of words used to express ideas), memory, and pronunciation (more specifically, delivery). For Aristotle the most important of these was probably invention, which he also classified into *topoi* or lines of argument, which are generalizable across all subject areas.

A discussion of the Greco-Roman tradition of rhetoric, however brief, is quite incomplete without a discussion of ethics and the "sophistic"—

an incredible parallel with contemporary American society. Because material and social success in the ancient Greek culture with its oral tradition was so dependent upon rhetorical skills, teaching those skills developed into a flourishing business. The rhetoricians who headed these schools were called sophists. At one time, sophists were highly respected educators and scholars, who included among their number such notables as Plato, Aristotle, and Socrates, to name just a few.

As is true of contemporary educational institutions, the worth of the school was often judged on a purely pragmatic basis. Did the students successfully defend themselves in court? Become successful businessmen or politicians? Soon logography (ghostwriting) flourished in response to these pragmatic demands for successful persuasion. Although logography was looked down upon and even outlawed, ethics eventually gave way to pragmatics and sophistry, thereby endowing the latter term with its present implications of specious reasoning and deceptive argument. Pragmatically, a sophist earned his living and reputation on the basis of the success of his students. And if that meant teaching the students or ghostwriting speeches by using techniques that made the worse appear the better, so be it.

It requires little imagination to see a highly similar sophistic principle operating in modern advertising. The success of an advertising agency is based on pragmatics—do its products sell?—and hardly at all on ethics. Today advertising agencies package sensual experiences and sell them as products; they package images of people and sell them as political candidates. In fact, the title of a recent best-selling book suggests that advertising agencies, in the role of twentieth-century sophists, sell even the president of the United States. Of course, I do not mean to imply that all advertising agencies are unethical and make the worse appear the better. Nor were all sophists evil. Nevertheless, the reputation of the sophists is, in many ways, being transferred to the reputation of the advertising agencies.

Aristotle was keenly aware of the ethical dangers in the sophists and emphasized character as an essential component of ethos. Given the culture of his day, if modern factor analysis of credibility scales could have been performed on ancient Greek audiences, character might well have been the key factor of communicator credibility. The Roman Quintilian also emphasized the character of the rhetor and laid out an entire educational program to develop such ethos. His analysis of rhetoric has been summarized as a blend of ethics and skill—the good man speaking well.

Through the twenty-four centuries since Aristotle, each of the five canons has been emphasized at one time or another with the exception of disposition and memory (considered to be the "lost canon," certainly precipitated by the vastly increased ability to package and store information). Style or elocution achieved its greatest prominence in the nineteenth century, and the distinction between the rhetorical and the poetic blurred with the subsequent emphasis on figures of speech, tropes, and schemes. Even as late as the early twentieth century, style seemed in vogue as a principal canon of rhetorical discourse. (Read some of the speeches of Daniel Webster, William Jennings Bryan, or even Everett Dirksen, for example.)

The elocutionary movement of the nineteenth century (and early twentieth century in the United States) emphasized the canon of pronunciation or delivery. Such emphasis increased still further the distrust of the too eloquent speaker, the glib of tongue, the stereotypical pitchman. The elocutionary movement nurtured a newer and more modern sophistic era.

The current study of communication includes the oral tradition, but evolutionary differences in cultures have broadened the study to include phenomena other than just public speaking and persuasion. The tradition remains prominent in the term used by former speech departments to identify themselves in many universities—departments of "speech communication." Malcolm MacLean (1969) scoffed at the term and considered it redundant and superfluous. He is, of course, quite correct. But the term *speech communication* clearly identifies the study of communication that has evolved directly from the rhetorical tradition and is quite meaningful for that reason. I presume that eventually the word *speech* will be eliminated from the departmental titles, leaving only *communication* as the distinguishing term. That change is probably inevitable, quite natural, and eminently sensible. But the rhetorical tradition underlying the evolution of the contemporary study of communication will never be discarded.

The Sociopsychological Influence

Clearly the most natural area of concern common to communication and social psychology was the psychological study of attitudes and attitude change. For twentieth-century "communicologists" (for lack of a better term) nurtured on the Aristotelian version of rhetoric as persuasion, the psychologists' research exploring the development of attitudes, beliefs, images, and values along with their modification was certainly relevant and a logical starting point for an interdisciplinary study of communicative phenomena. To a great extent the interdisciplinary cooperation has been unilateral, with communication specialists acknowledging and borrowing from the psychologists much more than psychologists' acknowledgment and borrowing from communication specialists. Nevertheless, the study of persuasion and attitude change has been a major specialty within both fields.

Perhaps the greatest influence of psychology, principally social psychology, on the study of communication has been the expansion of research methodologies employed in communication research. Whereas critical methods characterized the bulk of communication research several decades ago, contemporary communication research includes a vast array of methodologies and techniques. A cursory review of professional journals specializing in communication research over the past decade or two would reveal the prolific use of laboratory experimentation, field observation, case studies, natural history, and participant observation (among many others), along with a full complement of various critical methodologies.

One of the advantages of eclecticism would appear to be the resistance to a unimethodological approach to research problems. Although many would probably disagree, no single methodology nor even a few methodologies have clearly demonstrated any degree of superiority as most appropriate to researching the various phenomena of human communication. Although many, if not most, people actively involved in the study of communication (and I include myself) have emphatically declared their preferences for using certain methodologies, no rational basis appears to exist for denying others the right to use other methods to study fruitfully those same phenomena. The general issue of methodological approaches is the subject of further discussion in Chapter 3.

The development of symbolic interaction as a rather broad perspective from which to view human social behavior has demonstrated enormous impact on the study of human communication. Although symbolic interaction is broader in scope than the study of communication (unlike attitude change), the theoretical and philosophical assumptions of interactionism have proved so potent that some communication scholars identify themselves as interactionists, even though they may possess little comprehensive understanding of symbolic interactionism itself. In fact, symbolic interaction serves as the philosophical basis for one of the perspectives of human communication discussed in Part Two.

The contributory influence of sociology and psychology on communication is too pervasive to receive more than a cursory examination. Certainly, the impact of sociologists' writing on social movements has affected movement studies in the field of communication. The research in diffusion of information and innovations and persuasive campaigns has been reflected in communication research. The sociopsychological study of groups—that is, group dynamics, encounter groups, group problem solving, reference groups, and so on—has exerted enormous impact on the study of group phenomena in communication (an outgrowth of the Greco-Roman study of dialectic). The mathematical approaches to decision making, such as game theory, behavioral decision theory, utility theory, decision modeling, and so on, have been employed by communication researchers. Therapeutic or medical communication is only recently coming into its own as a consequence of communication scholars' bridging the gap between communication and psychotherapy and clinical psychology. A relatively new field of communication, sometimes termed "personal communication," reflects the impact of humanistic psychology, among other influences from various aspects of sociology and psychology.

This list could be much longer, but the point should now be emphatic. For the most part, these influences are peripheral, though clearly relevant, to the primary focus of this book: broad perspectives used to explain the process of human communication. With few exceptions, such influences have been more methodological than theoretical, or they can be incorporated within a more general theoretical framework. It is sufficient to say that the sociopsychological influence on communication has demonstrated a significant impact on all areas of communication study—theoretical, methodological, and technical. A more complete description of that impact should be increasingly apparent in the later discussion of perspectives in Part Two.

The Language Influence

An entire field of study directly relevant to the broader framework of human communication is the emphasis on language and language use. Although the study of language is, like the broader field of communication, interdisciplinary, several approaches are discernible. One approach attempts to relate linguistic structure and use with social structure and social institutions. Such an approach raises such intriguing questions as the interaction between linguistic structure and development with cultural development, the functions of language in social conflict, social control, social status, or group solidarity. Such a field embraces many linguistic systems and may even draw parallels or contrasts between one language system and another as well as observe the problems unique to multilingualism.

A second approach to language study involves a direct observation of the structure or syntactics of a language in an attempt to discern semantic aspects or meanings implicitly contained within the structure. Though this approach is not divorced from cultural phenomena or the use of language within a culture, the greater emphasis seems to be on understanding semantic (that is, meaning) aspects of language rather than social institutions.

A third approach traces language acquisition and development within a selected linguistic community. Such studies might involve observing patterns of linguistic socialization of persons entering the system (for example, newborn infants through adulthood, persons moving from one language-using community to another as immigrants) or the linguistic development of a primitive or emerging culture (or possibly subculture).

A fourth approach to language study is that of general semantics, an attempt to alleviate misunderstanding generated by language use. General semantics has decreased in popularity in recent years but still boasts many adherents who seek to uncover linguistic origins of ineffective meaning transference and to manipulate language use for the purpose of clarifying those meanings. The key purpose of general semantics is apparently to alleviate misunderstanding among communicating individuals.

The influence of psycholinguistics, sociolinguistics, anthropological linguistics, ethnolinguistics, general semantics, and the other varied forms of language study is still being felt in the field of human communication. The number of people who consider themselves "communicologists" with a specialty in language or language behavior is growing steadily. The study of communicative phenomena through the viewpoint of language is clearly an increasingly important area within the field of human communication.

The Mathematics Influence

The year 1949 marked an important event in the historical development of the disciplinary study of human communication. The publication of Shannon and Weaver's *The Mathematical Theory of Communication* provided two elements that gave impetus to those scholars who considered themselves communication specialists. First, Shannon and Weaver's book brought increased scientific respectability and interest to the study of human communication in the minds of many formerly disinterested scholars. It further spurred vast amounts of theorizing and research directly and indirectly attributable to that single book.

Second, Shannon and Weaver's book signaled the clear advent of information theory as a methodological tool as well as a quasi-theoretical

perspective of communication. Although information theory borrows heavily from the earlier cybernetics, this book provided a formalization that theretofore had not been present.

Ironically, Claude Shannon was an engineer—not a "communicologist" or even a social scientist. It is not surprising, then, that his overall view of human communication was highly mechanistic and of minimal direct value to the study of human communication as a social science. His mathematical formulations that provide the basis for information theory, on the other hand, have proved extremely valuable to other fields, such as computer science, as well as to communication in the form of analytical techniques. The concept of binary digits (that is, information "bits," for short), removal of uncertainty, and $\log_2$-based statistics have experienced wide usage in subsequent analyses of language structure and patterns of interaction. Though not universally or directly applicable to all perspectives of human communication, information theory is a significant and highly useful milestone in the development of a theory of human communication. Its value will be more apparent in the discussion of specific perspectives in Part Two.

In conclusion, one can state without fear of contradiction that the eclecticism of communication as a disciplinary study is at once a blessing and a curse. Similarity, rather than unity, is the hallmark of the many and varied approaches within the discipline of communication. Borrowing loosely from a criterion of "scientific method" suggested by Diesing (1971, p. 319), we might suggest that the field of human communication as a disciplinary study implies "regular, effective collaboration with other members" of the scientific community. Certainly, such collaboration is more the exception than the rule. For example, one of the top-rated papers presented to the Western Speech Communication Association in 1975 was a critical analysis of research into source or communicator credibility—still a major focus of many communication scholars. By contrast, Backman and Secord, nine years earlier in 1966, suggested that for the field of social psychology, "the focus . . . is on dynamic processes rather than such older problems of the influence of the [perceived] characteristics of the communicator, [although] these older questions have by no means been fully answered."

One hopes that the years ahead will see more collaboration and greater unity among scholars involved in communication research and less misunderstanding and polemics within the ranks. One giant step in this direction is an understanding of the diverse perspectives currently being used to understand and organize the phenomena of human communication.

The present volume is directed specifically toward that end—greater understanding.

BASIC ASSUMPTION—COMMUNICATION IS A SOCIAL SCIENCE

One assumed premise underlying the writing of this book is important to an understanding of its purpose. That premise, simply stated, is that the formal study of human communication can be accurately characterized as a social science. At first glance, this assumption seems noncontroversial, superfluous, and not particularly meaningful. Speaking quite generally, *social* implies that communication involves people. Of course it does! And *science* implies a systematic scholarly inquiry. Little to quarrel with at this point. Nevertheless, some issues remain unresolved with this broad characterization of the dualistic term—social science.

"Humanistic" Studies Versus "Scientific" Studies

For years the tendency to dichotomize has constituted a typical human endeavor. We tend to perceive entities in relation to their opposites. A person is either liberal or conservative, right-wing or left-wing, good or bad, young or old. To the true believers, others are either with them or against them. The tendency to portray observables in black-and-white terms (literally, as well, as witnessed by the official apartheid policies of, for example, the Republic of South Africa) may be the result of some negative imperative inherent in language (see Burke, 1952). But for whatever reason, a clear schism has been drawn between scholarly approaches as being either humanistic or scientific. Implicitly, that which is humanistic isn't scientific and vice versa.

Brodbeck (1968, p. 2) succumbs to the pressure to sustain this dichotomy by depicting a scientific faction as one that "embraces the scientific ideal" whereas the humanistic faction "exalts its own intuitive understanding as being superior . . . to scientific explanation." She labels "a scientific study of man" in opposition to "the literary tradition" and clearly implies the superiority of the former. Although Brodbeck is guilty of gross oversimplification, she does provide a valid statement, nonetheless, that a "barricade" often separates humanists from scientists even within the same social discipline.

That two (or more) factions exist within the field of human communication is an obvious truism. It seems only natural that what Brodbeck calls "the literary tradition" should exist when one recalls that one national organization of communication specialists, namely the Speech Communication Association, came into being by separating themselves from the National Council of Teachers of English over sixty years ago.

In psychology the branch of humanistic psychology was brought about, allegedly, as a reaction to experimental psychology.

Generally speaking, the humanism-science dichotomy in communication has generated more name-calling than cooperation. Radical extremists on both sides have created a formidable barrier between factions of scholars who are, after all, involved in the same basic pursuit—inquiry into an increased understanding of the phenomena of human communication. And some attempts to bridge the gap have aided the situation little. For example, Bowers (1968) attempted to ameliorate the distinctions between experimental research methods and critical methods, but in so doing he established a distinct hierarchy of methods by considering criticism to be only prescientific, functioning merely as a prelude to the ultimate research method—experimental. Miller's (1975) more recent amelioration seems more defensible and infinitely more valuable.

I, for one, deplore this separation between humanism and science and consider the dichotomy to be a false one. I can see little rational basis for sustaining this dichotomy except in extreme cases in which one type of inquiry is carried out to the absolute exclusion of the other. Research methods are simply neither scientific nor humanistic exclusively. Highly similar, if not identical, research questions can be formulated from allegedly disparate humanistic or scientific concerns. Statistical analyses of quantified data may be and have been applied to allegedly humanistic phenomena. And studies that are considered truly scientific have employed some phenomenological techniques without necessarily involving any statistical treatment of the data.

Consequently, I have personally rejected the necessity (although not the possibility) of dichotomizing humanism and science so that the assumption of communication as a social science is not intended to exclude humanistic concerns. If there is a sustainable distinction between science and humanism, I shall maintain that it is merely a "problem of communication"—not one of definitional analysis.

Science Versus Nonscience

Some readers may find the rather glib definition of science provided earlier to be unsatisfying. Such a reaction is perfectly understandable. More fruitful, though, than belaboring the cliché about the alleged separateness of science and humanism is probably to focus on those characteristics that render some discipline of study "scientific" as opposed to one that is "nonscientific." Although such a distinction is more fruitful, it is by no means very simple. Fortunately, some philosophers of science have addressed themselves to this issue and have provided some direction.

Shapere (1974, pp. 524–525) stipulates three assumptions inherent in the identification of science: rationality, generalizability, and systematizability. Such general assumptions raise additional issues that constitute the domain of the next chapter. For example, do the characteristics of systematizability of scientific principles and scientific rationality require overt axiomatization of laws within a formal logical system? (Kuhn, in the same 1974 volume, p. 513, considers formalism, that is, axiomatization with a semantic interpretation, much less important than does Shapere and by no means essential to science.) Such an issue is a matter of dispute among some science philosophers and is the subject for discussion in the chapter immediately following.

Whatever Shapere implied with his three assumptions, he clearly intended that a science include the principle of testability, that is, that any scientific concept or principle is subject to refutation or even falsification. Such a principle was advanced earlier by Popper (1959) and reinterpreted by Bartley (1968) to include the capacity for a scientific theory to be critical of itself and not immune to critical evaluation.

Alfred Schutz (1962, pp. 342–343) provides three postulates of science as it is applied to the social world. His postulates differ rather significantly from Shapere's in that Schutz incorporates essentially all three of Shapere's into a single postulate of "logical consistency." But Schutz goes on to suggest two additional postulates: "subjective interpretation" and "adequacy," in which the former requires that the social science account for the subjective meanings that actors may have for their own and for others' human actions or their results. Such a postulate broadens the nature of scientific explanation beyond that of deterministic antecedent causes and places the explanation of observed facts within, for example, the mind and its ability to interpret "a fact."

The third postulate, "adequacy," requires that science remain consistent with the "common-sense experience of the social reality." This third postulate prohibits scientific concepts and principles from remaining analytically divorced from reality within some instrumental sense and requires scientific explanations of human actions to be understandable to nonscientists and, therefore, compatible with a "common-sense interpretation of everyday life."

What, then, characterizes a nonscience in the light of these postulates and assumptions? Certainly, the concepts of a nonscience are not "observable," at least in some sense, nor are they subject to the criterion of falsifiability. Some claims made by some nightclub psychics for their extraordinary extrasensory powers are incapable of being refuted. When such performers are unable to "read someone's mind" or when they fail to manipulate a physical object with their mental powers despite their obvious exertion of mental concentration, they often respond that the conditions were not appropriate or that some unavoidable factor mitigated against their efforts. There is simply no way to invalidate their alleged power. They are truly dealing in a nonscience, incapable of scientific falsification. And they would probably be proud to admit it.

A nonscience is also divorced from reality—to some extent at least. To the extent to which explanations do not reflect real-world phenomena or events, these explanations are nonscientific. A science must inevitably return to those things or events that actually occur and cannot indefinitely remain analytically separated from proceedings in the real world without soon being rejected as fruitless. One might speculate that the anthropological "missing link" must eventually be discovered, or else Darwin's evolutionary theory of the origin of the human species will cease to be credible.

It should be clear by now that the assumption of communication as a social science serves not so much to exclude some modes of inquiry as it serves to provide some general framework within which to base the perspectives of human communication. Under no circumstances is the term *social science* a highly restrictive term intended to provide some rationale for discarding a multitude of current practices as unimportant or inappropriate to the "scientific" inquiry into communicative phenomena.

The term *social science* does not exclude humanistic studies, phenomenological techniques, or "the literary tradition" (whatever Brodbeck meant by that term). It does exclude unsystematic inquiry that leads to no generalizable results or explanations that can never be applied to reality. Specifically, what the implications are for viewing communication as a social science is the subject of the next chapter. How these implications of social science specifically affect the study of human communication is the subject of the third and final chapter of Part One.

— 2 —

Communication and Scientific Theory

For the past several years I have been lecturing students in introductory graduate research classes on the nature and meaning of theory—what it is and what it does. For years I have been asking graduate students during examination procedures to describe the nature of theory and even to apply such principles to communication—in short, to develop a full communication theory in about two hours. What incredible arrogance! Arrogance of students to attempt such an answer (as if they had a choice) and even more arrogance on my own part to ask such an unaskable question. At the risk of revealing myself to past, present, and future graduate students in my classes, I have no choice but to confess that I, too, am no longer sure what exactly constitutes a theory. I have a fairly good idea of what a theory does (or should do) and how a theory is used (or should be used), but beyond that is mere speculation. My sole consolation is that no one else appears to be any better off than I am.

The word *theory* appears in our vocabulary in a broad variety of usages. For example, the television private detective has a "theory" about his unsolved murder case. As he (or she) uses the term, a theory implies a hunch, a guess, an hypothesis. The stereotypical undergraduate student takes courses in what he considers to be "theory" as opposed to other courses that are "practical and relevant." To the undergraduate student

24

the "theory" is the stuff that the student must wade through to get to the good stuff that he or she can use. According to the cliché, "It may work in theory, but it won't work in practice." Theory may also imply simply contemplation or speculation about some puzzling phenomenon. But when one discusses theory in the sense of a "scientific theory," he implies something far more than hunches, impracticability, or speculation. And he is correct—not that scientific theory differs from hunches, speculation, or even sometimes impracticability; but that it involves more—much more.

Ernest Nagel (1967, pp. 5–6), one of the leading proponents of what we shall later discuss as the "received view" of theories, supports the necessity and desirability of theory in any scientific inquiry by pointing out the limitations of the only other alternative, namely, common sense. He indicates that common sense is generally imprecise and inconsistent, so that the choice to believe in similarities among various phenomena, differences, or in one of several conflicting beliefs is purely arbitrary and without rational guidelines. His most damning criticism of common-sense knowledge is its overwhelming emphasis on being utilitarian for common every day experiences. (Recall the stereotypical undergraduate.) Because common sense originates from and applies directly to issues of practicality, its range of applicability does not extend much beyond the routine of day-to-day experiences. Moreover, the emphasis on being useful tends to cause our knowledge to stagnate, leading inevitably to inflexibility. Such knowledge too quickly becomes customary and traditional (at least familiar), so that the ability to handle novel problems or situations never before encountered is impaired. Common sense is simply ill-equipped to deal with the unfamiliar—that which doesn't seem to "make sense." Nagel's point seems clear. The necessity and desirability of a theory in order to organize knowledge and provide direction for increasing knowledge is simply not a matter of dispute. It is a truism.

That communication does not now possess a guiding theory and, furthermore, needs a theory has been the expressed opinion of more than a few specialists on human communication. The most obvious place to seek assistance in the quest for a theory of communication is the philosophy of science. Just what science philosophers have to contribute to the field of communication is, of course, a matter of some conjecture. Science philosophers, it must be remembered, are not scientists, nor do they claim any expertise in any field of science. They are philosophers who deal with philosophical issues related to theoretical development in general and development of a discipline's scientific theory specifically. Never does a science philosopher tell the scientist, in an a priori fashion, what to do. For any given scientific field, philosophers of science can organize and systematize existing knowledge within some theoretical framework of one sort or another, explain scientific principles already confirmed or widely accepted, and trace the historical development of those principles.

Robson (1968, p. 369), a sociologist, paraphrases Lakatos, a philosopher of science, as characterizing the contribution of science philosophy "as telling scientists what they did and why they did it after they had done it." Although it may be disconcerting to some, Robson (p. 370) goes on to observe that "philosophers of science themselves appear to be divided on the kind of advice and counsel they would give us." And as Frederick Suppe (1974, p. 4) states in the introduction to his superbly edited book, "For more than fifty years philosophy of science has been engaged in a search for philosophic understanding of scientific theories; today it still is searching."

For students of communication to reap the maximum benefits from philosophy of science requires some understanding of this search for philosophical understanding of scientific theories. The ensuing discussion of issues raised by philosophers of science bears directly or indirectly on every facet of our understanding of human communication—the structure of theories, how theory is related to reality, observation of communicative phenomena, participation in communicative activities, methods of observing communication research methodologies, identifying communicative phenomena, analyzing data from the observation of communication, ad infinitum.

THE NATURE OF THEORY

It is one thing to espouse the need for theory; it is another to know what to do about it. In discussing the need for theory in the field of human communication, nearly all critics (including myself) seem to have no clear idea of what constitutes this ethereal goal. The professional journals are rife with pleas for theory, reconceptualizations of theory, new models, and toward-a-theory-of analyses. We seem to be saying that we are all for it. We say the right words and use all the right jargon (occasionally even inventing additional jargon). But when the smoke clears, we remain with little more than a collection of generalizations and semiconfirmed hypotheses drawn from research.

A fundamental issue could probably be phrased, "What does a theory look like?" Is it a list of axioms phrased in some order of logico-mathematical calculi? Is it a comprehensive morphology and taxonomy of communicative phenomena? Is it a list of fundamental concepts joined together with some list of connective relationships? The answer to questions such as these is not apparent at the present time. In fact, as the following discussion of theory and philosophy of science shall attest, these questions are basically unanswerable. More accurately, the answers to these questions differ significantly and often conflict with each other. A more fruitful starting point might be to discuss the issues related to the functions of a theory, that is, how people (or scientists) use a theory, and to lay aside momentarily those issues pertaining to the actual identifying structure of theories.

Heurism and Justification

To one viewing the march of scientific progress in the traditional manner, the process might go something like the following: Scientist X possesses an hypothesis. This hypothesis might originate from any of a variety of sources. The scientist might have logically deduced it from some set of axioms and now possesses a potential new truth. Or he might have generated this hypothesis from an earlier research study, which produced some unexpected or peripheral result. Or X might have arrived at this hypothesis in a blinding flash of insight or some intuitive leap while jogging around the block or watching television. (Recall the fabled story of the apple that fell on Isaac Newton's head or of Achimedes' taking a bath.) From whatever source, X must then transform his hypothesis into terms or concepts amenable to observation. Finally X submits his hypothesis to observational testing and either confirms or falsifies its validity or truth value. (Karl Popper, 1959, among others, suggests that no hypothesis can be directly validated, verified, or confirmed. It can only be falsified. But to the extent that numerous attempts by numerous scientists fail to falsify the hypothesis, it is considered to be confirmed. Actually, Popper prefers the term *corroboration* to validation or confirmation.)

This traditional description of scientific inquiry, in abbreviated form, of course, has been labeled the "hypothetico-deductive" approach to science. Central to hypothetico-deductivism is the bipartite division between generating hypotheses and validating them. Validating hypotheses is central to the traditional approach to philosophy of science. But although science philosophers acknowledge the importance of the heuristic function of theories, they provide little assistance to the scientist who desires to generate new hypotheses. Nor do the philosophers of science provide or intend to provide any method to assess the significance of hypotheses.

The hypothetico-deductive method of the traditional view of philosophy of science focuses on the validation of hypotheses through some form of deductive explanation. And you will recall that a valid conclusion of a deductive argument must be true if the premises from which it is drawn are true. In the form of experimentation, considered by many traditional science philosophers to be the only true scientific method, the attempt is to phrase a null hypothesis (that is, observations of the dependent variable in conditions of the presence and absence of an independent variable yield no difference between them) and attempt to prove it false.

Thus, the deductive form is established. If the hypothesis (H) is correct, then the prediction (P) of some effect will be true. The predicted effect (P) is observed. Therefore, the hypothesis is confirmed. The problem with attempting to confirm the hypothesis directly is a purely formal problem within the calculus of conditional (if . . . then) logic. The direct form is as follows:

$$H \supset P \quad (\text{If } H, \text{then } P.)$$
$$P \quad (P \text{ is observed.})$$
$$\therefore H \quad (H \text{ is confirmed.})$$

The above form of the deduction commits the fallacy of affirming the consequent (P). No valid conclusion can then be drawn. Hence, the prediction is phrased in the "null" form, which typically predicts no differential effects. Observation then seeks to deny the null (absence of effects) consequent, thereby confirming the hypothesis indirectly.

The deductive form of the typical experiment thus takes on the following form. If the hypothesis is not correct ($\sim H$), then the predicted difference will not be expected ($\sim P$). Observation then seeks to reject the state of no difference ($\sim P$), thereby denying the falsity of the hypothesis. The double-negative form of the deductive logic of the experiment is thus established:

$$\sim H \supset \sim P \quad (\text{If not–}H, \text{then not–}P.)$$
$$\sim(\sim P) \quad (\text{Observation rejects the null prediction.})$$
$$\therefore H \quad (\text{The hypothesis is indirectly confirmed.})$$

The point of this little exercise is simply to demonstrate that when hypotheses are confirmed within the hypothetico-deductive framework, the logical system being employed is exclusively deductive. Furthermore, the hypothesis is not directly observed or confirmed. Rather, it is assumed to exist after the attempt to falsify the hypothesis failed—a double negative.

The hypothetico-deductive model of doing science clearly places greatest emphasis on justification—the confirmation or corroboration of hypotheses. Such a model is admittedly ill-equipped to deal with the process of heurism—generating hypotheses and new research ideas. Traditional philosophers of science, acknowledging the significance of the heuristic function of science, dismiss the problem rather flippantly by decrying the absence of a "logic of discovery." Of course, if discovering hypotheses requires a logic with deductive rigor, no such logic is apparent or even possible. As Max Black (1967) demonstrates, any form of inductive logic (required for discovery) cannot be "justified" by meeting the standards of deductive reasoning. The heuristic function of science, then, becomes extrascientific in the sense of hypothetico-deductive science. For example, McGuire (1973) suggests guidelines for generating research hypotheses that do not include any trace of a logical calculus, inductive or deductive.

Some nontraditional science philosophers, along with some scientists, had addressed themselves directly to the problem of providing some systematic approach to discovering new research questions. Hanson (1961), for example, suggests viewing the justificatory and heuristic functions of scientific inquiry in terms of "reasons"—reasons for accepting an hypothesis and reasons for suggesting that hypothesis in the first place. Kaplan (1964, pp. 12–18) prefers to consider the two functions as separate "contexts." Hawes (1975, pp. 114–115) implies that the use of models might satisfy the heuristic function of a theory. And McGuire's (1973) list of guidelines is more pedagogical than theoretical.

Max Weber's (1949) proposal of a method of intuitive understanding, namely, Verstehen, is a logical candidate for systematizing the heuristic function of scientific theory. But as Nagel (1953) accurately points out, the proponents of Verstehen sometimes fail to distinguish between the heuristic and the justificatory use of Verstehen. Moreover, he goes on to report, the heuristic fruitfulness of Verstehen is a matter of considerable debate among philosophers and scientists alike.

One can safely conclude at this point that the philosophy of science in its "traditional" form has emphasized the justificatory function of a theory at the expense of its heuristic function. As a result, some social scientists (see, for example, Znaniecki, 1934, and Glaser and Strauss, 1967), recognizing this oversight, have sought to provide new conceptualizations and methods of scientific inquiry. Although one can debate the merits of what Znaniecki calls "analytic induction" and what Glaser and Strauss call "constant comparative method," specific explanations of which are not particularly pertinent to our purposes, one cannot question the importance of the heuristic function of theory and its relative neglect within the traditional mode of philosophy of science. Clearly, we need to guard against the myopic view that science is solely or even primarily concerned with validating hypotheses. Such a view, though currently too popular, is not only false but, in terms of scientific progress, is self-defeating.

Scientific Explanation

If a single goal exists for all varieties of scientific inquiry, that goal might be to understand the unknown; that is, science uses theory to assist in understanding phenomena that don't have obvious explanations. Throughout all of recorded history and certainly before that, mankind has been fascinated with asking and answering the question, "Why?" Even the small child develops at an early age an insatiable curiosity and proceeds to "why" everything, often to the aggravation and loss of patience of adults. Ultimately, such a question becomes unanswerable, and the final response becomes a frustrating, "Just because!"

When scientists ask why-questions, they are involved in seeking explanations. But there is more to scientific explanation than a simple *why*. For example, if someone were to ask you why you are reading this book, you might reply that you are filled with intellectual curiosity, and this book serves to alleviate some of that curiosity. Such a reply is, of course, quite flattering to an author's ego. More likely, you would respond that you were only fulfilling some arbitrary requirement set down by some identifiable instructor. Whatever your reasons for reading this book, this type of question is hardly a proper consideration for science. For one thing, the question is disgustingly anthropocentric and deals solely with motivations that understandably vary from one person to another although the result (reading the book) might be identical. In other words, some explanations may be perfectly valid and may certainly answer why-questions. But not all why-questions require scientific explanation. Consequently, scientific explanation involves more than a simple response to the question, "Why?"

A why-question often involves nonmotivational issues; that is, why implies "How come?" in the sense of why candidate X won the election? Implicit in such a question is the existence of some phenomenon or occurrence of some event in the election of X. The question then seeks to understand what other phenomena or events are related to the phenomenon or event in question, so that the explanation will lead to an understanding of election results. In this sense, how-come questions seek scientific explanation in that the explanation *accounts for* the existence of phenomena or changes in phenomena by relating other phenomena to them. And this accounting procedure involves relating classes of phenomena to each other in some understandable fashion.

One of the key issues in scientific explanation is whether explanations imply predictions and vice versa. Science philsophers do not agree on this issue. Grünbaum (1962), for example, indicates that explanation and prediction are virtually synonymous. Rudner (1966, pp. 60–61; see also Brodbeck [1968], pp. 9–10) indicates that explanation and prediction have the same deductive form and proceed from the same premises—virtually equivalent except that the prediction is of an event yet to occur whereas explanation need not presage the future.

That is to say, Grunbaum and Rudner would agree that all explanations probably imply predictions, but they would not necessarily agree that all predictions imply explanations. For example, one is able to predict with more than reasonable assurance that the sun will appear on the eastern horizon tomorrow morning. Such a prediction does not, however, imply any explanation. The explanatory principle of planetary rotation on an axis in a revolutionary orbit around the sun does imply the same prediction that the sun will appear in the east tomorrow morning. The first is prediction without explanation; the latter, fully explanatory.

Scriven (1959, 1963), on the other hand, does not consider explanation and prediction to be equivalent. To the contrary, Scriven cites explanations—specifically, evolutionary explanations—as highly satisfactory, although they do not involve any prediction of future events. Using Darwin's evolutionary explanation as a model, one might consider this explanation extremely significant and certainly explanatory as to how human beings (as well as other species) developed historically to their present form. Nevertheless, such an explanation can in no way be expected to predict what human beings will look like 500,000 years hence. Although Scriven would certainly agree that many, if not most, scientific explanations do indeed provide predictive power, nevertheless, a good scientific explanation need not directly imply any prediction.

The issue, then, of whether scientific theories provide predictions along with explanations remains unresolved. Of course, most scientific theories do include predictions, and many philsophers, even scientists, believe that prediction is at the core of science. But can an explanation be scientific without predicting? Probably so, but controversy surrounds this issue. We shall not resolve it at this point.

Meehan (1968) contributes yet another issue to this discussion of scientific explanation. He considers the pervasive purpose of all social science to be *control*, and the desire for social control necessitates explanation. If the scientist is able to intervene and change social phenomena or trends in social phenomena, according to Meehan, he has control. And the social theory is satisfactory. For Meehan the theory provides the scientist with the ability to alter relevant variables and thus alter the social outcome. Certainly, such a view of theory is consistent with the currently popular "social engineering." But does explanation necessarily lead to the ability to control? There is ample evidence (for example, Stein, 1968) that social control is virtually nonexistent in actual practice, although social theory is rich in explanation. If control were the sole (or even primary) consideration, explanation might be considered superfluous. *Robert's Rules of*

Order endow a legislative assembly with control, but they provide no explanation of the decision-making process. The issue of control through explanation does not seem to be a significant issue in scientific explanation.

What, then, is the essential character of scientific explanation? To Scriven (1962), "It is a topically unified communication, the content of which imparts understanding of some scientific phenomenon." Any scientific explanation is ultimately a way of organizing experience. We develop categories, which we then use to classify phenomena. At a superficial level, we all possess categories or topics that we can use to classify objects with which we are familiar, such as persons, animals, plants, minerals, and so on. We can also show relationships between classes of these phenomena in that some persons are classed as tall, short, dark, pale, and the like. We even invent abstract and virtually indefinable categories of properties, which we also use in conjunction with other phenomena, for example, pleasing personality, love, original, creative, handsome, and so forth. Under any circumstances, an explanation does not provide our experiences, but it does allow us to organize them and to show how one is related to another.

An explanation is never final, never certain. For, according to Meehan (1969, p. 80), "When everything that can be done has been done, uncertainly will remain." In other words, the extent of knowledge is infinite. We will never understand all that there is to be understood. We use our classificatory scheme, not because it represents the ultimate truth of our experiences, but because it allows us to understand our experiences, that is, to provide some meaningful order to those experiences. A different classificatory scheme would provide a different order, a different understanding, a different explanation. In this way, according to Meehan (1969, p. 81), "Faulty methodology or reasoning can destroy an explanation, but no amount of methodological skill can establish an explanation." Only humans can explain. Methodological tools are just that—tools. They are adapted to our explanations. Different kinds of explanations, of course, may require different kinds of tools. As Scriven (1962) points out, ". . . the only ultimate element in the logic of explanation is understanding itself, and that comes in many ways."

Explanation and Causation

The issue of whether scientific explanations imply a causal relationship among or between phenomena is more complex than it appears at first glance. On a superficial basis, the issue of causal relationships between social phenomena requires only a simple analysis. Causations requires that a relationship be temporally distinct and meet the criteria of sufficiency and necessity; that is, a cause must precede its effect and constitute both a necessary and sufficient condition for the effect to occur. No known social relationship meets these three criteria. And even if some explanation did meet the criteria of causation, there would be many more explanations or potential explanations that would not. Specifically, then, one might conclude that social scientific explanations, not necessarily those of physical sciences, do not imply any causal modality. Unfortunately, the role of causation in the social sciences is more complex than this superficial analysis indicates.

The influence of teleological explanation renders the temporal separation of cause and effect indistinct. For example, the behavior of goal-oriented phenomena can be explained through a causal relationship existing in the future. One eats and breathes in order to sustain life. A business engages in manufacturing and marketing activities in order to make a profit. A student studies and learns in order to acquire knowledge (or at least to acquire an acceptable grade). Under any circumstances, causes may not necessarily precede the effect, but the effect may actually precede the cause.

The necessity criterion is often ignored in social scientific explanations; that is, if you will pardon the phrasing, the sufficiency criterion is often sufficient for scientific explanation, whereas the necessity criterion is unnecessary. For example, if a ball is thrown with great force at a window-pane, the windowpane will break. The thrown ball is a condition sufficient for the window to break, but it is not necessary, given the existence of multiple conditions sufficient for the window to break; that is, any number of other antecedent conditions (for example, a fist, a thrown brick, heat-cold contraction, twisting, and so on) can cause the window to break without the thrown-ball condition. But the thrown ball is a condition sufficient for the effect (the broken window) to occur. In fact, many sufficient conditions may exist for the same result in social scientific explanation, but few, if any, conditions are ultimately necessary.

In addition to the three criteria suggested for causal relationships is the requirement that there be no exception to a causal law. If A causes B, then B will always occur in the presence of A without exception. In this sense, causation is inherently mechanistic or deterministic. But virtually all explanations in the social sciences do not lend themselves to such deterministic certainty. To the contrary, explanatory principles are typically phrased as statistical probabilities. Although some science philosophers cling to deterministic laws (for example, Bergmann, 1962, and J. J. C. Smart, 1963), the consensus appears to favor the use of both mechanistic determinism and statistical probabilities as interchangeably valid explanatory principles in the social sciences (for example, Hempel,

1967, and Brodbeck, 1968, p. 10), as well as for many explanations in the natural sciences.

What, then, is the status of causation as a criterion for scientific explanation in the social sciences? Winch (1950), for example, believes that causation is not operative in social scientific explanation and that only a "logical relation" between events is relevant. Hanson (1958, pp. 50–69) discusses causality as a conceptual basis for some theories but is largely detrimental to the development of scientific explanation in general that may or may not involve causal presumptions.

Nevertheless, a strange and incongruous phenomenon exists in the social sciences. Explanations do not admit of causal relationships. Yet such explanations seem somehow to appear to be causal. Even Dore (1961), who argues against causal explanation in sociology in favor of functional explanations, concludes that functionalism "blurs the precise causal relations imputed and yet descriptions in terms of functions seem somehow to be causal. . . ."

The situation is this. Explanation in the social sciences does not and cannot consistently satisfy the criteria for causation. Social explanations are often atemporal, employ only sufficient but not necessary conditions, and typically include statements of statistical probability (that is, if A occurs, B will occur with a probability of p). Yet, in practice, social scientists use their explanations as though they implied causal relationships. Cohen (1968, pp. 413–417) contends that social scientists cannot avoid using causal assumptions—that whether they admit it or not, the principle of causation is implicit in social scientific explanations. He indicates that causation, in the precise physical meaning of the term, has no referent in the social world but is nonetheless implicit in social explanation.

One reason, perhaps, for the assumption of some form of causation may reside in the logical form of the conditional, which pervades scientific (including the social sciences) explanation. The conditional expresses a relationship that some antecedent event implies the existence of (or is a sufficient, though not necessary, condition for) some consequent event. "If A, then B implicitly contains a linear relationship between A and B, which, though not precisely causal, is often treated as a causal relationship in actual scientific practice. As long as conditional (that is, if . . . then) relationships are the *sine qua non* of explanatory form in social sciences, the quasi-causal implications of explanation in social sciences will probably persist.

Rudner (1966, pp. 64–65) indicates that causation is not inherent or particularly important in scientific explanation. Rather, he suggests, "lawlike regularity" is the key element of scientific explanation; that is, if any phenomena are related in any way and if that relationship is observable with some regularity, then an explanation can be said to exist. The greater the regularity of observation confirming the relationship, the more potent the explanation. Any relationship can be regular, including causal relationships, but the key factor is the regularity of the relationship—not the causal or quasi-causal linear character of the relationship.

Instrumental Versus Realistic Interpretation of Theories

When a theory does exist, a scientist may interpret the theory in several ways. First, the scientist may interpret a theoretical concept to be an entity or an attribute of some entity that actually exists in the "real world." In this sense, a psychologist would consider the concept of "personality" to be some actual phenomenon possessed by an individual and manifested in certain behavioral attributes. Such a view suggests a realistic interpretation of theories.

The term *realistic*, however, does not imply that the theoretical concept actually possesses some material substance; that is, the most ardent realist would never claim to be able to see or touch a personality, to pick it up and examine it. Such a view, more appropriately termed "physicalism" or "idealism," would require direct physical observation of an entity. A realist's interpretation of a theoretical concept implies only that a theoretical concept does possess some observable referent in the form of direct or indirect observation of attributes.

On the other hand, the observation of attributes (from a realist's view) may not be complete in that the concept may possess other attributes, which have not yet been discovered. Then, too, the realist also assumes that observations that are attributed to one concept may be inaccurate in that they may be attributes of some other concept that are incorrectly assumed to be the attributes of the former concept. A realist claims some knowledge of nature, but he does not claim that his knowledge is total, ideal, or even accurate. Nor does he assume any ultimate goal of achieving final and perfect knowledge of nature in some Platonistic sense.

A second interpretation of theories makes no such knowledge claim. Rather, the instrumentalist would view theoretical concepts only as useful tools, which can be used to explain observable phenomena. Toulmin (1953), for example, considers theoretical terms to be only rules or guidelines for drawing inferences or making predictions. Suppes (1967, p. 65) regards theories as "methods of organizing evidence." A theory, then, is never true or false, nor can it ever be. Nor does a theory claim any knowledge of existence.

A theory can only be *adequate* in that it contains all the theoretical concepts necessary to derive explanations. When explanations no longer explain observations to the satisfaction of the inquiring population of scientists, the theory is modified or discarded in formulating another theory that is more adequate. Loosely speaking, phlogiston was an adequate explanation of combustion prior to the discovery of oxygen. An instrumentalist would not consider research into phlogiston or oxygen to constitute some claim of realistic existence. Rather, such research is only useful in explaining the phenomenal activity of combustible substances.

It is often difficult to distinguish a realistic from an instrumental interpretation of theories. Certainly, the theory itself is neither realistic nor instrumental in its choice of concepts, its structure, its logical form, and so on. Rather, the interpretation of the theory by the scientist who uses it is realistic or instrumental. But the distinction remains problematic. Both realists and instrumentalists, for example, would revise a theory of combustion following the discovery of oxygen. Both realists and instrumentalists in psychology would utilize personality variables in their inquiry and might conceivably be performing identical research projects. In fact, the distinction between instrumentalism and realism in interpreting theories is frequently a trivial distinction serving no useful purpose in scientific inquiry.

Shapere (1974, pp. 566–570) suggests a different distinction, which is tantamount to, or substitutable for, instrumentalism and realism. He considers a distinction between "existence claims" and "idealization claims" to distinguish among the concepts of terms within the theory itself. Some might consider that the notion of existence claims provides a defense for a form of realistic interpretation of theories. That might well be true, but the issue is more fundamental in that existence and idealization claims can exist within the same theory and serve to distinguish between the terms or concepts of the theory—not between how a theory is to be interpreted. Under any circumstances, Shapere's discussion of existence claims is significant to the purpose of this book.

Shapere (1974, p. 569) suggests that when one deals with existence claims, he implies that a phenomenon may exist about which "we can have different and competing theories." An idealization claim does not allow for different theoretical treatments of the same concept or phenomenon. Rather, the only type of existence claimed for an idealization term is its definition and function within the theory itself, that is, the idealization.

One fundamental assumption underlying Part Two and Part Three of this book is that human communication does exist. But our understanding of the phenomenon of communication may differ significantly from person to person. In other words, we do have quite different and frequently competing theories (I shall use the term *perspectives* rather than *theories* for reasons that shall become apparent in Chapter 3 of Part One) of this phenomenon such that many of the theoretical concepts describing communication are dissimilar. Furthermore, some terms that are identical within different perspectives imply quite specific attributes and meanings that differ significantly from one perspective to another. For this reason, only the distinction between "existence claims" and "idealization claims" (as substitutes for instrumental and realistic interpretation of theories) is important in the ensuing discussion.

THE "RECEIVED VIEW" OF THEORIES

One must remember that the contribution of the philosophy of science to scientific inquiry lies not in the *doing* of science but in the structuring of scientific theories. One must also remember that the philosophy of science is able to provide no assistance whatsoever in understanding the scientific theory of a given discipline of study until that discipline develops a rather substantial body of information in the form of empirical generalizations and underlying principles that account for those generalizable observations. After all, like the term *communication,* the term *theory* resists even definition. Shapere (1974, p. 556) points out, for example, that philosophers of science have consistently been unable to define the concept of "theory" itself. In fact, he goes on, "the usages to which philosophers . . . have put the term 'theory' are often so vague and ambiguous as to be scandalous." But like definitions of communication, definitions of theory fail to provide much assistance in the *understanding* of scientific theory.

To engage in argument over whether some body of principles is or is not a "theory" is quite fruitless. Our purpose is, rather, to delve into the issues related to the nature of scientific theorizing. An understanding of these issues is deemed much more fruitful to scientific inquiry than to establish criteria for developing and identifying theories within some specifiable format.

The issues relative to the nature of theories arise from the standard conceptualization of theory within the philosophy of science. Although we shall treat the following conceptualization as a coherent whole, the science philosophers who subscribe to this view are by no means unified. Our purposes can best be served, however, by considering the issues from the view of an historically "normal" or standard usage of theory within science philosophy and then proceeding to develop additional issues as departures from this norm.

The standard conceptualization of theories within the philosophy of science is directly attributable to the philosophical school of logical positivism most typically associated with the philosophers of the Vienna Circle. This standard conceptualization of science philosophy is identified under a myriad of terms, most typically the "covering law" model or hypothesis, but it also includes such labels as logical positivism, logical empiricism, radical empiricism, or the traditional view of theories. O'Keefe (1975), in his incisive article detailing its implications for communication research, uses the term *logical empiricism*. Suppe (1974) uses the term *the received view*, which he attributes to Putnam (1962). I have opted for the latter term in order to suggest the broadest interpretation possible for this standard conceptualization of scientific theory.

What follows, then, is a generalized discussion of issues raised by the philosophers of science in understanding the function and value of theory in scientific inquiry. A far more detailed description and summary of the issues are available in Suppe (1974), who undoubtedly gives the most comprehensive and valuable summary of the development of philosophy of science for the nonphilosopher. Whereas Suppe presents five summary "conditions" to define the received view, Krimerman (1969) organizes the received view (covering law model) under nine "propositions"—specifically for the purpose of rendering the covering law model applicable to the social sciences. The following discussion is not nearly so complete, and the interested reader is directed to these sources for a more detailed explication.

One elemental principle of the standard version of the nature and structure of scientific theory must be clear at the outset. The received view is by no means a clear-cut and unified body of information. Among proponents of the received view there is considerable controversy over specific interpretations and issues. Nevertheless, the proponents generally agree on a few fundamental principles underlying the rationale for their views. Contemporary philosophers most consistently and clearly identified with the received view include Carnap (see Schilpp, 1963) and Hempel (see, for example, 1965), although many other science philosophers are in substantial agreement, for example, Nagel (1961), Brodbeck (1968), Kaplan (1964), J. J. C. Smart (1963), Suppes (1967), Blalock (1969), and Dubin (1969).

Components of the "Received View"

Historically, according to Suppe (1974), the received view can be traced, in part, to a philosophical reaction to Hegelian metaphysics such that empirical verification of theoretical entities became central to the historical development of science philosophy. Subsequent to the publication of Whitehead and Russell's *Principia Mathematica* early in the twentieth century, the logical positivistic school of philosophers in the Vienna Circle possessed an elegantly precise language in which to phrase scientific relationships. Thus, mathematics in the sense of a logical language is fundamental to explicating the structure of a scientific theory.

Typically, but probably not absolutely necessarily, the logic adopted for use in scientific theory has been conditional in form. Sometimes termed "implication," the conditional statement stipulates antecedent conditions that imply the presence of some specified consequent conditions. Conditions are expressed as "if . . . then" propositions. According to this logical form, *if* certain conditions exist, *then* certain consequences will accrue. Conditional statements are often construed as causal statements, although such a construction is, strictly speaking, not accurate. At best, a statement, "If *A*, then *B*" (that is, $A \supset B$) implies that the antecedent condition of *A* is sufficient to bring about the consequential condition of *B*. To use a trivial example, one might say, "If a football game is on television this weekend, then I will stay home to watch it." The author of such a statement does not imply that the televised game *causes* him to stay home but that the condition of the game's being televised is sufficient to bring about his decision to stay home to watch it.

At the risk of belaboring this trivial example of a football freak, the analogy also contains another principle of a formalized (that is, a relationship stated in a logico-mathematical calculus with semantic interpretation) theoretical statement. The conditional relationship between the antecedent and consequent relies upon an underlying universal principle. Scriven (1962) points out that a formalized "law" assumes some universal principle that resides in "nature" (defined differently according to the specific discipline of study) and that serves to explain the lawlike regularity of the conditional relationship. (See also the discussion of descriptive and theoretical laws in Kaplan, 1964, pp. 113–115.) The football example implies that avid football fans take advantage of every opportunity to watch a televised football game. Only in a comprehensive statement of a scientific theory, however, are such principles explicitly stated. In the day-to-day practice of doing science, such principles are rarely explicit but remain as implicit and underlying assumptions that are rarely stated.

A second component of the received view is the existence of theoretical concepts that, when related to each other by the connectives of the logical calculus, form theoretical "laws" or "axioms." Concepts, by virtue of being theoretical, are largely independent of reality. Their existence is defined within the theory itself and not necessarily because of or related to any empirical (that is, observable) phenomenon. Hawes (1975, p. 29) describes this separation of theoretical concepts from observational concepts by asserting that a theory is "conceived" whereas an observational fact is "perceived."

Kaplan (1964) clearly maintains the contrast between theoretical and observational terms (pp. 54–62), as well as a contrast between laws composed of theoretical terms as opposed to laws composed of observational terms (pp. 113–115). In this sense, the theory exists apart from the evidence that serves to verify the theory. A theory's value lies not in reflecting the reality of observations but in explaining the reality that is not susceptible to observation.

Clearly, however, a theory possesses scientific value only to the extent that it does serve to explain reality. The received view thus postulates rules for converting theoretical terms into observable phenomena. A theory, then, serves a "mapping" function by organizing observable phenomena into identifiable classes, rendered identifiable by certain specified procedures. The procedures used to perform this mapping function and thereby relate theory to observation are termed "correspondence rules," so-called because they specify the correspondence between theoretical laws and empirical phenomena.

Typically, at least in the social sciences, correspondence rules take the form of operational definitions; that is, a theoretical concept is "defined" in the sense that the definition specifies certain procedures to follow in order to observe it. Often an operational definition assumes the form of a mode of measurement so that "attitude" might be operationalized as a specific set of Likert scales, Remmers scales, or even semantic differential scales. The "leader" of a group has been operationalized as the perceptions of members, the group member receiving and transmitting the most messages, or the member with the highest score on some specified test of leadership "abilities."

Numerous operational definitions can, of course, exist for the same theoretical concept. Thus, operational definitions suggest several implications. First, a correspondence rule provides only a partial interpretation or definition of the theoretical term and should never be considered to define or interpret all of the concept, that is, to exhaust the attributes of the theoretical concept. Second, operational definitions do not realistically uncover the meaning of the theoretical term. Rather, an operationalization attempts only to provide a method for applying the term. In other words, if it walks like a duck and talks like a duck and swims like a duck, you will be able to recognize "it" as a duck. But you won't know anything about the nature of "duckness."

One final implication of operational definitions concerns the equivalence of different operationalizations. Strictly speaking, two different operational definitions constitute two different concepts, although they may be quite similar. For example, if "attitude" is operationalized in one study as a specific set of Likert scales and in another study as a specific set of semantic differential scales, can one assume that the two different measurements are indeed measuring precisely the same concept? Such a question is basically unanswerable. Certainly, in scientific practice we do not make such discriminations but tend to assume that even significantly different procedures are measuring the same phenomenon. The only clear alternative to such an assumption is empirical chaos.

Suppe (1974, pp. 18–27) indicates that the received view has evolved from the use of operational definitions to reduction sentences as the basic logical form for correspondence rules. Such may indeed be the case for physical science. But for the social sciences, at least, operational definitions are undoubtedly the standard form of correspondence rules. Whatever conceptual problems exist in equivocating differing operational definitions of the same theoretical term, the fact remains that operational definitions are a fact of scientific practice and unlikely to change for some time.

Within the received view, theoretical terms have empirical existence only as correspondence rules exist for them. But because correspondence rules do not define *all* of a theoretical concept and provide only *partial definitions,* the concept itself always exists somewhat apart from its correspondence rules and is thus inevitably independent of empirical existence to some extent. Then, too, correspondence rules often change over a period of time as new techniques of observation are developed and methods become more sophisticated. But a modification in correspondence rules does not create a new or a different theoretical term. The concept remains; only its correspondence rule is altered.

For example, the concept of source credibility is over 2,000 years old. Aristotle discussed ethos as a persuasive impact of the source. That same term was used as recently as 1963 by Andersen and Clevenger in their summary of contemporary research on credibility. Aristotle, however, conceived of ethos as a collection of traits (specifically character, sagacity, and goodwill) possessed by the source him/herself. Quintilian later modified the correspondence rule by defining ethos as the educational experience developed by the source. The more recent correspondence rules define ethos as characteristics of the source as perceived by receivers.

Centuries of evolution have not eradicated the concept, nor have they significantly modified the role of the concept of ethos (or source credibility) within some theoretical perspective of persuasive communication. The correspondence rules or operational definitions of the concept have changed drastically, however, to the point that the locus has even shifted

from the source to the receiver. Oddly enough, the theory remains basically Aristotelian whereas the observational techniques reflect twentieth-
century sophistication.

Critical to the standard view of theories is the nature of explanation
as hypotheses deduced from or subsumed by a more general law. Thus,
any scientific explanation contains a law that is sufficiently general and
precise to derive testable hypotheses (typically in the form of predictions). In other words, scientific explanation takes the form of a deductive argument that contains as one of its premises a universal law or
lawlike statement. Hence, explanations employing such a deductive logical form requiring the inclusion of such a law are often called explanations from a "covering law."

Although covering-law explanations have undergone numerous modifications in response to philosophical criticisms, the basic deductive form
remains unchanged. The law included in the explanation, of course, may
be either analytic or synthetic; that is, an analytic statement is true by
definition as it is subject only to the postulated theory independent of
any possible empirical manipulation. For example, an analytic statement
such as, "Every triangle contains three angles" is true because it was
defined to be true within the logical system. It is, for all practical purposes, tautological in that it contains within itself all the information
needed to verify it. No amount of empirical testing can prove it to be
false. On the other hand, a synthetic statement is subject to empirical
testing procedures and may be proved false. For example, "Every leader
occupies a central position in a communication network" is a synthetic
statement that is subject to observation and description as to its uniform
or universal nature. (For our purposes, the discussion need not include
the controversy surrounding the tenability of sustaining the distinction
between analytic and synthetic statements. For more information concerning this controversy, see Quine [1953] and Putnam [1962].)

Hawes (1975, pp. 38–43) distinguishes between formal and substantive
theories on the basis of whether statements within the theory are subject
to the falsifiability criterion. Such a distinction is similar to Suppe's
(1974, pp. 113–114) distinction between axiomatization and formalization, the latter being subject to semantic (empirical) interpretation and
not exclusively tautological. In any case, the basic covering-law form is
the same; that is, the logical form is deductive, hypotheses are generated,
and a law (of some sort) comprises one of the premises of the argument.
This form of explanation is sometimes used to characterize a theory as
"hypothetico-deductive."

In point of fact, covering-law explanations in the social sciences
characteristically utilize covering laws that are what Krimerman (1969,
p. 44) calls "empirical laws" or "statistical correlations" rather than laws

that are analytically true. The nature of social explanation virtually requires such lawlike statements of the form that, given specific antecedent conditions or circumstances, some phenomenon or event can be expected to occur with more or less high probability. Hempel (1967) refers to such explanations, apparently equivalent to explanations within Hawes's (1975) "substantive theory," as "probabilistic explanation by covering laws." Hempel (p. 84) asserts that " all scientific explanations of empirical phenomena are basically covering-law explanations of the deductive or of the probabilistic variety," the sole distinction being based on whether the law is deductively certain or empirically probable. An explanation of any other form would apparently consist of what Krimerman (1969, p. 44) terms "mere description or clarification" or "intuitive hunches." According to O'Keefe (1975), the assumptions implicit in the form of covering-law explanations dominate contemporary research in communication. There appears little reason to doubt his conclusion.

Although this brief discussion is not intended to be a comprehensive explication of the received view of scientific theory, one final characteristic is worth of mention. Though not strictly a component of the received view, the development of theory by reduction is a characteristic belief among its adherents. Theory reduction implies two fundamental elements. First, science seeks to establish laws to explain events and phenomena in an ever-increasing succession of greater generality. Thus, one law may be subsumed within another law (or even one entire theory subsumed within another theory) of greater scope and precision. In this sense, the laws included within the theory hypothetically decrease in number, which apparently prompted Hawes (1975, p. 39) to observe that the fewer statements or laws within the theory, the more "parsimonious" the theory.

If this element of theory reduction is carried to its illogical extreme, one might expect the theory eventually to include only a single statement of a law that explains the universe. Such an expectation is clearly unjustified and even suggests an image of some cartoon figure clawing his way up a steep mountain in search of some wizened old guru who would, in a single statement, provide him with the secret of the universe. Clearly, such reduction is unreasonable even though reduction does seek to discover laws of greater generality if not universality.

A second element of theory reduction assumes the historical development of theory in a vertically inductive fashion; that is, a scientific theory begins with some observation of the real world, which develops in combination with other similar observations into a generalization of empirical facts, which, in turn, leads to an empirical law, which is then used to explain and predict further empirical facts or to make additional empirical predictions. Such an inductive view of theory construction suggests that observations lead to laws that lead to further observations and predictions.

Science philosophers are not in agreement as to whether progress in scientific theory actually develops historically in such a methodical vertical manner (See Kuhn, 1970). Nevertheless, implicit in the standard view of scientific theory is the assumption that theories are reduced but never actually disconfirmed; that is, once a theory achieves a substantial amount of confirmation (for example, numerous predictions from the theory prove to be valid), it is relatively incapable of being disconfirmed or falsified with further empirical testing. Rather, the empirical search is for a more inclusive theory or more inclusive laws. Phrased in another way, the practice of science is not to search for a better theory but a more parsimonious one. Such is the history of scientific progress in the received view.

At the risk of repeating myself, I consider it important to note that the preceding discussion of the standard view of scientific theory is not intended to be comprehensive. Its purpose is to provide only a "feel" for scientific theory construction and to lay the foundation for the philosophical issues of theoretical perspectives upon which this book rests. It is only with this foreknowledge that an understanding of the later discussion of communication perspectives is possible.

SHORTCOMINGS OF THE "RECEIVED VIEW"

The positivistic approach to scientific theory has not proved to be acceptable for a variety of reasons. Although the issues surrounding a suitable alternative to the covering-law model continue to be debated, several of them merit further consideration. Philosophers of science continue to attack the "received view" and, in so doing, have provided important observations about the nature of theory and research significant to every serious student of social science. Although the issues remain unresolved, they do provide an essential basis for the subsequent discussion of communication perspectives as well as criteria for selecting the most fruitful perspective for future progress in furthering knowledge.

Theory-laden Observation

Like any other specialized activity, science possesses its own mythology —assumptions unchallenged by even the most critical of social observers.

One of those pervasive myths concerns the objective neutrality of science, that is, the belief that scientific osbervation, by virtue of its methodolgy, resists subjective interpretation of data. When a scientist observes a phenomenon scientifically, she allegedly has no choice but to observe that phenomenon without prejudice and without any presuppositions. Only the most hard-core of positivistic scientists, however, would insist that such objective neutrality is anything but a myth.

Achinstein (1965) argues convincingly that the scientist has no choice but to observe within some theoretical framework, which serves to organize material into a pattern, which then becomes understandable and intelligible. The very terms used to describe and record what the scientists observe are definable only within that theoretical framework. In other words, the theory itself provides the language and the definitions used in the observation, so that the observation is inseparable from the theoretical framework.

It is a truism of perception that one perceives by abstracting parts and organizing what is unavoidably incomplete into some coherent whole. And past experiences and expectations will direct the individual in his perceptual organization. A similar process occurs during scientific observation. The theory directs the scientist beyond his conscious control to observe the phenomenon within certain categories, terms, or concepts. Furthermore, his observation is limited to those theoretical concepts. For without the ability to conceptualize his observation of an X, the scientist is simply not capable of observing that X.

We often think of observation and interpretation of that which is observed as two separate processes; that is, we see some object and then, separately and after having seen, we assign some meaning or interpretation to that object. Hanson (1958) argues that seeing and interpretation are not two separate processes but rather two aspects of the same process. One sees and interprets at the same time and in the same activity. One is precisely the same as the other.

Hanson (1958) employs numerous optical illusory drawings to illustrate his notion that seeing and interpretation are inseparable. His most telling illustration, perhaps, is the example of Johannes Kepler and Tycho Brahe together watching the sun rise at dawn. He stipulates that Kepler believed the sun to be stationary in space with the earth's revolving around it. On the other hand, Tycho Brahe theorized quite the opposite —that the earth was stationary and the sun revolved around the earth. Thus, Kepler saw the earth's revolution allowing the sun to come into view, while Tycho Brahe saw the sun actually move and rise above the horizon. Hanson argues that the actual sensory impression, that is, the image that appeared on each man's retina, may have been quite identical. But a human does not have merely a sensory image; he sees that image *as* something or other. Thus, for Kepler to have the retinal image of the rising sun is equivalent to Kepler's having the impression of the rotation of the earth on its axis. To see is to interpret and vice versa.

Kuhn (1974, pp. 473 ff) expresses a similar viewpoint when he indicates that sensory data operating on a human's "neural processing apparatus" set in motion the process of seeing/interpreting, which, although learned, is absolutely unavoidable. Moreover, it is a process to which the human has "no conscious access." The observing human being has no choice in the process and cannot avoid seeing and interpreting at the same time.

In fact, Kuhn describes this cognitive process as one of processing "similarities"—new phenomena that are familiar to us in that they are similar to other phenomena that we have encountered previously. The process is not, according to Kuhn, one of processing "criteria" that we would then apply to phenomena as definitive standards allowing us to make an interpretation. Rather, one processes sensory data by interpreting those data within the framework of previous interpretations. The small child who is beginning to learn the alphabet sees the shapes of letters throughout his/her environment. I can recall my youngest daughter in her preschool years elated at seeing a huge *H* on television while I was watching a football game. My similarity-processing had interpreted the object as a goalpost, but hers prompted her to see a letter of the alphabet.

When one applies the joint process of seeing/interpreting to scientific theorizing, the truly objective observation of any phenomenon becomes problematic, to say the least. As Feyerabend (1965, p. 180) points out, "The meaning of every term we use depends upon the theoretical context in which it occurs." If my context were the football game, I saw a goalpost. If my context had been the English alphabet, I would have seen an *H*. The processing of similarities within some context is simply unavoidable. As a geologist, I might view a volcanic eruption as a subterranean disturbance explainable within the framework of my geological theory. As a member of some "primitive" (so-called because of its "unscientific" nature) tribe, however, I might view that same eruption as some recompense of the gods for my past transgressions. I would then explain the same phenomenon within my theological theory.

The issue is not which theory is "correct" or which theory is the most explanatory. Indeed, the theological theory could be used to explain more phenomena than the geological theory. The more important issue is that my observation and my interpretation occur simultaneously so that the observed phenomena are explainable within the terms and labels of some theoretical explanation. Moreover, those terms are definable only within that theoretical perspective. To remove any term from its theoretical context is to place it within another context and thereby change its meaning —perhaps drastically.

Feyerabend (1963, 1965, 1970) insists that theories are "incommensurable" with each other, so that a term in one theory cannot be compared with a term in another theory—even the theory that developed from an older one. Bohm (1974, pp. 375 ff) is even more emphatic. He indicates that to call two theories incommensurable is redundant and irrelevant. He compares *incommensurable theories* with the term *nonquadrangular triangle,* which is obviously meaningless. Because any term or concept owes its meaning, its observation, its truth value, and even its very existence to its theoretical context, it cannot meaningfully be compared with any concept or term within another theory, even though the term may bear the same label.

Thus, conceptualizations of any phenomenon can be observed within one theory, or it can be observed within another theory. Furthermore, the different observations cannot meaningfully be compared one with the other in order to say which observation is more accurate or "better." The inevitable conclusion is that the observations are simply different. The differing theoretical contexts (and all theoretical contexts differ) render the observations inherently and unavoidably different. And one cannot go beyond that conclusion.

Alternate Theoretical Perspectives

From the preceding discussion of theory-laden observation, it seems obvious that different theories might exist simultaneously to explain the same phenomena and render different conclusions and explanations of the phenomena. Whether this state of affairs is desirable is a matter of considerable philosophical debate. Whereas the positivists would argue for the covering-law explanations, which would regulate scientific theorizing within a framework governed by a vocabulary and a logical system (or systems) for theorizing and observing, the philosopher-critics of the received view are not in agreement as to how scientific theorizing should proceed.

Kuhn (1970) believes that the development of a "mature" science leads to unification of members of the scientific community around a single theory. And, thus, maximal progress in science occurs within a unified scientific paradigm. Feyerabend (1963, 1965, 1970), on the other hand, argues for the development of "mutually inconsistent theories," which are "factually adequate" and "partially overlapping." But he believes that the greatest progress in science occurs within the competing and parallel development of different scientific theories, each one keeping the other "honest." Lakatos and Musgrave (1970) differ slightly from Feyerabend by advocating simultaneous but differing "research programs," which function within potentially different theoretical contexts and which develop differing explanations.

Despite the disagreement among critics of the received view, one element of agreement is abundantly clear: alternative theoretical contexts with differing concepts and explanations of the relationships among the same phenomena are distinctly possible within scientific research. The disagreement evolves around the desirability and acceptability of simultaneous differing theories and whether one or more should gain the acceptance of the bulk of practicing scientific researchers.

Why, then, does one choose which theory is most credible or most valuable? The obvious answer is that the theory that is most correct should be the one that gains the greatest acceptance among scientists. Certainly, the geological explanation of a volcanic eruption, recalling an earlier illustration, is preferable to the theological explanation based on the wrath of some gods. But the choice between scientific theories is rarely, if ever, one that involves an issue of the "accuracy" of a theory. Representing a philosophical truism, Suppe (1974, p. 215) boldly states that any choice between competing theories can be made only "on some basis other than their factual adequacy." Representing a different philosophical position, Kaplan (1964, p. 312), nevertheless, agrees: "Truth itself is plainly useless as a criterion for the acceptability of a theory."

To a nonscientist, such an assertion seems absurd. How can more than one theory explaining the same phenomena be true? The answer to such a question involves issues that are much too complex to be discussed in this brief overview, even if such a discussion were central to our purposes. But part of the answer lies in the earlier discussion of theory-laden observation. Whether any observation is "true" (that is, whether it is a "fact") must ultimately be determined within its own theoretical context, which stipulates how observations are to be made, what interpretations are to be phrased on the basis of the observations, and what criteria are to be applied to those observations/interpretations in order to determine their status as "fact." On a common-sense level, what is a fact to one person is not necessarily a fact to another. The criteria for judging something as a fact ultimately depend on the theoretical context in which that something is conceived, perceived, defined, and observed.

Kaplan (1964) suggests that scientific research is essentially autonomous in terms of the concepts that may be used for explanation (p. 79) or the form and content of the theory itself (p. 322); that is, no concept or theory is more "scientific" or more "pure" than any other. And the scientist is essentially free to choose what concepts and what theoretical structure or terms he is to employ to guide his research efforts. Whatever basis is used to make this choice may vary widely among scientists or scientific communities. The scientist may choose concepts and a theory because of its simplicity, its parsimony, its scope, its precision, its stage of development—in short, its fruitfulness. And judging to what extent a theory is fruitful is problematic. No clear-cut and consistent objective standards exist for assessing the "fruitfulness" of a theory. The choice ultimately boils down to a subjective choice of the scientist as to what is fruitful for him/her.

Feyerabend (1963) suggests that the best method to determine the acceptance-values of two or more theories is to perform a "crucial experiment" in which the same objective situation yields different observational phenomena. Within one experimental situation, then, Feyerabend suggests the testing of both observations (from competing theories) at once and comparing those different observations within some theoretical context of greater generality, that is, a theory that would encompass both theories being employed in the crucial experiment. Unfortunately, according to Feyerabend, such a crucial experiment is impossible—not because it is too difficult to establish but because no way exists to compare the observational statements of the differing theories.

Smart (1968, pp. 81–87) criticizes Feyerabend's notion of a crucial experiment by indicating its logical structure within a covering-law model. But he misses Feyerabend's point that the two different observational statements are simply not comparable given any methodologies currently employed in science. According to Feyerabend, then, anyone can perform a crucial experiment for the purpose of simultaneously cross-testing different theories. But no one knows how to interpret the results to conclude anything from the results of the cross-testing.

Feyerabend (1963) goes further to argue against arguments based on "synonymy"—that is, criticizing one theory from the perspective of another theory. As Feyerabend suggests, such criticism does not evaluate the theory's ability to explain realistic phenomena but evaluates instead the theory's ability to provide an explanation similar to another theory. But if the theory were similar in the first place, there would be no reason for it to be a competing theory in existence. The very fact that it differs from another theory (which it must, for theories are inherently incommensurable) makes it immune to criticism from the context of another theory. To criticize a theory is to evaluate it against reality—not against the assumptions or observations of another theory.

Mandelbaum (1957) indicates further that the nature of the conclusions as theoretical laws may even differ from one theory to another. This difference among laws would render such laws incapable of being compared with laws of a different kind; that is, laws themselves (especially those explaining social behavior) differ in how and what they explain. Mandelbaum distinguishes, for example, between "global" laws and "abstractive" laws, both possessing equivalent lawlike predictive power.

But abstractive laws stipulate some regularity of relationship between two (or more) properties or components of a system that holds true in the presence of specified initial or boundary conditions in a variety of situations. An example of such an abstractive law from communication research might concern the lawlike regularity of relationship between two variables within a specified communication: "Given a moderately high amount of education and an initial favorable attitude, two-sided persuasive messages exert greater persuasive impact on receivers than one-sided messages." The emphasis of such a law is on properties of components and their linear relationship to each other in the presence of specifiable initial conditions.

A global law, on the other hand, concerns the properties of the system as a whole (rather than properties of components) and how these component parts behave and reflect changes in the system over time. An example of a global law (assuming potential lawlike regularity) from communication research might stipulate, "The verbal interaction patterns of decision-making groups achieving consensus reflect discernible progressive phases of orientation, conflict, emergence, and reinforcement." The emphasis of a global law is on holistic properties changing over time in a variety of situations.

It is important to note that these examples are not meant to illustrate the actual presence of "laws" in communication theory but (despite the question of whether they possess the status of "law") that explanations of phenomena are obviously different in terms of what they are about. Abstractive laws are about properties of components linearly related in the presence of initial conditions. Global laws are about holistic properties changing over time and generalizable to many similar situations. The two kinds of laws differ as to form, content, and purpose and are thus incomparable.

The increasingly clear conclusion of this discussion of alternative theoretical perspectives is a basic tenet underlying this entire book. Multitudes of human beings, including social scientists and scholars, obviously disagree as to their understanding, explanation, and even definition of human communication. As students of communication, we should not attempt to discover which explanation, understanding, or definition is "correct." Such a "discovery" would, of course, render all others incorrect. Rather, our task is to understand the various perspectives and judge their relative fruitfulness in extending our knowledge.

After all, we are all convinced that the phenomenon that we have chosen to call "communication" does exist. And the phenomenon of communication does not change merely because different people define it differently. Humans see the same phenomenon and interpret it within some theoretical context. Changing one's theoretical perspective does not change the world, but it does change what we consider significant in the world; that is, what any individual sees in the world and how that same individual interprets what she sees are dependent upon her theoretical spectacles. In other words, communication (the phenomenon) does not change from one theoretical perspective to another, but our understanding of communication (the same phenomenon) can change drastically.

Formalization of Theories

Up to this point our discussions have concerned themselves with how one uses and is used by a theory. We have been less concerned with the actual structure or form of a theory itself; that is, what does a theory look like? If we had a theory of communication, how would we express it? On this point, the positivists are clear and emphatic. Theories are subject to formalization within some deductive logical language of mathematics. Furthermore, deductive logic leads directly to explanation within the covering-law model. The critics of the received view, however, are not so convinced and have suggested some inherent flaws and shortcomings of deductive formalization.

You will recall that deduction is tautological in that the premises of a deductive argument contain all the information necessary to draw a conclusion. Moreover, because a valid conclusion drawn from true premises cannot be false, the task of scientific research within the hypothetico-deductive paradigm is to attempt to discover the truth-value of the premises, thereby rendering the deduction true. The advantages of the hypothetico-deductive paradigm are clear. It lends precision to the explanation, resists extraneous error, and allows scientists to utilize the benefits of sophisticated mathematical formulations.

But some critics believe that the same elements that are advantages of hypothetico-deductivism are disadvantages as well. Merton (1957), for example, argues that the precision allowed by deductive formalizations may be a blessing in disguise. He argues that the pressures of precision and logical coherence often contribute to an increasing sterilization of research. Scientific questions are formulated in terms of variables selected for their ease of measurement. Problems of operationalization and measurement become more important than the imaginativeness of the research hypotheses. Statistical techniques and design come to outweigh the significance of the research question being asked. The resulting attempts at theorizing scientific relationships are either overly trivial or become so far removed in abstraction from their empirical content that they become useless as guidelines for further inquiry.

Meehan (1968, pp. 2–3, 120–121) goes further than Merton in suggesting that the hypothetico-deductive paradigm of scientific explanation is ill-suited to the social sciences and should be rejected—not on the basis that a social scientific explanation is weaker than an explanation in the physical sciences, but that the deductive paradigm simply isn't very useful. The question is not whether a social theory is capable of being formalized; of course, it is. As Suppe (1974, p. 63) points out, any theoretical statement can be formalized by being expressed within some logical language—typically a predicate calculus. More importantly, however, formalizing a theory is often very trivial and contains only generalizations from scientific research—results that are available without their formalized expression. The greater issue is whether formalization is fruitful—not simply whether a formal theory of communication is possible.

If there is any question as to whether formalization is necessary to the existence of a theory, an analogy might suffice to remove any doubt. The music we play and sing is written in a score—the language of music. However, being writable in a score form does not indicate that music might well exist that is not capable of being scored in the language of music. Music from some of the countries of the Middle East (for example, Iran, Turkey, Syria, and so on), I have been told, is played on instruments that are capable of playing pitches of infinite variability. In fact, the synthesizer, increasingly popular in contemporary music, is also capable of playing pitches of infinite variety, that is, in the "cracks of the piano." Is music from such instruments not music because it cannot be phrased in the language of music, that is, the score? If it cannot be so formalized, is it no longer music? Regardless of our attitudes toward Middle Eastern and rock music, I think we would all agree that such music is still music, even though it cannot be formalized within the language of music.

Some valuable varieties of explanation in the social sciences resist formalization within any known logical system. An example of such an explanation is that derived from functionalism (see, for example, Demerath and Peterson, 1967). To be sure, some aspects of function can be represented mathematically, but mathematical representation does not always assist explanatory power. Nor are all aspects of functionalism equivalent to mathematical functions.

A second variety of social explanations is evolutionary explanation. (See, for example, Malcolm [1968] and Jantsch [1975].) Such explanations are virtually incapable of formalization within existing logical systems. The essential difference is the basis of explanation—probabilities of expectation based upon retrospective examination versus prediction from initial conditions based upon prospective examination. The logic of the conditional (if–then) is simply not appropriate for evolutionary explanations. Requiring such an explanation to be force-fit into a logical language is problematic, if not downright foolish.

Kaplan (1964) and Monge (1975) have suggested a way of preserving formalization of theories through the invention of idiosyncratic symbolic systems of logic to meet the specific needs of a given field of inquiry such as communication. Such new symbolic systems, termed "logics-in-use," may indeed be the answer to formalizing theories without being tied directly to the hypothetico-deductive paradigm of predicate calculus—specifically conditional statements.

On the other hand, developing new logics-in-use may create as many new problems as it solves old ones. Scientists may well proliferate the number of logical systems as they have proliferated the variety of concepts and variables used in research. Moreover, a new logic does not solve the inherent problem of reductionism found in any logical system. As Naess (1975, p. 193) points out, among other things science restricts the nature of "facts" and that which is considered "factual" by the criterion of whether it is expressible within the framework of the logical language. Can a different logic alleviate the problem of positivistic reductionism, or will it merely provide a new variety of reductionism?

In this entire discussion of formalizing theories, the most fundamental issue has not yet been mentioned, and that is, What is the value of a formalized theory? Why does any scientist wish to express theoretical statements within some logical format in the first place? Bohm (1974, p. 389) states emphatically that our tendency to regard mathematical formalisms as some sort of truth is blatantly false. Mathematics provides only an extension of ordinary language in order to endow the expressed relationships with greater precision, thereby allowing the drawing of inferences. The logic is only a tool—no more and no less—and has no truth value in and of itself.

Hempel (1974, p. 250) stipulates that formalization is possible only *after* a theory has been developed and does nothing more than provide the theory with a precise statement of the information that is available with or without the formalization. Hempel (p. 257) goes even further and states that "at some point, there will have to be an interpretation [of the formalized statement] in terms already understood that does not in turn rely on formalization." Hempel, whose positivistic bias is well known, is clear on this point when he states emphatically that scientists can agree on, understand, and utilize any scientific term or relationship without having to rely on any formalized statement. His position also seems clear that a logical formalization of a theory is not necessary for theory and, in fact, must ultimately be interpreted outside the formalization.

The question of whether a theory should be formalized is certainly not resolved. To be sure, if communication (for example) were a formal theory, the concepts would be clear, and empirical measurements would be precise. A consequence of such precision, however, would be a restriction on what "facts" of observation and relationships are allowable. In other words, the desirability of formalization remains an open question. But whether formalization is necessary does not seem at issue. The implication is clear that a theory can exist without formalizations or axioms. More accurately, a theory can be expressed in ordinary language without the benefit of some logical language, whether an existing predicate calculus or a logic-in-use. Definitions of terms included in the theory would be more problematic, but the increased richness of explanation should more than compensate for the difficulty in achieving precision.

The Theory Versus the Practice of Science

One fact of communication study—no exception among the social sciences—is indisputable. The relationship between theory and research is not a close one by any stretch of the imagination. The bulk of research aims not at the confirmation or development of any general theoretical framework but at the confirmation of specific hypotheses. Communication research is variable-oriented rather than theory-oriented. Moreover, the few explicit attempts to discuss a communication theory of any generality discuss the issues at such a high level of abstraction as to inhibit empirical inquiry of specific research questions. Clearly, the need for a closer connection between specifically communication theory and research should be a foremost consideration of any serious student of communication. The only problem remaining is the question of how to go about such an endeavor.

The most obvious place to begin such an attempt to bring theory and research together is to discover what scientists are now doing. Kuhn (1970, 1974) suggests that a scientific paradigm exists only because some community of scientists are practitioners and specialists within that paradigm. Diesing (1971, pp. 319–320) suggests that a membership in a scientific community consists of "regular, effective collaboration with other members." Kuhn (1974, pp. 461–462) expresses a similar view. Diesing suggests further that the boundaries of the community "are marked by non-interaction, misunderstanding, and polemics." The identification of communities of scholars within a given field of inquiry provides a logical starting point for the study of communication theory and how research naturally follows theoretical guidelines.

The fact is that active scholars are members of a scientific community with an identifiable theoretical "set" even though they may be unable to articulate that theory with much explicitness. Kuhn's (1970, 1974) notion of shared exemplars provides the clue. He posits the belief that scientists generally imitate the past successful practices of other scientists through an almost subliminal acculturation into the scientific community. The scientist is exposed to the same literature as fellow members and learns the same techniques of observation and measurement and research methods. Logan (undated) suggests, for example, that in the instance of psychology, students in even the basic experimental psychology course become acculturated to a considerable extent in what research looks like, how it is to be performed and evaluated, and what variables or potential variables exist for empirical inquiry.

Even the beginning student in any basic course of any scientific specialty knows that the first job is to learn the jargon of the new field much as one learns a foreign language. Surely, then, any field of inquiry that has any degree of specialization possesses shared exemplars—*exemplars* because they serve as criteria-models upon which to perform and judge past and future research in their likenesses; *shared* because they enjoy to some extent a standardized usage among members of a scientific community.

Burgess (1972), analyzing the field of psychology, suggests that many paradigms (in the sense of "shared exemplars") exist within that scientific community. And I shall take a similar position regarding the field of communication. The scientific community of communication scholars is by no means unified. Techniques vary widely. Terms are not consistent from one segment of the community to another. And more importantly, perhaps, the conceptualizations and operational definitions of the same term are distinguishably different when used by different communication scholars.

One must be careful, though, not to confuse Kuhn's concept of "paradigm" with theory. Kuhn (1970) is explicit on that point as is at least one of his critics (see Masterman, 1970). A paradigm is not nearly as sophisticated as a theory and is rarely formalized. Nor should a paradigm be confused with research techniques or methodological techniques. To be sure, paradigms are definable by what scientists do with their techniques and methods rather than what techniques and methods they use. A given research method can stultify, or occasionally further, the development of scientific intuition and explanation, but it is far from being equivalent to intuition and explanation.

It seems obvious that the relationship between theory and practice within a given scientific research specialty is not close. The field of communication is certainly no exception. It seems equally obvious that the connection between theory and research practices should be much closer than it is in order to ensure true scientific progress. One way to assist this closer relationship is to discover what subfields or sub- specialties exist within the scientific community—those scholars actively engaged in the study of human communication.

If it is true that one's theoretical viewpoint determines the relevance and significance of concepts and properties (see Bohm, 1974), the task becomes one of surveying the scientific community with an eye to locating the essential *differences*, not similarities, among subcommunities. Discovering the specialized subfields within the community of scientists should enable us to understand more clearly the broad spectrum of communication study. Certainly, what we have come to call "communication theory" is not a unified phenomenon. Nor is it a "theory" in the sense of any school of thought among philosophers of science. But it is an intriguing and traditional discipline of specialized study eminently worthy of our increased understanding.

— 3 —

The Nature of Perspectives

Several years ago I recall watching a professional football game on television. In the later stages of the game, the referee ruled that an apparent touchdown catch was out of bounds and, therefore, was incomplete. Naturally, a heated controversy ensued as to whether the receiver was actually out of bounds when he caught the ball. In an effort to settle the controversy (and, of course, improve its ratings), the network reviewed the same play repeatedly on their marvelous innovation— the instant replay. I, along with the other viewers, was subjected to the déjà vu experience of watching the same event from three different angles—the original overhead long view, a ground-level camera angle from the sidelines, and a ground-level camera angle from the opposite side of the end zone.

In slow-motion frenzy, the receiver repeatedly caught the ball and tumbled over the sideline as I watched from three different angles. In fact, I watched with no small amount of anxiety in order to determine whether I could see both of his feet in bounds for even a fraction of a second. The overhead view was inconclusive—insufficient detail. The sideline camera clearly showed the second foot out-of-bounds as the receiver landed. The controversy seemed over when I saw the same play from the end zone camera. That angle appeared to indicate that the foot was inside the white sideline marker as the receiver fell down. Being a rabid Vikings fan, I felt inclined to accept the conclusion drawn on the basis of the end zone view. (The receiver, you see, was a Viking.) But, as is inevitably the case, the referee's perception of the event prevailed, and the Vikings lost the touchdown (but, as I recall, won the game).

This trivial event (although it seemed significant at the time) illustrates a truism of observation/interpretation. Knowledge of any reality depends on one's observing/interpreting it. (You will recall that observing and interpreting are the same process.) That is, whatever one knows or can know of a thing depends on the observation/interpretation of that thing. And the observation/interpretation of a thing is dependent upon the perspective used to observe/interpret. The event of the pass reception did not change merely because a different camera angle recorded it. But our understanding of that event (that is, our observation/interpretation of the event) is eminently worthy of change. Whatever our understanding of the event, it is dependent upon the perspective we have in observing the event. And part of our perspective includes the "set" or conceptualization we have of the event as it occurs.

This football example may lead some of us to conclude that one perspective is better than another because it, unlike some others, actually reflects the reality of the event. Indeed, the receiver either was or was not out-of-bounds. He could not have been both. Nor could he have been neither. In this sense, the football analogy may be misleading. In problems of scientific inquiry, many of the questions that are posed simply do not have such yes-no answers. (Elsasser, 1966, terms this aspect of social scientific phenomena the "radical inhomogeneity" of the phenomena of life.)

When I was an undergraduate student in an art appreciation course, I must admit to having been something of a cultural "clod." But one instance did impress me at the time. The instructor began a unit on expressionism by illustrating the period with a particular painting (by Picasso, as I recall). That painting included a table, which showed at once the top, bottom, and all four legs. As a typical recalcitrant student in art appreciation, I immediately considered the table to be "unrealistic" —that is, when one sees a table from a directly overhead view, the bottom and legs are simply not visible. And from an angle in which all four legs of the table are visible, the top and bottom are not. In other words, when a perspective or view is "realistic," some parts of the phenomenon being viewed are omitted, and others are distorted. After all, objects farther away appear smaller, even though they may be the same size or larger than objects in the foreground. But that is an elementary precept in the nature of perspective.

In other words, any perspective is to some extent incomplete and distorted, even though it is very "real." The obvious conclusion is that the nature of *reality* is simply not an issue. This fact is indisputable even though it may be disconcerting to the idealist. As true scientific inquirers, we should be more like the Picasso who wanted his observation to be as complete as possible even though he needed to distort reality to some extent. Furthermore, we have little choice but to utilize some perspective that is incomplete and distorted but is as complete as possible. We should also keep in mind that the value of our perspective does not reside in its truth-value or how well it reflects reality. All available perspectives will be true, generally speaking, and reflect reality. Our search, ultimately, is for the perspective that provides for us the most fruitful conceptualization of reality for our purposes.

The term *perspective* was not idly chosen. *Theory*, of course, is an inappropriate term, given the current development of the field of human communication. Kuhn's (1970) term *paradigm* has so many different interpretations as to inhibit any neutral usage. However, his term *disciplinary matrix* might be appropriate. Shapere (1974) uses the term *domain* to refer to a field of multidisciplinary inquiry, which is certainly suitable for communication. Unfortunately, the term connotes that the inquiry has no identity as a discipline in and of itself. Rather it exists as a phenomenon of interest only within other disciplines.

Other terms were suitable for the title of this book, including *models, approaches, intellectual strategies, conceptual frameworks,* and *Weltanschauungen.* None provides the instant awareness of the common usage of the term *perspectives.* Nor do the other terms suggest the possibility of differing views of the same phenomenon. The understanding of human communication, as Parts Two and Three illustrate, is a matter of the perspective used to understand it.

PROPERTIES OF PERSPECTIVES

The significance of theoretical perspectives is probably greater in the social sciences than in the physical sciences. At least, differences among theoretical perspectives are more evident in the social sciences. Some consider this variability a symptom of the different nature of the phenomena unique to the social and physical sciences. Some consider such variability to be a weakness of the social sciences; others see it as a symptom of their strength. Under any circumstances, perspectives of any area of science (but typically the social sciences) contain certain inherent properties. These properties accrue whenever perspectives are applied, regardless of whether that specific field of inquiry is communication, psychology, sociology, anthropology, history, or political science.

Relevance Determining

Bohm (1974, pp. 376–377) typifies the incommensurability of theories with a brief historical description of malaria research. That same example also illustrates the inescapable fact that the perspective one uses to view any phenomenon determines to no small extent what aspects of that phenomenon are considered to be significant or relevant and, conversely, which aspects are deemed trivial and irrelevant.

The word *malaria* itself, according to Bohm, derives from the early association of the disease with "bad air." Thus, it was believed that anyone exposed to damp night air would contract malaria. As a matter of fact, we might hypothesize that the early theorists may have noticed swampy areas and pools of water and speculated that this excess water might contribute to the dampness of the air. Subsequent drainage of the ground water may even have resulted in decreasing the number of malaria cases and thus served to confirm their perspective.

We now know, of course, that the cause of malaria is not a humid atmosphere but bacteria carried by mosquitoes. Draining the swamps may have reduced the numbers of mosquitoes by destroying their breeding grounds, but the dampness of the air is certainly irrelevant to the disease—its cause or its cure. In fact, knowing that the mosquito population contributes to the incidence of malaria may well have led later theorists to drain excess groundwater in addition to employing insecticides and antibiotics. But in the two perspectives of malaria, such action is based on totally different conceptualizations of the disease, leading to quite different conclusions—even though the action (draining groundwater) and the results (reduced incidence of malaria) may have been identical.

If you have ever been to an auction, a rummage sale, or an antique shop, you are probably aware of the adage that one person's junk is another's treasure. The person selling an old table at an auction, for example, may see it as a piece of discarded old furniture inherited from parents and last used as a platform for mixing paint. I might view that same table as a piece of used furniture with minimal utilitarian value because it reflected an outmoded design and would take considerable refinishing work in order to render it usable. An aficionado of antiques, however, might view the same table as a valuable collector's item representative of a specific period of furniture making. The table itself remains constant within all three of these perspectives; only the person's understanding of the table changes. And our understanding is based wholly on our conceptualization of the phenomenon, that is, our perspective.

Meehan (1968, p. 83) is emphatic on this point when he writes, "The most important and most difficult part of explanation.is the selection of concepts to load the system." Meehan goes on to indicate that we really have no guidelines to assist us in conceptualizing. Rules and principles related to methods and techniques of explanation abound in virtually every scientific field of endeavor. But we are left on our own to develop our concepts.

Clearly, a concept that is trivial or irrelevant or even ignored in one perspective may suddenly leap into importance when one applies an alternative perspective. For example, most of us would not even notice the behavior of smoothing hair, straightening a tie, brushing lint off clothing, and so on, in a casual conversation. If we did notice it, we would probably consider such behavior random and perhaps distracting movements but certainly not significant in establishing a communicative relationship. In Scheflen's (1965) perspective of a "quasi-courtship" context, though, such behavior is called "preening" and assumes great significance in establishing social relationships.

After all, when one views a communicative event, one does not view people who believe in certain theories of communication or who hold certain axiomatic propositions in mind. One views people making certain movements and sounds. The relevance or significance of those movements and sounds is a direct result of the concepts used to understand the communicative event. Those concepts determine what is relevant in the event. In terms of what they do not include, concepts also determine what is irrelevant.

We often tend to think of the quest for knowledge or understanding as the *discovery* of some truth that exists. If we do not know or understand, we like to think that we will someday, for it is "out there"—somewhere—to be discovered. Actually, scientific knowledge does not conform to such a naïve view of the world. What we now know or can ever know is not truth but *understanding*—an understanding *created* by humans. And because our understanding is the result of our humanness, it is subject to conceptual changes historically as our concepts and perspectives used in creating our understanding change. In this sense, our knowledge/understanding of the world is like a moving picture—constantly changing and fallible. We should not conceive of knowledge as a snapshot—a truth discovered, static and unchanging. Today's fact may be tomorrow's folly.

Time/Culture-bound

Generations of philosophers and scientists have concerned themselves with the basic paradigm of science as that of the physical sciences. The guidelines of controlled experimental research and hypothesis testing from axiomatic laws have emanated directly from the physical sciences —notably physics and chemistry—and have been the bases for comparison with the social sciences. But such a view naïvely ignores a fundamental aspect of the social sciences—the concepts of the social sciences, unlike those of the physical sciences, are nonconstants. They vary from one period of history to another and from one culture to another within the same time period.

Weaver (1953) describes a property of nineteenth-century rhetoric/communication, which he terms "spaciousness." At the risk of oversimplifying Weaver's analysis, I would suggest that the spaciousness of a century ago is not extinct but has merely evolved into a variety of contemporary spaciousness. In the nineteenth century, Americans maintained a strong and virtually unquestioned conviction and faith in the precepts of the Bible and the United States Constitution. Because they did not "enjoy" the technological marvels of radio, television, and motion pictures, their view of mass media was one of public speakers and platform entertainment. Information that came to them from these forms of mass media, as well as newspapers, probably, was clothed in the language and the lawlike principles of God and Constitution. And they believed.

Our modern sophistication leads us to scoff at the naïveté of our ancestors. But they would probably scoff, too, at our equally incredible naïveté and manipulation by the spaciousness of contemporary rhetoric/communication as illustrated in contemporary political campaigns. Candidates for political office today are merchandised as products, as "things." We vote not on the basis of issues but on the more naïve basis of "image." Books such as *The Selling of the President* and movies such as *The Candidate* paint a disturbingly real picture of today's reality. The principle of spaciousness may be not so much a matter of historical interest but a concept that has only changed in character through time.

Certainly, the variables and concepts of social behavior may lose or gain significance across time or cultural boundaries. What must not be overlooked is that the time/culture-bound character of the principles of social sciences is a fact of life. As Machlup (1961, p. 184) points out, "these are not defects to be remedied but fundamental properties [of social sciences] to be grasped, accepted, and taken into account."

This variability of social scientific principles across the boundaries of time and culture may suggest that evolutionary explanations may be more significant than they are in the physical sciences. In physics, for example, evolution is a far slower process, requiring eons rather than centuries or even decades to note discernible change. Time/cultural variability may indicate a need for a multiple-perspective approach to the social sciences. It may also indicate a difference between social sciences and physical sciences. But whatever the indications, we must take into account the time/culture-bound nature of social concepts and principles in order to understand adequately what we are about.

Interchangeability

If we return to the earlier example of the table being sold at an auction, the conceptualization used by the three people (the seller, myself, and the antique expert) are not the sole possessions of those three people. In fact, the seller (or even I) could utilize the perspective of the antique aficionado and find antique-value in that piece of furniture. In other words, we can view the same phenomenon (in this case, the table) from different perspectives at different times; that is, perspectives used to conceptualize a phenomenon are interchangeable among people. Moreover, as a person utilizes a different perspective, that new conceptualization will yield different results, which are, to a considerable extent, not comparable with the results of the former perspective used.

Now this notion of the interchangeability of perspectives does not imply that every scientist can or should employ different perspectives for every observation in order to be a good scientist. In fact, the converse is probably more representative of good scientific practice; that is, a scientist typically uses one perspective, the perspective that he or she believes to be the most appropriate and that will yield the most fruitful results.

A good scientist is not an intellectual or theoretical dilettante who changes his or her perspective, his or her theoretical conceptualization at will. The good scientist understands all available perspectives and accepts them as viable alternatives. But he/she also has a mind of his/her own and has opted for that perspective that appears to be most fruitful. Depending on scientific interests and purposes, that perspective may be different from one scientist to another. Therefore, a scientific community taken as a whole probably reflects the usage of a number of different perspectives. But a single practicing scientist has probably settled on one perspective.

The point to be gleaned from the interchangeability of perspectives, then, is not simply that one perspective is as good as another; so take your pick. A much more fundamental issue is involved, an issue that appears throughout this entire volume and that is worthy of repetition. No theory (or perspective) can be considered to reflect truth, rendering all other theories (or perspectives) false. Perspectives are autonomous. They are, generally speaking, all true. But, then, truth-value is of little significance. The fruitfulness of the perspective is the prime criterion for its acceptance and use.

Phrasing this interchangeability principle in yet another way, we may say that knowledge is not an absolute reflection of reality—even scientific knowledge. Knowledge is inevitably social—what people believe to be true or have found to be true—but inevitably social nonetheless. As is the case with any kind of knowledge, scientific knowledge is not independent of the people who know; it cannot be separated from this inherently social element. Grasping this fundamental aspect of knowledge is the first step toward acquiring understanding.

Models and Analogies

In nearly every field of scientific inquiry (communication is no exception), models play a vital role. A model is basically an analogy that abstracts or selects parts from the whole, the significant elements or properties or components of that phenomenon that is being modeled. The model then allows the scientist to observe the interactions of these vital elements free from the confounding of the insignificant elements.

In this sense, the model airplane tested in the wind tunnel is aerodynamically equivalent to the full-sized airplane but is much smaller, made of different materials, and not equipped with all the interior accouterments of the "real" airplane. But for the purposes of testing the plane's aerodynamic properties in the wind tunnel, elements such as interior design, size, and so on, are not significant. Only those properties of the aircraft relevant to the wind-tunnel-testing procedure are selected for inclusion in the model. The advantages of using the model rather than the full-sized airplane are obvious.

Like the model airplane, scientific models are also quite valuable. Campbell (1920) and Scriven (1962), a physicist and a philosopher, agree on the value of models as informal descriptions to explain and apply a theory. Hawes (1975, p. 8) argues that the most valuable use of models is in the inductive or discovery phase of inquiry as an heuristic aid in conceptualizing the facts. Whenever models are most valuable— in applying the theory or in generating a theory—seems a trivial point of debate. That models are valuable in understanding scientific phenomena and their interrelationships seems a matter of undisputed agreement. The perspective, then, should probably include some model or analogical device in order to describe and explain the conceptualization. Such a model will select those elements and properties considered crucial to the phenomenon and organize them into a clear framework for understanding. The model locates what is important and describes the nature of the relationships among component elements. Although many models, particularly of communication, include some pictorial description, such a depiction is not essential to the model. Certainly, models may be in verbal form—in words rather than the all-too-familiar circles, lines, arrows, Greek letters, and the like. Each of the perspectives of human communication in Part Two will include a model—even a pictorial depiction of a model. But you will soon discover that some perspectives are, much more than others, adaptable to pictorial representation.

PHILOSOPHICAL ISSUES OF PERSPECTIVES

Numerous issues, many unresolved and many unresolvable, exist in every field of scientific inquiry regardless of the perspective utilized. Some of these key issues surround the distinction between what is science and what is nonscience. Others involve the doing of science—the act of scientific inquiry. Still others involve the conceptualization of phenomena under scientific scrutiny. Although our task is not to resolve such issues arbitrarily, foreknowledge of the issues involved is essential to applying the perspectives to the field of communication study.

Methodological Bias

The mystique of "science" has pervaded intellectual Western thought for several centuries. Most of the general populace is in awe of science and scientists. Sometimes that awe even takes the form of fear. Sometimes awe is in the form of great expectations of new discoveries that will revolutionize industry, transportation, education, and our very way of life. The mystique pervades our imaginations in the form of science fiction—the logical extension of scientific progress into the future. We fear science. We respect science. We worship science. We endow the very word with a mystique all its own and, fundamentally, don't understand it. But, above all else, we do know that science is methodical with a method that pretentiously bears its own name—*the* scientific method. But precisely what is the scientific method? The answer to such a question is unclear. Bunge (1967, p. 12) points out clearly that the scientific method is "a mark of science." That is, it provides "the difference between science and non-science." But it is not a single method. Rather, science proceeds by employing a variety of "special methods adapted to the peculiarities of the subject matter." Clearly, then, *the* scientific method is a misnomer. It is only the method used by the scientist, whatever it is. And Kaplan (1964, p. 27), citing Bridgman, has already suggested that "the scientist has no other method than doing his damnedest."

But the advice of "do your damnedest" is probably less than totally satisfactory for the student who desires to learn how to do science. He or she will demand more guidelines than that. Such guidelines apparently involve the learning of many techniques that can be applied to the observation of scientific phenomena. If they are part of a scientific method, the techniques probably possess some characteristic properties in common.

Nagel (1967, p. 9) suggests that one such characteristic is "control." But Nagel may be overly restrictive. He stipulates that his view of scientific method is not necessarily "overtly experimental" but must include some "eliminative procedure [;] the differential effects of a factor that is assumed to be relevant to the occurrence of a given phenomenon can be ascertained." Frankly, I cannot discern the crucial difference between Nagel's description of scientific method and that of experimentation. And certainly an experiment is not the only method that scientists have at their disposal.

H. R. Smart (1931, pp. 44–45), on the other hand, indicates one general characteristic of scientific method that should arouse no question. He believes that the key to a scientific method "is simply to proceed in an *orderly* manner, and in the light of some clear *guiding principles,* with the investigation of a given subject matter." (Emphasis added.) Scientific inquiry, then, is orderly, systematic—governed by some clearly understood principles that, of course, may vary from one method or technique to another. For a method to be scientific, one must be able to understand what was done, how it was done, and how the conclusion was achieved. Given this characteristic, virtually any method is scientific if the inquirer is able to defend the observations and results as systematic and orderly because of the clarity of the guidelines.

The prime characteristic of scientific methods, however, is objectivity. The scientist, so it is said, views the world with an unjaundiced eye, lets the chips fall where they will, and then records the placement of the fallen chips. For years some philosophers have accused the social sciences with failing to be objective—that is, that the methods of the social sciences do not provide the objectivity of those in the physical sciences.

The charge is, of course, unfair and fails to consider what the social sciences are about. But this comparison was the subject of an earlier discussion.

To be objective, we would say, the scientist must not be subjective. But what subjectivity implies is as imprecise as what objectivity implies. Rudner (1966, pp. 68–83) suggests four possible meanings employed to distinguish the objective from the subjective: (1) whether ideas and concepts are the same from one person to another; (2) whether statements are true; (3) whether methodologies used in science are reliable; and (4) whether the scientific investigator employs or believes the ideas, statements, or methodologies used in the act of scientific inquiry. Rudner argues convincingly that social science is clearly objective in the sense of minimizing error, even though social phenomena continue to be laden with excessive meaning.

But the issue at hand is still not whether social sciences are or can be objective, but what objectivity of scientific method implies for the scientist using perspectives. If it implies that the scientist is totally devoid of subjectivity, then the concept of objectivity is not only absurd but worthless. Meehan (1969) illustrates clearly how scientists, in every field of inquiry, employ value judgments, cannot avoid making value judgments, and benefit significantly from the making of those value judgments.

Rudner (1953) states clearly that the issue of scientific objectivity requires being aware of those value judgments—not only those that "are being and might have been made in a given inquiry, but more importantly "what value decisions ought to be made." He goes even further to state, "The slightly juvenile conception of the coldblooded, emotionless, impersonal, passive scientist mirroring the world perfectly in the highly polished lenses of his steel rimmed glasses—this stereotype—is no longer, if it ever was, adequate." Nor are Meehan and Rudner alone in this philosophical view of scientific objectivity. Those in essential agreement include Churchman (1948) and Braithwaite (1955).

Perhaps the most telling argument against objective purism comes from McGuire (1973), himself a social scientist. McGuire even goes so far as to say, "Experiments . . . turn out to be more like demonstrations than tests. If the experiment does not turn out 'right,' then the researcher does not say that the hypothesis is wrong but rather that something was wrong with the experiment. . . ."

McGuire's accusation rings all too true. I cannot recall reading any report of research that, upon not achieving the sought-for significant differences, did not attempt to rationalize why those differences did not occur. The first, and typically only, response of the investigator is to search for extraneous circumstances—some uncontrollable event, an error in the design, another variable unaccounted for, inappropriate selection of subjects, and so on—that prohibited the expected discovery of significant differences. Occasionally, the scientist even employs other statistical tests in order to discover the differences that must be there but that are not discoverable with the former too stringent test. In other words, the investigator typically discovers that his original hypothesis was correct after all, or he experiences some sense of having failed in his research.

McGuire argues that such research attitudes lead to research that does not "test" the hypothesis so much as it "demonstrates" it—either successfully or unsuccessfully. A review of articles published in our scholarly journals would tend to substantiate such a claim. The investigator clearly illustrates a presumption on the side of the hypotheses under test. If they are confirmed (more accurately, if the null hypotheses are rejected), the investigator assumes the research to be successful. If they are not confirmed, the investigator tends to rationalize the "failure" of the study to reflect the expected results. Such reports of research do not emanate from the spirit of scholarly inquiry, that is, to discover aspects of reality, but from the spirit of confirming one's own predispositions. And that is not very scientific or objective regardless of what method is used in the investigation.

The key to the objectivity of a scientific method is not the absence of subjectivity in the sense that the investigator seeks to remove himself or herself from the observation. Nor does the objectivity of scientific methods involve restricting the investigator's capacity to make value judgments or even reducing the number of value judgments made. To the contrary, achieving objectivity absolutely requires the investigator to make value judgments. The purpose of the method's objectivity is to reduce the probability of error, and every step taken by the investigator to reduce error entails a value judgment of some kind. Essentially subjective choices are not only necessary to the application of a scientific method, but they are crucial to the success of reducing error—in short, to the objectivity of the method itself.

In the sense of making value judgments, subjectivity and objectivity are two sides of the same coin. For example, the choice of the critical value of the statistic at which the investigator will reject the null hypothesis is a necessary value judgment. When the investigator attempts to control mediating external variables that may affect the outcome of the observation, she must choose which variables to control. The choice is inherently subjective and crucial to the reduction of error in any controlled inquiry. The choice of which statistical tool is to be used to analyze results or which design to organize the study is also crucial to error-free research.

The researcher also reduces error in drawing conclusions when she not only allows for, but searches actively for, potentially disconfirming data—a judgment too rarely made in most social scientific research. And most significant of all is the judgmental choice of the research question itself. The application of a scientific method that is truly objective considers each of these choice points—value judgments all—as integral to the doing of research.

Most of these judgments, to be sure, are governed by norms; that is, the community of scientists, through repeated practice of doing research, tend to establish standards or rules of research practice. Hence, many investigators make their value judgments without necessarily being consciously aware of having made a subjective choice. Such norms of scientific practice aren't necessarily harmful, although too often they may result in decreased objectivity if they occur for unscientific reasons. For example, I have the feeling that some variables and statistical techniques are selected not on any objective scientific basis but because of their ease of application or because "positive" results are more likely to be obtained. If my impression is valid, much of social scientific research may be leading nowhere. More importantly, it is not scientific—regardless of the particular method used.

In short, the "scientific method" does not inhere in any particular method or variety of methods. In this sense, there is no such thing as a scientific method per se. Rather, a method is considered to be scientific on the basis of what the investigator does with it, that is, how he applies it. For example, Popper (1968, p. 96) illustrates that even the method of trial and error is applicable as a scientific method. Moreover, contrary to the naïve beliefs of some alleged scholars, a scientific method need not rely on statistical analysis of data (although many do). Nor is a scientific method necessarily experimental. A scientific method is a research method that is applied scientifically and may be descriptive, experimental, qualitative, quantitative, ethnomethodological, critical, analytical, historical, phenomenological, ad infinitum.

Fortunately, only a few alleged social scientists remain who are sufficiently narrow-minded to believe that theirs is the only or even the best method for studying communication. One of the strengths of the communication field is the multiplicity of methods used in its study. But the scientific community of communication scholars could still benefit from what Kaplan (1964, pp. 29–30) calls a "catholicity of outlook." According to this viewpoint, no method and no instrument are identifiable as the core of scientific method. The problem lies not in what methods are used but in the view that some methods are inappropriate to scientific inquiry. As Kaplan says, "All of them are right; what is wrong is only what they deny, not what they affirm."

Operationism

The logical positivistic view of science philosophy, you will recall, considered the separation of observational and theoretical terms to be necessary for science in order to eliminate any metaphysical entities from scientific theory. As a result, philosophers considered operationism as a means to bridge the observational-theoretical gap. Thus, operational definitions enjoy wide usage among social scientists as *the* means to translate theoretical concepts and constructs into empirical phenomena. Thus, the operational definition today holds a central position of importance in the doing of social scientific research.

But philosophers (for example, Hempel [1949], Scriven [1956], and Heidelberger [1969]) have attacked operationism as inherently distasteful. Because operational definitions translate a concept into observable entities, these philosophers note that the concept is invariably defined in physical terms. Such a translation reduces all of science to physics and a common observational language—the language of physics. Although some philosophers argue that operational definitions and a common observational language are both undesirable and impossible, others (for example, Chapin [1939] and Carnap [1955]) argue that operational definitions are essential in order for social science to be either intelligible or scientific.

Despite the philosophical controversy surrounding operational definitions, several practical and conceptual problems are indisputable and inherent in operationism. Are different operational definitions (and many definitions exist operationally for each concept) equivalent with each other? Of course, they are not. Yet scientists treat different operational definitions as if they are equivalent. Simply put, they have no choice but to do so. As Suppe (1974, p. 19) points out, the interchangeability of operational definitions is absolutely essential for science. The only alternative is conceptual chaos. Members of the scientific community have no recourse but to treat the problem of the difference in meaning created by differing operationalizations as insignificant. Then the problem becomes one of choosing which operational definition of a concept to use in a specific research study. Too often the choice is made on purely arbitrary and unscientific bases, such as ease in administering the measurement. But that is a different problem.

A second inherent problem involves the nature of the definition itself. All existing operational definitions taken together do not exhaust the meaning of a concept. Some residual meaning always remains, indicating that no matter how good the operational definition, it does not reveal the true nature of the concept. Nor does it reveal all of a concept. Operational definitions serve only to translate a concept, but they do not define the concept adequately, completely, or conceptually. Phrased in yet another way, an operational definition may increase knowledge of the concept, but it does not allow for an adequate understanding.

A third problem of operational definitions is the tendency among members of the scientific community to confuse the concept with its measuring technique. Such confusion has led some scholars to insist that the only legitimate scientific model is one in which all the terms and concepts can be operationalized. As Dubin (1969, pp. 186–187) stipulates, such a conclusion is patently absurd. Operational definitions are applicable only when the model is tested not before and not after.

Many theoretical concepts are extremely valuable in conceptualizing relationships and providing scientific explanations, even though directly observable indicators of them are simply not available. One might speculate further that an operational definition is merely a convenient tool to use in testing the concept, but it is neither a substitute for the concept, nor is it particularly valuable to the theoretical model from which it is drawn. It is valuable only as a means to allow testing of the model and has no other usefulness or any significance. (See Maxwell, 1968, pp. 159–160.)

The final problem is indisputable when dealing with social scientific phenomena. Interpreting the results of operational observation requires increased involvement of the investigator. The results of the operations do not stand by themselves; they require symbolic interpretation. Interpreting the physical length of an object operationalized with a tape measure requires little interpretation beyond the results of the measurement itself, but a set of attitude scales marked by an experimental subject requires further interpretation beyond the pencil scratches on the paper; that is, 6′ 2″ requires little further interpretation to be meaningful as a measurement of physical height. But what does it mean when a person marks some attitude scales at the midpoint but others at one of the two extremes of the continuum? The social scientific measurement inherently requires symbolic interpretation by the researcher.

What then is the status of operationism in the perspectives of social scientific inquiry? Clearly, the use of operational definitions is fraught with inherent difficulties and seemingly insurmountable problems. Nevertheless, operations are absolutely essential and not to be discarded out of hand, at least until something better is developed. Concepts must be amenable to empirical observation. Operationalizing allows observation. The definition of concepts must be reliable. Operationalizing allows for testing reliability among different observers and observational events.

There is simply no alternative to operationalization at the present time. As Mischel (1969, p. 267) indicates, common sense provides only "rough and ready categories," which are not explicit and are notoriously unreliable. Despite its inherent flaws, operationism is with us for some time to come. Our only recourse is to be aware of the problems created by operational definitions and not allow these problems to inhibit scientific progress.

Individualism and Holism

Philosophers have long treated the controversy between individualism and holism as a methodological issue—which it is, of course. For the purpose of furthering an understanding of perspectives, however, the issue is a conceptual one as well. In fact, the concept of holism exists in the currently popular trend in the field of communication that views communication as a "transaction." The increasingly popular use of system theory to conceptualize communication also smacks of the issue of holism. These contributions to communication perspectives receive more complete treatment in Part Two of this volume. The present purpose is to consider the issue of whether a perspective might utilize an individualistic or a holistic view of social phenomena.

Briefly, individualists (for example, Bergmann [1962], Morgenbesser [1967], and Watkins [1957]) maintain that holistic entities such as group, culture, society, and so on, are not independent of individual persons who comprise them. More specifically, they would maintain that the holistic phenomenon is symptomatic of idealism and is explainable and reducible to scientific principles or laws that explain individual behavior. The social phenomenon, in other words, has no existence beyond that of the individual. The individual imposes the structure on the social entity. The social entity has no capacity to impose structure on the individual.

Holists (for example, Durkheim [1938], and Gellner [1956]) argue that individualism does not account for social regularities that are not discernible in the observation of individual behavior. Moreover, they argue, social phenomena are created by the existence of the social entity, so that, for example, the existence of a group created what Collins and Guetzkow (1964, p. 58) call the "assembly effect." In the words of the adage, the whole is different from the sum of its parts. Such a holistic view should not be confused with the "group mind" concept, now outdated (see Gellner, 1956); that is, the social entity does not take on a property equivalent to that of an individual (for example, a group personality or a cultural ego). Rather, the social entity reveals properties and phenomena unique to the structure of the social unit and unidentifiable in the individual.

To engage seriously in any argument pertaining to the superiority of either individualism or holism would be fruitless, not to mention trivial and self-defeating. As a methodological stance, we should leave it to the philosophers to quibble over. And often the quibbling takes on an arrogance that borders on the incredible. For example, Bergmann (1962) says of holism, "Such nonsense we can dismiss without further ado." He also states flatly, "To the extent one thinks teleologically, he does not think scientifically." One must admire the conviction, if not the subtlety, underlying such all-or-nothing statements.

Our purpose is not to judge holism and individualism but to illustrate their conceptual differences and where the perspective embodying either concept leads the investigator. In fact, we shall take the view that the issue of individualism/holism is not which conceptualization is more correct or even more fruitful, but that the difference between them is a matter of perspective. Weick (1969) points to different sociological levels of analysis (for example, individual, group, organization, society), each of which is a legitimate focus for scientific investigation. Furthermore, he indicates that lower levels serve to constrain higher levels in the sociological hierarchy, thereby relating each level to the one above and below it. Mandelbaum (1957) indicates that the issue is not which (individualism or holism) is more correct than the other but what is the difference in what they are about. And they are about different lawlike statements —specifically, global laws and abstractive laws, a distinction that was discussed earlier.

The issue that individualism and holism raise for the understanding of different perspectives of communication centers on the locus issue to be discussed later in this chapter. To the extent that one conceptualizes communication as an individualist, he focuses attention on the individual and individual properties relative to communication and vice versa. On the other hand, the holist would locate the study of communication at the social level and considers social phenomena as central to the study of communication. Such differences should be apparent in Part Two in comparing one perspective with another. In other words, to be a holist or an individualist is a matter of one's perspective.

Theory and Research

A major philosophical issue concerns the relationship of research and the unified process of scientific inquiry. The consensus among scientists and philosophers alike appears to favor the view that verification of theory is the primary function of research. Popper (1959) pointed out that research functions to verify theory by attempting to prove it false; that is, the peculiar logic of the conditional is such that scientific research cannot directly confirm hypotheses generated from theoretical laws. Rather, it attempts to prove an hypothesis false. After numerous attempts to falsify have proved unsuccessful, scientists may then consider the theory to be confirmed.

Whether falsification or direct verification is the function of research relative to theory, the prevalent belief is that research is the means to test a theory—to confirm or deny hypotheses. Some social scientists, however, have disputed this viewpoint—not denying that theory verification is a viable role for research but holding that research also serves to generate or initiate theory as well. Glaser and Strauss (1967) argue strenuously for theory to proceed from a cumulative research program aimed at developing theoretical advances. They stress the fact that verification has been given far too much emphasis by scientists and that scientists should develop a greater interest in generating new theory. They go on to provide guidelines for such a research program centered in their "constant comparative method of analysis." In the light of contemporary development of theory (or lack of it) in the field of communication, their argument is persuasive. And their goal of increased theoretical development is infinitely acceptable.

At least one leading theorist in the social sciences, Robert K. Merton (1957), agrees with Glaser and Strauss in advocating a broadened role for research. He states bluntly that "empirical research goes far beyond the passive role of verifying and testing theory." In fact, Merton lists four major functions performed by research: "It *initiates*, it *reformulates*, it *deflects* and it *clarifies* theory." His point is well taken.

Research is, simply put, far more than a mere technical exercise in hypothesis testing, although it is that also. Research should serve also to broaden knowledge and understanding of phenomena and lead the investigator to new phenomena, new ideas, new concepts, and new observations. In short, the report of a research project that goes beyond mere verification includes a lengthy and significant "discussion" section. Such a section serves to provide new answers to so-what and where-do-we-go-from-here questions, which are unknowable and even unaskable prior to the investigation.

PHILOSOPHICAL ISSUES
IN COMMUNICATION

Applying perspectives specifically to the field of human communication raises additional issues, which focus on the nature of communicative phenomena. Although such issues are not realistically resolvable as correct or incorrect, they indicate points of analysis that distinguish among the perspectives to be discussed in Part Two of this volume. These issues raise questions regarding the concepts to be used in the perspectives and, more abstractly, how the entire phenomena of communication are to be conceptually organized.

Rules and Laws

A good share of the reaction in the social sciences against the received view of theory construction focuses on the heart of the theoretical structure—the covering *law;* that. is, a number of philosophers and social scientists have suggested an alternative to the law (and its corresponding postulates, axioms, and theorems) as the fundamental unit of a scientific theory. These scholars have suggested that social scientific theory may revolve around explanations based on rules rather than laws.

Although the following discussion will tend to dichotomize the concepts of rules and laws, we should be aware of the fact that this issue is far more complex than a simple choice among dichotomous alternatives. Toulmin (1974) has illustrated clearly that rules themselves cannot be conceived as a unified concept but exist with considerable variety and complexity. Some of that complexity is evident within several perspectives outlined in Part Two.

To review an earlier discussion, a law is construed as an analytically true statement of the relationship between two (or more) classes of phenomena. Typically, a law is expressed in the language of a predicate calculus such that all A are B ($A{<}B$) or If A, then B ($A{\supset}B$). Indeed, the typical expression of a scientific law is in the logic of the conditional —if (antecedent condition), then (consequent effect). In such a case, the relationship between the antecedent and the consequent is causal or quasi-causal so that the presence of the antecedent requires (in the sense· of the criterion of sufficiency) the subsequent presence of the consequential effect.

The law is said to "govern" the relationship among phenomena; that is, the investigator can only discover a law that conforms to the regularity of the relationship between phenomena. If water is raised to 100° C at sea level, for example, then it will boil. The phenomena do not conform to the law in the sense that were water at sea level not to boil at 100°, we would consider that the water had made a "mistake" or "failed" to conform to the law. Indeed, if investigation revealed an exception to the law, only two explanations would be possible: (1) some error existed in the observation, and (2) the law is invalid. The investigator cannot impose lawlike explanations on the phenomena but can only discover lawlike regularities that exist inherently in nature.

Rules, on the other hand, do not "govern" relationships. Rather, regularities are said to "follow" or "conform" to rules; that is, rule-following behavior inherently involves choice on the part of the behaver. Given a situation in which a rule is invoked, the behaver chooses to conform to the rule. (Obviously, water is not capable of making a choice.) Choosing not to follow a rule does not invalidate the existence of the rule but serves only to assess the strength of the rule as an explanatory device. In this sense, we would say that the regularity of behavior exists *as a rule,* which has exceptions, of course. The fact that they are exceptions (that is, so indicated because they occur significantly less frequently) illustrates the existence of the rule.

Rule-following regularities, of course, do not necessarily involve any antecedent conditions in the sense of the conditional (if–then) statement. In fact, the conditional logic is probably inappropriate and even irrelevant to the statement of a rule. Any antecedent condition does not require (either as a necessary or as a sufficient condition) a consequent. The occurrence of a subsequent event in the presence of an antecedent event is inherently probabilistic. Thus, one might stipulate that if A, then B will occur 80 per cent of the time; that is, if A, then B *as a rule.* The remaining 20 per cent are observed exceptions to the rule.

The next logical question would probably involve how rules are discoverable in observation. The answer to such a question is similar to that of laws—regularity of occurrence. An obvious example of one regularity is the greeting ritual practiced in American culture, which goes something like this:

> "Hi! How are you?"
> "Fine, thank you. How are you?"
> "Fine!"

As children, we learn this ritual early in the acculturation process. I recall an old comedy routine of Shelley Berman that involves the comedian's talking on the phone to a very small child. We, the audience, hear only one side of the telephonic conversation, in which Berman repeats with ever-increasing frustration the line, "Fine! Thank you. Fine!" It takes little imagination on our part to know that the child is repeating by rote memory the ritualistic how-are-you greeting.

Is this regularity of greeting an instance of rule-following behavior? Of course, it is. Regardless of the state of your health, you are expected to answer and, as a rule, do respond to the inquiry, "Fine." Whether you are suffering from the swine flu, a sore back, and the heartbreak of psoriasis, you respond with "Fine." And if you still don't think that you are conforming to a rule, try responding to the how-are-you greeting with an accurate assessment of your physical and mental health. The other person will consider you something of a nut! At the very least, your rule-nonconforming behavior will serve to disrupt the sequence of interaction.

Some people (for example, Braybrooke, 1968) distinguish between rules and social habits and would probably consider the greeting ritual as habitual rather than rule-following. To engage in any debate over whether a phenomenal regularity is or is not related to rule-following behavior or habitual behavior seems inordinately needless and trivial. The fundamental issue is whether rationality or awareness is necessarily involved in rule-following behavior. That issue is again not an either-or proposition. As Toulmin (1974) illustrates, the question is not a dichotomous choice but a "heptachotomy."

Despite Toulmin's obvious skill as a wordmonger, his point is clear. He visualizes a taxonomy of seven (hence, the word *heptachotomy*) varieties of rule-conforming behavior, ranging from a total absence of awareness at one extreme to conscious attentiveness to explicit rules being followed at the other extreme. In other words, rule-following behavior may or may not involve rationality or awareness. The significant issue of the greeting ritual, then, is not whether it exemplifies a rule or a social habit, but whether it is a rule sufficiently significant or interesting to be worthy of study.

One further issue related to rules concerns the source of the rules themselves; that is, laws are universal principles that inhere in nature (for example, the law of gravity) and are unalterable by human actions. Rules, on the other hand, are products of human actions and are probably "learned" regularities. Where, then, do rules come from? Where do we search if we wish to discover rules? The answer is, in a word, enigmatic. Cushman (1975) believes the individual's self-concept generates the rules that lead to regularity of behaviors. Harré (1974) believes that rules emanate from the individual's cognitive processes achieved through cultural learning. For Weick (1969), rules are located in behaviors and probably retained in some "memory" of a social organization. Toulmin (1969, 1974) is not completely clear on this point but probably focuses on the person as the genesis of rules.

This volume will certainly not alleviate any of the confusion over the source of rules. In fact, I will probably add to the confusion by asking the provocative question, "Is it absolutely essential to a rule-following explanation of human communication to locate the source (or, to use Cushman's term, *generative mechanism*) of rules?" Frankly I don't know!

Perhaps we formulate rules through trial and error; that is, in early stages of interacting behavior, the interactants may not be following rules and may not even know what the rules are or are going to be; that is, they don't know which sequences of interaction are to be regularized and which are to be prohibited. After a nearly random interaction in the early stages of interaction, rules begin to emerge with increasing regularity of recurrence of some sequences with other sequences (that is, those not conforming to the rules) correspondingly reduced in frequency.

If trial-and-error methods do explain the emergence of rules, then certain definable types of social situations will reflect similar rule-following behaviors as interactants find the situation (after trial and error) to be of a certain familiar type, that is, a similar type. I know of no clearly defined taxonomy of social situations with any significant measure of empirical support, but perhaps such a taxonomy is an alternative to the search for universal mechanisms that serve to generate rules.

The use of rules, rather than laws, to explain the phenomena of human communication is a relatively recent and increasingly popular mode for conceptualizing communicative phenomena. In fact, Cushman and Whiting (1972) may have been the first communication scholars to advocate such conceptualization. But even a cursory review of journal articles and convention papers of the past few years will reveal an increasing popularity of rule-following explanations. The importance of rules in discussing contemporary perspectives on human communication cannot be denied.

Human Choice

One elemental fact of humans is their capacity for choice. Unlike other animal species without symbol-using capabilities, humans possess the capacity for choice—choosing what to respond to (or not) and what to attend to (or not), choosing what behaviors or actions to perform, choosing what to think or recall, ad infinitum. In no other biological species is the capacity for choice so great as that of humans.

Some social scientists have suggested visualizing human choice as a vast repertoire of acts, messages, behaviors, thoughts, actions, responses, or some other phenomena. In this sense the human communicator then chooses from among this array of alternatives, deciding what to do, say, or think in a given situation. Shannon and Weaver (1949), the noted information theorists, conceptualize communication as comprised of choices. For example, they view a message as representing a choice or a series of choices made by the source. And, of course, decoding a message involves choices on the part of the receiver. In fact, the fundamental aspect of information theory is choice from among a finite set of alternatives.

If we grant the human's repertoire of alternative choices, one task of communication will be to explain what choices are made from among the alternatives and why they are made. At least two possible approaches to explanations of choices are evident at the outset. The covering-law model would serve to explain a certain behavior or set of behaviors by seeking some antecedent condition (possibly a cause) that determines the choice to be made. Thus, a person behaves in a certain way because of a personality factor or because certain aspects of the situation or context influence that behavior. This explanation of choice is the basis of several of the perspectives discussed in Part Two.

Watzlawick, Beavin, and Jackson (1967, p. 131) proceed from tenets of information theory in order to explain behavioral choices in an evolutionary form of explanation. They explain how humans choose a behavioral alternative in terms of a "limitation" principle of communication, so that "in a communicational sequence, every exchange of messages narrows down the number of possible next moves." (Emphasis omitted.) Each choice that is made continually restricts the range of available choices remaining. The "cause" of the initial choice thus becomes increasingly irrelevant. Once made, each choice tends to restrict the range of alternatives of each subsequent choice. Such an explanation stems from information theory rather than antecedent explanation and is central to the "pragmatic perspective" of communication discussed in Part Two.

It is important to remember that choice as an inherent part of human communication does not necessarily involve rationality. Nor is the communicator necessarily aware of either making a choice or what the alternative choices are; that is, the choice to act, speak, think, and so on, may or may not be a rational act made by careful weighing of the alternatives. And the communicator may or may not even be aware of making the choice to act, speak, think, and the like. Moreover, the choice may or may not be intentional. The irony of human choice in communication is that a human has no choice but to choose. Whether that choice is or is not performed with awareness, rationality, or intent is of little relevance to the fact that choice is inevitable at every stage in a communicative event. After all, one cannot not communicate.

Time

Time is, without a doubt, one of the most crucial, yet most neglected, variables of communication. Actually, the problem is not so much one of neglect by communication investigators as much as it is one of failure or unwillingness or inability to deal with the complexity of time, its varied aspects and dimensions. We are accustomed to treating time as an uncontrollable variable bound by the physical demarcations of the earth's rotational movement on its axis and its revolution around the sun. Thus, we can speak of time in terms of physical duration (for example, one hour long), or we can speak of a physical instant in time (for example, exactly 3:30 P.M.). Many philosophers (for example, J. J. C. Smart, 1968) view any other aspect of time as metaphysical and consequently unrealistic—at least, unscientific.

Physical time, of course, serves as the standard against which all other aspects of time are compared, and physical time is relevant to social scientific knowledge in the sense that standards and norms of human behavior are probably time-bound as well as culture-bound, a topic discussed earlier in this chapter. The time-bound nature of social scientific knowledge may indicate that part of what we consider progress in scientific knowledge may actually illustrate differences in time as well as scientific progress.

For example, the concept of ethos or source credibility has changed significantly since the time of Aristotle. As illustrated in an earlier discussion, the concept of the persuasive impact of the source has changed little as a concept in 2,000 years, but the correspondence rule has undergone drastic modification; that is, Aristotle conceived of ethos as properties of the source who embodied such characteristics as character, sagacity, and goodwill. The twentieth-century concept of ethos has modified the correspondence rule so that observation lies within the receiver's perceptual impressions of the source.

Normally, we would consider this shift in correspondence rule indicative of progress, that is, increased knowledge and sophistication of measurement techniques, vertical theory reduction, and the like. On the other hand, perhaps the shift in operationalization indicates a difference in the cultures separated by 2,000 years of cultural differentiation; that is, the credibility of the source in ancient Athens could well have been attributable to the characteristics of the source himself. (Athens was a chauvinistic society.) Ethos today, however, might well place greater emphasis on the image that is perceived by an audience. Indeed, our changing conceptualizations and operationalizations may well indicate not scientific progress exclusively but the time-bound characteristic of principles of social behavior as well.

But more important than physical aspects of time is the recent trend to conceptualize time in other more novel ways. In no way do such reconceptualizations invalidate physical time. Rather, the concept of time is merely thought to be more complex than was previously thought. And if aspects of increased time complexity appear metaphysical on the surface, so be it. As measured by Newtonian physics, time is symmetrical —constant and unidirectional; that is, each unit of time (one minute, for example) is precisely the same as any other unit (that is, another minute). Time moves physically at a constant and unchanging rate. Moreover, time moves in only one direction—forward. Physical time cannot stop or go backwards—notwithstanding the "time machines" of science fiction.

But humans utilize and conceptualize time in ways not always congruent with physical time. Alvin Toffler's *Future Shock* illustrates how contemporary humans find time moving too fast for them and have difficulty comprehending this rapid acceleration of time. Then, too, we often compress time that has existed in the past. For example, we talk of the fall of Rome as "an event"—implicitly an overnight sensation. In point of fact, Rome's decline extended over three centuries—half again as long as the United States of America has been in existence. Human manipulation of time does not substitute for physical constancy and unidirectionality, but it does suggest that time is symbolic as well as physical. Time is thus a rather complex phenomenon.

Brodey (1969), a psychiatrist, discusses several aspects of time relevant specifically to human communication. One characteristic, which he terms "time graining," suggests that different persons and different social systems possess different time periodicities; that is, we tend to conceptualize and measure time in terms of novelty. When nothing new or different occurs, time proceeds at a slower rate. In the presence of numerous novel events, time moves more rapidly. Brodey suggests that the child's time span of one hour may be the equivalent of a full day for the grandmother. The effectiveness of social interaction thus depends on whether the graining or the "texture" of time is equivalent or compatible among interacting individuals or groups.

Brodey goes on to suggest that time is measurable in ways other than Newtonian physics. He suggests that the assessment of effective dialogue could be enhanced by the use of "information time": "Information time means setting two time periods as equivalent when the same amount of data is processed [p. 241]." The implications of information time for human communication are obvious. Information time leads to the increased importance of the "timing" of information exchange; that is, *when* the information is exchanged may be more important to communication effectiveness than the sheer quantity or quality of the information itself.

Information time as a function of communication exists in some perspectives, implicitly or explicitly, but is absent from others. These implications will be evident in Part Two.

Kolaja (1969) also discusses the complexity of time in terms of directionality. He suggests that all events occur in the present, of course. But when the event occurs, it may involve elements of the past and the future as well; that is, if the present event is similar to other events that have occurred and is recognized as similar, then the present contains elements of or memory of the past. In addition, if the present is compared with some projection of a future event in the sense that the present is compared with some desired goal, objective, or end state, then the present contains elements of the future. These "two-layer presents," to use Kolaja's term, suggest that the directionality of time is more complex in the explanation of human behavior than purely physical aspects of time might suggest.

Let me emphasize once again that physical time as symmetrical, that is, constant and unidirectional, remains the standard for conceptualizing and measuring time. Additional aspects of time render physical time more complex but no less valid; that is, such aspects as time graining, information time, and two-layer presents should be conceptualized as overlays on physical time and not substitutes for Newtonian physics.

No one can deny that human communication is an event. It occurs in time as well as in space and is said to be a process. The consideration of time as an important variable in the study of communication is certainly indisputable. But such consideration brings with it a marked increase in empirical difficulties. The observation and measurement of time complexity is problematic at best.

To observe is to comprehend through the senses. And time data are not easily comprehended as sensory data. Space data are clearly less problematic. Space possesses at least three dimensions—height, width, and depth—and no directionality at all, whereas time is dimensionless and directional. Space data are observable through senses of touch, sight, and hearing, but none of our senses clearly comprehends time data. Clearly, the empirical quality of time data is not a simple matter.

In the sense of the physical sciences, time data are said to be less "real" than space data. After all, space data are enduring; they are not directional. But time data do not endure. They must be recalled from some memory-type device and are less capable of being reobserved. Only recently have scientists been capable of reobservation of time data with the development of storage devices for time data—notably, the motion picture and video tape recorders. But the empirical problem persists in that the camera abstracts time data from the event. Time data are then susceptible to camera angle or microphone placement and are restricted to that sensory perspective with all its physical distortions. (For example, the television picture is "flat" in its severe physical compression of depth.) But increased empirical difficulties are the inevitable price to be paid when considering time as a more complex phenomenon.

The Locus Issue

Kaplan (1964, pp. 78–80) suggests one of the key factors that will be used to distinguish among the perspectives of human communication in Part Two—the locus issue. So far we have discussed various empirical questions associated with communication as a social science. Such questions have included *what* (problems of definition), along with *why, how,* and *what for* (problems of explanation). One question that is often overlooked but that is vitally important to the use of a perspective is *where.* To ask the where-question is to ask what the observable phenomena are that serve as the basis for any empirical science.

Let us employ once again our recurring example of ethos (or source credibility) in communication: the operationalized concept has a different locus (the receiver) from its former locus in ancient Greece (the source). The semantic interpretation of the empirical concept depends primarily on the locus of that concept. Take, for example, the concept of *meaning* itself. The semantic empiricism of meaning (the concept) depends on its location (its empirical interpretation). To ask *what* is meaning is equivalent to asking *where* is meaning; that is, what does one look for to determine what meaning is? A number of possibilities present themselves immediately.

Does meaning exist in the language patterns of the linguistic community? Does meaning exist in the language used? In the mental processes of the language users? In the patterns of behaviors of the interacting individuals? The resolution of such questions depends on the perspective used to conceptualize communication, and a difference in perspective leads to a difference in locus and, consequently, a difference in semantic empiricism of the phenomena. Those differences are explicit and serve as a basis for distinguishing among the various perspectives of human communication.

Where is communication? The locus issue is fundamental to the study of any social science. Communication is no exception. Spielberger (1965) suggests for psychology a "cognitive renaissance," which seeks to explain human behavior in terms of mental processes. Although Spielberger is reacting against radical behaviorism, which locates psychological explanation in the reinforcement schedules of humans, his argument with behaviorism centers on the locus issue. Some communication scholars agree with Spielberger's notion and consider the locus of communication to be within the individual—perceptions, cognitions, and so on. Other communication scholars argue for different loci and, hence, different empirical phenomena. The issue is not who is correct and who is mistaken. All of them are, of course, quite correct. Only their perspectives differ —not their validity.

To ask for a definition or an explanation of human communication inherently involves the question, "Where is communication?" What does one look for? What are the basic phenomena or components of communication that serve as the focus as well as the locus of its empirical being. Once the locus issue is settled, other concepts fall into place in the theoretical framework. The locus is fundamental to the perspectives and serves as a distinguishing characteristic of the perspectives discussed in subsequent chapters.

CONCLUSION

At this point we are ready to turn our attention specifically to the understanding of human communication. At the outset of this volume, you will recall that a distinction was drawn between knowledge and understanding. That distinction should become increasingly clear as you progress in your reading. Knowledge of one of the perspectives (or even a little knowledge of all of them) is certainly commendable. But it is insufficient.

I hope that you have resisted the temptation to plunge directly into the reading of the perspectives of communication. I realize fully how difficult it is first to mull over the philosophical issues involved in a multiperspective (or multiparadigm or multitheory, if you prefer) field such as communication. An understanding of communication includes knowledge of the various perspectives but is not synonymous with that knowledge. Indeed, understanding human communication involves an appreciation for the multiplicity of the perspectives used in understanding it.

Appreciating this multiplicity, of course, does not preclude choosing a perspective that is most appealing and fruitful to you. But that appreciation mandates that your choice does not rule out the other perspectives as either invalid or less valuable. In other words, "different strokes for different folks." As long as we don't carry this attitude too far and lose sight of the empiricism upon which each perspective rests, the key to multiple perspectives is the inevitable adaptation of how one views any phenomena to the purposes of the viewer.

Mischel (1969, p. 36) suggests that increased dialogue between psychologists and philosophers is of value to both. I would paraphrase the philosopher's comments and suggest that the field of communication is also ripe for such a dialogue with philosophers. A greater attention to understanding the complexity of the field with less emphasis on advocating one's own pet perspective will prove to be of maximum benefit to increased understanding and empirical-theoretical progress. And that in a nutshell is the rationale underlying this volume.

— PART TWO —

THE PERSPECTIVES

Introduction to Part Two

During this final quarter of the twentieth century our world finds itself in the midst of another revolution. Berlo (1975) dubs the present era a genuine communication revolution brought about largely by the remarkably rapid development of technological advances in the media of communication. One of the most notable facts about recent decades is the incredible explosion of information—new advances in virtually every field of scientific and humanistic endeavor and increases in population in virtually every sector of the globe. The explosion of information has necessitated the discovery of some means of coping with this information.

Nowhere is the explosion more pronounced than in the scientific communities. For a student of communication or any other field of scholarly inquiry to keep pace with the new research, the new discoveries, and the new information demands the development of some means for coping with the vast quantities of information available. Weick (1970) has suggested the compensatory device of "twigging" in dealing with information overload at the individual psychological level. His article should be required reading for any serious student, whatever his or her academic specialty. Technology has been brought to bear on the mass level with the development of sophisticated computerized systems (for example, ERIC) to store and retrieve information systematically. In a very real sense, ERIC is little more than a computerized coping mechanism.

Technology has also increased the "portability" of information in that each succeeding year has witnessed more people receiving more information faster. Merely three decades ago the American public waited for days only to receive sketchy information about the progress of World War II. By comparison, some people have described the war in Vietnam as the longest-running series on television. The public was saturated with war news in gory color every evening on the 5:30 news—events in words and pictures only hours after they had occurred halfway around the globe.

The portability of information has increased steadily from the invention of the movable-type printing press to the speedy and efficient photo-reproductions even in coin-operated machines in supermarkets. The portability of information has become an object of study in itself. A number of communication scholars consider their primary specialty the study of how innovations (specifically, information about innovations) spread or diffuse throughout a society. (See, for example, Rogers and Shoemaker, 1971).

The contemporary revolution of communication has focused on non-print mass media, that is, the electronic media of mass communication. The influence of television, for example, is rampant in our society. Some of television's most outspoken critics have gone so far as to suggest that for the present generation of students, literacy is no longer particularly relevant. Given the concern over the apparent inability and disinterest of high school and college students in spelling and grammatical usage, this observation may not be unfounded. Under any circumstances, we must agree that the electronic media have changed the character of information. Information is now as much visual as linguistic, prompting a distinction between visual and print literacy. The quasi-subliminal influence of this visual character of information is the underlying assumption behind McLuhan's (see, for example, 1962 and 1964) catchphrase of the sixties: "The medium is the message."

Becker (1968) has portrayed the modified nature of information as a time-space mosaic symbolizing a conglomeration of numerous "bits" of messages available. The individual moves almost randomly through the mosaic and is bombarded with these minimessages. Becker views the concept of message, in the sense of a unified whole, as an archaic concept in present times. Rather, the contemporary communicator is exposed to multiple pieces of messages from multiple sources. Any unification of these minimessages into a semicomplete message is performed after the fact by the communicator within self. Moreover, because message "bits" may conflict with each other or may be redundant with others or vary in the amount of time (that is, gaps) between exposures, the character of information as we once knew it is modified considerably.

Contemporary information certainly includes the vicarious and the secondhand. We glean much information from other people when we buy a new automobile, choose a family dentist, decide which candidate to vote for, and so on. Contemporary information is abstract and often very visual. Recall the dispute over the height of the podium used in the Ford-Carter presidential debates of 1976, the camera angle allegedly favoring Ford in the first debate and Carter in the second debate. The inevitable result of the communication revolution of today is that understanding the nature of human communication is even more difficult yet more crucial in contemporary society.

THE COMPLEXITY OF COMMUNICATION

Ubiquitous, pervasive, and *equivocal* are three esoteric adjectives often used to describe the phenomena of human communication, and these adjectives are certainly appropriate. Even in everyday usage we employ the term *communication* often and in a variety of ways. For example, we consider communication a *process*—"We are engaged in communication." We consider communication a medium or *media* of transporting information, as in the term *mass communications.* The potential for communication to be pluralized (that is, adding *s*) is also evident in the use of the term to refer to *messages*—"I received many communications from her." We also consider communication as an *event*—"We were in communication just yesterday." We consider communication as a state of *connectedness*—"We have established communication with the downed aircraft." We even consider communication as a state of *mutual understanding* quite distinct from the transfer of information or messages—"We talk, but we just don't seem to communicate." And, of course, we consider communication a *discipline* or field of study—"This volume is a textbook in communication."

Many people unfortunately tend to consider communication to be something quite different when it occurs at different sociological levels; that is, interpersonal communication is different from group communication is different from organizational communication is different from mass communication. One fundamental axiom underlying the philosophy of this book is that communication is a process that is variable only as a function of one's theoretical or conceptual perspective. But communication is precisely the same process no matter at what sociological level or setting it occurs—interpersonal to societal.

Consider, by the way of analogy, how the ground appears from an airplane. The checkerboard pattern of agricultural fields and the line of lights along a city street are the same phenomena as those viewed from ground level. They appear to be different only because the field of vision takes in differing ranges of abstraction. In other words, only the scope of the visual field differs from ground level to 20,000 feet in the air—not the phenomena themselves. The same is true of communication. The uniqueness of the individual may be extremely important in a face-to-face setting but certainly less significant in a societal setting where he or she is considered one of many within, for example, a reference group.

Many of the examples and explanations of human communication included in Part Two reside in an interpersonal face-to-face setting. Under no circumstances should this be construed as an attempt to view the perspectives as restricted to the interpersonal setting or that interpersonal communication is more important than other social settings. Rather, these examples signify only my own very arbitrary choice and are chosen simply because they are more familiar to me. They neither represent nor do they imply any difference among communication occurring in different social settings.

ON UNDERSTANDING THE PERSPECTIVES

The four perspectives of human communication to be presented in subsequent chapters of Part Two are not, strictly speaking, theories of communication. Although Part Two characterizes these perspectives as relatively distinct approaches to communicative phenomena, they should not be considered to be mutually exclusive. To the contrary, a majority of communication scholars would probably subscribe to a dual perspective that unites the perspectives that I have labeled *mechanism* and *psychologism*. Other members of the scientific community, a distinct minority, have united the perspectives of interactionism and pragmatism. Nevertheless, Part Two treats the four perspectives as separate, although not necessarily exclusive, from each other. Although certain perspectives may reasonably be utilized in combination, a full understanding of the perspectives should demonstrate the infeasibility of using all four perspectives at once.

Nor should the four perspectives be considered exhaustive of all conceptual approaches to the study of human communication. Other approaches are available and have been employed by past and present scholars in order to understand more clearly some aspect of the communicative process. These other approaches, however, are either not as popular or as influential in scholarly inquiry. Nor are the other approaches typically as comprehensive as the four presented. The minor approaches often focus on specific elements relevant to or within the communicative act but are not as useful as an explanatory framework for the entire process of human communication. The four major perspectives are readily discernible in the scholarly literature of human communication and are currently popular, although varying in popularity, among members of the scientific community.

An Epistemological Basis

Any attempt to analyze the various theoretical or quasi-theoretical perspectives of communication must reflect some common-denominator basis used to distinguish one perspective from another. One possible basis for differentiating among theoretical approaches is the theoretical structure used in formalizing a theory. Such an approach might have included such categories as an axiomatic or covering-law perspective, a rules perspective, a taxonomic perspective, a graphical perspective. A second alternative might have opted for distinguishing among perspectives on the basis of the relatedness of the communicative phenomena as reflected by content-free theoretical approaches, which are then applied to communication. Such categories might have included cybernetics, structural-functionalism, functionalism, or general system theory.

I have chosen not to impose other theoretical structures or categories on the field of human communication. Rather, I began with the field of communication itself and attempted to characterize the regularities or similarities of the lines of scholarly inquiry actually being practiced in the study of human communication. Consequently, the basis used in organizing this book is more epistemological than structural or syntactic; that is, beginning with a global view of communication and working backwards from that viewpoint allow for a philosophical-theoretical characterization of how communication scholars agree or disagree on the nature of communicative phenomena, how these phenomena relate to each other, and what phenomena are most or least significant to the process.

Although the approach used to organize the four perspectives is clearly not the only appropriate means of classifying communication perspectives, I believe that it reflects more accurately the current scholarly inquiry in the field of human communication. Furthermore, a specific syntactic formalization such as covering laws or rules should be applicable within any of the four perspectives with only slight modification. I hope the perspectives arise from the field of communication itself and are not imposed, in the sense of a content-free, cookie-cutter approach, on the field in an attempt to force-fit the field into a priori categories.

The "Impurity" of the Philosophical Bases

Communication is eclectic—a cliché to every student of human communication. For years scholars have sung the praises of communication's eclecticism, interpreted as the pervasive significance and applicability of communication to nearly every human endeavor and social scientific discipline. Eclecticism, in this sense, also implies broad-mindedness. Although we have already discussed the identity problems associated with the eclectic nature of communication, another problem is self-evident. Communication has borrowed heavily, though haphazardly, from other disciplines. Consequently, the borrowing has not necessarily preserved accurately the intentions or the precision of those concepts from other disciplines from which the borrowing has taken place. The apparently sole purpose in borrowing has been to apply those concepts directly to communication. However, in applying the disciplinary approaches of others, communication scholars have modified (by omission, neglect, oversimplification, or overt commission) the original philosophical basis.

Part Two, then, discusses four perspectives of communication, not from the viewpoint of physics or sociology or biology, but from the viewpoint of communication. The reader who desires a solid grounding in psychology, symbolic interactionism, or general system theory is thus advised to look elsewhere. This volume is a book on and about human communication specifically. Psychology, symbolic interactionism, and general system theory are merely points of reference and are significant only as they relate to and are applied to the study of human communication. No attempt is made to preserve the "purity" of the positions founded by scholars from other disciplines. Part Two consistently maintains the view of communication and not the view of another field.

A psychologist would undoubtedly find Chapter 5 unsatisfying. It contains no in-depth discussion of psychological principles or issues, no consideration of the various schools of behaviorism, variations in conditioning paradigms, or controversies such as that between the cognitivists and the behaviorists. A symbolic interactionist would be dissatisfied with the discussion in Chapter 6. It fails to consider the issues dividing the Chicago and Iowa schools of symbolic interactionism and to distinguish between dialogists and symbolic interactionists. A similarity of philosophical basis abstractly related to symbolic interactionism is considered sufficient to unite otherwise disparate approaches to human communication.

A "pure" system theorist will be disappointed in the absence of an in-depth discussion of systemic principles in Chapter 7. It includes no consideration of the widely varying applications of system theory, no discussion of functionalism or cybernetics, and no consideration of the philosophical differences rampant among system theorists. It begins with an approach to communication and relates it to a specific interpretation of general system theory.

In short, Part Two does not attempt to apply psychology, sociology, or biology to the study of communication. Rather, it seeks to label the similarities that are discernible within the field of communication. Those labels identify a philosophical basis. In the uniting of these communication scholars under a somewhat amorphous umbrella of mechanism, psychologism, interactionism, or pragmatism, the "pure" integrity of the original philosophy/theory may not be maintained. The present volume is not intended to be a textbook in psychology, symbolic interactionism, or general system theory. Nor does it seek to explain how these philosophies can be applied to communication. This is a book attempting to describe the study of communication and toward that purpose employs identifiable, albeit imperfect, philosophical-theoretical underpinnings borrowed and bastardized from other disciplines.

Do not confuse the perspective with the broader theoretical framework of its philosophical basis. The psychological perspective of communication is not psychology. The interactional perspective is not symbolic interactionism. The pragmatic perspective is not general system theory. Each perspective emanates directly or indirectly from its philosophical basis but departs, sometimes radically, from a pure interpretation of that philosophy. Indeed, the scholar of communication need not be consciously aware of the philosophical basis used in conducting a specific study, but a broad view of the field of communication allows one to discern a philosophical train of thought common to many communication scholars. Those commonalities are identified as the four perspectives. The attempt is to organize under reasonable rubrics the efforts of the scientific community of communication. In attempting to provide a richer explanation of communication, those scholars may have sacrificed the purity of integrity of original philosophical bases. That sacrifice is deemed insignificant to the purposes of this volume.

The Locus of Communication

A final comment on the locus issue is appropriate. The discussion of each perspective identifies that perspective's location of communication. Recall that the locus is not necessarily the most important or significant element of an explanation. Rather, it is the central location of *where* communication takes place. It provides the *place* of where to look in order to explain the communication process. Schramm's familiar model of communication as source-message-destination, for example, does not even mention channel as a major component. Nevertheless, every one of the three basic elements has one commonality. They are related to each other by a channel and are located at various points on the channel. The channel, then, is the locus of communication in Schramm's mechanistic model.

Recall that these perspectives of communication are competing in the sense of Feyerabend's (1963) and Bohm's (1974) incommensurable theories or Lakatos and Musgrave's (1970) research programs. Each perspective includes its own exemplars and disciplinary matrix. (Recall the earlier discussion of Kuhn, 1970 and 1974.) Central to distinguishing explanations from differing perspectives is to determine where to look for phenomena that are deemed most crucial to the explanation. That is the locus issue.

Ultimately, these perspectives compete for popularity among members of the scientific community. For many practical purposes, a scholar's choice of a perspective is often subjective and even arbitrary. Some are even led to believe that a combination of perspectives is always better because it takes more things into account. But such a view is overly naïve. The combining of two or more perspectives is neither inherently superior nor inherently inferior to a single perspective. Although a combination does indeed broaden the scope of explanation, it also may increase confusion and make empirical investigation more difficult. Dealing with a single locus is simply more parsimonious than having to take into account two different loci, and, of course, utilizing all four loci of the four perspectives is not only theoretically contradictory but empirically impossible.

AN IDENTITY PROBLEM

Members of the scientific community of communication suffer from an identity problem, if not crisis. The public (including other members of the university community) often have no clear comprehension of the identity of communication as an academic discipline or field of scientific inquiry. When I identify myself as a faculty member of a communication department, I am often asked whether I repair television sets. New acquaintances occasionally tell me that they had better watch their grammar when they speak with me. And a psychologist-friend once asked me quite seriously whether it wasn't true that communication was merely a branch of social psychology.

I am still uncomfortable when I attempt to identify the field of communication. For one thing, we have no single label to call ourselves. Unlike psychologists, sociologists, biologists, and physicists, we do not agree on a common, single-term label for a person whose primary specialty is communication. The obvious term *communicologist* remains foreign to most of us. Like many others, I personally don't feel comfortable with that label.

But beyond the linguistic label, communication as a field suffers from the lack of a clear-cut identity both within the field and with the general public. In a very real sense, this book stems from a fervent desire to provide some identity, at least within the scientific community of communication itself. Ours is a broadly based discipline covering everything from writing news stories and producing television programs and taking photographs and giving public speeches to the most sophisticated scholarly inquiry into verbal behavior, linguistic symbolization, societal effects of mass media, and human perceptions. Once we have established an identifiable order out of the eclectic chaos within our own scientific community, we can then concern ourselves with our public-relation image with the mass society.

— 4 —

The Mechanistic Perspective

Social theorists and science philosophers generally agree that the social/ behavioral sciences borrowed heavily from the physical sciences as the newer disciplines underwent development during their formative years. Certainly, no one should be surprised that the study of psychology and sociology, for example, is an extraordinarily modern phenomenon, little more than a century old. The more established sciences of physics and chemistry had made great strides in their theoretical development for several centuries earlier. Then, too, the early social scientist felt a strong need to gain the academic respectability of the term *science* in its most academically reverent sense. For a multitude of reasons they shunned the title of *art*, considering it metaphysical and unworthy of their endeavors.

As the social sciences sought entrance into the scholarly community of science, the first logical step was to emulate the theoretical and methodological guidelines of the physical sciences. Dominating physics for several centuries was the perspective of mechanism, generally recognized today as the era of "classical physics." Physicists developed constructs and conducted research within the mechanistic ideal developed principally by such scientists as Laplace and, later, Newton. Although physics has proceeded to newer theoretical perspectives, vestiges of the Laplacian ideal of mechanism linger—perhaps more so in the social than in the physical sciences.

TENETS OF MECHANISM

Like most scientific perspectives, mechanism proceeds from the conceptualization of an "ideal" state; that is, mechanists would subscribe to certain epistemological and axiological assumptions about the state of the world (more accurately, knowledge of the world) that may never exist as reality in terms of observability of actual phenomena. The purpose of scientific inquiry, then, is to determine the extent to which the ideal conceptualization approximates reality or vice versa.

The ideal state is an assumption or series of assumptions—an analytical rather than an empirical truth. Its purpose is to function heuristically in constructing testable hypotheses and formally in specifying the relationships among concepts and constructs. Max Weber (1949) provides a more comprehensive discussion of ideal types and their role in theory construction and empirical methodology. Mechanism is such an ideal type —a collection of assumptions and tenets to guide scientific research and theoretical development.

Quasi Causality

Theorists and philosophers (for example, Bergmann, 1957) often associate mechanism with causality; that is, the mechanistic ideal assumes causality to be the principal relationship between concepts or phenomena in the sense that a theoretical statement, stated mechanistically, would stipulate, "A causes B." Although causal thinking does appear to characterize mechanistic reasoning, such a gross characterization of the mechanistic ideal is probably not completely accurate. If we could back a radical mechanist into a corner, he would probably equivocate his theoretical position somewhat and define a brand of determinism that we shall term "quasi causality."

To call the mechanistic ideal deterministic is to say that mechanism assumes a temporal constraint of the present upon the future; that is, present events determine future events. Bergmann (1957) suggests that such a determinism characterizes probably the whole of science. But you will recall that Bergmann subscribes to the received view of theories —the covering-law model—and views a law as a conditional (that is, if–then) statement. Thus, mechanistic determinism assumes that given some antecedent event/condition or combination of events/conditions, then some prediction of some future event/condition is possible. In the mechanistic ideal, to know the present is to predict the future.

Determinism, in the sense that the present determines the future, is the mechanistic ideal of "process." In other words, within the mechanistic ideal the concept of "process" is little more than a temporal sequence of events within a closed system. Although ensuing chapters shall deal more specifically and extensively with the principles of general system theory, some mention of closed systems is relevant to the present discussion. If a system is closed (that is, no interaction is allowed between the system and its environment), then the present state of the system will determine the future state of the system. No other alternatives are possible because the closed system is incapable of self-regulation and control and because no variable or influence from the environment (outside the boundaries of the system) is capable of interfering. A system is said to be "open," then, to the extent to which it is capable of self-regulation and interacting with its environment.

Kick a stone and you will be able to predict fairly accurately the future actions of that stone. Your prediction will be based upon the initial conditions of our stone-kicking system—the weight and volume of the stone, the velocity of the kick, the direction of the kick, the pull of gravity, the friction of the surface over which the stone travels, and so on—a closed system. But kick a dog—an open system capable of self-regulation— and your capability of predicting the actions of the kicked object (that is, the dog) markedly decreases. The dog might run away, or he may turn and bite. Or he may lay his ears back, wag his tail, and seek affection. You just can't predict how the dog will react from knowing only the initial condition of kicking.

Lest I incur the wrath of the SPCA, perhaps another example would illustrate more clearly the notion of determinism inherent in a closed system. An archer shooting an arrow at a target may do so on an indoor target range or on an outdoor range. Indoors the environmental conditions are relatively constant and controlled from outside variations (for example, wind)—hence, a closed system. The archer can predict with reasonable accuracy and certainty where the arrow will land on the target (assuming she had the proper measuring instruments) by determining the initial state of the system—for example, the aim of the arrow, the velocity of the arrow at the point of release, the arrow's balance, the pull of gravity, wind resistance, and so on. On the outdoor range, however, environmental variables may interact with the system and invalidate the prediction based on assessment of initial conditions. For example, a gust of wind could arise after the arrow was released and blow the arrow off its computed trajectory. Even a bird could fly in its path and deflect the arrow. And the target could be blown over by the wind. When the system is open, in the sense that environmental variables can enter the system, the present or initial condition does not determine future or subsequent conditions.

Add one more element to the archery example—the ability of the system to regulate itself. We can equip the target's bulls-eye with a radio transmitter and the arrowhead with a homing device. The arrow is then capable of correcting its trajectory in mid-flight and home in on the signal transmitted from the bull's-eye. Perhaps the archer's aim is off when she released the arrow. No matter! The arrow changes its flight path and corrects itself to achieve the desired goal-state—hitting the bull's-eye. The system is thus open and no longer determined by the initial conditions.

It takes little imagination to realize mechanism's profound appeal to the practicing scientist. If prediction is a desirable goal of scientific inquiry (and you will recall that prediction is the *ultimate* goal of some scientists), then conceptualizing the observed system as closed and thus deterministic is a natural theoretical perspective for the conducting of empirical research. For example, Gerald Miller (1972, pp. 44–49) has recognized this theoretical advantage of prediction within a mechanistic perspective and has conceptualized communication as a process (a la Bergmann's mechanistic ideal), thereby "necessitating" closure of the system of human communication. This deterministic (quasi-causal) tenet of mechanism is clearly relevant and significant within at least one perspective used to view human communication.

Transitivity of Functions

Perhaps because scientists emphasize the causal or quasi-causal character of mechanistic explanation, we sometimes tend to overlook the fact that mechanism may include functional accounts of phenomenal relationships as well. Recall that functional explanations emphasize not only what A *is* but what A *does* as well. We have already treated the philosophical difference between function and cause—a distinction that is probably hazy at best. The relevance of functionalism to mechanism is not so much its differentiation from causality, but the characteristic manner in which functioning components or concepts are related to each other; that is, the functions of A, B, and C are transitively interconnected in such a way that the functioning of A leads directly to the functioning of B, which leads to the functioning of C, and so forth.

Fodor (1965) describes the association between mechanistic and functional explanations in psychology by means of a mechanical analogy. Fodor suggests that an internal combustion engine contains some components that are named by the function that they perform. For example, valve lifters are so entitled functionally. But in a very real sense, the camshaft is also a valve lifter in that its rotation functions to activate the valve lifters actually to lift the valves. Nevertheless, the mechanistic explanation does not consider the camshaft to be a valve lifter, nor does it reduce the two functional concepts into one. Rather, the functions of the two are transitive in that the function of the camshaft transfers to the functioning of the valve lifters.

If you are old enough (or nostalgic enough, perhaps), you may recall seeing one of the many Rube Goldberg cartoon drawings of a highly complex mechanism, which came to be associated with Goldberg's "warped" sense of humor. A Goldberg device was an intricate web of submechanisms, each transferring some function to the next submechanism until some final function was ultimately performed (usually, a trivial function such as lighting a cigar or watering a plant). A contemporary board game called Mouse Trap embodies the Goldbergian notion of transitive functions in an elaborate mechanism manufactured or plastic, which is assembled during the playing of the game. The linear transitivity of functions is exemplified in such contraptions and is clearly consistent with the mechanistic ideal.

Significant to the transitivity of functions are two corollative principles. As A affects B, B affects C, C affects D, and so on, mechanistic functioning is highly linear; that is, each of the component submechanisms transfers its functions forward to the next component in the sequence. This linear process functions unidirectionally: it cannot reverse itself, and it cannot skip a step. Each component is like a link in a chain—each link connected to the next link and connected to other links only through the intervening links. Taken together, all the links form a complete chain.

The second principle of transitivity relates to the functional identity of each component submechanism itself. To a great extent, each component or submechanism is independent of the others; that is, each component performs an identifiable function in the transitive scheme of things, but the component itself is not capable of modifying its preordained function or affecting any component except the immediately proceeding one or of being affected by any component except the immediately preceding one. Nor can any component "decide" to change its functional effect on the next component. Of course, the part may "wear out," in which case it can be replaced with a similar part. For example, a camshaft in the automobile may cease to function, and it is replaced with a new camshaft. Without that functioning camshaft, the automobile system ceases to operate at all. But the mechanic would not replace a camshaft with a carburetor, either. Its functional identity is quite different from that of the camshaft. The mechanism of a chain, of course, is less complex. One link is like any other link, but each is also replaceable in the event that it should "wear out." And the functions performed by all the links remain somewhat independent of each other and are related only by the transitivity of functions. We have even coined a cliché that emphasizes the transitivity of the links' functions in a chain system: "A chain is only as strong as its weakest link."

Mechanism, then, may be quasi-causal, but it may also include functional explanations within its guidelines. But if mechanism and functionalism merge, then the functions of mechanistic components are transitively associated with each other. Inherent within the mechanistic ideal is the assumption of transitivity.

Material Existence of Components

One of the key specifications of classical physics (and thus the mechanistic ideal) was the material existence of particular entities (see Laszlo, 1972a, pp. 23–25); that is, mechanism conceives of a universe composed of material entities possessing material form and substance whose structure can be ascertained and that are related to each other in terms of physical actions and reactions. Of course, a mechanistic model does not necessarily imply a molecular structure of subatomic particles—especially when applied to social phenomena rather than those from the physical sciences. But mechanism does imply a conceptual materialism, that is, entities that are conceptualized as material, semienduring phenomena related to each other by spatial attributes.

Several implications are clear from this materialistic assumption of mechanism. First, entities themselves endure through time as material substances—physical or conceptual. Relationships among entities thus emphasize spatial properties, for example, above-below, near-far, left-right, inside-outside, and so on. And the behavior of a material object is conceptualized as a movement or flow across space—a movement from one place to another. In the sense of spatial movement, the mechanistic behavior may be fast or slow, a straight line, or a deflected path. And movement can also be restricted, retarded, or stopped completely. Under any circumstances, mechanism imparts spatial characteristics to behavior and leads to a particular conceptualization of potential relationships and explanations of relationships among entities.

A second implication of materialism is the emphasis on physical actions. One of the first principles of physics known to nearly every junior high school student is the definition of matter; that is, matter takes up space, is extended. Consequently, as Solon's law states, no two objects can occupy the same space at the same time. Thus, when two material substances meet, they collide. Conceptually, the mechanist views the universe as a series of actions and reactions. In the words of the old song about an irresistible force meeting an immovable object, the result is a physical inevitability—something's gotta give. Looking ahead to a mechanistic model applied to communication, we should not be surprised to find a conceptual emphasis on the "effects" of communication.

A further implication of the materialistic tenet of mechanism concerns the functional concept of the aspects of time. The Newtonian concept of time, of course, is relative to the physical rotation of the earth on its axis and the planet's orbit around the sun. Mechanistic time is, simply stated, clock time. The mechanistic ideal, then, conceptualizes time as being of constant duration—sixty seconds to every minute, sixty minutes to every hour, twenty-four hours to every day, 365 days to every year. Time is thereby durational in the sense of "how long" it takes to get from one point to another. We use such a blend of time-distance in our everyday vocabulary. For example, we often conceptualize distance in terms of duration: I live about twenty minutes from my office. How far is it to San Francisco? That depends on whether I fly or drive. In our common conceptual framework, time and distance are often interchangeable.

Mechanism implies a further restriction on the concept of time in the sense that time is unidirectional and unrepeatable. The past always precedes the present, and the present always precedes the future. Time simply cannot reverse itself. It moves inexorably forward. Nor can time stand still or repeat itself. Remember the cliché, "You can't step in the same river twice." Mechanism, in terms of time, is strictly Newtonian—it goes by the clock. We cannot manipulate or control it. It is constant.

Even daylight saving time causes us to "lose" an hour in the spring, but we "gain" it back in the fall. I can recall the controversy a few years ago, before daylight saving time was nationwide, over whether my home state should adopt the new clock over the summer months. One author of a letter to the editor of my hometown newspaper (where all political battles are fought) found the change inconsistent within his apparently mechanistic conceptual model. That letter writer was disturbed that we would "lose" an hour during the day—an hour that was essential to agriculture. The crops would have one hour less to grow during each day; the chickens would have one hour less to lay their eggs; the farmers would have one hour less to work in their fields. Moreover, "gaining" the hour back during the winter was no solution—we needed the extra hour during the summer months, the growing season.

To this day I am not sure whether that letter writer was serious or just "putting us on." More importantly, however, the letter does emphasize the absoluteness of time—constant duration, inevitable unidirectionality, irreversibility, and unrepeatability. Mechanistic space and mechanistic time are intertwined in the physical laws of the universe.

Reductionism

A corollary, perhaps, of mechanism's tenet that all entities possess or are conceived as possessing material/physical existence is the tenet of reductionism. Reductionism assumes that reality is capable of being analyzed into ever smaller units. Because structure of entities is ultimately physical, so goes the rationale of the mechanistic ideal, then those entities are reducible to their structural components until the smallest individual component is realized.

In this way, physical reality is reduced to molecules and atoms (believed to be the smallest indivisible unit just a few decades ago) and subatomic particles; biological organisms are reduced to cells; perceptions, into sensations; behaviors, into reflexes or microkinesic units. Every high school student is familiar with the periodic table of elements—the reduction of the entire world into its various elemental substances. And what person has never had the compelling mechanistic urge to take something apart in order to see "what makes it tick!" The child takes apart the toy. The adult/child puts together a kit (reversing the mechanistic process) and makes a model airplane, a model automobile or rocket, a radio, a stereo set, a television set, and so on.

The mechanistic tenet of reducibility is conceptually advantageous for the researcher. Reducing an entity into component parts allows the scientist to isolate specific relationships and to discover the interactive effects of several isolated components. Reducibility is absolutely essential to experimental research, allowing the observer to determine the essential variables, isolate them from each other, and manipulate them at will. When wholes are reducible to component variables, then the scientist can select certain variables to be held constant and certain variables to be observed (that is, allowed to vary). The effect of one variable (independent variable) on another (dependent variable) is the hallmark of experimentalism and requires the conceptual possibility of reducible wholes.

This is not to say that all experimental research is necessarily mechanistic. Certainly, when the experimenter conceptualizes the effect of a single variable on another single variable, the experiment is totally consistent with the mechanistic ideal. As Bertalanffy (1968, p. 45) points out, the analytical tenet of mechanistic science appeared to have as its goal "the isolation of individual causal trains"—one variable causes an effect on another variable. Main effects are thus quite mechanistic. Multivariate analysis is a bit more complex, so that the causal trains are less individualistic and are more difficult to isolate. Nevertheless, the most complex and sophisticated form of multivariate analysis requires the tenet of reducibility—the prerequisite that a component variable can be identified, isolated, controlled, and observed. The chains of the effects of those variables existing in combination departs somewhat from the mechanistic ideal.

To a considerable extent all empirical inquiry requires some analysis, that is, some splitting up of reality into component parts. The mechanistic ideal of reductionism goes beyond the mere analysis of wholes and assumes the identifiability and measurability of causal or quasi-causal chains as the relationships among those analyzed parts. In this sense, the whole can be reduced to the effects of one part (or parts) upon another part (or parts).

The opposite of reductionism is not the inability of a whole to be analyzed into parts but how the relationships among the parts are to be interpreted. Reductionism assumes that parts affect other parts in a linear or one-way fashion. Holism (the opposite of reductionism) assumes that the level of interpretation must proceed from the whole—the mutual interaction and transaction of component parts. If reductionism implies one-way relationships among components, holism implies a nondirectional relationship (nonlinear).

It is significant to note that the opposite of unidirectionality (one-way) is not bidirectionality (two-way), but the absence of directionality altogether. This distinction has important implications for causality—implications that are quite novel and that are difficult to conceptualize at first thought. We can easily conceptualize linear causality of two entities —for example, A causes B or $A \rightarrow B$. With some effort we can even see two-way linear causality; that is, A not only affects B but is affected by B in the sense that $A \leftrightarrows B$.

But the causal chains in both cases are linear; only the direction of the linearity has changed. Hence, the direction of the causality does not deny the linearity of the causal chain. The opposite of linear causality, then, is mutual causality, so that the transaction between A and B creates not just discernible differences or effects in A and discernible differences or effects in B separately. Rather, mutual causality creates a single effect —a new entity, a third reality (AB), which is substantially different from A and B either separately or summed.

The nature of mutual causality is not particularly relevant to the mechanistic ideal but is significant to another perspective to be discussed later. This brief digression serves only as a prelude to later discussions and, in addition, the purpose of avoiding any possible confusion between mutual causal relationships (that is, AB) and simple two-way linear causality ($A \leftrightarrows B$). To say that mechanistic reductionism implies unidirectionality is to say that it can also imply two forms of unidirectionality at the same time, that is, bidirectionality. The key is not the difference between one-way and two-way directionality but in the assumption of a directionality at all. In that mechanism implies physical movement through space, then that movement must inherently have some direction. Within a nonmechanistic perspective, that is, one that does not imply physical movement through space, the direction of movement (either one-way or two-way) becomes superfluous and irrelevant.

A MECHANISTIC MODEL

Nearly every student of human communication, at some time or other, reviews the various "models" of communication. Typically, the student is asked to devise her own model of communication. Of course, every student wants to be as imaginative and as creative as possible—to devise a model that demonstrates to the instructor a new insight into this complex process called communication. I recall my own initial attempt at model building when I tried to incorporate into my model everything I knew (not all that much, as I recall) about communication. I was also keenly aware of an admonition from one of my colleagues, who absolutely detested the presence of arrows in a model. Fortunately for my self-esteem, I only faintly remember the specific appearance of my model, but I can remember the feeling of desperation as I attempted to illustrate the transmission/reception of messages without using any arrows.

When we think of a "model" of communication, our first response is to visualize some pictorial drawing linking the component elements of communication. Furthermore, we are apt to think of arrows as a key element of that model—if not arrows, at least some substitute to depict the transmission of messages among communicators. Perhaps because of our early training in communication as pictorial models, perhaps because of our conventional knowledge of communication, perhaps because of our growing up with television—but for whatever reason—we find it extremely difficult to conceive of a communication in any way other than the transmission process. Even the noted sociologist, Erving Goffman, (1969, p. ix) considered communication as strictly "socially organized channels for transceiving information" and went so far as to say that communication "obviously and centrally applies" only to that strictly mechanistic interpretation.

To phrase it in yet another way, the perspective of communication held by the vast majority of people, including laymen and scholars alike, includes a strong dose of mechanism. Moreover, the popularity of mechanism is perfectly understandable. It lends itself well to pictorial description in the form of a paper-and-pencil model, clearly owing to its inherent emphasis on spatial attributes. It is consistent with the classical conceptualization of the physical sciences. It is a convenient device to adapt to the growing technology of communication, for example, television, WATS telephone systems, transamatic banking, computerized packaging of information such as ERIC, and a whole range of futuristic notions such as electronic newspapers and thought transference. Some form of mechanism is a convenient and easily understandable tool for looking at the world in the twentieth and twenty-first centuries.

Typical Components

Viewing communication within a mechanistic perspective implies a form of conveyance or transportation across space. Something, usually information and typically called a *message,* travels across space from one point to another. The mode of conveyance, the "road" over which the message travels, is the *channel.* The channel connects the point of the message's origin, the source or the transmitter, to the point of destination, the receiver or the respondent. Because communication typically involves a continuous exchange of messages, the source becomes the receiver and the receiver becomes the source at once and simultaneously. Thus, the distinction as to which point in space is the source and which is the receiver is moot—hence, the term *source/receiver.*

The interchange of messages is demonstrated in Figure 1 as a continuous-loop channel. In fact, one can visualize the channel as something of a conveyor belt that is continuously and simultaneously running between both source/receivers. At either end of the conveyer belt is the

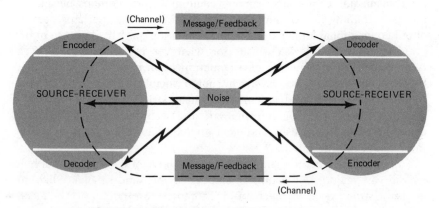

Figure 1.   A Mechanistic Model of Human Communication.

source/receiver, who serves as the "pulley" in our conveyer-belt analogy. And messages are constantly flowing over the conveyer-belt channel in an endless loop. In fact, a message can probably be visualized at every point on the channel rather than just the two points depicted in Figure 1. If we use the conveyor-belt analogy, the point of origin at which the transmitting-receiving process began becomes less important and less distinctive as the process continues. Hence, distinguishing one communicator as source and the other as receiver becomes not only impossible but trivial. The transmission and reception of messages, however, remains a significant and central element of the mechanistic model.

The conveyor-belt analogy breaks down somewhat when we realize that the channel or medium of transmission changes from one point in space to another. For example, between the source/receivers the channel may be in the form of a telephone line. Thus, the message is in the form of charges of electrical energy. But the message originated as a spoken voice in the telephone transmitter. That transmitter transformed the voice into electrical charges, which are then transformed back again at the receiving end of the telephone line as the electrical impulses vibrate a diaphragm in the telephone receiver, resulting in a sound which becomes distinguishable once again as a human voice. The process of transforming a message from one form to another at the point of transmission is called *encoding* and at the destination is called *decoding*.

Actually the encoding/decoding process of communication is much more complex than the telephone example would suggest when we remember that humans are doing the communicating and not the technological machinations of a telephonic system. In the simplest form of human communication possible—two persons engaged in face-to-face conversation—the channel between people is simply air. A source encodes a message by transforming some thought or idea into words, which are then transformed into vibrations of the air, that is, sound waves, and conveyed to the receiver, who decodes those sound waves into words by his receiving mechanism, the ear. But the transformation of thoughts into words and words into thoughts is a highly complex process involving linguistic codes, paralinguistic cues, learned behaviors, physiological interconnections within the human central nervous system, intentions, cognitions, informational biases, memories, sociocultural norms, ad infinitum. Disregarding the human element in the mechanistic perspective, thereby considering solely technological modes of transmission and receiving, is a serious error too often committed by students of human communication.

One key element in the transmission process of the mechanistic model of communication is the notion of fidelity. Before the advent of stereos and quadraphonic sound, the term applied to recording and playback apparatus for music buffs was "high fidelity." Only a few decades ago the rage was "hi-fi." Implied in this term was the concept that the music heard on your hi-fi set at home was nearly the same as the sound heard "live" in the recording studio. In terms of communication, the extent to which the message is similar at two points on the channel (say, the message encoded by the source and the message decoded by the receiver) is the fidelity of the transmission process. Anything that interferes with the transceiving process and thus serves to reduce the fidelity of the message is called *noise*.

It is natural to assume that a message that is transformed into so many different varieties, as it is in human communication, will inevitably result in lowered fidelity. In other words, the potential for noise to attack the fidelity of the transmitted message is extremely high, and something is bound to be "lost in the translation." And noise may attack message fidelity at any point on the channel—*between* communicators, as "static" or atmospheric disturbance on a telephone line or television signal, or *within* the communicator in the sense that one can say something (encoding) unintentionally or that one can interpret (decoding) something unintended in a message.

In this sense, noise reduces fidelity of a message by either subtracting some informational element previously contained in the message, adding some informational element not previously contained in the message, or substituting some informational element for another element previously contained within the message. Noise serves to reduce the fidelity of the transceiving process, but noise does not necessarily imply a reduction in the amount of information contained within the message.

Although *feedback* will be discussed more extensively in Part Three as an element included in several perspectives, it is worthy of mention here as a component of the mechanistic model of communication. Mechanistically, then, feedback is defined as any message that is a response to another message. And because communication typically involves a continuous and simultaneous interchange of messages, every message may be interpreted as a response to the previous message. Thus, during the exchange of messages the distinction between what transmission is a message and what is a feedback response becomes increasingly unclear and insignificant—hence, the term *message/feedback* in Figure 1.

Locus—The Channel

It should be readily apparent that central to the mechanistic model of communication is the element of transmission—movement of the message from one point to another. In the parlance of a few years ago, the channel is "where it's at" in the mechanistic perspective of communication. Every component of communication is located on the channel. Communicators are linked together by the existence of a channel. In fact, it is the channel and only the channel that provides any connection or relationship between any of the components of communication. Without the channel, the components would be left dangling conceptually in space. Hence, the mechanistic perspective clearly locates communication squarely on the channel.

Previous discussion has highlighted the idea that *channel* may exist in a multitudinous variety of forms—telephone lines, air, neurological connections, synapses in the nervous system, memory traces, and so on. Moreover, the number of channels conveying messages at any one time is also potentially large. Consider again the example of the simplest of all possible communicative situations—two persons engaged in face-to-face conversation. If we could freeze that conversation at one instant in time and consider only one of the communicators only in the role of receiver, we could simplify the example even further. But, even then, communication is not very simple.

When we speak of a channel, we tend to think of a single message-signal flowing over a single channel. If we focus on that frozen instant in a two-person conversation, the receiver is simultaneously receiving signals from the spoken words (the linguistically coded signal), the vocal quality and inflection and pitch (paralinguistic cues), all extraneous background sounds from the environment (for example, a radio playing rock music, another conversation nearby, traffic noises, and so on). So far our example has considered only the aural channel—sound waves. If we add the visual cues, the communicator is receiving cues simultaneously from the source's bodily movements, posture, and gestures (kinesic signals); the distance from the source, the face-to-face confrontation (proxemic cues); and other nonverbal cues, which might include such elements as the source's mode of dress, body odor, perfume or after-shave lotion, the intensity of lighting in the room, the size of the room as well as the color of the walls, interior design, decoration, and the like. Still to be considered in the multiple channels of the communicator's reception are the signals emanating from within the receiver, for example, the sensation of hunger or headache, association of the source with memories and biases, the discomfort from standing too long or remaining in the same bodily posture for too long, ad infinitum.

In fact, the simplest of communicative situations can be compared with an individual who is receiving signals from all channels of a CB radio or a TV set at the same time. A human being simply cannot process the information contained in viewing fifty television programs all at the same time. To consider all the simultaneous signals as being of equal importance or significance is to render the communicative situation totally chaotic. But the human communicator is a highly sophisticated communicative mechanism (intending no necessarily nonhuman existence). He can select out signals as irrelevant or insignificant and select in signals as being more relevant or significant than others. The human simply cannot and does not deal with all information or all signals in a communicative situation. She essentially reduces the fidelity of the messages received. Noise is, in a manner of speaking, not necessarily evil but is absolutely essential to every communicative act.

To say that much misunderstanding occurs in human communication is only part of the truth and probably unfair. The fact that so much understanding characterizes human communication (indeed, any understanding at all), given the potential for cognitive chaos that can occur from the multiple channels and signals inherent in the mechanistic perspective, is a tribute to the effectiveness of the human being as a communicative mechanism. Not even the most sophisticated digital computer known to human ingenuity can approach the mechanistic prowess of the human being.

Although we sometimes tend to oversimplfy the concept of channel in communication study, the channel is a highly significant element of communication viewed from the mechanistic perspective. Although we tend erroneously to consider the channel as only the link *between* communicators, the channel also exists *within* each communicator and serves to link the encoding and decoding functions. The channel is, simply speaking, the locus of communication within the mechanistic perspective.

The emphasis mechanism places on the transmission and the reception of messages clearly emphasizes the significance of the channel. Every function relevant to human communication occurs on the channel from encoding and decoding to noise and feedback responses. Where is communication? From the mechanistic point of view, the answer is "the channel." Communication study then focuses on the channel, and events or functions occurring on the channel become the fodder for research and theorizing.

IMPLICATIONS

As mechanism focuses attention on the channel, communication inquiry and theorizing also focus on the channel as the place to look for communicative phenomena. Once thought is directed to the functions performed on the channel and to what occurs during the transmitting/

receiving of messages, numerous implications for communication become prominent. Such implications should seem quite familiar and altogether sensible—a further indication of the impact that mechanistic thought has exerted on the field of human communication.

Emphasis on Effects

The mechanistic model depicted in Figure 1 strongly suggests a linear connection between communicators. The channel that serves to link the source/receivers is clearly directional. (Recall the conveyor-belt analogy.) Messages flow from one person or communicator to another in a specific direction, implying some impact on the receiving end. This directional linearity of the channel is clearly conducive to an inference of quasi causality, that is, that a source/transmitter (arbitrarily denoting a "beginning" of the communicative act) affects or does something to the receiver/respondent (an arbitrary "ending").

Clearly, the prerequisite conditions for a covering-law explanation are met by such an inference. For example, a time sequence is established in that the message is always encoded and transmitted before a receiver decodes and responds. Given the appropriate combination of environmental variables and specifiable noise sources, a law might then be phrased that would specify certain message and source variables that could, in turn, be used to predict certain responses on the part of the receiver. The phrasing would probably be in the conditional form of predicate calculus: *if* (specified message variables), *then* (receiver effects). In this way, a mechanistic perspective of human communication bears a close resemblance to explanation from the physical sciences (specifically, classical physics) within the received-view conceptualization of scientific theory.

A common conceptualization of communication is that a source *does something to* a receiver. Consider, for instance, all the verbs in the English language that correspond to communicative functions. Such verbs are typically transitive (that is, they convey action to some object or receiver of that action) and, therefore, emphasize the effect of communication. We *talk to* someone. We can *question* another person. Conversely, we *answer* them (in the sense of feedback as a response or reaction to a previous action). We *persuade, convince, sell, entertain, inform, stimulate, arouse, incite, cajole, beg* with communication. In addition, such verbs imply a receiver of that action. Certainly, communication is often viewed mechanistically in our language as some form of action-reaction, not unlike an explanation from the physical sciences.

Occasionally, our penchant for viewing communication mechanistically gets out of hand. Too often, communication takes on the aura of some strange and almost mystical power to control another human being. Schachter (1951, p. 191), for instance, refers to communication as "the mechanism by which power is exerted." A popular book a few years ago bore the title *Man, the Manipulator;* and former Vice-President Spiro Agnew, in his now infamous attacks on the mass media of newspapers and television, voiced the paranoia felt by many Americans. This paranoia stems from the overly naïve but nonetheless firm belief in the power of communication to exert power, to control receivers, to affect beyond their control the receivers of communication.

Frankly, I don't fully comprehend why we tend to endow communication with such overwhelming potency in its role as an instrument for affecting human behavior. Perhaps we are merely responding from the folk wisdom developed through years of acculturation in such aphorisms as "The pen is mightier than the sword" and in such novels as *Brave New World* and *1984.* That is certainly possible. Perhaps we are merely reacting from a state of "future shock" brought about by the revolutionary progress made in communication technology, which allowed us to view, for example, live pictures from the moon's surface as well as the bloody results of frontline combat in Vietnam—all in gory living color. We even know the winners of elections within minutes after the polls close and with only 2 per cent of the vote tabulated. The potential power of such technology is awesome—a subject for contemporary science fiction. Such an explanation is also plausible.

Perhaps we hold the power of communication to affect mass audiences in such esteem because communication does indeed possess such power. There are certainly numerous examples from contemporary history to suggest such power. After all, during this century Adolf Hitler rose to political power largely on the basis of his communicative capacity to incite the German people to follow him. On the other side of the coin, Burton (1969, p. 49) suggests that effective communication can solve the problems of international tension, and DuBois and Li (1971) suggest their form of "group conversation" as the cure for interpersonal disharmony. And the current image making of political candidates, implying that advertising agencies have the power to "sell" even the president of the United States through the mass media of communication, is now taken for granted in contemporary political campaigns. Perhaps communication does indeed possess a mystical and awesome power to affect people. But I don't think so.

There is little hard evidence to suggest that communication possesses such devastating power. In fact, Hovland (1959) suggests that people's attitudes are not so easily changed as we might be led to believe. Whether we consider communication to be a problem (in that it is a tool capable of manipulating human actions and beliefs) or a cure (in that it is the tool for solving every social problem from divorce to international warfare), we are grossly naïve in ascribing to the phenomenon of communication a quasi-irresistible power to affect human actions.

This disavowal is not to suggest that communication does not affect people at all. To the contrary, such a reaction is equally uncalled for. The beginning student of communication, steeped in the philosophy of mechanistic communication, too often overreacts in the direction of rejecting out of hand the value of the mechanistic perspective. Such an overreaction is particularly true if the student is also steeped in the values of the humanist (as everyone is or should be).

The slightest suggestion of the human being as some mechanistic automaton devoid of human will is clearly distasteful and quite unrealistic. Nevertheless humans are suspectible to being influenced by other humans. Child rearing proves that susceptibility. Moreover, after all, we do buy the toothpaste that we have seen advertised. Humans, simply speaking, have only one device at their disposal to influence other humans. That "device" is communication. As students of human communication, we should guard against the oversimplified conceptualization of the mechanistic effects of communication—not that communication cannot affect human actions, but that the effects of communication involve a rather complex process, which resists oversimplification.

Precisely what aspects of human communication contribute to effects is a matter for research inquiry and not idle speculation. The information transmitted via the medium is clearly relevant to effects accrued, and there are many variables of information. The brief popularity of McLuhanistic thinking of a few years ago suggests that the nature of the channel itself may contribute to observable effects. (Remember the slogan "The medium *is* the message" as well as the difference between "hot" and "cool" media.) When one discusses effects of communication, she is probably operating from within the mechanistic perspective, although mechanism is not absolutely essential. At the very least, mechanism with its emphasis on the linearity of the channel provides a perspective quite conducive to considering the effects of communication on receivers.

Barriers and Breakdowns

The mechanistic image of communication suggests the metaphor of a machine as the analogue or model of the communicative process. It is then only a small step to conceptualize effective communication as a well-oiled machine that must be kept "in tune" but that is capable of "breaking down" or needing some repair. Although the notion of "communication breakdown" is not unique to the mechanistic perspective, the concept probably originated from mechanistic thinking and still directs much of the popularized conceptualizing about human communication.

Visualizing the mechanistic model as a conveyer belt allows a clear picture of message-signals traveling along the belt in a constant, directional, and cyclical flow. However, like a conveyer belt, the machine can "break down" and then cease to function. Within this mechanistic train of thought, then, communication ceases with a breakdown. And in the sense that messages "flow" over the channel just as a river flows in its channel, some barrier or "dam" in the channel can restrict the flow of message-signals.

Unlike a breakdown, a barrier does not cause communication to cease, but it does retard the flow of messages. Some messages are "dammed up" and do not get through the barrier. Others, like water over a spillway, do get through to the receiver. But the character of these messages may be changed in the process of spilling over the barrier. They may be more uniform, be filtered, have greater force or significance, be distorted, and so on. Although mechanistic breakdowns suggest a cessation of communication, mechanistic barriers suggest a "dam" on the channel retarding the flow of messages and modifying their character and significance.

Then, too, a barrier may be stronger, that is, retard message flow more severely, between A and B (left to right in Figure 1) than it is in the opposite direction between B and A (right to left in Figure 1). This aspect of directionality might suggest that the communication barrier would affect B more than it affects A. But recall that communication continues in a circular fashion so that the messages flowing from A to B affect the subsequent flow of messages from B to A, which, in turn, affects message flow from A to B, B to A, and so forth. A barrier at any point on the channel thus affects all subsequent transmission and reception of messages (according to the mechanistic directionality of time) even in the strictest of mechanistic perspectives.

Perhaps the clearest example of mechanistic breakdown is found in Newcomb's (1948) psychological explanation of "autistic hostility." Actually, Newcomb is more interested in what occurs within a person's mind after a communication breakdown; that is, any prior hostile feeling or interpersonal conflict, however insignificant, might result in a communication breakdown (in the mechanistic sense of ceasing or absence of communication). With no more information flowing from the other person, the feelings of hostility or conflict are increased. After all, no contradictory information is received that would reduce the negativistic state of mind. Thus, according to Newcomb's explanation of autistic hostility, communication breakdowns function psychologically to exacerbate rather than mollify feelings of hostility and conflict.

Communication barriers are rarely discussed in purely mechanistic terms. Rather, the bariers are seen more as psychological barriers existing within the individual's cognitive and affective capacities for encoding and decoding messages. As such, barriers of communication are more prevalent within the psychological perspective and will be discussed in the next chapter. Within the mechanistic perspective, a barrier exists more as a consequence of the human's limited capacity to process information units received from multiple sources. The resulting barrierlike concept, called "information overload," will be discussed later in this chapter.

I suggested earlier that the mechanistic notions of barrier and breakdown occur more frequently in our day-to-day thinking about communication than in the practice of serious scholarly inquiry into communicative phenomena. We are more prone to oversimplify the complexities of human communication in our everyday life than to attempt to comprehend the myriad of forces at work in shaping our understanding of human communication.

Paul Simon's lyrical statement on contemporary American life, "Sounds of Silence," mentions people who talk without speaking and who hear without listening. We can all understand what those words imply. We use them frequently in such phrases as "It is only so many words" or "He just doesn't listen to me." The teen-ager says of her parents, "They don't listen to anything I say." The candidate for divorce says of the marital relationship, "We just don't seem to communicate any more." The disenchanted member of a minority group says of our public officials, "They continue to offer meaningless promises. They don't give us straight talk."

Thus we continue to speak, in highly oversimplified terms, of a "credibility gap" or a "generation gap," and we continue to oversimplify social problems, as did the character in *Cool Hand Luke*, by saying, "What we've got here is a failure to communicate!" The cry of "more communication" continues to be the cure-all, the panacea, the "formula answer" for social ills.

If such thinking possesses any validity at all, it is not to be found in the mechanistic perspective of human communication. This perspective of barriers and breakdowns simply cannot and should not be expected to pinpoint the difference between effective and ineffective communication. For the issue is clearly the difference in communicative effectiveness—not the presence or absence of communication. One of the concerns of this book is to highlight the strengths and limitations of each perspective of human communication—not to select the one true ideal. Some perspectives may be more appropriate than others, when applied to certain situations for certain purposes. But, more importantly, to oversimplify one of the most complex of all human activities—the process of human communication—can only lead to increased misunderstanding. A little knowledge is wonderful, but knowledge is no substitute for understanding.

The Gatekeeping Function

Up to this point we have considered only two communicators, both in the dual role of source/receiver (see Figure 1). Of course, this model could accommodate any number of additional source/receivers, every pair of whom would be interconnected with conveyor-belt channels. But a third element is still missing from the present model—the "gatekeeper." The term *gatekeeper* apparently originated in Kurt Lewin's (1951) exposition of field theory in social science and suggests its function in the term itself. The gatekeeping function exists on the channel (naturally) between source and receiver and serves as an intermediary between the two.

Figure 2 demonstrates the gatekeeping function in human communication in a simple three-element model of message flow. Naturally, this chain could be extended to four, five, or more communicators, each one of whom would serve a gatekeeping function except for the first and last source/receiver in the chain. The gatekeeper functions to receive information from a source and to relay that information to a receiver. This gatekeeping function can work in both directions, too. The concept of gate-

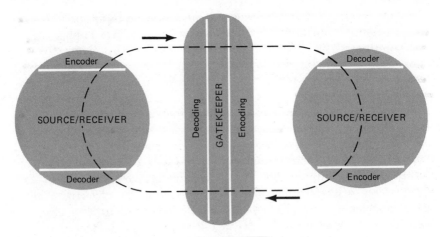

Figure 2.   The Gatekeeping Function.

keeper should be familiar to all of us in the sense of a "grapevine" of information or rumors being disseminated throughout a social system.

Often business, political, and educational organizations have utilized the gatekeeping function by formalizing it in the role of an omsbudsman. It is the function of an omsbudsman to filter messages in the form of suggestions or complaints from persons on a lower stratum of the organizational hierarchy and retransmit them to persons in higher levels of authority.

The gatekeeper, simply speaking, serves as a filtering source/receiver of information. The function is not as a source/receiver in the sense of the entire communicative process but as a receiver and *re*transmitter of messages. Like a gate on the channel, the intermediary allows some messages to get through and bars others. Of course, the messages that flow in may be quite different from those that flow out from the gatekeeper. The gatekeeping function regulates the flow of messages and may function to modify the messages so that the initiated message is quite dissimilar from the message that is ultimately received. The gatekeeper exerts great control over the message and affects the informational flow to every person after him in the chain.

Westley and MacLean (1957) formulated a model of mass communication and added the gatekeeping function (C) to the function of source (A) and receiver (B). They speculate that the gatekeeper's role can exist only so long as C retransmits messages that are appropriate to or desired by the receiver (B). They go on to suggest that in the complex communicative interrelationships in our society, there exist many gatekeepers that B may choose among. In a sense, then, many potential gatekeepers compete for B's attention. Thus B selects the C who gives him messages that are appropriate for him. Westley and MacLean visualize the function of the gatekeeper, then, as an extension of the receiver's environment.

The gatekeeping function is particularly important in dealing with a more abstract (that is, more generalized) sociological level of communication—mass communication. The gatekeeper can be a person, a group, a book, a newspaper, a TV program, a billboard—in short, any element capable of retransmitting a message from one source to another. In this sense, we "communicate with" the author of a book—not by a direct link to the author but through the gatekeeping function of the publisher and the printed page.

In fact, I am communicating with you at this very moment through the gatekeeper, Macmillan Publishing Co., Inc. And don't forget that you communicate with me, too, through that same gatekeeper—perhaps not always individually but as a collectivity in terms of book sales, book reviews, and conversations with professional colleagues (your instructors and other gatekeepers). And occasionally—too rarely—I even get messages directly from you, students, in the form of "ungatekept" messages. The gatekeeping function is also a significant element in much communication research. But more about that later in this chapter.

Mediated Communication

Occasionally, scholars who wish to distinguish clearly between interpersonal communication and mass communication will interject the concept of "mediated communication" to make that distinction. The essential elements of the explanation go something like this. In interpersonal communication, the face-to-face encounter allows for direct access between communicators. The mediation of a newpaper, magazine, book, television set, or radio receiver between source and receiver denies this accessibility. Consequently, the source of the message (the author, producer, newscaster, and so on) remains strictly as a source, and the receiver (the viewer, listener, reader, and the like) remains strictly as a receiver. They do not share the combined source/receiver role as they do in interpersonal settings. Apparently, then, one generally concludes from this explanation that interpersonal communication and mass communication are fundamentally different phenomenal processes.

Frankly, I find it difficult to accept this kind of explanation. The viewpoint of this book, you will recall, is that communication itself does not change; only our understanding of it is susceptible to change. A corollary of this maxim would be that the phenomenon of human communication exists at all sociological levels (dyad, group, organization, society) but does not differ fundamentally from one level to another. What changes is the complexity of the sociological level. Our level of generality changes, too, in the sense that we are dealing with a more abstract (that is, more general) process as we move upward from interpersonal to mass communication. But unless our perspective of human communication changes our understanding of communication, the phenomenon itself remains constant.

This corollary does not mean to imply that there is no discernible difference between interpersonal and societal levels of human communication. To the contrary, interpersonal communication "looks" very different from mass communication. What I am suggesting is that the concepts used within any perspective apply consistently to all sociological levels of the communicative process. But the correspondence rules, the operational definitions of those concepts, make them appear to be quite different even though they function in the model in precisely the same way.

For example, feedback responses in a face-to-face encounter between two persons may be in the form of a nonverbal facial expression or gesture or as a verbalized message (correspondence rules). Feedback to a television station may be in the form of a telephone call, a letter, a Neilsen rating, a *TV Guide* review. But feedback exists conceptually as a mechanistic response in both levels.

Is the feedback *delayed* in the mass setting as opposed to *immediate* in the interpersonal setting? Not necessarily. The durational aspects of time are not equivalent as one moves upward from one level of generality to another; that is, one day in mass communication may be equivalent to one second in the interpersonal setting. If one were to ask a direct question of another person in a face-to-face encounter and wait until the next day for the receiver to reply, we would probably say that the feedback response was delayed. But when a television network receives the Neilsen rating of programs broadcast the night before, we would probably say the feedback response was incredibly immediate.

What constitutes immediacy or delayedness of the feedback response is relative to the level of generality (for example, interpersonal or societal) of the viewpoint. But the function of feedback response remains unchanged. Only its operationalization (that is, what it looks like) changes. In the terms of philosophy of science, the specific theoretical concept of communication (in our example, feedback response) functions in the theory in precisely the same manner, regardless of how or where it is discerned in reality. But the correspondence rule for relating that theoretical concept to reality may differ from one sociological level to another.

Rather than consider "mediated communication" to imply some distinction between interpersonal and mass communication, we can more fruitfully utilize the concept to refer to the inherent gatekeeping function performed by a mass medium. And this is the more prevalent concept implied by the term *mediated communication*. In interpersonal communication, the gatekeeping function may or may not be present. In mass communication, implied by the presence of some mass medium such as newspaper or television, the gatekeeping function is always present. The medium serves inherently as the gatekeeper between the source (for example, principals in a news event, a public official making a statement) and the receiver (us—the consumers of the mediated information).

It is the sense of mediated communication that the mass media serve the C (gatekeeping) function in Westley and MacLean's (1957) model of communication. The newspaper, the book, the television set, the radio receiver, and the movie extend our environment beyond our immediate surroundings to include events, information, and observations to which we would otherwise not have access. For most of us, our knowledge of foreign countries in Africa, Europe, or Asia is restricted to the information we receive from the mass media; and unless some astronaut is reading this book (which I doubt), we all have only mediated knowledge of the surface of the moon.

In the role of gatekeeping, the mass media exert extraordinary power over a society in regulating the flow of otherwise inaccessible information items that it shall receive; they delete other items from the flow of messages. The criteria upon which media personnel perform those selections have come under severe attack in recent years as the technological revolution in mass communication has achieved enormous proportions. Much of that criticism has been in the form of accusations of interpretative bias on the part of the media. But that criticism is more appropriate within the psychological perspective of human communication and will be reserved for later discussion. It is sufficient at this point to state the obvious—the responsibility of the mass media in the role of gatekeeper is awesome. No one, least of all media personnel, takes that responsibility lightly.

One-Way Versus Two-Way Communication

Throughout the writing of this book, I have attempted (however successfully) to keep my biases under control regarding the various perspectives of human communication. However, when it comes to the issue of "one-way" and "two-way" communication, I simply cannot help myself. You, the reader, should be aware at this point that my biases are now consciously overt. I simply do not and cannot consider the difference between one-way and two-way communication to be either significant or conceptually realistic within any known perspective of human communication; that is, either there is no difference at all between one-way and two-way communication, or the alleged difference can be explained within existing concepts of the mechanistic perspective.

Clearly, the issue of one-way versus two-way communication applies only within the mechanistic perspective with its emphasis on the channel. The linearity of the channel that links communicators, along with its inherent directionality of that linkage, allows a distinction between a message flowing from source to receiver ($\rightarrow$) and an exchange of messages between source/receivers ($\leftrightarrows$). Only a clear-cut focus on the channel (the locus of Mechanism) with its spatial directionality renders this distinction possible.

Barnlund (1968, p. 230) illustrates a form of one-way communication as a situation in which receivers are "expected to listen and not talk back." Such situations probably result from an overly autocratic parent or teacher or boss. Such situations, however, are explainable by other existing concepts within the mechanistic perspective. The autocratic parent or teacher who thinks he is not receiving any feedback response from the child reflects not necessarily one-way communication but a limited capability for decoding messages. Surely, the autocrat is receiving sullen glances, passively obedient responses, ritualized "yessirlike" responses, and the like, which are simply not decoded as feedback responses. The autocratic boss in the factory probably also receives feedback responses if she were to decode the efficiency reports, production quality reports, absenteeism, labor turnover, employee morale reports, and so on, as feedback responses. If the autocrat in a bureaucratic organization receives no feedback responses at all, the situation is probably attributable to an overly restrictive gatekeeper mediating those responses to the autocrat from the worker.

Of course, zero-feedback conditions can be simulated in a laboratory setting or as a classroom exercise in which the experimenter or the instructor manipulates the environment so as to disallow any possible response from the receivers. But is this a realistic simulation of the real world? I think not. In fact, as an instructor, I have used a classroom exercise that specifies zero-feedback and feedback conditions. (You might be familiar with the exercise that involves two students who individually give instructions to the class on how to duplicate a drawing or a geometric design. The first student is not allowed to face the class or answer any questions—zero-feedback condition. The second student duplicates the instructions but faces the audience and is allowed to answer and solicit questions.) But I refer to this exercise as the difference between a complete act of communication and an incomplete act of communication. The zero-feedback condition, then, becomes nothing more than a misconception of the communication process. In this sense of a laboratory/classroom exercise, one-way and two-way communication is an artifact and is not applicable to the "real world."

Ruesch and Bateson (1968, pp. 197–199) suggest a different form of one-way communication. They describe a situation in which one person, in the role of an observer, views another person or organism and makes some inferential judgments about that person's or organism's codifying or evaluating process. If we use a simpleminded example of my own, a person may observe another student in a classroom working furiously on his schoolwork whenever the instructor is nearby and loafing when the instructor is not present. The observer is then, according to Ruesch and Bateson, receiving one-way communication about the student's codification/evaluation processes regarding the instructor/student relationship or the student's attitude toward school, but the student is not even aware that he is being observed. Ruesch and Bateson refer to this phenomenon of one-way communication as "the unobserved observer."

Whether the case of "the unobserved observer" is pertinent to communication is debatable. One of my colleagues would call this situation "eavesdropping"—an interesting event, but not communication. But the issue of whether it is communication seems trivial. More important is how the situation is relevant to human communication within the mechanistic perspective. Westley and MacLean's (1957) model of communication would subsume the source's involuntary or unintended behavior under their concept of "non-purposive message"—without A's intent to transmit any message to B (the observer). As a nonpurposive message, the student's behavior is not an integral part of the communicative process but is only an X (in Westley and MacLean's model)—an object in the environment to which a person may orient herself.

As an environmental object, X, the student's behavior is no more and no less significant to the communicative process than the temperature of the room, the color of the walls, or a fly buzzing around one's face. According to Westley and MacLean, the X becomes part of communication when a gatekeeper, C, selects that X and relays it to B, the receiver. Otherwise, the X remains in the environment, where it may or may not be accessible to the receiver. In the case of the unobserved observer, it is accessible to the observer only as the observer is orienting himself to his environment. But in his role as a source/receiver of communicative messages, the unobserved observer is not engaged in the transmission/reception of messages when he merely selects an X from the environment without benefit of receiving the X in a message relayed from C.

What, then, is the difference between one-way and two-way communication? My personal response to this question has always been a flippant arithmetic difference, that is, one-way. In other words, the difference between one-way and two-way is equivalent to subtracting the numeral one from two. What is the difference between "$\rightarrow$" and "$\leftrightarrows$?" The answer is equally simple (and trivial); the difference is "$\leftarrow$." Just more of the same—another one-way!

As a summary of this admittedly editorialized discussion, one-way and two-way communication both conceptually focus on the channel and its linear directionality (unidirectional versus bidirectional). The issue is thus relevant only to the mechanistic perspective. Any alleged difference between one-way and two-way communication can either be explained by other concepts within the mechanistic perspective or can be dismissed as unrealistic or not integral to the communicative process. The issue of one-way and two-way communication is nothing more than a straw-man issue and must be considered ultimately insignificant to serious inquiry into human communication.

SELECTED AREAS OF RESEARCH

Historically, far more research into phenomena of human communication has been generated within the mechanistic perspective than from any other. Perhaps because of the conceptual borrowing from the physical sciences (specifically, classical physics), a mechanistic view of communication was a natural extension of quasi-physical scientific research, utilizing similar research techniques and theorizing from the covering-law model. It is only natural that communication research should begin with the theoretical and research methods tested by previous decades of physical scientific development.

Not too many years ago, nearly all empirical research into human communication emanated principally from the mechanistic paradigm. Concomitant with an increasing sophistication in theoretical and research development in human communication was a growing disenchantment with many of the formerly popular areas of communication study. Such historical development should also be expected as old values seem inevitably to be discarded for new fads and interests. Nevertheless, research conducted within the mechanistic perspective continues to be a significant area for fruitful scholarly inquiry.

Persuasion

The field of human communication, with its strong foundation in classical rhetoric and public speaking, has long been involved in the study of persuasion. Communication, as a tool for social influence and affecting change in receivers' attitudes, has prompted literally thousands of studies attempting to shed light on the persuasive impact of the communicated message. Although not nearly so popular a research area as it was just a few years ago, the study of persuasion and attitude change remains an integral part of communication research. Moreover, much of the research in the field of persuasion and attitude change has proceeded from the mechanistic perspective. With its emphasis on effects and transmission/reception of messages, mechanism is a natural perspective for inquiry into persuasion, and persuasion is, after all, a study of communication's effects. (See Fotheringham, 1966.)

Oddly enough, the three means of persuasion (ethos, pathos, and logos) outlined by Aristotle over 2,000 years ago remain a convenient and suitable outline for analyzing contemporary research in persuasion. Of the three, ethos has probably received the most sustained attention of communication scholars. The impact of the source on the receiver remains a potent variable in persuasion research.

Generally termed *source credibility* or *communicator credibility*, after the equivalent variable in social psychology, this variable has not wholly been viewed in contemporary research as a mechanistic component conveyed on the channel. Rather, scholars have treated ethos as a multidimensional (for example, comprising dimensions of competence, trustworthiness, sociability, dynamism, and so on) variable exhibiting differential effects on receivers. In other words, much of the persuasion research into ethos has overtones of the psychological perspective of human communication.

Pathos refers to the largely implicit appeals in a message to nonrational frames of reference, for example, motives, needs, desires, and emotions of the receivers. Although such research is also consistent with elements of the psychological perspective, these appeals are allegedly identifiable in the message and are conveyed on the channel to the receiver. Probably the most prominent variable of pathos studied in recent years has been that of message appeals calculated to arouse fear in the receivers (see Miller, 1963). The use of appeals from pathos has often been perceived as somewhat distasteful. "Pathetic" (derived from pathos) appeals smack of sophistry and irrationality for many people and, accurately or not, carry with them connotations of unethical practice.

Like Aristotle, communication scholars have found reasoned discourse more to their liking. As humans we would like to think that we are ruled more by our intellect than by our emotions or instincts, whether we are or not. Consequently, a great deal of research effort into persuasive variables has been directed at variables of logos. Although such research has not proved conclusive, inquiry has gained some insight into the persuasive impact of such variables as evidence (see McCroskey, 1969) and logical argument (see G. R. Miller, 1969) contained in messages.

Perhaps the greatest impetus in the study of persuasion occurred during World War II, when we apparently discovered the role of propaganda and wanted to know more about its appeals. The result was a spate of studies into the persuasive impact of communicated messages exemplified best, perhaps, by the now-famous Yale studies (see, for example, Hovland, Janis, and Kelley, 1953) conducted largely by social psychologists. Never ones to shun borrowing from other academic disciplines, communication scholars continued to pursue the study of persuasion with even more vigor. Much of that research interest in persuasive communication has subsided in recent years, although it continues to intrigue many communication scholars.

And the mechanistic perspective continues to be popular as a point of departure for persuasion research. The 1969 New Orleans Conference on Research and Instructional Development in communication strongly emphasized "the centrality of messages" in communication research and called vehemently for the development of "more exact means of defining, manipulating and measuring message variables" as well as "new methods for identifying and measuring effects of messages." (Kibler and Barker, 1969, p. 35.)

Media Effects

One result of the explosion of communication technology is reflected in the public concern over the effects of the mass media on society. Prompting this concern is a 1984-like fear of some people that sophisticated electronics (objects worthy of fear in themselves) have the power to control minds. Fortunately, this fear has been tempered by serious scholarly inquiry into the effects of the mass media on the receiving public. Whereas the early research in media effects proceeded from a mechanistic interpretation of mediated messages, the area has resisted a purely mechanistic interpretation.

Although some inquiry has focused on the effect of the medium itself, most research is directed at the effect of the information carried on the medium. The most popular area of research seems to be assessing the effects on subsequent receiver behavior of violence and aggression depicted on television. No hard evidence exists to suggest a purely mechanistic effect. Rather, the potential effects have prompted a series of hypotheses to explain the results, and these hypotheses seem more relevant to the psychological perspective. The bulk of the research, much of it supported by governmental funding, provides little evidence to warrant the abnormal fear of an electronic medium (see Comstock and Rubenstein, 1971); but the research results have not completely allayed those fears either. In fact, these fears have been instrumental in increased governmental activity to uncover definitive answers as to the effects of media violence. That activity has included a presidential commission (Lange, Baker, and Ball, 1969) and a lengthy surgeon-general's report (Comstock and Rubenstein, 1971; and *Television & Growing Up*, 1972).

Much of the research into effects of media violence has been performed in laboratory settings, highly conducive to mechanistic explanation, and on probably the most susceptible receivers of all—children. If the results are inconclusive, they do suggest that the mechanistic perspective is probably not wholly appropriate to comprehending fully the complexities of the communicative process involved in assessing media effects on receivers. Although the concentration on violence and aggressive behavior is a matter of public concern, some critics of the research have suggested looking at the potential effects of other information conveyed by the media on the receiving public. For example, what about the socially desirable information transmitted by the media, for example, wholesome family life on "Father Knows Best," "Leave It to Beaver," "Partridge Family," "The Waltons," and a host of other family shows; interracial cooperation on "Mod Squad," "I Spy," "Ironside," to name just a few. But the effects of these kinds of televised information would probably resist mechanistic explanation as well.

Another stimulus for public fear was the recent concern over subliminal persuasion a few decades ago. Vance Packard's *Hidden Persuaders* unveiled the potential power of media to control the public by appealing to the subconscious recesses of the mind, uncontrollable by individual will or overt resistance. We were all worried whether some movie-house manager was flashing "Drink Coca-Cola" on the screen too quickly to be perceptible to the naked eye but processed nonetheless by our brain at an extremely low level of awareness. This public scare has also subsided, largely because subsequent research could provide no hard evidence to support subliminal effects. Again a strictly mechanistic explanation of receiver effects is probably oversimplified and incomplete.

One area of media effects that seems ripe for continued research is the area of advertising and marketing—selling products via commercial messages. Strangely enough, the explanations advanced to account for the effects of advertising are phrased in highly mechanistic terms although little research has demonstrated any consistent effects of various informational strategies in media advertising. Extraordinarily little theoretical development has occurred in the area of advertising, as a process of communication, and consequently little communication research. The principle that seems to direct current practices in media advertising is apparently the first principle of business pragmatics: "Whatever works, works." (See C. Leavitt, 1975.)

The communication research into media effects has not progressed with the sophistication and continued development as has similar research into persuasion and attitude change. Several reasons might account for the disappointing results of research on media effects. First, the technological revolution in the mass media, particularly electronic media, has so increased the number of variables available for study that the very act of designing a research project with any sophistication or comprehensiveness is nightmarish. Second, the research into media effects has experienced a very brief life—only a few decades—and has not had sufficient time to develop much sophistication.

Perhaps most important, however, is the nature of mediated communication itself. Emphasis on effects is clearly on the information conveyed. In an interpersonal or face-to-face setting, that information is relatively well understood. We have several centuries of study into language and paralinguistic cues of the spoken language. We have delved into the areas of nonverbal, nonlinguistic (for example, kinesics, proxemics, haptics, and so on) communicative phenomena with some success. But what is the language of the mass media? "English" is the obvious answer. But what are the paralinguistic cues of English conveyed over a television screen or a six-column newspaper page? These questions are highly perplexing ones and demand more investigation and innovation.

Mass communication researchers are just beginning to gain some insights into the visual elements of communication, whether one side of the television screen is more significant than another, whether one kind of typeface is more significant than another, whether background music affects the significance of the story, and the like. Research into media effects is truly in its infancy. That it has yielded so many insights is remarkable in itself.

Networks

Although research into persuasion and media effects has the flavor of the psychological perspective, research into communication networks is almost totally mechanistic. A network focuses clearly on the channels that allow communication to flow between individuals. The specific combination of channel linkages between communicators, then, is the structure of a communication network. Most research into communication networks has been performed in group and organizational settings, and the ensuing discussion will focus on these two levels.

In a group setting networks suggest the structure of the group by focusing on the channels that are used by the individuals when they communicate directly to other individuals. One key variable of network structure is the centralization of the network that pinpoints one or two positions in the structure as more central than others. Naturally, each position is occupied by a person in the communicative role as source/receiver.

The most centralized network is the "wheel," with one person in a central position. Every other member communicates only to that one person and to no other group member. Visualize a central position, designated A, at the hub of a wheel, with all channels connecting A to other members who would be positioned on the perimeter of the wheel. Those channels would then appear as "spokes" in the wheel, extending outward from A to B, A to C, A to D, and so forth.

The least centralized network is the "circle" structure, whose channels include no position that is more central than any other. Every individual in the "wheel" network communicates with only two other individuals. You can visualize the circle network by positioning all members on the circumference of a circle, each position connected to the positions on either side. In this way, B communicates only with A and C, C communicates with B and D, D with C and E, and E with A and D—a five-person group.

Most of the network research has been performed, not by communication scholars but by social psychologists interested in group phenomena. For a summary of this research, see Collins and Raven (1969, pp. 137–155). The prevailing assumption underlying this social psychological research is that communication network structure affects other variables of group activity. For example, leadership has been associated with the central positions, centralized networks are more efficient at problem solving, decentralized networks exhibit higher morale, and persons in the central positions experience greater satisfaction with their position.

The aspect of networks more interesting to communication scholars utilizing a mechanistic perspective is probably the function of central positions as gatekeepers. For example, the central position in the wheel network serves as the gatekeeper for every other member of the group. All messages flow to A from every other person in the group. A's task is, then, to filter those incoming messages and retransmit messages back to the other members. The central position in a wheel network is potent. The person occupying that position exerts sole control over the flow of information to the entire group. All messages pass through A. And all messages received by any other member of the group must come from A.

Any centralized position in a network serves a gatekeeping function. But along with that centralized position is a problem of information flow that emanates directly from the mechanistic perspective—"information overload." Overload refers to the state in which the input of messages or informational units exceeds the capacity of the individual to process them. If we recall an earlier discussion of multiple channels, the situation of overload is similar to the typical phenomenon of human communication in which every communicator receives more incoming signals than she is capable of processing; that is, the decoding process normally and always involves selection of relevant and pertinent information from among that mass of incoming signals. However, in the case of information overload, the flow of relevant and pertinent messages to be decoded and selected exceeds the decoding and selecting capacity of the individual.

One might consider an analogy of a circuit breaker in an electrical transmission, an analogy that might help to visualize the phenomenon of information overload. Every electrical circuit breaker possesses only a predetermined capacity to convey an electrical charge along the channel. At one point in each electrical circuit is a fuse or circuit breaker, which is carefully manufactured so as to allow only a specific amount of amperage to flow through. In the event that the circuit draws too much amperage or an intensified electrical impulse travels through that circuit breaker—that is, the transmitted electrical charge exceeds the capacity of the fuse—the fuse "blows" or the circuit breaker shuts down, thus halting the continued flow of electrical current. In a similar manner, information overload tends to disrupt the flow of messages and thus results in communication breakdown. Overload is clearly a mechanistic concept of human communication. It focuses on the transmission and reception of messages along a channel—consistent with mechanism.

Although networks have not been a primary emphasis of study among communication scholars doing group research, the basic elements of networks provide a significant emphasis of research efforts by scholars in the area of organizational communication. An organization is a fertile field for mechanistically oriented communication research. (See Goldhaber, 1974.) An organization, with its inherent division of labor and formalized structure, is acutely susceptible to a mechanistic interpretation. Specifically, the structure of an organization is hierarchical—a spatial conceptualization of levels in an ascending or descending order of status levels. Individuals at each hierarchical level have the responsibility for managing those individuals at each hierarchical level "below" (a spatial concept) them. Authoritative functions flow transitively from hierarchical level to the next—either upward or downward. The typical structure of an organization is quite mechanistic.

Communication channels in an organizational structure link individuals within each hierarchical level as well as serve to link hierarchical levels to each other. Directionality of the transmission thus becomes a significant variable of organizational communication, that is, a vertical flow of information (from one level to another in the hierarchy) and a horizontal flow of information (among individuals at the same level). The nature of the information, the disruptive elements of the information, gatekeeping functions, and other mechanistic concepts differ markedly, depending upon whether the flow of information is upward, downward, or horizontal.

Unlike group networks, organizations also have the capability to designate some specific channel links between individuals or positions as the channels that should be used for specific purposes. Other channels, consequently, should not be used. The networks comprising those organizationally designated channels are typically called the "formal" channels, network, or communication structure of the organization. We typically refer to the use of formal communication networks in an organization as "going through channels"—using the organizationally approved network to convey information. When channels other than those formally designated by organizational authorities are used, the flow of information is typically called "informal" communication. The now famous series of social psychological studies conducted at the Hawthorne plant of Western Electric some forty years ago demonstrated the potency of informal communication networks. The significance of the Hawthorne studies to organizational communication has diminished but little.

Organizational communication scholars have devised specialized measuring instruments for performing communication research in organizational networks. Among these instruments are communication audits and ECCO (episodic communication channels in organizations) analyses. Such techniques seek to assess communicative effectiveness, discover informal networks, locate information overloads, identify gatekeepers, relate communication to production efficiency and employee morale, and fulfill a myriad of other purposes. The field of organizational communication is a popular and still growing area of specialization in human communication.

Diffusion

How do rumors circulate so swiftly throughout a mass population? How direct is the impact of the mass media on a mass audience? How do people obtain information of major news events? How do people formulate opinions on political issues or candidates? Or, for that matter, on buying groceries or clothing? These questions are all relevant to the process of information "diffusion," sometimes called the two-step (or multistep) flow of information. Credit for discovering or, at least, confirming the diffusion process probably goes to Lazarsfeld, Berelson, and Gaudet (1948), who conducted an extensive study of voters in the 1940 presidential elections. They added a new term to the vocabulary of mechanistic concepts of communication—*opinion leader.*

Lazarsfeld and his colleagues discovered, to their surprise, that the role played by mass media in effecting voters' choice of candidates was minimal. Rather, face-to-face contacts with other individuals provided the most prevalent source of information and influence. These individuals, called "opinion leaders," exposed themselves more frequently to the mass media and retransmitted that information to other individuals, the majority of whom received the bulk of their information from these gatekeeping opinion leaders rather than directly from the mass media. The resulting two-step flow of information, then, suggests that information flows from mass media sources to opinion leaders to the majority of the mass audience, the less active segment of the population. Of course, several groups of opinion leaders may intervene between the media and the majority of the population, which suggests a multistep, rather than simply a two-step, flow of information.

Katz and Lazarsfeld (1955) discovered later that opinion leaders typically exert influence as a gatekeeper in only one sphere of influence (for example, political opinions, motion picture preferences, clothing purchases) and rarely serve as a source of information in another unrelated area. The interest of opinion leaders apparently influences them actively to seek additional information from the mass media, but only in that area of interest. As such, opinion leaders are not so much "leaders" of public opinion as they are convenient and informed sources of information, within a clearly defined subject area, for a larger segment of the population. In other words, opinion leaders are less likely to be community leaders. They are simply gatekeepers of information and, hence, influence other people.

Research interest in diffusion has also been prevalent in anthropology and rural sociology as a paradigm for planned social change. Particularly in regard to the dissemination of innovative technological advances in developing countries, the diffusion paradigm has guided research efforts to trace the adoption network of a new seed corn or a new farm implement, for example. (See Rogers and Shoemaker, 1971.) As a paradigm for diffusing innovations, the multistep flow must trace two elements of the communicative flow—information about the innovation and adoption or use of the innovation. Although anthropological interests have focused on other variables (principally culture), the diffusion paradigm of a mechanistic flow of communication from a mass media source to a larger population through gatekeeping opinion leaders is highly similar.

CONCLUSION

The mechanistic perspective of human communication emphasizes the physical elements of communication, the transmission and reception of messages flowing in a conveyer-belt fashion among source/receivers. All significant functions of communication occur on the channel, the locus of the mechanistic perspective. Mechanism is the perspective most frequently adopted by scholars whose principal interest is not human communication, for example, social psychologists, anthropologists, business management specialists, and the like. Nevertheless, vestiges of the mechanistic perspective permeate a vast quantity of communication research.

Although most communicologists (I still resist using that pretentiously awkward term) would resist labeling themselves "mechanists," many of them, nonetheless, utilize numerous conceptual or theoretical elements of mechanism to direct their thoughts and their research efforts. For all its allegedly antihumanistic faults, the mechanistic perspective is a pervasive, convenient, and valuable perspective from which to view the relationships among variables of human communication. Its importance should not be slighted, and its virtues should not be rejected out of hand. It remains simply one perspective, among several, as a framework within which we might conceptually organize and thereby understand the process of human communication. As students of human communication, we need to understand mechanism as *a* perspective for understanding human communication. It is not *the* perspective. Neither is it false. As long as people use mechanism to understand communicative phenomena, we need to understand it.

— 5 —

The Psychological Perspective

Much of the communication research in the empirical tradition of contemporary social sciences has borrowed heavily from psychology, but this phenomenon is understandable. Communication has for centuries borrowed from other disciplines, including, at one time or another, philosophy, English, theatre, history, political science, and sociology, among others. Defenders of borrowing have considered the practice a strength of the discipline and thus refer to communication as an "electric" discipline.

Others within the field of human communication, however, have been disturbed by the extensive borrowing and consider communication to be experiencing an identity crisis as a result. Are we really, they ask, an identifiable discipline of study? Or are we just a hodge-podge of disparate approaches to a rather common phenomenon called communication—a domain of inquiry of interest to several disciplines but hardly a discipline unique to itself? However, I have discussed this topic in an earlier chapter. I am not sure I resolved it then, and I can add little to the issue; therefore, I shall not belabor the subject.

Communication's borrowing from psychology has been rather superficial and sporadic. This is not to say that communication study from a psychological perspective is superficial. Rather, the interests of communication scholars are simply not those of psychologists. Therefore, certain psychological precepts have made the transition to communication study whereas others have been largely ignored. Communication research, for example, typically uses personality as a variable affecting communicative phenomena, but rarely is personality an object of study in and of itself.

Then, too, communication has not borrowed from all areas of psychology but principally from social psychology. But unlike social psychologists, communicologists have demonstrated little interest in the theoretical arguments surrounding the S–R (stimulus-response) tradition of modern psychology. Whereas cognitive psychologists and behaviorists argue over the theoretical and empirical merits of their allegedly disparate approaches, communication scholars have blithely borrowed from both. Moreover, we have borrowed while only rarely taking into account the nuances of psychological theory that do not bear directly on the phenomena of human communication.

The psychological perspective to be delineated in this chapter probably does not exist in any pure form. The perspective is one of emphasis and relative significance. In reality, the psychological perspective is an addendum to the mechanistic perspective, but in supplementing mechanism, the psychological perspectivists tend to avoid many of the theoretical limitations of the former perspective. Therefore, when the following discussion includes such mechanistic terms as *encoding, decoding,* and *messages,* those terms should be understood within the psychological perspective with connotations quite different from those in the purely mechanistic perspective.

Tracing the beginnings of the influence of psychology on the study of human communication inevitably becomes arbitrary. The interdisciplinary influence probably predates the 1938 publication of Eisenson's *The Psychology of Speech* (extensively revised in 1963 as *The Psychology of Communication,* coauthored by Eisenson, Auer, and Irwin) and the 1936 publication of Oliver's *The Psychology of Persuasive Speech.* Whenever the initiation of the psychological influence on communication took place, the psychological perspective is probably the most popular perspective of human communication today; that is, more people who claim to be students of communication as a discipline for empirical study would also find this perspective most similar to their own point of view.

CHARACTERISTICS OF A PSYCHOLOGICAL EXPLANATION (OF COMMUNICATION)

Like communication (perhaps more so), psychology is a diverse discipline of loosely connected specializations, for example, personality psychology, social psychology, industrial psychology, counseling psychology, abnormal psychology, physiological psychology, clinical psychology, architectural psychology, humanistic psychology, educational psychology, and so on. Certainly, no one theory or mode of explanation unites such disparate specialties. Popular theories in psychology include psychoanalytic theories (Freudian or Jungian, for example), behaviorism, field theory, role theory, personality theory, and cognitive explanations. The psychological perspective of communication, needless to say, does not include all these theoretical approaches.

As a matter of fact, the psychological view of communication does not include all of any single theory from psychology. The careful reader will note that this comparable section in the preceding chapter on mechanism was called tenets, whereas the present section employs the term *characteristics*. Those terms are used with purpose. Recall that communication's borrowing from psychology has been relatively superficial and sporadic. Consequently, the purpose here is not to stipulate the essential features of psychological explanation or even explanation within one psychological theory. Rather, the purpose is to characterize the features of psychological explanation that appear to guide the communication scholars who utilize it.

The major emphasis is a form of post-Skinnerian behaviorism with a strong flavor of cognitive explanation. The following characteristics, then, should not be construed as a comprehensive or a realistic definition of the form of explanation used by most psychologists. These characteristics, instead, are the central features of a principally S–R explanation adapted to human communication.

Sensory Reception of Stimuli

As human beings, we are highly restricted in our capabilities for relating to our environment and to each other. Physiologically, at least, we have at our disposal only our five senses—seeing, hearing, smelling, touching, and tasting. Those environmental phenomena intrinsic to many psychological explanations, including theoretical explanations beyond those with behavioristic tendencies, are the concept of a "stimulus" as a unit of sensory input. Thus, any ray of light falling on the retina, any atmospheric vibration imparting on the inner ear, or any substance contacting the taste buds is potentially definable as a stimulus. What makes an object a stimulus, however, is not that it exists in a human's environment but that it is received as a definable unit by one or more of the human's senses. Stimuli provide input for the senses and, consequently, the data used in the explanation of human behavior.

The fundamental concept of stimulus is more complex than it seems at first glance. Take, for example, a face-to-face encounter of two individuals. One person smiles and says, "Hi! How are you?" What is the stimulus for the second person? On the one hand, we can consider the stimulus to be the smiling person uttering the English-language phrase; that is, the stimulus may be considered an object that exists in the environment (and, of course, received). As an object, the stimulus is an environmental influence and may take the form of a person, a message, a noise, a color —in short, an object that influences. Conceiving of a stimulus as an environmental object leads to a semideterministic explanation in which the environment impinges upon or affects human beings residing within it. The human can resist the environmental influences, of course, but his behavior is explainable, essentially, as a product of the environmental context and the phenomena within it.

A second conceptualization of stimulus, however, is to focus not on the stimulus-object itself but upon the impact of the object on the sensory organ; that is, the stimulus is a visual pattern on the retina, an aural pattern on the ear drum, and so on. In this sense, the stimulus is basically a physiological concept—the apprehension of an environmental object by a sensory receptor. A stimulus is, then, the object converted to sensations, a particular variety or pattern possessing specific visual, aural, olfactory, tactile, or taste properties. Intrinsic to such an explanation of stimuli is physiology—relating the psychological experience to the physical experience and the physical to the psychological. This area of psychology, often called psychophysics, has also been somewhat popular in communication studies using instrumentation for physiological measurement—for example, heart rate, respiratory rate, brain waves, pupil dilation, secretion of sweat glands, and the like.

Still another conceptualization of stimulus is similar to Hanson's (1958) notion that observation and understanding are inseparable. If you recall an earlier discussion in Part One, Hanson noted that we don't just "see" some object; we see that object *as* something or other. In the example of the face-to-face encounter, the stimulus is definable as a ritualistic greeting of friendliness—an inference and a synthesis of the set of stimuli. But this notion of a stimulus requires that the observer be familiar with that cultural ritual beforehand; otherwise, he would see the stimulus as something else—perhaps a sincere inquiry as to the status of health. In this sense, a native American would see the stimulus as a cultural greeting whereas someone else might see the stimulus as an attempt to invade privacy. Clearly, the concept of stimulus is that of an inference directly from either the environmental object or the sensory pattern or both.

To ask which of the three conceptualizations of stimulus is "correct" or "best" is to miss the point. A stimulus may, in a given situation, be either an object in the environment, a sensory pattern, a unitary experience, or all three in combination. The specific nature of the stimulus is a rather complex concept, which may vary from one situation to another and which will certainly affect our understanding of the phenomena to be explained. The context in which inquiry is to take place and the specific purposes of the inquiry should indicate how the stimulus is or should be defined. Under any circumstances, to understand the explanation is to understand how the concept of stimulus is being used.

Still another problem potentially inherent in the concept of stimulus serves to increase still further the complexity of the theoretical concept. What constitutes a single stimulus? That is, what is the discernible unit of stimuli? How many units of stimuli are included in the hi-how-are-you example? Certainly, it makes a difference whether the stimulus is conceptualized as an environmental object, a sensory pattern, or unitary experience. As an experience, only one unit or stimulus occurs in the example, but as a sensory pattern, the number of units is nearly infinite.

This problem has never been solved adequately by psychological theorists. In most cases of applied research, the stimulus is defined and unitized rather arbitrarily even though the very arbitrariness of the definitional unit may render results of the research less interpretable. For our purposes, we shall recognize that the problem exists but shall attempt no resolution.

Internal Mediation of Stimuli

The term S–R is probably a misnomer in that virtually all contemporary uses of S–R explanations recognize the intervention of the organism between stimulus and response—hence, S–O–R. The S–R explanation, then, takes on the inherent characteristics of an input-throughput-output sequence. Rarely will a contemporary psychological explanation attempt to predict specific responses by considering only specific stimuli. Rather, the explanation will take into account the internal reception and processing of stimuli, which will consequently be transformed into some observable responses or set of responses.

For the most part, the mediation of the organism in S–R explanation is a "black-box" concept; that is, the specific structure and function of the internal mediational process are considered less significant than the transformation of inputs into outputs. In the sense of a black box, then, the explanation requires observation of inputs and outputs but does not require direct observation of the inner workings of the organism, as if it were even possible. In the first place, direct observation of the internal processing is virtually impossible; so we observe external behaviors and consider them to be manifestations of the internal state of the organism. The assessment of internal states is fundamentally an indirect observation—an inference from observable behaviors.

Our everyday world is filled with such inferences. When we observe someone laughing or smiling, clapping her hands, and using exaggerated movements, we are apt to infer from this combination of behaviors the internal emotional state of happiness. Another person who is yawning, constantly shifting posture, and gazing idly about the room would lead us to infer that the person is inwardly bored. This is not to suggest that external behaviors inevitably reflect internalized states, but only that we can only infer internalized states from externalized behaviors. We have no other means to observe the "black box." Furthermore, we do it all the time without being consciously aware of the inference.

The extent to which we expect behaviors to be consistent with internal states is the extent to which we say that the person is "sincere." We consider the stereotypical used-car salesman to be insincere because we attribute to him ulterior motives as a direct consequence of the situation—seller and sellee. In the same vein, we tend to view the frozen smile on the face of beauty-pageant contestants as phony—not really reflecting friendliness or happiness. In other words, we apparently have means at our disposal to detect discrepancies between outward manifestations and internal states of the organism. And those means arise from a knowledge of the situation.

This, then, is the nature of the black box. Observation of inputs and subsequent observation of outputs lead to an inference about the internal mechanism of the throughput. To observe a shark's dorsal fin in the water and the subsequent behavior of a swimmer heading posthaste to shore will lead us to infer that the stimulus (the fin) activated the mediational process internal to the organism (the swimmer experienced fear), which then led to a behavioral response (flight behavior). Responses, then, do not emanate directly from stimuli but are mediated through internal states within the organism, the human being. Furthermore, the mediational process need not be observed directly but can be inferred from the observation of inputs and outputs, that is, stimuli and responses.

The relationship between stimulus and response is occasionally characterized as a cause-effect relationship. Later in this chapter there will be a discussion of some apparent similarities between the S–R and cause-effect relationship. Nevertheless, an S–R explanation is not totally causal, for a purely causal explanation would not account for the significant mediational function of the internal states. An S–R explanation would then suggest that an organism produce certain behaviors, given certain stimulus conditions. That is to say, the organism's internal states function to produce certain behavioral responses, given the presence of specified stimulus conditions. It is important to remember, however, that the internal states are knowable only in terms of the role they play in producing behaviors.

Prediction of Response

The goal of an S–R explanation centers on prediction, and prediction centers on responses. Typically, a response is considered to be a behavior capable of being directly observed, and the psychological explanation attempts to account for, that is, to explain, behavior in terms of stimuli and internal states. It is clear that responses are unpredictable purely in terms of the physical properties of the stimulus. The response is attributable more to the internal states that are activated by the inputs.

One factor of behavioral response is important to understanding the psychologically based explanation. History of previous stimulus conditions encountered by an organism is important in predicting any behavior, given a specified stimulus situation. In other words, the internal states of the organism contain elements of prior stimulation, which affect responses in subsequent situations that are judged to be similar. If prior stimulation affects the response to a given stimulus condition, then at least some elements of the internal mediational states are themselves products or responses to previous stimulus experiences.

The knowledge that responses are predictable, at least in part, from past responses suggests another interesting facet of the S–R explanation —the concept of memory storage of past responses within the organism. Not only must psychological explanation account for the history of responses when attempting to predict a response, but such an explanation must also include principles accounting for the accumulation and degradation of S–R experiences in the past; that is, some conceptual principle must account for the recognition of a stimulus situation as similar to past experiences. And certain principles or laws are necessary to explain the development of that memorylike concept and how it changes with subsequent experiences, which may be dissimilar.

The concept generally used to account for recognizing similarities among S–R situations is *set*. A mental or psychological *set* may be conceptualized as a collection of criteria or expectations based on prior experiences that are inherently applied to each new experience as a means for determining the similarity or difference between the new situation and past experiences. If the stimulus situation is similar, then the set also provides the appropriate (that is, similar) response.

The concept of *set* implies a linkage between the past and the present and is thus relatively enduring over time. But the conceptual materialism of mechanism is not wholly applicable to the durational properties of the psychological set. Keep in mind that the set is a product of experiences and is thus susceptible to change over time as more and more experiences are collected. Although the set does not change immediately or even easily, it is not a concept that is mechanistically permanent. Rather than endure as a constant entity over time (a mechanistic concept), it endures only for a period of measurable time and may evolve into something quite different at a later date. We shall refer to the set, then, as a semienduring or semipermanent concept that is a function of experiences, that is, the past.

The psychological set, as a product of experience, contains elements of both stimuli and responses and is located in the organism as an internal mediational state. In this sense, the O (mediating between S and R in the S–O–R explanation) is itself a series of S–R relationships. Although the S and the R are events that do not endure over time, in effect they too are semipermanent because they are included as a memorylike property of O—the organism—and serve to convey the past into the present. It is in this way that behavioral responses are influenced not only by stimulus situations but also by previous stimuli encountered and the previous responses to those stimuli. An S–R explanation is not nearly so simple as one might be led to believe at first glance.

Reinforcement of Responses

Berger and Lambert (1968, p. 97) suggest that the term S–R is really a misnomer because it omits the more recent variations of S–R theory. These authors go on to suggest "that S–R psychology is of necessity at least an S–O–R-feedback psychology." In other words, a complete psychological explanation within an S–R framework requires the addition of the internal states of the organism (O) and the responses to the behavioral response (feedback) to the original S and R concepts. Rather than confuse Berger and Lambert's use of the term *feedback* with the same term as a communication concept, I shall use the term *reinforcement* to refer to the response to the organism's original response, that is, response to R.

S–R psychology can easily be extended to include the many varieties of psychology such as Pavlovian conditioning, operant conditioning, learning theory, and social exchange, among others. Adding the fourth principle of reinforcement to the S–O–R relationship allows a dimension similar to teleology, which allows a present event to affect the past or a future event to affect the present. If the reinforcement serves consistently to reward a particular response to a specified stimulus event, then we might hypothesize (in a rather simpleminded fashion) that that particular S–O–R relationship will be strengthened. Conversely, if subsequent reinforcement consistently punishes a particular response to a specified stimulus situation, then that S–O–R relationship will weaken and eventually lead to an extinction of the response.

Probably the most significant effect provided by the addition of the reinforcement principle to the S–O–R explanation is the reversing of the unidirectionality of time effects. Not only does the stimulus situation affect the organism's internal states and hence the response, but the reinforcement affects the organism's internal state in the reverse. That is to say, the organism is affected not only by past events but by the future as well. The consequence of this bidirectionality of time is to place greater emphasis on the internal states of the organism. In a sense, the organism is not merely at the mercy of the environment. Rather, it can control the environment and its influence, to some extent, through the application of the mediational function of the internal states. But the degree and nature of the organism's control over its environment is not all that clear in conceptualizing the S–R explanation.

It might be safer to say that the internal states of the organism become more significant to the S–O–R conceptualization than in the S–R formulation. Endowing O with greater significance is at once both a conceptual strength and weakness. As a strength, the internal states of the organism possess greater explanatory power and can thus account for a greater variety of situations than ever before. The weakness lies in the capacity of the S–R explanation to explain everything by accounting for any result (typically after the fact) with reference to the inferred internal states of the organism. Recall that the O is a black-box concept observable only in terms of behavior produced. By explaining everything, the internal states do not discriminate as well among differing results. The end result is that they essentially explain nothing. The inevitable consequence is a potential conceptual dilemma, which any psychological explanation must recognize and compensate for.

A PSYCHOLOGICAL MODEL

A psychological model of communication is rarely evident in the literature of communication theory as a unitary view of the communicative process. Generally, those communication theorists who would subscribe to a psychological perspective combine the psychological attributes of communication with those of a mechanistic model. The most fruitful method of viewing the model which follows, therefore, is to overlay this model on a mechanistic model which was introduced in the preceding chapter. Specifically, a psychological model focuses on the source-receiver, the individual human being, and delves into the internal cognitive and affective makeup of the communicating agent.

Typical Components

An S–R orientation is quite prominent in the psychological perspective of human communication. The perspective, first of all, assumes that humans exist in a *stimulus field*, loosely defined as an informational environment. Surrounding each person is a nearly infinite array of stimuli (see Figure 3), all capable of being processed through the sensory receptor organs, that is, seeing, hearing, touching, smelling, or tasting. In a sense, these stimuli compete for reception in that they are so numerous that they far exceed the human's capacity to receive and process.

The communicating human being, of course, not only receives stimuli but produces stimuli as well. Similar to the source/receiver concept in the mechanistic model, the human is characterized in the psychological model as embodying both the productive and the receptive functions— thus, the human is a *communicator/interpreter* of informational stimuli.

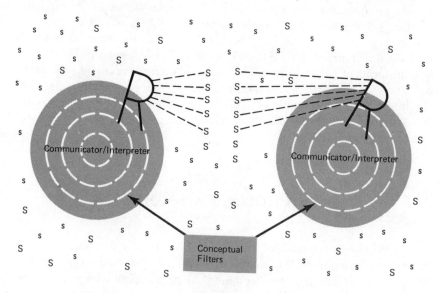

Figure 3.   A Psychological Model of Human Communication.

(Later in this chapter there will frequently be a reference to the communicator/interpreter as simply communicator. The term *communicator* also implies the dual functions of producing and receiving stimuli.)

The psychological model of communication differs from a psychological model explaining all behavior in the assumption that all human beings in the stimulus field produce a significant portion of the stimuli that are perceived by the other person. To some extent, then, each communicator is psychologically oriented toward the other. Unlike a psychological model to explain any behavior, the communicative situation implies some degree of purposiveness or instrumentality on the part of the behavioral stimuli produced by communicators, and that purposiveness is oriented toward another communicator.

Obviously, any attempt to describe communication within a psychological model begins at a rather arbitrary point. Because we began the description of the mechanistic model at the point of encoding a message, the present description of a psychological model can easily be initiated at a comparable point. Every communicator is capable of producing stimuli in informational form, that is, in the form of signs and symbols. Although the bulk of the informational environment, the stimulus field, is randomly ordered and unstructured, the stimuli produced by the communicator are structured or organized and are more easily identifiable and interpretable as a body of informational stimuli that is produced by that communicator. In fact, Goyer (1970) develops a psychological model of communication by including the cognitively structured discriminative response by the interpreter as the *sine qua non* of human communication.

As the interpreter intakes these (and, of course, other) stimuli, she automatically processes them through various *conceptual filters*. These filters comprise the internal states of the human organism and are essentially black-box concepts. They are not directly observable, of course, as internal states, but are assumed to affect the communicative event significantly.

Depending upon the purpose of the inquiry and the specific theoretical predisposition of the inquirer, the filters may be described as attitudes, beliefs, motives, drives, images, cognitions, self-concepts, percepts, orientations, sets, or any of a host of other hypothetical constructs. Their specific identity or their specific modes of functioning as conceptual filters are determinable only within a specific school of psychological thought. Neither is their specific identity or functioning directly pertinent to our present purpose of delineating the various perspectives used to view human communication. More important for our purpose is the observation that the conceptual filters are inherently internal—within the individual communicator—and, as black-box concepts, their functioning is only indirectly observable through the modification of stimuli input into behavioral output.

After filtering communicative stimuli, the communicator then responds to those stimuli by producing additional stimuli, which are then added to the stimulus field as a behavioral *response*. The response, symbolized in Figure 3 as R, is also a structured set of informational stimuli identifiable as signals and symbols produced by a communicator and susceptible to a subsequent discriminative response by the other interpreter. As a matter of fact, the original (that is, "original" in the sense of our arbitrary starting point) production of stimuli is also a response in Figure 3, symbolized by the R converted into a body of Ss.

You will note in observing Figure 3, however, that the R is located on the circumference of the circle representing the communicator/interpreter. Only a portion of that big R is outside the circle, and a substantial portion remains within the communicator/interpreter. In other words, all of a response is not capable of being directly observed. Some of the response remains hidden and thus not observable in the communicative event. For example, the normal communicative event does not allow for observation of certain physiological responses, such as changes in brain waves, respiratory rate, body temperature, heart rate, muscular tension, and the like. If the individual were to be hooked up to a polygraph, an electroencephalograph, a galvanometer, and a pupillometer, then a greater proportion of the response would be observable. Nevertheless, some portion of the response inevitably escapes observation.

If every experience somehow changes the semipermanent internal states—the perceptual filters of the mental set—then experiences in the form of responses to stimuli must be retained within the communicator; that is, some of the response cycles inward to become stored in the memory, and some serves to strengthen or weaken the perceptual set. Under any circumstances, the effects of these retained portions of response remain within the individual and serve to modify the individual's behavior in later communicative events. Their effect may be long-range and, depending upon subsequent similar experiences, may affect observable responses at a later date.

Human communication in a psychological model is thus a continuous production and reception of stimuli added to and selected from the stimuli available in the informational environment. Although transmission is not necessarily included, in the sense of messages conveyed on a channel, each communicator is psychologically oriented to each other. This orientation probably assumes some awareness of each other and more. Goyer (1970) includes the criterion of discriminative response rather than simply a random or unstructured choice on the part of the interpreter. And Fearing (1953) incorporates the concept of "intent." The communicative situation, then, is characterized by a structured stimulus field and a certain degree of purposiveness on the part of the communicators. Certainly, a communicative situation from a psychological perspective differs from other S–R situations that do not imply the existence of communicative phenomena.

Locus—Conceptual Filters

The psychological perspective of human communication clearly focuses on the individual as the primary "place" to look for communication to take place. Moreover, in that the psychological perspective conceives of the individual as a black-box organism, focusing on the individual effectively locates communication within internal states and thus inaccessible to direct observation. Many clichés relevant to communication demonstrate this psychological locus. For instance, "Words don't communicate; people do." And, of course, the ever popular "Meaning is perception." The locus of communication in the psychological perspective is clearly and consistently within the individual—in S–R terms, the internal states of the organism.

I hasten to point out that the term *conceptual filters* is, to my knowledge, original with me. I use the term not to identify the nature of the internal states but as a catchall term, which is intended to include all the varying constructs that have been used to describe theoretically the internal workings of the human being.

Recall that a construct is not a demonstrable (that is, observable or provable) concept. Rather, a construct is a theoretical concept that is literally invented to explain otherwise inexplicable observations. A construct, in a manner of speaking, is an intellectual synthesis of numerous data or details and is utilized to account for those data. The very existence and measurement of constructs are, therefore, inferences drawn from other observables. Constructs that have been used to account for the resultant behavior in an S–R explanation include the following: attitudes, beliefs, needs, values, drives, motives, cognitions, feelings, emotions, perceptions, images, instincts, orientations, perceptions, and a host of others.

One might also describe the locus of the psychological perspective by its comparable locus in the mechanistic model—the encoding-decoding process. But in the psychological perspective in which transmission and channel functions are less significant, the difference between encoding and decoding becomes imperceptible. In other words, the process of receiving stimuli via conceptual filters is a process of interpretation. The interpreter must identify, structure or organize, and discriminate among the stimuli received. In this way, the interpreter assigns meaning to the stimuli, which is, in a manner of speaking, a function of encoding a message.

This process of interpretation through conceptual filters is precisely the same whether the communicator is producing a structured set of stimuli (that is, encoding a message) or receiving and structuring a set of stimuli (that is, decoding a message). The result is a blurred distinction between the mechanistic processes of encoding and decoding. It might be more accurate to think of the psychological locus of communication as the encoding process or simply the "coding" process. In any case, the encoding/decoding process is internalized.

Thayer's (1968) version of a psychological perspective of communication includes a distinction between "data" and "information." Thayer considers data as only stimuli existing in the stimulus field, but those data are of little significance to the communicator or the communicative event until the individual "takes them into account." When the individual internally processes data, those stimuli then become information and thereby relevant to communication.

Thayer's key term is the individual's capacity to "take into account" the data, and once that is accomplished, the individual is able to exert some control over the information. The communicator supplies the data with meaning. The information no longer "belongs to" the communicator who originally produced it. Thus, each communicator encodes the message value (that is, information) from the data, and the conceptual filters are the devices used to transform data into information.

A final observation is in order concerning the psychological locus of communication within the individual. Although the foregoing discussion implies that the psychological perspective is a singular approach to scholarly inquiry into human communication, the reality of the situation is not as neat and tidy as it appears. Remember that the individual is a black-box entity, in that the information-processing individual is "behaving" in ways that are quite covert and not accessible to direct observation. Therefore, the central focus of communication must inherently deal with some variety of conceptual filters, which are inevitably hypothetical constructs drawn from some particular brand of psychological theory. The result in the field of psychology has been a plethora of theoretical orientations generated by scholars and theorists with different interests and different theoretical assumptions.

The communication scholars with a psychological orientation may utilize instrumental and theoretical constructs that differ widely from one scholar to another. Although these scholars are quite similar in their general perspective and approach to the phenomena of human communication, the fact remains that they must inevitably choose from among the variety of theoretical conceptualizations of internalized filtering devices. There are at least a dozen different theoretical approaches to the study of perception alone. Add to that the multitude of theoretical approaches to attitudes, and the number of approaches available for inquiry into communicative phenomena increases dramatically.

Further discussion will continue to treat the psychological perspective as a unitary approach to communication. The reader is cautioned to consider that the psychological perspective of human communication is, for our purposes, an abstract perspective to be distinguished from mechanism and the rest and does not necessarily imply unanimity of agreement among the community of scholars who might be identified within a psychological model. Certainly, all psychologists are not unanimous in their assessments and practices of psychological inquiry. There is no reason to assume that communication scholars, borrowing from psychology, should reflect any greater agreement.

IMPLICATIONS

The psychological perspective of human communication has generated many new issues and directions, which have characterized a significant portion of research efforts in the field of human communication in recent years. Some of the issues raised within the psychological perspective are rather knotty conceptual problems, which have not been totally solved. Nor are any final solutions likely to be found in the near future. Other implications, however, have supplied direction for a considerable quantity of communication research.

One general tendency seems to be a direct treatment of the communicator as a human being—a return to humanistic principles. To some extent, the popular belief that S–R psychology tends to dehumanize people and render them virtually defenseless against their environment —unrecognizable from rats, guinea pigs, or rhesus monkeys—is a "cheap shot." Certainly, such an accusation is not wholly accurate. Without an attempt to generalize to the whole of psychological inquiry, the psychological perspective of human communication is typically a perspective consistent, for the most part, with abstract humanistic principles emphasizing the individualism and the dignity of the human communicator.

Receiver Orientation

A few years ago there was talk of several leaders of the American Indian Movement planning to celebrate the American Bicentennial by traveling to Italy in order to "discover" it. After all, they reasoned, the history books credit an Italian, Christopher Columbus, with the "discovery" of America even though it had already been "discovered" and inhabited hundreds of years before by the natives then residing on the North American continent—the American Indians. Turnabout being fair play, it seems only natural for native Americans to "discover" Italy and Europe and even claim the "new territory" for themselves. Of such is formed the "Columbus syndrome"—claiming discovery of the already familiar or previously "discovered."

As recently as 1964, Raymond Bauer (in true Columbian fashion) "discovered" the receiver as an active agent in the process of human communication. His notion of the "obstinate audience" was familiar to I. A. Richards (1936) some thirty years previously and not particularly novel to a number of rhetoricians in ancient Rome and Greece dating back another 2,000 years. But, then, Bauer's point of view was quite different. His perspective was that of psychology and advertising, fields that do not consider rhetoric as part of their historical tradition. In a sense, Bauer was the Christopher Columbus of psychology; and the rhetorical theorists, the native Americans of communication.

The numerous attempts to assess the effects of communication, particularly those of mass media, led to some second thoughts about the purely mechanistic model. The overly simplified notion that a communicative source "does something to" the receiver seemed, upon reflection subsequent to research, to be an incomplete and rather inaccurate picture of the communicative process. Similar to the view of "one-way" communication, the viewpoint became infamous as the "target model" of communication and was encouraged by the popularized belief in manipulation of the masses through such familiar notions as "propaganda," "brainwashing," and (once again) "hidden persuaders." But results from research indicated that receivers were not so susceptible to mass manipulation and were even capable of strong resistance to manipulative attempts.

Fearing's (1953) psychological model of communication includes the concept of "intent" as inherent to the communicative situation. By intent, Fearing implies that the communicator structures and directs the content of message-stimuli with the interpreter in mind. The interpreter (or receiver, if you prefer) thus affects the "original" message-stimuli by being "always in the psychological field of the communicator" (the source, in mechanistic terms). But more than that, the control over the communication event (control over content as well as social control over the other person), according to Fearing, is not centered in the communicator/source. Nor is control centered in any one person in the communicative situation—communicator or interpreter—but is "complex and interdependent." The result is a view of the receiver as an equally (perhaps even more so) active participant in the communicative process and a participant who serves to influence the event and the informational stimuli. As such, the interpreter partially determines the entire process of communication. The target strikes back!

To a considerable extent the receiver orientation of the psychological perspective of communication is a reaction against the mechanistic model and its inherent directionality of the channel. Although mechanism (in an oversimplified but easily accomplished conceptualization) encourages a target-model view of the receiver, the psychological perspective and its accompanying locus of communication within the individual conceptualizes the receiver as an active encoder of structured stimuli affecting the message and the source. Because the receiver has an element of control (through assigning meaningful interpretation) of information that he processes, the conceptual capacity of the communicator to control another communicator is severely restricted.

Intrapersonal Level

A corollary to receiver orientation is the increased significance of the intrapersonal level of communication. A commonly heard controversy among students of communication is whether such a thing as intrapersonal communication can exist. The controversy includes such issues as whether a person can communicate with himself or whether a person can communicate with inanimate objects such as trees. I am always reminded of the song from *Paint Your Wagon,* which includes a line about talking to trees but their not listening. I am always tempted to say, "Of course not, you turkey! And trees can't talk back to you, either." Arguing over whether intrapersonal communication exists seems such a waste of time as well as being disgustingly trivial.

It is infinitely more valuable to think of communication occurring at different "levels"—intrapersonal, interpersonal, group, and so on. As a "level," intrapersonal communication is an analytical focus rather than a one-person social setting for communication to take place. For example, if four people are engaged in conversation, one could focus on the communicative level of the group in terms of group values, group attitudes, and the like—those elements shared among the group members by virtue of their membership in that social level. At the intrapersonal level, however, the focus would be on the values, attitudes, and such, held by each individual in the four-person group. Rather than being a one-person setting or event for communication to occur, intrapersonal communication embodies the phenomena going on within the individual during any communicative situation regardless of how many people are involved.

The question should not be whether intrapersonal communication exists but, rather, to what extent are intrapersonal processes significant to human communication? In a psychological perspective they are highly significant. Mortensen (1972, Chapter 4) suggests that the communicator can be viewed in terms of his orientation—self-directed, other-directed, and coorientation (that is, similar orientation of self and other to a third entity). In discussing self-directed orientation, Mortensen suggests that the communicator is unique, integrated, consistent, and active. Without our going into detail, the implication is strong that every communicating individual is actively engaged in considerable introspection in the process of relating herself to other people and to the world around her. In addition, the very concept of self (for example, self-esteem, self-concept, self-disclosure, and so forth) is a significant variable in human communication.

With the emphasis on the intrapersonal level of communication and what goes on inside the person is the conceptualization of the human being as a highly sophisticated processor of information. When the locus of human communication resides within the individual, the intrapersonal level of communication is virtually omnipotent. Of special significance are the conceptual filters—how they are acquired, how they process sensory data, how they are modified, how they affect behavioral responses, how they assign meaning, and so on. The study of human communication becomes centrally the study of intrapersonal processes—attitudes, cognitions, perceptions, and the like. The uniqueness and the activeness of the individual render the variable of individual differences (for example, personality, sociocultural background, and so on) extremely vital to the performance of inquiry into communicative phenomena.

Although the intrapersonal level of communication is relevant within the mechanistic perspective, it is not of central significance as it is within a psychological perspective. In fact, no perspective of human communication places nearly so great an emphasis on intrapersonal levels of communication as the psychological perspective. To the communication scholar viewing the process of human communication psychologically, the pragmatic perspective will seem blasphemous, and another controversy is born. More on that in Chapter 7.

Attitude-Behavior Relationship

We have made much of the fact that the psychological perspective guides the study of human communication to "black-box" variables internal to the individual. The locus, of course, does not imply that communication scholars utilizing this perspective completely ignore overt behaviors. Rather, the perspective is one of emphasis. Communicative behavior, then, is explainable and attributable to a knowledge of the internalized variables—conceptual filters. Because all black-box study is inherently inferential, the specific nature of the relationship between covert variables and overt behaviors is a matter of considerable theoretical conjecture.

The most significant discussion concerning this overt-covert relationship centers on the relationship between attitudes and behaviors. As McGuire (1969, p. 156) points out, the concept of attitude is probably a multidimensional (including cognitive, affective, and behavioral elements) construct in that "the verbal report of his attitude has a rather low correlation with his actual behaviors. . . ." In a survey of psychological studies of attitudes and behaviors, Wicker (1969) came to a similar conclusion—that research has demonstrated no clear consistency between covert attitudes and overt behaviors. The problem has become popularly known as the "attitude-behavior discrepancy." The precise nature of this relationship (or lack of relationship) remains undefined although communication scholars, among them Burhans (1971), Larson and Sanders (1975), and Seibold (1975), have made numerous attempts to resolve the apparent discrepancy.

To some extent the debate over the attitude-behavior relationship reflects a theoretical struggle in psychology over cognitive and S-R psychology. To some psychologists, the struggle represents a search for a single theory uniting the bipartite study of psychology—behaviors and cognitions. That theoretical union is apparently well in the future, for the numerous attempts in the past that have attempted to discover a clearly linear relationship (for example, that cognitions "cause" behaviors or that behaviors "cause" cognitions) have met with little success. Apparently, the relationship between the covert and the overt is multidimensional, too—an interdependent and highly complex relationship, which resists clear explanation. The attitude-behavior issue remains unresolved but significantly evident, implicit or explicit, within the psychological perspective of human communication.

Quasi Causality

Although mechanistic functions are clearly transitive in nature and lead directly to inferences of linear relationships, functions within the psychological model are not transitive. Nevertheless, the theoretical and methodological implications of the S–O–R–R perspective lead to a form of linearity that we can term quasi-causal. Clearly, a purely causal relationship simply is inappropriate in the psychological perspective. Stimuli do not lead directly to responses as some critics of S–R have alleged. Equating S–R relationships with causal relationships is a classic misconstruction of behaviorism. Remember that the organism, the human individual, intervenes as an active controlling element between S and R.

The fundamental model for investigation of the internal states of the organism (the individual's conceptual filters) is an input-output paradigm. The investigator typically plies the subject with controlled stimulus variables and then attempts to observe the resultant modification of response variables or, inferentially, changes in the internal states. Consequently, the investigator assumes a certain linearity between (1) the stimulus and response mediated by conceptual filters or (2) the conceptual filters and subsequent behaviors often precipitated by initial stimuli.

Measure what goes in (input), and observe what goes out (outputs). The result is an inference about what happened in between (throughput). The information flows unidirectionally forward in time and is changed systematically by the mediational black-box concepts within the individual. The paradigm is quite linear in regard to time and resembles a type of linear or quasi-causal assumption.

Most importantly, the quasi causality of the input-output paradigm of psychological inquiry is easily adaptable to the covering-law hypothesis of science philosophy. The antecedent states in a conditional statement represent input, and the consequent states represent output. Internal mediational states could be represented by auxiliary hypotheses or, inferentially, either the antecedent or consequent conditions in phrasing the research hypotheses. The significant element in the input-output assumption is the adaptability to traditional science philosophy and, consequently, to experimentation as the methodological setting for scholarly inquiry.

Proliferation of Measuring Instruments

Like the quasi-causal assumption of the psychological perspective, a further implication is most pertinent to the methodologies and techniques used in research practice. When observation of any phenomenon is inevitably indirect or inferred, such as observation of internalized conceptual filters, proving the superior validity of any measuring instrument is highly problematic, to say the least; that is, if you don't know what an attitude "looks like," then how do you know when you are measuring one? Add to this conceptual difficulty the additional one of conceptual multidimensionality and complexity of cognitive, affective, and behavioral components (see McGuire, 1969, pp. 155–157), and the difficulties in measurement of attitudes alone increase dramatically. The problem of assuring the validity (that is, whether the instrument actually measures what it purports to be measuring) of any technique for measuring a covert concept is virtually insurmountable. The real question becomes the degree of invalidity you are willing to tolerate.

The result of the conceptual difficulty of observing the directly unobservable is a proliferation in the number of instruments and techniques to measure or observe the same concept. Consider, for example, the instruments available for measuring just one variety of conceptual filters—attitudes. If we do not count the virtually infinite subspecies (that is, specific combination of scales) of each type of measuring device, techniques used to measure attitude include verbal reports, Likert scales, Thurstone scales, Guttman scales, semantic differential scales, physiological indexes (for example, heart rate, brain waves, galvanic skin responses, capillary circulation) and various other behavioral indexes unique to a specific research setting (including contribution of money, doing volunteer work, recall of information, and other unobtrusive measures).

Validation of such inferential measures is probably inevitably inconclusive. Factors such as sociocultural bias, empirical bias, and demand characteristics of the experimental setting are difficult to recognize or resolve in formulating measuring instruments. The problem is the age-old philosophical one of providing correspondence rules for theoretical terms; that is, the problem is one of operationalizing (making observable) theoretical concepts so that differing operations are equivalent. Do Likert scales, Guttman scales, or Thurstone scales, for example, measure the same thing, which we have called "attitude"? We assume that each of these techniques measures "attitude," even though operational definitions in any two studies may be quite different.

Several consequences accrue from this proliferation of measuring instruments in the psychological perspective. One result is an overwhelming emphasis on method in scholarly inquiry. And as Platt (1964, p. 351) has written, "the method-oriented man is shackled." Rather than assess the value of research implications, the greater tendency is to defend one's own pet "theory" or operationalization by attacking the validity of the methods used by others, and no inferential measure is immune to attack on the basis of validity.

A second consequence of on overemphasis on method is the sacrifice of attention to the research question being asked. If the method of analysis is sufficiently sophisticated, then the research is judged to be sufficiently worthy. Dunnette (1966, p. 344) has suggested: "It is common for psychologists to apply so-called sophisticated methods of analysis to data hardly warranting such careful attention." The reverse is also true—that we tend to discount research with crude analytical methods even though the research question asked may be quite innovative and potentially significant. Sophistication of methodological techniques is certainly important.

There is no implication intended that analytical methods should be discounted. But to place so much emphasis on analytical methods as to obscure the research purpose is unwarranted. No analytical technique, regardless of its level of sophistication, should take precedence over the significance of the research problem. Remember, from an earlier discussion, "What is not worth doing is not worth doing well."

I can still remember one of my former instructors telling us graduate students, "If you want to know what's going on inside someone's head, ask him." At the time that bit of sage advice seemed simple but quite reasonable. But the complexity of the issues surrounding the operationalization of "what's going on inside someone's head" resists such oversimplification. These methodological implications precipitated by the proliferation of psychological measures are not trivial. Every student of human communication, particularly from a psychological perspective, needs to be aware of them and understand their role in scientific inquiry. (For a more specific discussion related to some of these issues, see Seibold, 1975.)

Selectivity of Information

A final implication emanating from a psychological perspective of human communication centers on the "activeness" of the communicator/interpreter. The input-output model has clearly demonstrated that the mere availability of information does not guarantee that the individual receives it or retains it. In other words, communicators actively control the information they process. The most important control tactic at their disposal appears to be that of selectivity in which the individuals may choose for themselves what information they wish to receive, what information they will remember, and what information they will relay to others.

Typically, selectivity has been explained as an ego-defensive device in which the individual seeks out information that is consistent with prior beliefs and retains (that is, remembers) information that is also consistent with prior beliefs, thereby forgetting discrepant information. A corollary to selective exposure and retention principles is selective avoidance, which suggests that an individual will tend to avoid or ignore information in the environment that is not consistent with existing beliefs.

Although these principles are rather widely accepted as empirical support for cognitive balance theories (to be discussed in a later chapter), the results of past empirical research do not unequivocally support the ego-defensive explanation for selectivity of information. Apparently, other factors (for example, confidence in the belief, feeling of open-mindedness, relevance or significance of belief, utility of the information, and conformity to social pressures) also serve to interact with the individual's selective processes.

Whatever the principles that guide and serve to explain the human's incredible power to exercise selectivity, it must be remembered that there can be no doubt that individuals do possess and exercise selectivity whenever they encode/decode information. The capacity of the individual to process information is simply inadequate and deals with only a small portion of the information available in the stimulus field. Perhaps selectivity is a function of ego-defensiveness. Perhaps selectivity is a function of assimilation with past informational experiences. Perhaps it is a function of coping with environmental stress. Whatever the basis for the explanation, the mere availability or even reception of information guarantees nothing in the way of predictable response. The selective capacity of the individual, via use of the mediational conceptual filters and psychological set, is a potent variable in communication research from a psychological perspective. (See Katz, 1968.)

SELECTED AREAS OF RESEARCH

Communication research from a psychological perspective has been largely, though not exclusively, experimental. Although the input-output model has typified such research and is easily adaptable to the experimental method, that factor alone does not account for the prevalent usage of experimental designs in communication inquiry. Probably more than any other single factor, such research stemmed directly from the experimental bias existing in the field of psychology. As communication scholars have borrowed the concepts and the operational definitions from psychology, it is only natural that they should also reflect the typical methodologies used by the psychologists.

Persuasion and Attitude Change

A great deal of the communication research in the area of persuasion and attitude change has stemmed from one or more of the various balance models of psychology. Although the nuances of the different balance models differ greatly, all of them (including cognitive dissonance, cognitive consistency, congruity, equity, and so on) reflect the principle of internal equilibrium; that is, the human being prefers to maintain an internally equilibrial state. Imbalance is inherently dysfunctional to the individual and cannot long be maintained psychologically. Hence, the individual cognitively, affectively, or behaviorally, seeks to restore and maintain a state of internal equilibrium.

About a decade ago cognitive dissonance theory enjoyed a period of popularity among communication scholars (see Goyer, 1964). More recently, communication research has reflected a bias toward Sherif and Hovland's (1961) social judgment approach with its accompanying concept of ego-involvement (see Sherif, Sherif, and Nebergall [1965] and Sherif and Sherif [1967]). According to the social judgment approach, ego-involvement refers to the degree of significance or relevance of a particular attitude to the individual. To the degree to which information is similar to that attitude, the individual assimilates the information, including that new information within her latitude of acceptance. Conversely, to the extent to which the information differs or is in contrast with the ego-involved attitude, the individual places it within her latitude of acceptance. The individual is neutral to all other information (latitude of noncommitment).

Persuasion research, then, shifted in emphasis from seeking to discover what appeals result in change of attitude or behavior to looking for those factors that account for resistance or susceptibility to attempts at attitude change. Related factors included such variables as innoculation, counterattitudinal advocacy, and source valence. The emphasis shifted to the individual as a processor of information, and research sought to explain those internalized conceptual filters used in information processing. In other words, empirical recognition was given to the activeness of the interpreter as a participating member of the communicative event.

Research into ethos or source credibility also demonstrates this emphasis on the information-processing capacity of the individual. Characteristics or dimensions of source credibility became operationalized as those characteristics of the source *perceived by* the information-processing interpreter. As the emphasis on the interpreter became clearer, credibility researchers attempted to relate perceived characteristics of source credibility to specific populations of interpreters. The result was a theoretical term borrowed from a mechanistic perspective (source characteristic) operationalized within the psychological perspective (source characteristic as perceived by the interpreter-receiver)—a blend of two perspectives.

In terms of communication research in the mass media, the research question has changed, too. Instead of seeking exclusively to determine the effects of mass media of communication on a body of receivers as in the mechanistic perspective, mass communication research is now asking additional questions seeking to determine how audiences use the media, that is, what purposes or functions the media serve for a body of active receivers. A target-model approach to mass communication is losing much of its popular appeal among researchers in mass communication. The increasing tendency is to view the receiver as an active consumer of radio, television, and newspapers. From the perspective of the receiver, the investigator seeks to explain media effects in terms of their purposes, functions, or uses (that is, uses and gratifications) as controlled by the choice patterns of receivers.

Organizational Communication

Although the bulk of organizational communication research is probably quite mechanistic, some of the organizational research in communication has reflected a psychological perspective. Particularly in terms of the gatekeeping functions, communication network studies in organizational settings have attempted to explain properties of the individual's information-processing performance. For example, gatekeeping individuals exercise selectivity in allowing certain information to pass through them in the network. Often this information is selected out in the upward flow of messages so that information to pass through in the upward flow of messages so that information negative to the organization (in the sense of negative feedback responses) has difficulty being processed upward in the hierarchy. Communication across hierarchical levels of an organization is difficult and explainable by the differences in values, attitudes, images (that is, conceptual filters) between individuals at different hierarchical levels.

A common assumption and finding from organizational communication research is that communication across hierarchical levels is often ineffective. The reason for such ineffectiveness stems from the differences in conceptual filters possessed by organizational members at different hierarchical levels. Thus, when the subordinate communicates with a superior (or vice versa), the two will be utilizing different conceptual filters, different perceptions, and will consequently be interpreting information quite differently. (See Redding, 1972.) Although perceptual congruence has been a common assumption of effective communication in the psychological perspective, some scholars (for example, Sussman, 1975) have questioned this assumption even within the psychological perspective. (The notion of perceptual congruence will be discussed in more detail in Part Three.)

Another aspect of a psychological perspective overlaid on the mechanistic view of organizational communication is the concept of organizational "climate." Faules (1976) defines defensive and supportive climates in organizations as a function of values (one type of conceptual filters) that characterize the organization. Furthermore, Faules goes on to define conceptually an organizational climate as a function of communicative behaviors performed by active interpreters (individuals) of information in the organizational setting. The concept of "values," then, may characterize a specific organization as well as a larger mass culture.

The human relations school of organizational communication utilizes a psychological perspective to explain employee behavior in organizational settings. Some conceptual filters are unique to the organization in terms, for example, of the individuals' commitment to the goals of the organization. Some organizational researchers term this individual commitment in clearly psychological terms—"internalization" of the organizational goals.

The Hawthorne studies illustrate the importance of psychologically selected and individually evaluated rewards and punishment of the organization. The individual may find a longer coffee break more rewarding then increased pay, clean washroom facilities more valuable than profit sharing. Working in a reverse direction, the reinforcement (remember S–O–R–R) of responses is evaluated and filtered by the individual's internalized conceptual filters as are stimuli. In short, organizational communication research is coming to realize that the individual employee in an organization is an active participating human in the social setting, even a bureaucracy, and not merely a passive recipient of information and thus subordinate to organizational rules and authority.

Group Communication

Communication scholars delving into group phenomena have often utilized a psychological approach in their inquiry. The social exchange model advanced by Thibaut and Kelley (1959) has conceptualized interpersonal interaction as a ratio of rewards to costs or an economic model of alternative social choices. Their conceptualization of social interaction emanates directly from a psychological perspective and blends elements of S–R and cognitive balance psychologies. Although of significant theoretical import to the study of group communication, the social exchange model has generated little research by communication scholars focusing on the group setting.

A high-priority variable in group research among scholars in both psychology and communication is that of cohesiveness—the degree of satisfaction, group loyalty, esprit de corps, commitment, and so on— experienced by individual members in regard to their group membership. Gouran (1973, p. 25) has urged communication researchers to pursue more actively an inquiry into the concept of cohesiveness—particularly those characteristics of communication that determine, promote, and sustain high levels of cohesiveness.

The influence of the individual in terms of leadership, cognitions, affective attributes, personality traits, and the like continues to play·a significant role in group communication research. Those characteristics of leadership, as perceived by members, remain an important means of assessing leadership in group settings (for example, Geier, 1967). The role of communication in increasing the tendency of group members to make choices involving greater risk than do individuals is still of interest (see Applbaum and Anatol, 1975). Homophily (that is, perceived similarity among group members or interacting individuals), as a selective determinant of group communication, enjoyed a brief period of popularity just a few years ago (see Rogers and Bhowmik, 1971). Clearly, the psychological perspective in group communication remains a potent influence in directing the research efforts of communication scholars.

Miscellanea

Some additional areas of communication research are currently enjoying a modicum of popularity but are not included in the preceding discussion, even though they seem to be consistent with the assumptions of a psychological perspective. They have been excluded for one or both of two reasons. First, they deal with specific variables of limited generalizability to the communicative process; that is, they are relevant but of questionable theoretical import in the realm of communication inquiry. Second, these variables have not generated widespread research interest among a significant portion of the scientific community to the extent that numerous scholars in numerous parts of the community are involved in their study. For the most part, each area represents the efforts of a relatively small but identifiable membership of communication investigators.

Phillips (see, for example, 1968) and his associates from Pennsylvania State University have for some time been investigating the phenomenon of reticence. The concept is similar to the phenomenon of stage fright, a term applied to the overt and covert nervousness of a public speaker or actor. In normal communicative situations the phenomenon of stage fright would be called reticence. When an unfamiliar social situation or a public communicative event is encountered, reticence appears as a pathological deterioration of communicative effectiveness or competence. Phillips suggests that reticence is a pathological characteristic that can be treated and either improved or eradicated. Moreover, as in the case of a physical malady, treatment can overcome or cure reticence in the same sense that a physician treats or cures physiological symptoms of bodily dysfunctioning in a patient.

McCroskey and his associates (see, for example, 1975) deal with a communication variable similar to reticence, which they term "communication apprehension." But, unlike reticence, the concept of communication apprehension is defined as a broader term similar to a personality trait. The result is similar as a phenomenon of social stage fright—selective avoidance of social-interactive situations or feelings of tension in a communicative situation. Rather than treat apprehension as a pathology, however, apprehension research tends to assess the intensity of the personalitylike trait (for example, high apprehensive individuals and low apprehensive individuals) and observe its effects of or correlation with other more common variables of social interaction.

CONCLUSION

A psychological perspective of human communication focuses theoretical and empirical attention on the individual—the communicator/interpreter. More specifically, the internal mechanisms of perception and information processing are the prime focus of communication. This focus has led to a receiver-centered orientation for human communication. Although the precise area of psychology from which this perspective is borrowed remains unclear, elements of S–O–R's mediational behaviorism and cognitive psychology, particularly balance theories, tend to dominate the research efforts of communication scholars utilizing a psychological perspective.

It should be apparent to even the casual reader that the foregoing depiction of a psychological perspective does not imply a single unified perspective for communication inquiry. To the contrary, within this perspective is a wide diversity of methodological approaches, concepts utilized, and operational definitions employed. To some degree this disparity reflects much of the turmoil existing within the corresponding discipline of psychology. The emphasis on the black-boxlike conceptual filters (such as attitudes, perceptions, beliefs, and wants), of course, precipitates these disparate directions.

It should also be clear that much theorizing, modeling, and investigating in communication do not employ a psychological perspective in its purest form. In fact, the bulk of writing on or about communication is probably a blend of mechanistic and psychological elements, probably with greater emphasis on the psychological. If we were to poll all members of the Speech Communication Association and the International Communication Association, for example, we would probably find that the far greater number of members would characterize themselves as subscribing to some variety of a psychological perspective. A psychologist-friend of mine just a few weeks before this writing asked if it were not true that communication is a branch of social psychology. I knew immediately what prompted his question.

Such a poll as that described above would not, of course, render the psychological perspective any more valuable or more credible than another perspective, but it would certainly make it more popular. Moreover, according to Kuhn, the most popular paradigm within a field of science is the most notable and the odds-on favorite to be *the* paradigm of that science. Certainly any serious student of communication must be fully aware of and familiar with a psychological perspective.

— 6 —

The Interactional Perspective

I use the word *interaction* in the title of this chapter with some trepidation. The word itself takes on a variety of meanings that are not intended by this title. For example, Goffman (1969) has distinguished interaction from communication, so that the two terms imply something quite different from each other. As I have discussed earlier, I personally do not make that distinction and consider interaction and communication to be synonymous. Stewart (1973, pp. 9–10) uses *interaction* to signify "two-way" communication. That usage is obviously not implied in this chapter. I use the term *interactional perspective* to refer to the view of human communication that has developed indirectly from that branch of sociology known as *symbolic interaction.*

Symbolic interaction is a relative newcomer to the study of human communication, with its historical origin dating back only to the late nineteenth century. But the influence of symbolic interaction is even more recent than that. Manford Kuhn (1964), a sociologist and not to be confused with Thomas Kuhn, the science philosopher, suggested 1937 as the real beginning of symbolic interactionism owing to the failure of early interactionists to publish their philosophical perspective. Kuhn centered on 1937 as the middle of a four-year period, which witnessed the publication of some noteworthy books detailing SI. These publications spelled the end of the "oral tradition" of symbolic interactionism—that is, disseminating the perspective haphazardly and incompletely by word of mouth.

George Herbert Mead, generally considered the major figure among the early interactionists, published nothing save a few articles during his lifetime. The major statement of Meadian interactionism, *Mind, Self and Society* (1934), was one of four books bearing his name as author that were published posthumously by his former students. Although Mead was a faculty member at the University of Chicago, he apparently did not feel the pressures of the contemporary publish-or-perish syndrome of academia. In what is a rather bizarre publication venture, his students felt the need to inform the scientific community of their mentor's philosophy. The four books, then, are composed of an edited collection of Mead's lecture notes, old manuscripts, unpublished essays, and anything else the students could get their hands on.

There were other symbolic interactionists during Mead's time, to be sure. They included such luminaries as Charles H. Cooley, William I. Thomas, William James, John Dewey, James M. Baldwin, and Ellsworth Fairs, among others. But only Mead left a legacy of a relatively comprehensive and systematic treatment of his philosophical position. To Mead, then, goes most of the credit for the philosophical tenets of symbolic interactionism. Though some controversy exists among schools of thought in symbolic interactionism (see Meltzer and Petras, 1970), the discussion of symbolic interactionism that follows in this chapter remains quite consistent with Mead's original formulations.

At the risk of appearing redundant, I wish to emphasize that the treatment of interactionism presented in the following pages is not intended as a comprehensive treatment of symbolic interactionism as a theoretical position in sociology. If the reader is interested in knowing symbolic interaction, he/she is directed to Meltzer et al. (1975). Nor are the differences between the Chicago (Blumer) and Iowa (Kuhn) schools of symbolic interaction considered pertinent to this chapter.

The interactional perspective of human communication should not be interpreted as an *application* of symbolic interaction to communication. Rather, a number of approaches to the study of human communication appear to reflect some common or similar philosophical assumptions. Those assumptions appear consistent with some general and basic principles from symbolic interaction. The emphasis of this book is on an attempt to analyze the field of human communication. Differences between the interactional perspective and symbolic interaction, as well as differences among the interactional scholars of communication, certainly do exist. But a discussion of them would be self-defeating—a trivial exercise in theoretical minutiae.

The interactional perspective, based on emphasizing similar philosophical assumptions, will include under this umbrella a number of scholars who would not consider themselves conversant with the symbolic interactionism of sociology. But, then, they should not be expected to be sociologists; they are communication scholars who operate within an interactional perspective of communication. In other words, they have not learned symbolic interactionism and then decided to apply it to communication.

CHARACTERISTICS OF INTERACTIONISM

Relating symbolic interaction to the study of human communication can precipitate additional controversy. Hulett (1966), a sociologist, intentionally formulated an interactional model of human communication. Looking beyond the titles of his two articles, however, leads to the conclusion that Hulett's model is a rather intriguing blend of the mechanistic and psychological perspectives with a generalized addendum of concepts drawn from symbolic interactionism. But a truly interactional perspective of human communication it is not!

The present discussion of symbolic interactionism is drawn from Mead (1934) and Blumer (1969), probably the leading symbolic interactionist of this generation of scholars. Furthermore, Blumer's brand of symbolic interactionism is clearly consistent with the Meadian philosophy. Supplementary material was also drawn from Manis and Meltzer's (1972) collection of related essays.

The Nature of Self

Of all the perspectives that have been applied to the study of human communication, the one that is most "humanistic" is probably that of symbolic interactionism (at least, the tradition of SI espoused by Mead and expanded by Blumer). The interactional perspective exalts the dignity and worth of the individual above all other influences. The human embodies the essence of culture, of relationships, of society, of mind. Every form of social interaction begins or ends with a consideration of the human self. This is the principal characteristic of the entire perspective.

Contemporary scholars in the interactional tradition typically avoid direct discussion of Mead's separation of self into the dual entities of the "I and the me." Nevertheless, the duality of self is fundamental to the process of interpretation that is the keystone assumption underlying symbolic interactionism. Within every individual, then, the embodiment of self implies the existence of an "I" and a "me"—distinguishable only through theoretical analysis but in reality interdependent and inseparable dimensions of self.

The "I" is the active portion of self capable of performing behaviors. The "me" embodies within self the concept of "other"—social mores, definitions, attitudes, values, and behavioral tendencies. Only the "I" has the capacity to behave. To some extent the "I" is unpredictable and unorganized, containing all the possible behavioral choices available to the person. But the "me" provides the "I" with direction and serves to bring the "I" under control, which results in making human behavior more predictable or, at least, less random. Within the notion of self, then, is the essence of social interaction—interaction between the "I" and the "me"—the embodiment of self and other within the self. The individual inherently reflects a social process—a miniature society—within the concept of the single individual's self.

The process of experience and interpretation is a process termed *self-indication*. The "I" may initiate an act or may experience some stimuluslike reception, and the "me" allows the self to observe that fact or stimulus as being performed or experienced by an "other"—an outside observer. The individual, then, both acts and observes the action at the same time. The "me," through self-observation of the act and relating it to past observations of other people's actions, builds "I's" behavior. In giving direction to "I" on how to behave in a given situation, the "me" performs jsut like an outside person giving direction to an individual. This process of self-indication, inherently a social process, allows the individual to transcend the immediate situation and to go beyond the limitations of individual experiences, past and present.

It is in this process of self-indication that Mead's dual concept of social self takes on additional meaning. The self is both an object ("me") and a subject ("I") of action. "I" acts, but "me" exists; that is, the "me" contains the consciousness of the actor, the past experiences of "I," and the observed experiences of others. Throughout the process of self-indication is a continuous introspection. Within the "me" consciousness are the experiences and the reactions to the experiences of "I." As Mead (1913, p. 375) writes, "If the 'I' speaks, the 'me' hears. If the 'I' strikes, the 'me' feels the blow." This introspective process is inherently social in that the self does it all—acts, acts upon itself, and calls out the behavioral action that is appropriate to a given situation. The self also evaluates the appropriateness of that response and retains it for future reference.

The self not only functions as a social process but also originates as a social process; that is, the individual can achieve any comprehensive development of self only through interaction with other people. The individual develops through his conduct of behaviors a repertoire of responses and interpretations not only from observing self-conduct but from the conduct of others, too. The child, for example, develops her self, inherently a social being, in normal group and interpersonal experiences with family and playmates. She acts toward herself in a manner analogous to her actions toward others. One of the clichés drawn from our often fallible wealth of conventional wisdom reflects this interactional truism—"He cannot like others until he learns to like himself." The cliché misses the point somewhat by assuming that actions (or feelings) toward others are implicitly different from actions toward one's self. According to the interactional philosophy, they are identical. Introspection is a social process that is absolutely identical to extrospection. Only the object (self or other) changes.

Occasionally, the I-me duality of Mead is confused with the Freudian tripartite division of self into id, ego, and superego. That comparison is unfortunate. To Freud, self was more like a structural definition of self into three separable entities, which, to some extent, warred or struggled against each other, each fighting for expression. Thus, the self comprised a triadic structure that maintained a virtually continuous state of internal tension. But to Mead, the I-me duality of self reflects not a structure but a process—self-indication, which includes action and acting upon actions. As a structure of self, Mead's I-me duality is relatively meaningless.

Mead's concept of self, then, is a reflexive process quite different from behavioristic psychology. The individual does not filter experiences through acquired and semipermanent concepts. She acts upon the experience and organizes past, present, and future actions on the basis of interpretation of experiences. The actual behavior is not so much a response as it is one facet of the interpretative process of self-indication in which the individual constructs the experiences of self rather than responds to forces either internal or external to the organism. In this sense, interactionism does not view the individual as a unique and integrated entity with internalized cognitions and beliefs but as a social being. The human does not merely exist in a stimulus field as a selective receptor but acts toward environmental phenomena creatively and reflexively.

The Nature of Symbols

Mead distinguished two levels of interaction—gestures and symbols. Blumer refers to these levels as nonsymbolic interaction and symbolic interaction. The distinction is the same for both Blumer and Mead. A gesture, or nonsymbol, is an impulsive and spontaneous action in the sense of a reflex response. For example, if I place my hand on a hot coal, I will immediately withdraw it—unthinkingly and almost instinctively. If I see a snake, even a nonpoisonous snake, I will immediately experience internal discomfort and will probably flee. (I am that way about snakes—any snakes—only slightly less phobic than one of my colleagues.) The key to nonsymbolic interaction is the absence of the interpretative process. Action or object leads directly to another action —no self-indication and no interpretation. In short, a reflex.

Symbolic interaction, on the other hand, requires the internal social process of self-indication and interpretation. Though nonhuman animals are capable of nonsymbolic action (as are humans, too, of course), only the human possesses the capacity for symbolic interaction. A human will respond to another person's action on the basis of what the action or symbol represents. An individual can see an object as food, but he has socially created the symbol to be food. There is nothing in the nature of the object itself that makes it food. The experience or behavior of eating and digesting it renders the object food. As an object that is interpretable as food, that is, as a symbol, the nature of "foodness" is created by the thought processes of self-indication, of interpretation, of action on action. In addition, that social process embodies how the "I" can act toward the symbol-object as well as how others have been observed to act toward it.

Mead (1922, pp. 160–161) adds the concept of "significance" to symbol and thus broadens the social context of the symbol:

> But it is not enough that he should indicate this meaning—whatever meaning is—as it exists for himself alone, but that he should indicate that meaning as it exists for the other to whom he is pointing it out. . . . We must indicate to ourselves not only the object but also the readiness to respond in certain ways to the object, and this indication must be made in the attitude or role of the other individual to whom it may be pointed out. . . . It is through the ability to be the other at the same time that he is himself that the symbol becomes significant. . . .
>
> But signification is not confined to the particular situation within which an indication is given. It acquires universal meaning. Even if the two are the only ones involved, the form in which it is given is universal—it would have the same meaning to any other who might find himself in the same position.

Mead clearly illustrates that the significance of a symbol is solely dependent upon the ability of the individual to place himself in the role of an "other"—a typical member of a larger society—and ask himself how that "other" would respond if he were in the same situation. (This phenomenon is called "role taking" and will be discussed in more detail later in this chapter.) Furthermore, any member of that larger society would perform the same self-indication process and arrive at the same or similar interpretation in the same situation. Significance of a symbol, then, is directly related to the sharedness or commonality of the interpretative process. This criterion of sharedness leads Meltzer (1972) to equate "significant symbol" with language—a codified set of symbols whose interpretation is shared by members of the language-using society.

Keep in mind that the process of interpretation of a significant symbol requires role taking, which is the subject of discussion in the next section. But, for now, the process of interpreting the signficant symbol leads to a clearer picture of what Mead regards as the concept of "mind." Mind is definitely not conceptualized as some internalized physiological process. Rather, it is inherently action—a behavioral process in which the human being is capable of acting toward and even creating her environment—or at least objects in her environment. This mental activity is inherently a social process, too—in a sense, symbolic interaction with oneself. As Mead writes (1922, p. 163), "Mind is then a field that is not confined to the individual much less is located in a brain. Significance belongs to things in their relations to individuals. It does not lie in mental processes which are enclosed within individuals."

The interactional concept of mind is thus antithetical to the internalized conceptual filters of S–O–R–R psychology. The nature of this antithesis is most evident in the concept of "meaning" as defined within the psychological and interactional perspectives. But that subject must await discussion in Part Three. At this point, we can only say that the familiar phrase *shared meaning* has a different meaning, depending upon whether one uses the psychological or the interactional perspective.

The Nature of Human Action

The previous discussion has alluded to the process of role taking in the interpretative process regarding a significant symbol. In any process of self-indication, the individual is himself an object of interpretation. In this way, the interactional perspective is similar to the psychological perspective in that the individual's past experiences can affect present actions, which, in turn, can affect subsequent actions. But the similarity ends at that point. The interactional perspective goes far beyond this inference from the S–O–R–R interpretation and becomes quite different.

Because of the internal social process of self-indication, the interactional perspective allows the individual to see himself as others see him. In order to become an object of self-interpretation, the self must go outside the self to do the interpreting; that is, the individual can assume the interpretative processes (called *standpoints*) of others in order to define the self. The individual thus takes on the role of someone else—some "other" outside the self—and engages in interpretation just as he would any other object, physical and social.

In this process of role taking, the individual may take on the role of a specific other person (Mead's "play stage"). For example, the student could see herself from the standpoint of her instructor. (Have you ever observed a youngster playing "school"?) Or the individual could take on the role of a specific organized group (Mead's "game stage"). A student defines himself as a member of the class or the student body and engages in self-assessment. A faculty member defines himself from the standpoints of his departmental colleagues. A voter asks herself what a Democrat (or Republican) would do in this situation.

The most informative form of role taking, perhaps, is the role of "generalized other." The role is much more abstract than the specific individual or group and probably relevant to more aspects of human action. The generalized other represents typical members of a society or culture with which the individual identifies herself. In the example of a language, the individual takes on the role of the language-using community—the typical average language user. But you can probably see the difficulties entailed by this abstraction. There are numerous subgroups within the English-speaking "generalized other" who use the language quite differently—from regional dialects to Black English. Which is the generalized other? This concept has been defined more concretely in theoretical and empirical development subsequent to Mead's lifetime— notably research in "reference groups" (see Hyman and Singer, 1968), a research area to be discussed later in this chapter.

The importance of role taking to symbolic interaction, however, is not diminished merely because of Mead's failure to define more clearly the role of "generalized other." It is through role taking that the individual, inherently a social self, achieves individuality. In this apparent paradox, the human who engages in self-interaction with self as an object and an active interpreter, both at the same time, is a dynamic being whose principal characteristic is action—on the environment and on the self. The individual creates her environment and creates her "self" at the same time rather than being merely the product of past experiences and past environmental stimuli. To a significant degree the interactionally viewed human being is master of his own destiny. But without other people, he is severely hampered in gaining his individual self—his humanism.

The Nature of Social Action

As earlier discussion has emphasized repeatedly, symbolic interactionism places great emphasis on the individual and is, perhaps, the most humanistic of the four perspectives included in Part Two of this volume. But the apparent emphasis on the individual may be misleading if the reader is led to believe that a society or group or culture does not affect individual behavior to a significant degree. Remember that the individual is by definition the embodiment of a minisociety whose action is a direct result of and, in fact, an integral part of self-interpretation and role taking. Thus, the individual embodies a social entity, including all the social pressures toward conformity in addition to the capacity to deviate from those conformity pressures.

Moreover, the social process of self-indication and role taking allows for mutual interaction and action by identifiable members of a group entity. As the individual engages in role taking, she can allow the "other" to direct her individual actions so that, as a result, the actions of several or more people become interstructured with each other to form group action; that is, the individual role taker aligns her actions with those of another, even a generalized other. In this way, different actions by different individuals are organized into a social collectivity that is discernible by those nonmembers as a set of acts organized to form the identifiable actions of the collectivity—not simply the separate acts of distinct individuals.

Another way of describing this phenomenon of self-alignment of actions with those of an "other" is to say that the actions are now identifiable as collective actions rather than a random combination of individual actions; that is, each individual's separate actions, together with the individual actions of the other, comprise a third set of identifiable actions—group action or collective action. Moreover, that group action is different, by virtue of its organization, from the separate actions of the individuals who comprise it. This view is consistent with the cliché that the whole is greater than the sum of its parts. More specifically, the collective action is identifiable as the identity of the collectivity to the extent that we characterize the joint action as a single entity such as family, jury, friends, or something more abstract such as blue-collar workers, Democrats, liberals, and conservatives. Most importantly, we identify collective action without necessarily any reference to individual actions that comprise the collectivity.

An important characteristic of social action, however, is the explanation of why collective action is formed in the first place; that is, why do people align their actions to form groups or families or organizations? Symbolic interactionism would disavow any explanation from an antecedent quasi-causal factor that would necessitate the formation of collective action. To the contrary, collective action is not the result of some environmental force or influence but is directly attributable to the individuals who align or "fit" their actions with those of others. Of course, the creation of the collectivity arises from the prior actions of the individuals who engage in role-taking interpretations. But, as McHugh (1968) illustrates, these actions are their own best explanation. To the extent that individuals seek to define the situation—and hence the appropriate behaviors—they tend to find commonality with others and subsequently align their behaviors into a homogeneous pattern with others. In a very real sense, to ask *how* individuals form collectivities is equivalent to asking *why*.

Collective action in the philosophy of symbolic interactionism is certainly not conducive to covering-law explanations, as you have probably surmised by this time. In fact, rules are probably more applicable to explain social interaction than are laws. It is important to note, however, Blumer's (1969, p. 19) observation: "It is the social process in group life that creates and upholds the rules, not the rules that create and uphold group life." The rules, then, are not the same as those a priori regulations that govern how players move on a chessboard or the rules of playing basketball. Rather, the rules are principles that develop during the playing of the game and achieve their status as rules by being reaccomplished in a repetitive fashion during the playing of the game.

Blumer (1969, p. 2) has suggested three "simple premises" that underlie symbolic interactionism. They serve as a summary of the philosophical/theoretical position of symbolic interaction. First, "human beings act toward things on the basis of the meanings that the things have for them." Second, those meanings are directly attributable to "the social interaction that one has with one's fellows." Third, these meanings are created, maintained, and modified through "an interpretative process used by the person in dealing with the things he encounters." Fundamental to symbolic interaction are two vitally significant characteristics. Human behavior is, more than anything else, "social" and composed of "actions." The human being is inherently, then, a socially active organism whose interpretative process, that is, symbolic capacity, renders him unique among the animal species—a human.

AN INTERACTIONAL MODEL

Depicting an interactional model of human communication in a two-dimensional drawing is not a simple task. Although Figure 4 is alleged to represent an interactional model, it is misleading in many respects. For one thing, it suggests a separation of self, other, and object when in reality the orientations to all three are simultaneous and inseparable— more a gestalt orientation, each one influencing and being influenced by the other. It also implies pictorially a unidimensional singularity of self, other, object, and cultural context that is also unrepresentative of reality. It also does not allow for a clear representation of action, the *sine qua non* of the interactional perspective.

In other words, Figure 4 may be a drawing of an interactional model, but drawings are subject to the two-dimensional limitations of paper— height and width. As an earlier discussion of models suggested, some perspectives are simply not easily adapted to the typical concept of a communication model as a pictorial drawing. The ensuing discussion of an interactional model will allude to the drawing represented in Figure 4, but the greatest clarity of representation of interactionism is the verbal rather than the pictorial model.

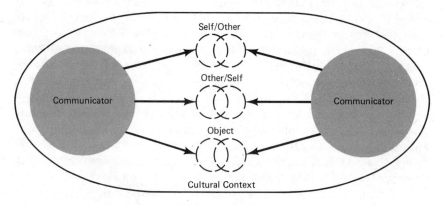

Figure 4.   An Interactional Model of Human Communication.

Typical Components

The interactional communicator is a complex blend of social individualism, that is, an individual who develops humanistic potential only through social interaction. As a social self, the term that more accurately describes the communicator's individuality is probably that of *role*. An immediate digression regarding the concept of "role" is in order. Mead probably viewed role and self (that is, social self) as identical in the sense that self develops exclusively through interaction with others. In other words, as an individual is carving out her societal role in dealing with others, she is in the process of developing self by taking the role of "other" and observing "self" as an object of orientation. The crux of this fundamental assumption of interactionism remains unquestioned. But later research developments in what has come to be known as *role theory* have added substantially to the explanation of how self and role develop.

Sarbin and Allen (1968, pp. 522–527) suggest that research developments in the past twenty years have tended to separate self and role rather than to maintain their conceptualization as identical terms. But this separation should seem quite reasonable. Observing self from the role of other should be no different from observing another person. And to the extent that one can err in assessing the "other" of another person, one can similarly err in assessing the "other" of self. Then, too, repeated or prolonged experiences and behaviors of self in undesirable situations (for example, not liking one's job or work-group peers) will tend to affect one's own assessment of self.

The numerous studies that have consistently discovered cultural role differences between men and women clearly demonstrate incongruence between role and self. Why, for example, are males discovered to be superior to females in performing problem-solving tasks? There is clearly no evidence to warrant any difference in problem-solving ability attributable to sex, merely a physiological difference. Researchers have suggested that the cultural expectation of women as "feminine" is somehow inexplicably related to the inferior problem solving. Thus, the self (as assessed by a woman's observation of self from the role of the generalized other) is incongruent with the role function. The result is a deterioration of task performance—attributable to self-role (female-problem solving) incongruence rather than any natural or innate ability or skill in problem solving of the female individual.

The communicator in the interactional model is thus performing or acting a role. Part of his role behavior involves *role taking*. The communicator views self from this perspective of "other" as well as the other from the perspective of self. The communicator, then, can adapt her behaviors to the other person by aligning those actions with those of the other person. Of course, alignment of behaviors and thus collective or joint action are not possible without active role taking.

Williams (1973) suggests that the research methodology required to observe human communication from an interactional perspective is for the researcher to take the role of participant-observer. We can expand Williams's view of the investigator's role to include the roles of each communicator as well; that is, the communicator is, at once, an active participant in the communicative situation and an analytical observer of the process. As a role taker, the communicator is an actor in and observer of the communicative process. The task is to observe the behaviors of both self (as object) and other and to adapt behaviors accordingly.

A third component vital to role taking and the interactional perspective is (for lack of a better term) *orientation*. Nwankwo (1973) employs Newcomb's (1953) *A–B–X* model of communicative acts to illustrate his interactional definition of communication. If we ignore Newcomb's assumption of cognitive balance and "strain toward symmetry," we can also borrow the *A–B–X* orientation to illustrate an interactional perspective.

In the process of role taking and behavioral alignment, the communicator clearly relates to an "object," directs his attention to an "object," and formulates an assessment of the "object." If we visualize Newcomb's *A* and *B* as communicators (a minimal two-person setting), each communicator in the process of communication and collective action orients herself to each—self as well as other. Figure 4 illustrates those orientations as arrows toward the dotted circles. That is, *A* orients to both *A* (self) and *B* (other), and *B* orients to both *A* (other) and *B* (self). Orientation, then, simply implies a directiveness in the process of role taking.

The *X* in Newcomb's *A–B–X* approach implies a third object of orientation that is separate from the behaviors of the communicators. In any normal communicative situation, of course, there are numerous *X*s. The *X* might be an envirnmental object, a task, the social relationship itself, a goal, another person, an event—in short, anything that might be called a topic of conversation or an object of interest and mutual orientation. Naturally, the *X* need not be a physical object but could be something as abstract as the nature of "love" or "quality of life" or even the *A–B* relationship itself—any topic of conversation. Keep in mind, however, that each of the three objects of orientation (*A–B–X*) is not necessarily a singular entity but encompasses multiple and constantly changing elements. Although Figure 4 also represents each entity as a separate object of orientation, the greater likelihood is that of a gestalt orientation. The *A–B–X* is a single, multifaceted, and multidimensional object separable only for purposes of analysis but probably interdependent.

In order to avoid any possible misinterpretation by the casual reader, I shall reiterate the admonition that Newcomb's *A–B–X* model is definitely not consistent with an interactional perspective. His approach to communicative acts is clearly from a psychological perspective with a cognitive-balance assumption implying a need for the individual to achieve "symmetry" in the various values (that is, positive or negative) of the orientation. Our use of the *A–B–X* model is strictly for the purposes of identifying the three-dimensional nature of objects of orientation and does not suggest that any semblace of cognitive balance exists in the interactional perspective.

An additional component integral to an interactional perspective is *congruence*. Figure 4 suggests congruence in the overlapping of the dotted circles of *self/other*, *other/self*, and *object*. To the extent that the interpretative orientations of the communicators are similar (that is, overlap), congruence exists. Nwankwo (1973) describes the notion of overall congruence as "mutuality." We might also use the term "shared-ness" to suggest the same concept. Clearly, congruence is not an all-or-nothing concept in which the communicators' orientations are either congruent or they are not. Congruence is a matter of degree and can range from nearly complete overlap to nearly no overlap at all. The two extremes (that is, total congruence and total incongruence) are probably not empirically possible. Moreover, total incongruence would probably imply the absence or impossibility of human communication.

Nwankwo also warns that congruence should not be confused with accuracy of interpretation. There probably exists no outside or external element or source to verify whether the orientations of self or other are true or valid. Under any circumstance, the accuracy of orientation toward an object is not the same concept as that of congruence. To the extent that one's orientation to an object reflects the reality of the facts (that is, the "true" other or the "true" characteristics of the conversational topic), then the orientations are accurate—but they are not necessarily congruent.

Two people could be in total agreement and develop a highly stable relationship while being ignorant of many facts; that is, their orientations could be congruent and shared, however inaccurate. Nwankwo does not suggest that accuracy is unimportant or irrelevant to communication but that it is simply not the same concept as congruence and should not be confused with it. And though congruence is inherent in the communicative act, accuracy may be a measure of communicative effectiveness; but it is not an integral element of the process of human communication.

Perhaps the most significant indication of Figure 4's inability to represent an interactional perspective is the omission of *symbols*, a component integral to the interactional perspective. But how do you draw a symbol? Symbols are, of course, actions and may take the form of any representative behavior—verbal and nonverbal. We can probably agree that most symbols possess a linguistic element through the medium of spoken or written words. But the anthropological studies of nonverbal behavior suggest that language possesses a nonverbal element, too, in the sense that learning a native language reflects learning the cultural nonverbals as well. Whether the symbols are verbal or nonverbal, however, it is probably fair to depict them as human actions.

A final component of interactionism is essential to the significance of the symbol. Recall that a symbol is significant to the extent that more than one individual in the same situation could role-take with similar results. The similarity of role-taking experiences performed by different individuals implies the existence of some unifying social system to which these individuals belong or with which they identify themselves. Figure 4 depicts this social system as the boundaries or the parameters of the communicative situation so that human communication always occurs within some identifiable *cultural context.*

Identifying the parameters of the communicative event is not so simple as Figure 4 might imply. The term *culture* should be interpreted in the broadest possible sense. For one communicative event, the context may be the broad national culture. In another, the context might be that of family or community or neighborhood. Every individual belongs to many overlapping cultural contexts and adapts to the one that is most relevant to the communicative event. For example, my black friends interact with me quite differently from the way they interact with each other. We apparently define the cultural context differently for different communicative situations, adapt our symbols to that context, and perform actions that we consider appropriate to that context.

One final element symptomatic of an interactional perspective is that of *adaptation.* Adapting is not a component of communication so much as it is a guiding principle. The communicator adapts to the other, to self, to the object, to the situation, to the role. Every communicator has the capacity to perform many more behaviors than she actually does perform in any situation. But she organizes those behaviors into sets that she utilizes as an appropriate group of behaviors depending upon self, other, context, and so on. This adaptation of behavioral sets is consistent with the concept of "role" that implies only a part of the total person is reflected in any given situation. Which "part" of the person is reflected in any specific communicative situation is a function of the communicator's processes of adaptation—judging the appropriateness of the various behavioral sets, selecting one, and performing actions accordingly.

Locus—Role Taking

For the most part, the interactional perspective in the field of human communication is a humanistic reaction to mechanism and its accompanying assumption of linearity located in the channel. The psychological perspective of S–O–R–R behaviorism would not be as repugnant as mechanism, but the model of conditioning implicit in behaviorism renders that perspective unacceptable within a humanistic philosophy. Either perspective possesses the implicit linearity of quasi-causal factors that determine human behavior. Regardless of which perspective (mechanistic or psychological) is used, the view renders the individual to some extent a "victim" of external influences.

The interactional perspective of human communication is most often expressed as "dialogical communication" or communication viewed as dialogue. Matson and Montagu (1967) view dialogical communication as an outgrowth of an existential philosophy of religion that is reflected in "sociological interactionism." Of course, the wellspring of a dialogical approach to communication dates back to classical Greece and the field of "dialectic." Among the Greek sophist-philosophers, we tend to give most credit to Socrates (for example, "Socratic dialogues"). To quibble about the philosophical origins of dialogue, however, is to miss the point that dialogic communication is quite consistent with the interactional perspective, and that consistency is most evident in the locus of human communication—"role taking" and its corollary of "congruence."

Communication as monologue (the antithesis of dialogue) implies a mechanistic notion of someone (or some environment) "doing something to" another person. The individual is then downgraded to a stimulator or a recipient of communication, whether active or passive. The communicator is destined to be either a "doing to-er" or, even worse, a "done to-er." But dialogue implies the expression of self and the development of mutual understanding (that is, congruence) along with the development of self through social interaction. But the key to dialogue is the elevation of the individual self to a position of prominence. And the concept of role taking allows for the individual to discover and develop self through social interaction.

Johannesen (1971, p. 375) illustrates clearly the focus of dialogical communication: "The essential movement in dialogue is turning toward, outgoing to, and reaching for the other. And a basic element in dialogue is 'seeing the other' or 'experiencing the other side.'" In short, the fundamental process in dialogue is the interactional perspective's concept of role taking. The existentialist, Marcel (1960, p. 9) emphasizes the point when he writes, "The fact is that we can understand ourselves by starting from the other, or from others, and only by starting from them."

Neither the mechanistic nor the psychological perspective can account for this "seeing the other" in any specific manner. Only interactionism not only accounts for the phenomenon of "going outside self" but also lends it prominence as the central focus of the communicative event. Mead's duality of self (I–me) allows the individual to place himself in the role of both participant and observer, to see himself as others see him, and to see the other as he himself sees him. Role taking makes that possible, and interactionism endows role taking with primary significance.

The dialogists in the field of communication do not always use the term *role taking* in describing communication. Nor is the term *congruence* the term consistently applied to the result of role taking in human communication. Dialogists and interactionists may refer to an "emphatic bond," "identification," or "mutual understanding." Furthermore, they typically tend to view role taking as an *ability* of the individual—an ability that may be called *empathy, social or interpersonal sensitivity,* or *social understanding* or even *communication skill.* Defining role taking as an ability of the individual renders the individual that much more prominent in the communicative event and even more consistent with humanism. (Role taking as an ability is a significant implication of the interactional or dialogical perspective and is the subject of further discussion in Part Three.)

IMPLICATIONS

The humanistic emphasis of interactionism leads to profound modifications of viewing the process of human communication. As suggested earlier, the interactional perspective represents a humanistic reaction against mechanism and S–R psychology. As a negative reaction, many of the implications represent a search for something new in the sense of what Matson and Montagu (1967, pp. 1–11) term an "unfinished revolution." Other implications, particularly for research methodology, reflect the antithesis of the covering-law model of either of the first two perspectives. As a result, the interactional perspective represents new directions and different emphases.

Search for Self-understanding

To say that we live in an age of "future shock" is to reiterate the obvious. Our civilization is on a crash course heading for the future and picking up speed almost uncontrollably. We live in the age of the greatest technological revolution so far in history. But ours differs from past revolutions in the sense that the new technological advances deal directly or indirectly with the explosion of information. As a result, we live in implicit fear of being "controlled" by our technology, manipulated by our machines. The recent trend in science fiction visualizes the future as an era beyond Armageddon. Contemporary novels and movies depict the future in apocalyptic terms—humans eating other humans to stay alive, living underground or in the midst of widespread devastation from a nuclear holocaust, killing everybody over thirty to control the size of the population in order not to exceed available food to eat or air to breathe.

I can remember reading *1984* as a best seller and thinking that Orwell's future was possible, perhaps, but a far cry from the present. But that was then. Now, 1984 is almost upon us—both the year and the future. Who would have predicted then that we would be rationing gasoline because of a worldwide oil shortage or that we would be victimized by our national leaders indulging in Watergatelike activities as well as illegal surveillance and harassment of loyal American citizens (and to this day claiming to have done nothing illegal or even immoral!). Small wonder that we become confused and overwhelmed by the need to understand —to come to grips with ourselves and the world in which we live.

The search for understanding is obviously an antitechnological and antiscientific reaction. To many, this translates as humanism. A substantial portion of this quest has taken the form of escapism—a withdrawal from the larger society in a return-to-Walden endeavor. In the 1950s such people were called beatniks. In the 1960s they were hippies or flower children. But these countercultural movements could be attributed to the disillusionment of youth with an adult society not of their own making. However, the search for self-understanding is not restricted to those under the age of thirty.

The past decade has witnessed a revolution in the sense of a phenomenal growth in popularity of alternative philosophies. Although the philosophies reflect a diversity of beliefs and approaches, they all have one thing in common—seeking to understand one's self and to relate that self to those of other people. This trend toward increased humanism takes the form of encounter groups, sensitivity training, creativity workshops, interpersonal awareness training, and so on. Together with the T-group syndrome is the increased popularity of transcendental meditation and the influence of the mystical religions of the Far East. Still other forms of the same quest include transactional analysis, psychotherapy for "normals," and est (Erhard Seminar Training) and in organized religion a trend toward fundamentalistic back-to-the-Bible Christianity.

For the most part, this search for self-understanding is not directly observable in academic and scholarly inquiry. Nor is it directly associated with either interactionism or the study of human communication. But placing interactionism in the intellectual milieu of increased self-awareness as a reaction to the technological revolution and future shock should serve to clarify the factors contributing to the developing popularity of communication as dialogue. Both the interactional perspective and the alternative philosophies are symptomatic of the times in which we live. But though the antitechnological social movement does not reflect a commitment to scholarly inquiry, the interactional perspective and dialogic communication symbolize an increasing popular movement within academia. The research implications of this perspective are the subject of the next section.

The Role of the Researcher (and of Research)

I hate to disinter the alleged distinction between science and the humanities, but I am reluctantly about to do it. I have already argued that the alleged separation is nonexistent at worst, trivial at best, and stems from a fundamental misunderstanding by extremist representatives on either side of the academic fence. The hard-shelled scientist views the humanist as a bespectacled, stooped scholar in a worn tweed coat with leathered elbows. (Of course, all stereotypes are sexistly male.) According to this distorted view of humanism, the humanist's methodology is confined to literary-aesthetic experience or dead orators with an "unscientific" if-it-feels-good-do-it approach to triviality. The equally hard-core humanist depicts the scientist as a bespectacled (why do stereotypical scholars always seem to wear glasses?) fellow wearing a white lab coat who stimulates experimental subjects like cattle (or rats) with impersonal stimulus prods, reducing every human to a number, each indistinguishable from another. This view of scientist lives in the laboratory and has forgotten what the "real world" looks like.

Obviously, both stereotypes are grossly erroneous. In the language of the interactionist, the extremists (both "scientists" and "humanists") demonstrate a deplorable lack of role-taking ability. As representatives of scholarly inquiry, both humanists and scientists are in the empirical tradition of objective observation tempered by issues of validity and reliability. Although the criteria for what constitutes appropriate tests for validity and reliabilty vary considerably, as they must for differing methodologies, the scholarly goal of methodological inquiry is the same. The nature of the data also varies, but both humanists and scientists use data (although the extremists will quibble over what constitutes appropriate data). In short, true scholarly inquiry is not so much *either* humanistic or scientific as it is *both* (or at least it should be).

So what is all the fuss about? The answer lies in what has been called *scientism*—the elevation of science to paramount significance, the belief that science can discover everything, the mole's-eye view of the scientific method. Only the greenest of new students in any field of social science seriously believes in the possibility of utter objectivity. Particularly in social science, the common truism asserts that all observation is unavoidably subject to error and bias and interpretation. Some empirical methods (which we arbitrarily designate as "scientific" but only for purposes of this discussion) recognize the problem of objectivity in empirical observation and seek to minimize error, that is, account for the inherent loss of objectivity. Other empirical methods (arbitrarily designated "humanistic" only for present purposes) overtly acknowledge subjectivity and incorporate it into the methodology. The latter approach is consistent with, though not limited to, the interactional perspective.

The key to understanding the difference between these two approaches to empiricism is understanding the role of the researcher. Denzin (1970) clearly illustrates an interactional research perspective by emphasizing that the investigator herself must engage in role taking and be empirical from the standpoint of the observer—the human subject. Williams (1973, p. 242) echoes Denzin's observation that the communication researcher "must view human transaction from the perspective of the communicants under study." Williams goes on to depict the researcher as a participant-observer. As an empiricist, the researcher is an outside observer *in addition* to a role-taking other, that is, an inside participant in the research setting.

The result of this new role for the investigator is what Williams (1973, pp. 244–245) terms "naturalistic inquiry." The empiricist enters the act of inquiry with as few preconceptions or *a priori* assumptions as possible. His organization of the data and even assumptions of what constitute data arise during and as a direct result of the act of observational inquiry. Notice the similarity between Williams's "naturalistic inquiry" and Glaser and Strauss's (1967) "grounded theory" or Znaniecki's (1934) approach to method called *analytic induction.*

Denzin (1970) refers to this same phenomenon in discussing "sensitizing concepts" as opposed to "operational definitions." In operationalizing a concept, by definition one identifies a priori procedures as to how to discover and measure the concept. Denzin suggests that a concept should only sensitize the investigator to the inquiry, giving him an idea toward discovering what the subjects believe to be the definition of the concept. The investigator then observes how the subjects define the concept and the processes they perform to illustrate it. Then, and only then, does the investigator seek to operationalize it. The phenomenon of operationalization occurs in either case, but the point in time when operationalization is performed—a priori or a posteriori—is the difference between the two empirical approaches.

It should be superfluous to point out that the interactional perspectivists would not rank experimentation at the top of their list of most favored research methodologies. The principal criterion in choosing a methodology to perform research from the interactional perspective is the freedom allowed the researcher to enter into the research setting as a participant-observer. The philosophy of phenomenology has proved to be popular. But its popularity has been more as a philosophical stance than as a source for generating research techniques.

More specific research methods include participant observation (see Bruyn, 1966), of course, as well as a range of other methods still being used tentatively in communication inquiry. Scheflen's (1965) "context analysis" has been more talked about than utilized as a research method. Ethnomethodological (see Garfinkel, 1967) approaches are becoming increasingly popular, along with "conversational analysis," indirect or unobtrusive observation, hermeneutics, and various methods of criticism. For some discussion of one aspect of the interactional perspective and adaptation of research methods, read the dialogue between Hawes (1973, 1975) and Grossberg and O'Keefe (1975). See also Blumer (1969, pp. 21–60).

In more ways than one, the revolution in communication research methodologies is yet unfinished. It is still a seeking process providing more of a research attitude than specific methods. That attitude is also reflected in several chapters included in Part Three.

Sharedness

Every student of communication soon confronts the ubiquitous phrase *shared meaning*. To some, this phrase bears the connotation of an entire viewpoint or theory of human communication. Actually, the phrase has been used so much by so many that the meaning of "shared meaning" has come to be a function of the perspective used to define it. (Perspectives' accounts of shared meaning is the subject of more extended discussion in Part Three.) In other words, the definition of shared meaning differs from one perspective to another, but the concept of "sharedness" is an intriguing notion for many communication students who should be aware that it arises directly from the interactional perspective.

Nwankwo (1973) focused on "mutuality" as a principal concept in an interactional perspective. The interactional model described in the preceding pages included the concept of "congruence." The dialogists pay philosophical homage to "mutual understanding." Implicit in each of these terms is the principle of "sharedness." That is, each communicating individual "reaches out" to the other person reciprocally. The result is a sharing of behavior to form a new entity not present and not possible in each person's behavior taken in isolation.

The principle of "sharedness" is a uniquely human capacity. Nonhuman animals can respond to other's behaviors and can even "communicate" in the sense of transmitting a message to another. But only humans can develop a symbolic relationship. It is not the actions alone that involve sharing, though. Nor is it the individuals' minds. It is more. Sharing creates a single experience that involves all those who participate in the experience. The "meaning" of the words or actions are quite indeterminate unless and until they are interpreted—not in the psychological sense of individual perceptions but interactionally within the mutuality of the experience itself.

Emphasis on Action

A corollary to the principle of sharedness implied within the interactional perspective is the emphasis on action—particularly social or joint action. The role-taking individual performs actions that arise out of the situation and, in shared combinations with other's actions, provide the meaning and the significance of the entire process of human communication. As the individual behaves in social action, he develops his definition of self, other, and consequently the situation during the ongoing process of social interaction. His behaviors within the scheme of the interaction reflect his self-definition and his situational definition. In the process of the developing of those definitions, the behaviors serve also to reflect the nature of his or her definitions.

Blumer (1969, p. 72) suggests that symbolic interactionism and its accompanying emphasis on joint action through role taking are antithetical to the psychological perspective. In the latter perspective, the individual carries the conceptual filters around with him. These filters are then activated (at least a portion of them) by antecedent conditions and stimuli upon his entering into a given social context. The internalized motives, attitudes, images, values, expectations, perceptions, and so on are semipermanent and change only slowly over time. Most importantly, the internalized "set" of the individual in a psychological perspective reflects the self of the individual.

But, according to Blumer, the self is reflected only through social interaction (including self-interaction), which is a function of the social situation and the alignment of behaviors with "other." In Blumer's words: "By virtue of self-interaction the human being becomes an acting organism coping with situations in place of being an organism merely responding to the play of factors." Action is thus not merely a response to antecedent stimuli mediated through internalized filters but is a direct result of development through social interaction—and only through social interaction.

Furthermore, if the ongoing process of role taking in collective action can develop definitions of the situation, then the ongoing process can change over time as the interactional pattern changes. The definition of the situation or self during one period in time reflects that period of time and not the situation or the individual in any enduring sense. Part of the emphasis on action, then, is the changing over time as well as the initial development. Given this longer-range view of communicative phenomena, it is not difficult to perceive another reason why the empirical method of experimentation, notably the one-shot-effects study, is anathema to the interactional perspectivists.

Compared with the implications of the first two perspectives discussed in Part Two, the implications of the interactional perspective are profound and far-reaching. Not only are the philosophical/theoretical foundations at variance, especially the view of self and role, but the approach to scholarly inquiry is equally disparate. Those who utilize the interactional perspective are, in a way, rebels. They dispute the fundamental assumptions of the traditional science philosophers, and they consider lack of objectivity a virtue rather than a methodological weakness. Those scholars in the field of communication who are committed to the interactional-dialogical perspective are true believers—not in any pejorative sense but in the sense of ideological commitment. Interactionism in communication is still a developing perspective—a revolution that is yet unfinished.

SELECTED AREAS OF RESEARCH

The interactional perspective in the field of human communication has not generated the amount of research even approaching the reams of studies from the mechanistic or psychological perspectives. The perspective has generated more discussion and fervor than actual empirical investigation. More than anything else, interactionism has resulted in a heightened awareness or consciousness among members of the scientific community of the shortcomings of more traditional perspectives. If nothing else, the benefits of this heightened consciousness include serious consideration of humanistic principles that had too long been stifled in the nearly scientistic rush of communication scholars to achieve what they considered to be the academic respectability of science. Until more research is performed within the interactional perspectives so that trends are clearly discernible, the ensuing discussion must be considered woefully incomplete.

The areas of communication research to be discussed are clearly not areas of research in symbolic interaction. Indeed, such scholars as Fromm, Rogers, and Garfinkel are not symbolic interactionists. But they are scholars who have viewed communicative phenomena in a perspective consistent with many of the philosophical assumptions that we have labeled the interactional perspective. The communication scholars who function within an interactional perspective have bridged the gaps existing between symbolic interactionism, ethnomethodology, phenomenology, therapeutic transaction, and dialogue.

In this eclectic borrowing and combination of otherwise disparate areas of inquiry, a "family" of theoretical positions is discernible. We have dubbed this family of positions the interactional perspective, which implies a common philosophical basis traceable to symbolic interactionism, the speculations and research of such neosociologists as Fromm and Rogers, and the specific research applications to communicative phenomena that even include the concept of self-disclosure (a concept certainly not directly associated with symbolic interactionism). At the risk of again repeating what should be abundantly obvious, the interactional perspective is a part of communication and is not sociology (that is, symbolic interactionism).

Self-disclosure

A heightened consciousness of self has contributed to the recent surge of research interest in the phenomenon of self-disclosure. Self-disclosure can be defined, however broadly, as the revelation of information about the self that would otherwise be unknown by the other. Though the bulk of the studies treat self-disclosure from a rather awkward psychological perspective and utilize traditional research methods, there seems to be an increasing tendency to view the self-disclosing phenomenon (defined as actions) in more interactional terms.

Most of the research into self-disclosure has tended toward a psychological explanation with psychological attributes. For example, two popular attributes of disclosure appear to be *amount* (that is, how much information about self is disclosed?) and *valence* (that is, is the information positively or negatively valued?). (See Gilbert and Horenstein, 1975.) These characteristics are quite consistent with the psychological perspective's emphasis on conceptual filtering (valence) of informational input (amount). Moreover, the research tends to link these characteristics to the outcomes (output) of self-disclosure, typically in an experimental research setting.

Closely linked with self-disclosing communication is the aspect of *intimacy*, that is, the degree to which the information reflects the private person or the self's innermost feelings. Observing intimacy, however, is a methodological bugaboo. How does the investigator determine how personal or private the information is to the individual who discloses it? Taylor and Altman (1966; see also Altman and Taylor, 1973) developed a list of topics that, based upon testing hundreds of subjects, are distributed across a range from highly intimate topics of conversation to nonintimate or "safe" topics. This method assumes that the intimacy levels of the topics are generalizable across a variety of situations. Such an assumption thwarts the interactional notion of the role of the researcher who must view the research setting from the standpoint of the subject. Achieving that role-taking behavior of the investigator is, at best, minimally reflected in the literature of self-disclosure research.

Interest among communication scholars in the topic of self-disclosure, particularly the dimension of intimacy, continues to accelerate. That interest is reflected not only in research (for example, Hancock, 1977) but also in the recent publications of books emphasizing this perspective in human communication (for example, Phillips and Metzger [1976] and Villard and Whipple [1976]). In all likelihood, the interest will continue to escalate as new methods and procedures for conducting research from an interactional perspective are developed and utilized more widely. This area seems to be a research topic of the future as well as the present.

Persuasion

The interactional perspective has not been a potent contributor to the study of persuasion and attitude change. That phenomenon should not come as much of a shock, however. Remember that one can view the act of persuasion as a source's manipulating a receiver or as a perceiving receiver who filters manipulative messages and thereby controls his responses to persuasive attempts. But the pragmatics of persuasion are inherently related to effects of some kind of another. The previous perspectives account for effects in terms of stimuli or in terms of receiver perceptions. Nevertheless, the concept of persuasion is typically cause-effect, stimulus-response, input-output, that is, some discernible result or change in receivers.

If we were to analyze realistically the typical setting of persuasive acts, we would discover elements that are quite incompatible with the interactional perspective. Persuasion implies a process of social influence—a directiveness of communication that is not wholly consistent with interactionism. Furthermore, the roles of the communicators in a persuasive context are complementary—differentiated as to persuader-persuadee, seller-buyer, or manipulator-manipulatee. Consequently, the motives or intentions of the communicators in the persuasive context seem to suggest an inherent disparity when compared with each other. In other words, the orientations of the communicators are probably disparate, too.

One way to circumvent this conceptual problem is to conceive of the social influence process as inherently one of self-persuasion; that is, the persuader role-takes the standpoint of the persuadee in an attempt to discover those elements that the other finds most important. The persuader then possesses the advantage of knowing what the other wants. The result, at least in a sales situation, is for the persuader to make the product available and consistent with the expectations and orientations of the buyer. In other words, the act of persuasion is ultimately an act of self-persuasion on the part of the persuadee.

Although this approach to persuasion is consistent with interactionism, some die-hard dialogists would argue that there is no sharedness—no mutuality—but manipulation simply masquerades as dialogic role taking. Of course, this assessment may be quite accurate, but it does not invalidate either the viability of the approach or the fruitfulness of such a perspective for the study of persuasion. One must keep in mind that the persuadee also engages in role taking and will just as easily "psych out" the orientations of the persuader in order to accommodate his orientations and expectations. In other words, sharedness or mutuality does not necessarily imply that the roles or statuses of the communicators are equivalent. Both communicators can share the same definition of the situation as a highly complementary role relationship in which the person in the submissive role accepts that definition as well as shares it with the dominant other.

The area of social perception (or person perception, if you prefer) has also been linked with social influence processes—at least in communication research. If we think of the process of perceiving another person (along with other's motives, interests, orientations, and the like) as a process of role taking, social perception is simply another term for the interactional concept. Hastorf, Schneider, and Polefka (1970, p. 91) suggest that there is a trend toward such an emphasis: "The research in person perception has shifted in interest from the stimuli and the accuracy with which they are recorded to the ways that perceivers actively process those stimuli to create interpersonal meaning" (authors' emphasis deleted). In other words, the trend in research seems to be away from the nature of the stimuli and the internalized conceptual filtering implicit in the psychological perspective and toward the actions of the communicators as they relate to each other interpersonally over time.

Of course, the view of Hastorf, Schneider, and Polefka remains markedly psychological—conceptually filtered stimuli that are interpreted by an active receiver. Nevertheless, the trend seems clearly to reflect an interpersonal or shared characteristic, that is, between individuals rather than merely within a single individual. This view seems much closer philosophically to an interactional perspective.

A further indication of the interactional perspective in communication theory is the use of attribution theory as an explanatory framework for social influence through communication. Attribution is simply making inferences about other on the basis of other's actions during communication. It is but a small step to conceptualizing interpersonal attributions as a specialized form of interpersonal role taking. Although attribution research in communication has generally utilized methods more closely aligned with those of traditional psychology (see, for example, Ellis [1974] and Berger [1975]), the groundwork has been laid for a major emphasis of communication study from an interactional perspective.

A final area of research is the area of reference groups. A reference group is the result of collective action in which role-taking individuals align their behaviors to "fit" with those of a specific group or generalized other. In persuasion, that group or generalized other then becomes a frame of reference or orientation for the individual to judge his own actions. Some evidence (see, for example, Charters and Newcomb, 1958) suggests that the strength or ego-involvement of an individual's expressed attitude is a function of the individual's valuation of membership in a reference group. If this premise is true, then ego-involvement of attitudes is not so much a function of the individual's internalization of attitude as it is the individual's role-taking ability that generates collective actions. In other words, the same concept (ego-involvement) assumes a character or definition that changes according to the perspective from which it is viewed—further indication of the perspectival approach to theory and research that underlies this volume.

Miscellanea

For the most part, communication research reflecting an interactional perspective consists of relatively isolated groups of studies within a broader framework of study principally oriented to a different perspective. As a result, this review of typical areas of research highlights fragmented and rather idiosyncratic collections of studies on a variety of topics. Though there appear to be some trends in persuasion and self-disclosure, the remainder of the studies is relatively isolated and resists identification as a full-fledged trend.

One such area of communication research is the approach to organizational communication in which the investigator enters the organization as an interactional researcher, that is, with as few preconceptions as possible and sensitized toward variables to be defined rather than operationalizing them beforehand. Schein (1969) describes this procedure as "process consultation," and Hawes utilized the procedure in an extended organizational study (as yet unpublished) of a regional planning commission. Though process consultation has not generated voluminous research, the potential exists for fruitful communication research in the organizational setting.

Another area of research involves the concept of "interpersonal confirmation," an area of interest that seems to be restricted to communicologists at the University of Denver (see Cissna, 1976). Interpersonal confirmation involves the acceptance of other's definition of self, sometimes operationalized as a favorable comment about other's self-concept that would lead other to value himself more highly. Though the concept itself emanates directly from interactionism, the research so far appears to include a strong methodological emphasis on outcomes—typically, individual outcomes—so that the interactional character of the concept deteriorates as a consequence of the research design. Nevertheless, the concept is consistent with the perspective of dialogic communication and is eminently worthy of further exploration.

SUMMARY

Although the origins of the interactional perspective of human communication can be traced to existential philosophy and even to Socrates, the specific and comprehensive wellspring of this perspective comes directly or indirectly from symbolic interactionism in sociology. Mead and Blumer have served as the major sources for the basic philosophy underlying the interactional model of human communication described in this chapter. More specifically, the trend in the scientific community of human communication that treats communication as dialogue is the clearest indication of interactional approaches to the study of human communication. This chapter has not dealt directly with the influence of psychotherapists in dialogic communication, reserving discussion of their influence for Part Three.

The popularity of interactionism stems, in part, from a humanistic reaction to mechanism and psychologism. More importantly, however, is the humanistic emphasis on self as a principal element of the interactional perspective. But rather than view self as a mere internalization of individual experiences, interactionism accounts for the development of self through a process of "self-indication" in which the individual can "go outside" self and engage in introspection from the standpoint of other. In a similar manner, the individual can engage in role taking and define self as well as other both from the standpoint of other. It is this phenomenon of role taking that allows for the development of self solely as a social process—within the process of either introspection or extrospection. Only through social interaction, then, can self or relationship be developed. And it is role taking that is not only the central element of the interactional perspective but the unique element as well.

The interactional perspective emphasizes action and symbolic action in a processual development of human communication. The emphasis on actions allows role taking to develop joint action or linking of individual actions with the actions of other individuals to form a collectivity. The joint actions of the collectivity reflect not only a social grouping but a sharedness or mutuality of the individuals, described in the model as "congruence" of the individuals' orientations toward self, other, and object.

Perhaps the most significant implication of the interactional perspective for the study of human communication is the revised emphasis of research methodologies. The first implication involves a revised notion of the role to be taken by the researcher. Rather than be portrayed as an impartial, unbiased, and disinterested observer of empirical phenomena, the interactional researcher takes on the role of a participant-observer in the act of doing research. She engages in role taking herself in order to discover the standpoints of the research subjects. From their standpoints the investigator then operationalizes the concepts and performs empirical observations. But the validation of the research concepts shifts from some external criterion (that is, a source outside the specific research setting and generalizable to many such settings) to the standpoints of the research subjects themselves.

The interactional perspective is definitely a source of excitement in the sense that it is in a stage of continuing development. In the sense of an "unfinished revolution," every research discovery is relatively new and leads to many new directions. Contemporary research reflects the true spirit of inquiry in the sense that investigators are not so much engaged in confirmation or verification of hypotheses but in discovering what the hypotheses should be. Interactional research has yet to answer many questions or yield many answers, but it has raised many new questions that heretofore have not even been recognized as questions for research.

On the flip side of the coin, interactional research has little direction or focus in its efforts. Researchers have yet to develop the new methodologies necessary to the interactional/dialogical guidelines and have instead attempted to force-fit interactional research questions into traditional methodologies—typically, psychological. Then, too, interactionally motivated researchers have not developed a common focus of what variables are most significant, what concepts need to be developed or studied, and in what direction their efforts should take them. In short, programmatic research yielding a cumulation of research findings does not characterize communication research in the interactional paradigm.

Consequently, some members of the scientific community have tended to downgrade the interactional perspective. That is certainly their right and even their obligation to view disciplinary inquiry with a critical eye. But much of that criticism is based on the wrong criteria—disparate or unfamiliar methodologies that do not reflect the more traditional approaches to the doing of research. Such arguments from synonymy—criticizing one paradigm from the viewpoint of another—are self-defeating and not in the spirit of scholarly inquiry. They lead nowhere.

The interactional perspective is relatively new to the discipline of human communication. The ultimate value it demonstrates is yet to be realized. Its potential for new insights into the process of human communication is enormous. In one way, the interactional-dialogical view of human communication is on an intellectual honeymoon. It can be evaluated only on the basis of its potential. We must adopt a wait-and-see attitude. At the present time, the approach is revolutionary and excitingly different. What happens in the next twenty years will demonstrate to the scientific community the value of the perspective—directly attributable to the discoveries from research studies. Under any circumstances, whatever happens—whether increased popularity and significant research or the intellectual demise of interactionism in communication—the interactional perspective provides a fresh humanistic look at human communication.

— 7 —

The Pragmatic Perspective

Over thirty years ago, Charles Morris (1946) laid the foundation for semiotics—the theory of languages or symbols. He divided semiotics into three areas of general study: syntactics, semantics, and pragmatics. By syntactics, Morris intended the area to include a study of how symbols relate to each other—symbol-to-symbol relationships. By semantics, Morris defined a study of how symbols relate to their referents, that is, the things (objects) that symbols represent—symbol-to-referent relationships. Pragmatics, then, is the study of how symbols relate to people (that is, symbol users)—symbol-to-user relationships. These general divisions of semiotics remain to this day a reasonable and popular analysis of language study.

Relating Morris's tripartite division of semiotics to the broader study of human communication is but a simple step. Syntactics refers to the grammatical structure, word order, message construction, and so on of communication—basically, the coding process. Semantics focuses on the meaning of messages, primarily a receiver-oriented interpretation but also including the cultural conventions of shared meanings. Both syntactic and semantic aspects of human communication have received widespread attention by researchers in the scientific community of human communication study. Pragmatic aspects of communication have until recently been relegated to a subordinate role—typically, as a result or outcome of communication, commonly associated only indirectly with communication study.

The pragmatic aspect of communication concentrates on the behavior of the communicator as the fundamental component of human communication. Rather than view behavior as an outcome or effect of the communicative act, pragmatics implies that communication and behavior are virtually synonymous. Oddly enough, the principal impetus to the pragmatic perspective of human communication came not from members of the scientific community of communication but from a group of psychotherapists involved in the "domain" of communication, as a variable of study but outside the discipline of human communication. Watzlawick, Beavin, and Jackson (1967) also provided the term *pragmatics* (indirectly from Morris, of course), which serves to name this perspective to view the process of human communication.

The pragmatic perspective is by far the newest of the four perspectives outlined in Part Two. In fact, as a force in the discipline of communication study, nearly its entire development dates from the 1967 publication of Watzlawick, Beavin, and Jackson's *Pragmatics of Human Communication*. Like the interactional/dialogical approach to human communication, the pragmatic perspective is still in the process of developing. Moreover, the perspective is steadily increasing in popularity among scholars of human communication. And like interactionists, those members of the scientific community who are utilizing the pragmatic perspective possess the fervor of "true believers," apparently highly committed to this new approach to communication. They, too, are "rebels" in the field of human communication.

PRINCIPLES OF PRAGMATICS

Despite the fact that the term *pragmatics* has its origin in the study of semiotics, the pragmatics perspective owes no allegiance to semiotics for its theoretical/philosophical principles. Rather, such principles come directly from general system theory, a multidisciplinary blend of assumptions, concepts, and principles, which seeks to provide a general framework for the study of many different kinds of phenomena—physical, biological, and social. Our concern, however, is not to satisfy the desire of some theorists who seek to unite all the scientific inquiry within the rubrics of *general* system theory, a desire strongly held by Ludwig von Bertalanffy (often considered to be the father of general system theory) until his death in 1972. Our only interest is applying certain principles of system theory to the study of human communication.

Before we outline the principles of system theory, it is necessary to understand at the outset that these principles are quite abstract (that is to say, general). Consequently, they can be applied in numerous ways by different theorists with equally different results. In fact, system "theory" is probably a misnomer. Although Mesarovic (1972) and Wymore (1972) consider system theory to be a "formal theory," other advocates are not so convinced. Churchman (1968), for example, refers to the "systems approach." Boulding (1965) prefers the "systems point of view." For Laszlo (1972), it is a "systems philosophy"; for Zadeh and Polak (1969), a "systems discipline"; for Bertalanffy (1968), a "systems perspective" (a term most consistent with our view, of course); for Emory (1969), "systems thinking"; for Alfred Kuhn (1974), "systems logic"; and for one of my psychologist-colleagues, "systems opinion."

In short, system theory is a loosely organized and highly abstract set of principles, which serve to direct our thinking but which are subject to numerous interpretations. The model of communication outlined in this chapter is but one way to apply system theory to the study of human communication. It is a model shared by a growing number of communication scholars but is by no means to be considered the sole representation of system theory applicable to the discipline of human communication.

Because of the high level of abstraction implicit in system theory, this section is divided into three parts. The first section abstracts from the enormous body of literature in general system theory and outlines some fundamental tenets that are relevant to the study of human communication. Because the ensuing discussion of the pragmatic perspective of communication demands it, the second section outlines a few principles selected from information theory—a subsidiary quasi-mechanistic approach to communication, which also stems from general system theory. A final third section then translates the foregoing set of abstract principles into terms that are applicable to human communication and sets the stage for a description of the pragmatic model that follows.

Tenets of System Theory

As suggested earlier, the high level of abstraction of general system theory allows for a diversity of interpretations within its parameters. Under no circumstances should the following tenets be considered a comprehensive definition of system theory. Rather, they reflect only a few overall tenets that reflect some principal axiomatic assumptions generally held by system theorists. The tenets themselves and the interpretation of them are drawn from a range of sources representing scholars from such diverse fields as philosophy, economics, biology, engineering, sociology, physics, and psychology in addition to communication. This diversity serves to point up the multidisciplinary interest, popularity, and applications of general system theory.

THE PRINCIPLE OF NONSUMMATIVITY.   The first principle of system theory is the definition of system itself—a whole, the "all of a thing." Rapoport (1968, p. xvii) defines a system as a "whole which functions as a whole by virtue of the interdependence of its parts." Hall and Fagen (1956, p. 18) reiterate the principle of wholeness by defining a system as "a set of objects together with relationships between the objects and between their attributes." In other words, the components of a system do not characterize the systemic nature of the whole, but the relationships—more specifically, the interdependent relationships of the components—provide the system with its unique characteristic of wholeness. Interdependence, of course, implies mutual dependence among components such that any change in one component automatically and inherently affects every other component.

Nonsummativity and wholeness are but two sides of the same coin; that is, wholeness implies that the system is different from the sum of objects or components that, taken together, form the system. But when the component parts are related to each other interdependently, the result is a collectivity that takes on its own identity separate from the individual identities of the components. For example, two adults and three children may constitute a mere "aggregate" or a "heap" (system-theory jargon for a nonsystem). But when they live together as a family and affect each other in the day-by-day living together, they constitute a collective system called *family*—identifiable as a single unit. The individual identities of family members become amalgamated into the collectivity— father, mother, son, daughter—such that what happens to one (for example, an illness, a broken teen-age heart, a loss of job income) affects every other member of the family unit.

A system may take on a clearer meaning if it is contrasted with a nonsystem ("aggregate" or "heap"). A heap implies no interdependence of relationship among components so that they do not function as a single entity (whole). Contrast, for example, an artificial collectivity, such as all the left-handed people in school, with all the members of a labor union. Left-handed people simply do not relate to each other in any interdependent fashion. The sum of their individual activities constitutes the entirety of their existence as a collectivity. There is simply little or no consistent effect of one left-handed person on another because of their left-handedness. But the labor union does function as a whole in many significant ways. Its members all go on strike as a whole. They all go to work, perform assigned jobs, and in other ways honor the labor contract as a whole. In short, the actions of one affect the actions of others.

Of course, the boundaries of systems overlap considerably, so that some components of one system are also components of other systems. For example, every person is a member of multiple social systems, for example, family, friends, work group, neighborhood, political party, church, and school. Consequently, the existence of any given system is a function of a specific time and place; that is, when the individual is home with her family, her membership in the family system is most prominent. When the child goes to school or a parent goes to work, she is a member of the school system or the work group system.

For the purpose of laying the groundwork for a perspective on human communication, the discussion that follows will concentrate on social systems—systems composed of people. Other systems (for example, physical systems and biological systems) are also part of general system theory, but they will not be discussed as directly in the following paragraphs.

STRUCTURE, FUNCTION, AND EVOLUTION.   The interdependent relationships among components can be described according to the three interrelated elements of structure, function, and evolution. Structural relationships imply a spatial relationship among components in the sense of *beside, above, under, face-to-face,* and so forth. For example, one structural relationship in a social system could be two persons sitting across the table from each other—face-to-face. Another structural relationship is that of status; that is, one person could be a subordinate to the other in the sense of foreman-worker or could have equivalent status as co-workers. If you recall the earlier discussion of mechanistic (inherently involving spatial relationships) networks, the structural relationship allows for such spatial or structural concepts as communication *distance* or *centrality* within a network. Both distance and centrality are structural relationships that depict components as material or quasi-material objects enduring through time.

Functional relationships imply a time-oriented relationship among components. Thus, components are inherently events rather than material objects. As events, the components are transient, fleeting, potentially repetitive occurrences. In a social system, functional relationships deal with actions so that a person may be identified by his functional relationship with other people, for example, information giver, questioner, energizer, and respondent. In other words, the person is not so much the component as are the actions he performs in relationship with other.

And as an action, the occurrence is repeatable. For example, a person may ask a question more than once. Thus, functional relationships are associated with actions or behaviors—events and not material objects.

Evolutionary relationships trace the entire system's history through time. The evolution of a system contains within it structural and functional relationships along with changes in those relationships that occur during the passage of time. As the term *evolution* implies, changes are typically very gradual rather than sudden or immediate—continuous small changes rather than massive revisions. And, of course, evolution also traces periods of no change, that is, maintenance of the structural and functional relationships over a period of some time.

The structural, functional, and evolutionary relationships in a system might seem more understandable with the assistance of an example. Considering the government of the United States of America as the social system, we can depict the general structural, functional, and evolutionary relationships in that system. Structurally, our national government is divided into three major components: legislative, judicial, and executive branches of government. Their functional relationships occur as a process of "checks and balances," in which the legislative branch makes the laws, the judicial branch interprets the laws, and the executive branch enforces the laws. These functions are interdependent so that each function affects and is affected by the other. For example, during the era of prohibition of alcoholic beverages, the law was passed by the legislative branch but not well enforced by the executive branch. The evolutionary relationships, of course, trace the two hundred-plus years of the development of the system of checks and balances, the changing laws, the increase in structural size of the government, periods of large-scale social welfare such as the Great Depression of the 1930s, periods of international isolation, expansion, warfare, peace, and so on.

If we focus on structural relationships momentarily, such relationships can vary along a continuum from highly structured to highly random. To the extent that the system possesses structure, we can say that the structural relationships reflect *order*. To be a system, of course, the components must inevitably possess some order, but the degree of order can vary. In terms of a social organization that is highly structured (that is, a high degree of order), we consider it to be bureaucratic—clear-cut separation of status relationships, clear division of labor based on role specializations, well-defined rules and regulations, clear procedures for performing organizational functions, and so on.

The more order in a system, the more predictable is the system's behavior. For example, the physical system of the pendulum reflects a high degree of order, so that we can predict the length of the arc and the periodicity of the swing, if we know the structural variables of the pendulum. On the other hand, the pendulum is not very interesting, either—precisely because it is so disgustingly predictable.

Functional relationships can also vary along a continuum. To the extent that they do vary, the system is said to possess *complexity*. Remember that functions are events that are transient, repeatable, and even reversible. The person who is identified as a questioner may, from time to time, perform an action that is not a question. When he does, his functional role becomes more complex. The more complexity in the system, the less predictable are the functional relationships. Another word for complexity is *differentiation* in the sense that differences in actions increase the level of complexity existing within the system. To the extent that all behaviors are the same, the system is "simple" (the opposite of complex). And, for me, another word for a simple system is *dull!*

Obviously, social systems are not totally predictable. In other words, every social system realistically possesses order to some degree (but not fully ordered) and complexity to some degree (not a very simple system). Relating system theory to social systems (and thus to communication) must eventually involve some assessment of the degree of order and complexity in a system, along with tracing evolutionary changes in order and complexity over time.

THE PRINCIPLE OF OPENNESS.   All systems are classified according to some degree of "openness." Reasonably enough, the opposite of an open system is called a *closed system*. Theorists have used several characteristics to distinguish an open system. The most common of these characteristics is the free exchange of energy or information between an open system and its environment (see for example, Rapoport, 1968, p. xviii); that is, an open system has permeable boundaries that allow for considerable commerce with the system's environment. For example, the biological system of the human body takes in food and oxygen from the environment and expels bodily wastes into the environment. The family, of course, is an open system with members frequently entering and leaving the system whenever someone goes to work or school. Information from the environment enters the system whenever someone turns on a television set, a radio, reads a newspaper, or answers or uses the telephone. But the fact that open systems interact with the environment, an obvious truism, taken by itself is insufficient to describe the nature of openness.

At the risk of introducing more jargon unnecessarily, we need to be familiar with the concept of *equifinality,* an inherent characteristic of an open system. Conversely, the principle of *equilibrium,* along with *entropy,* characterizes the closed system. According to the equilibrium principle, the final state of a closed system is determined by the initial state, that is, the structure of the components antecedent to a subsequent condition. Thus, knowing the antecedent conditions allows one to be able to predict the consequent—an assumption that is highly consistent with the now-familiar conditional statement common to the covering-law model of science philosophy and inherent in experimental methodology. On the other hand, the principle of equifinality, according to Bertalanffy (1968, p. 40), stipulates "the same final state may be reached from different initial conditions and in different ways." Then, too, different open systems with the same initial conditions could well achieve different final states.

The practical difference between the principles of equilibrium and equifinality can be demonstrated in a simple example. Kick a stone, and you will be able to predict within a reasonable measurement error the consequential behavior of the stone. All you need to know is the state of the initial conditions, that is, the force and trajectory of the foot, the mass and volume of the stone, the friction between the stone and the surface over which it skids and so on. The kicked stone characterizes a closed system governed by the principle of equilibrium. But kick a dog, and your ability to predict the dog's subsequent behavior is severely limited. The dog may run away, turn and bite, seek affection, stand still, or do any of a number of other possible behaviors. The latter is more like an open system with equifinal states.

The difference between equifinality and equilibrium resides in the "second law of thermodynamics," which spells out the concept of *entropy*. Roughly stated, entropy implies the presence of a natural and irreversible force or tendency within a system to decrease its order over time. Entropy is thus a destructive force, which leads ultimately to the disintegration of a closed system. In the same sense that a burning building cannot be "unburned," the entropic process of increasing disorder (disintegrating structure) cannot be reversed. Entropy and consequently disorder inevitably and irrevocably increase until the system eventually disintegrates.

Closed systems combat the disintegrative force of entropy with an opposite force known as *negative entropy*—more familiarly called *negentropy*. Though negentropy cannot reverse the process of disintegration resulting from entropy, it can stalemate disintegration by balancing the force of entropy. The resulting balance of the disintegrative force of entropy with negentropy is termed *homeostasis*. The balanced state of homeostasis, however, does not suggest an increase in order or structure, only a slowing down or stoppage of the disintegrative process. One can douse the flames on a burning building and prevent further destruction, but in doing so, one has not restored the burned portion of the building to its original state. That damage has been done and cannot be undone.

If entropy exists in a closed system, why does it not also affect an open system? The answer lies in the ability of the open system to import additional information from its environment. Furthermore, many open systems have the capacity to generate their own information within the system—particularly, many social systems. Stated another way, open systems are purposeful (see Ackoff and Emery, 1972) and possess the ability of self-regulation. They can make assessments of the structure and functioning of their own systems as well as the state of the environment and can act accordingly. As Rapoport (1968, p. xix) puts it, open systems operate "on the principle of *correcting* their performance on the basis of taking stock of what is happening." The open system "compares its current state with some preset goal state and adjusts its performance on the basis of the 'observed' difference." Consequently, open systems may actually decrease entropy so that order (that is, structural organization) actually increases in the system. (See also Bertalanffy, 1968, p. 150.)

Up to this point, the discussion of openness has focused on changes in structure and order. However, another characteristic of open systems is increased "complexity," that is, differentiation of functions. Pringle (1951) discusses increased complexity as a function of evolutionary process. He indicates a parallel between human learning and such evolutionary processes. The analogy of Darwin's biological evolution, which leads to increased complexity (greater differentiation) among animal species, is relevant to the evolutionary processes of differentiated functions (behaviors) in social systems. Through natural selection or other evolutionary processes, open systems possess systemic processes that evolve into a pattern of increasing differentiation of functions within the system. In other words, open systems tend toward increasing levels of complexity.

Some students of system theory unfortunately tend to consider the openness principles in dichotomous terms; that is, a system is either open, or it is closed. There is no "in between." But openness is not an attribute or trait of a system in the sense that a system either possesses it or it doesn't. Openness is a variable property, which a system possesses to some degree—from 0 per cent (or totally closed) to 100 per cent (totally open). But the totally open or totally closed system is an ideal type that probably can be maintained only under severely controlled laboratory conditions. When one is considering social systems, rather than physical or biological systems, there is no question. Social systems are never closed but must be viewed as more nearly open.

Miller's (1965, p. 203) view of living (including social) systems characterizes them as inevitably open systems. And Berrien (1968, p. 16) is also explicit on this point. Nevertheless, it is important to remember that although social systems are characterized as open systems, the degree of openness may vary considerably among different social systems. Though some social systems are more susceptible to change and more capable of adapting to changes in environmental conditions, other systems (for example, bureaucracies) are less open and tend to resist change.

In summary, then, social systems are open systems. The principle of openness implies that their boundaries are permeable, thereby allowing systems to interact with their environments in the sense that the systems can import information or energy from the environment. Furthermore, open systems are characterized by equifinality and are thus less subject to the irreversible destructive force of entropy. Consequently, the initial or antecedent state of the open system does not determine the final or subsequent state; that is, the open system is capable of importing and generating information or negentropy and can evolve to increased structural organization, impossible in closed systems. Finally, a social system, because it is open, tends to evolve toward increasing complexity or an increase in differentiation among functional relationships. Of course, because the degree of openness varies from one social system to another, social systems vary in their self-regulating capacities and thus also vary in their ability to adapt to environmental changes.

HIERARCHICAL ORGANIZATION. Most of us can probably recall a childhood experience of addressing a letter to name, street, address, city, state, U.S.A., Western Hemisphere, planet Earth, Universe, Solar System, the "mind of God." We learned long ago the principle of a hierarchical organization of systems. If you can picture a series of concentric circles or a virtually infinite series of boxes, one inside the other so that each time you open one box there is another box inside, you have the idea of smaller systems existing within larger systems. For every system there can be a larger system that encompasses it—a suprasystem—and there is also a smaller system (subsystem) included within it.

Naturally, systems, subsystems, and suprasystems are all systems. A system becomes a suprasystem or a subsystem only because of its relationship with another system. A suprasystem or subsystem is a system nonetheless. Stated another way, every system is a suprasystem to the systems within it, and every system is a subsystem to the system that environs it. The hierarchical organization of systems is an axiomatic assumption of system theory and itself the subject of considerable theoretical and empirical speculation (see Pattee, 1973).

All right. So systems exist within an hierarchical organization. So what? Remember that open systems interact with their environments (the suprasystem). The flow of information across the boundaries of the system suggests that the nature of the functional relationship between the system and its suprasystem affects to no small extent the structural-functional behaviors of the systems. A full comprehension of this informational exchange is essential to understanding the system. Because systems are capable of generating their own information (from subsystems), the relationship between system and subsystems is also vital to understanding the system. Ozbekhan (1971) is emphatic on this point—that any understanding of a given system must involve an understanding of the transfer of information across systemic boundaries both upward and downward in the hierarchy. This point has implications for human communication, too. But those implications will have to be held in abeyance for a few more pages.

Tenets from Information Theory

The mathematical and mechanistic approach to communication bears the name *information theory,* which stems philosophically from Norbert Wiener and cybernetics and statistically from Shannon and Weaver's (1949) mathematical theory of communication. Though the mechanistic philosophy of information theory is not particularly significant or even relevant to the pragmatic perspective, the functioning of information is very central. It is information that energizes the social system and allows the system to survive. It is information that is exchanged between subsystem, system, and suprasystem, consistent with the principle of openness.

"The "mortar" that holds physical systems together is energy; for social systems information is the energy. Structural and functional interrelationships among components imply the existence of information. When communication occurs in a social system, the individuals are engaged in the processing of information. Prerequisite to discussing communication pragmatically is a comprehension of the nature of information. Information theory provides one way to gain such comprehension.

CHOICE AND UNCERTAINTY.   One of the characteristics that sets the human being apart as being a unique species among the animal world is the human capacity for choice. Only the human possesses the capacity to conceptualize the range of alternatives, assess the relative value and consequences of each, and then choose one of the alternatives. Rothstein (1958, p. 34) considers the existence of alternative choices as integral to the functioning of elements in a system: "Each element must be associated with its own set of alternatives. Were there no freedom to choose from a set of alternatives, the corresponding element would be a static, passive cog rather than an active unit." In a social system, then, a population of choices exists for every human being (that is, element). The human, as an active component in the social system, is constantly making selections from this population during social interaction.

Selecting from a population of choices implies, of course, that the individual does not choose randomly what actions to perform. Rather, the human somehow reduces the number of available alternatives to a manageable number and eventually to a single alternative. As the human acquires information, she is able to make those reductions. It is through this functioning of information that reduces the range of alternatives that information is said to be, the opposite of uncertainty. The amount of information necessary to reduce the range of alternative choices is, of course, related to the number of alternatives that are available to be chosen.

Information, according to the maxims of information theory, exists only as an amount; that is, the meaning or significance of a particular item of information is totally outside the realm of information theory. It measures information in terms of "how much" uncertainty is removed —uncertainty as to which choice should be selected from a range of alternatives. The basic unit of information is called a *binary digit* (that is, information "bit"), which is defined as a reduction of uncertainty by 50 per cent—reducing the number of available alternatives to half their original number.

For example, if you are to pick a number between one and ten and can ask only yes-or-no questions in order to select the correct number, you will discover the correct number by asking 3.3 questions. (No, I don't know what the .3 of a question sounds like, but such is the wonder of mathematics.) Of course, each question asked must reduce the number of remaining alternatives by half. Thus, if the population of choices is ten, the amount of information contained in the set of ten is 3.3 bits.

The first question might ask if the number was five or less. If the answer is affirmative, you have eliminated half the numbers—six through ten. The second question cannot arithmetically acquire 1.0 bits of information, for half of five is not a whole number; Is it three or greater? No. (You now know what 1.3 questions look like.) Only one information bit remains to reduce certainty to zero. You need to ask only one more question (the third question asked) to discover the exact answer, Is it two? No. You know the number is one without asking another question; that is, you can acquire only zero bits of information by asking whether the number is one. No more uncertainty remains. You have reduced the population of alternatives to that single choice, and you have all the information available in a population of ten choices. Uncertainty is zero —no more information remains to be processed.

Information theory assumes several requisites before its statistical measures are applicable. First, a finite and specifiable number of possible alternatives must be available for choice. In other words, the population of choices is never infinite. Second, individuals use information to reduce their uncertainty. Implicitly or explicitly, every individual, even in a friendly conversation, asks, "What did he mean by that?" or "How should I respond to that?" Consequently, the information-processing communicator asks questions or in some way continues interaction with the other person in order to acquire a sufficient amount of information to answer those questions and thus function appropriately in the communicative setting. This process of inquiring and using information to reduce uncertainty is a natural, though not necessarily conscious, and inevitable characteristic of human communication.

REDUNDANCY AND CONSTRAINT. The nature of information, in the sense of a social system that processes information, suggests that the system deals with events rather than material objects. As occurrences in time, events are associated with each other in terms of a chronological sequence—a chain of events. Uncertainty, then, is associated with whether or not an event occurs or will occur at some level of expectation. Information theory specifies that past adaptations of the system impact upon the present so that the information-processing behaviors tend to repeat themselves over time in tried-and-true patterns. When a given sequence of behaviors or events occurs again and again, that sequence can be said to exhibit a regularity of occurrence at some level or probability.

Consider, for example, a chain of events in which every element has an equal probability of occurrence—a random chain of alphabetical letters typed by a small child playing with a typewriter. This chain of letters shows no impact of past regularity of occurrence and can be said to contain no information. But a letter typed in words, sentences, and paragraphs does show the impact of English language usage. Certain letters occur so frequently in a pattern with other letters that we recognize them as words and are even able to decipher typographical errors because a particular letter does not "fit" the expected pattern. Even an omitted word, such as in the sentence "The bat —— the ball" can be interpreted *within the probable pattern of the sentence* as a verb —a transitive verb such as *hit*.

The probability of occurrence of any sequence can be computed directly from past sequential occurrences. To the extent that the sequence is repeated consistently over time, the system exhibits "redundancy." The more redundant the sequence, the less uncertainty is contained in the sequence; that is, the higher the probability of occurrence (that is, the more redundancy) of any given event in the sequence, the more "constraint" is placed on the range of available alternatives. When sequences achieve sufficient levels of probability, we can discern the sequence as a recognizable "pattern," for example, the subject-verb-object pattern of the English sentence. Therefore, as Watzlawick, Beavin, and Jackson (1967, p. 34) point out, the three terms of "redundancy," "constraint," and "pattern" are virtually synonymous in information theory and can be used interchangeably.

Relating information theory to system theory, Orchard (1972, p. 214) indicates. "If the system is observed over a sufficient time interval, it may be possible, if desired, to associate each part of the behaviors (relation) with its probability of occurrence." Because redundancy serves to constrain the selections made from the population of choices, a sequential pattern of events is discernible only by observing the system of behaviors over a period of time. The repeatability of the past and the effect of past behaviors on present behaviors (also implying that present behaviors affect future behavioral sequences) illustrate the openness of the system and the importance of the time dimension in scholarly inquiry. (See also Watzlawick, Beavin, and Jackson's discussion of the principle of limitation, 1967, pp. 131–132.)

Application to Human Communication

At long last, this abstract discussion can get down to the task at hand —a manageable level of specific assumptions applicable to human communication. It will soon be apparent that the pragmatic perspective of human communication is quite different from the other three perspectives and requires some novel reconceptualizations of communicative phenomena. Some of these reconceptualizations precipitated by system theory are included not only in Watzlawick, Beavin, and Jackson's (1967) landmark volume but also in the collection of essays edited by Ruben and Kim (1975).

SOCIAL SYSTEM. To conceive of human communication as a system requires the existence of a social system within which communication takes place. This stipulation requires, first of all, the conceptualization of communication as a human activity not to be confused with the hardware (that is, technological developments) of communication, even though the hardware elements may be relevant; that is, the technological devices, particularly of mass media, are not integral to the study of human communication but are instruments, tools used by humans in the human activity of communication. As a social system, communication involves people who may or may not manipulate machines. But clearly the manipulation of humans by machines is not at issue.

A second function of the social nature of communication is to focus upon the information processing at the level of the system and not at the level of the subsystem, that is, the single individual. Essentially, the effect of the systemic focus is to reduce the significance of the intrapersonal level of communication. That effect is not particularly vital to our present discussion but will receive more comprehensive discussion in Part Three. However, some of the ramifications of the intrapersonal level of communication are relevant at this point.

The issue of the discrepancy between attitudes and behavior of individuals was a significant point of contention, you may recall, in a psychological perspective of human communication, but in the pragmatic perspective the issue simply ceases to exist. By focusing on the level of the social system, the smallest subsystem is that of an individual. Though attitude and behaviors may be subsystems of the individual, the pragmatic focus does not descend down the hierarchy to such a miscroscopic examination; that is, the focus is not on the individual but on the social system—a minimum of two people. Thus, the problem of attitude-behavior discrepancy is not "solved" within the pragmatic perspective; it is simply not recognizable as a problem.

BEHAVIORS.   When the individual becomes the subsystem in the focus on the social system, the hierarchical organization of systems comes into play. Three systemic levels are necessary for systemic analysis of communication—subsystem, system, and suprasystem (see Laszlo, 1972a, p. 47). Weick (1969, p. 45) points out: "If there are different levels of analysis (e.g., individual, group, organization, society), the only way we can learn much about any of these levels is if we know how they are tied together, that is, how one level interacts with another level." Weick goes on to point out that lower levels constrain higher levels. Thus, individuals constrain the social system. Ozbekhan (1971, p. 182) suggests that the suprasystem (also a social system, of course) gives "significance" or "meaning" to the system. In the viewing of communication as a system, then, it is vital to view the respective subsystems and suprasystem as well.

For example, a conversation between a mother and daughter may be the communicative system of interest. The mother and the daughter as individuals "constrain" the system; that is, they provide the pattern or the structure or the organization of the communication system. Moreover, the suprasystem of the larger "family" provides the perspective within which their conversation takes on significance or meaning. The example could also be a work group in a business organization, a class in a university, or two families in a neighborhood. In any case, the individuals constrain, structure, or pattern the social interaction of the communicative system; and the significance of that interaction is a function of the system's relationship with its suprasystem, that is, its environment.

Individuals possess only one means at their disposal to constrain the interaction in a social system—the behaviors that they perform; therefore, the units of interest to the function of information processing in the social system are the behaviors produced by individuals. In a social situation one person can affect another only by what the other can observe with sensory receptors, and that means behaviors. One person may think, feel, or believe something; but the other person will remain unaware of that thought, feeling, or belief unless or until some behavior reflects it. Even then the expressed thought or feeling is insignificant to the social system unless it "fits" into the structure of the interaction sequence; that is, it is redundant or patterned and thus possesses information.

Bloom (1975, p. 9), citing Charles S. Peirce, "the father of American pragmatism,' elucidates the fundamental principle of pragmatism— that "our conception of these effects is the whole of our conception of the object." Now this statement does not mean to imply an antihumanistic view of the individual but only that part of the individual, the part that is reflected in behaviors, is included in a social system. The social system neither wants nor demands any more of the individual than that portion of his behaviors, and the individual commits no more of himself to the system than the behaviors he performs in the communicative system. This is the familiar "law of partial inclusion," significant to the study of human organization.

The focus on behaviors as the fundamental units of the communication system is not to deny necessarily the relevance or significance of non-behavioral components of the individual (subsystem), but the relevance or significance of these elements to the social system as a whole is not to be assumed either. Fisher and Hawes (1971) call for research aimed at discovering potential correlations between the "Interact System Model" (behavioral relationships among individuals) and the "Human System Model" (nonbehavioral relationships, such as cognitive-affective relationships, among individuals). The pragmatic perspective focuses on human communication as a system of behaviors. Unless or until nonbehavioral relationships are manifested in interaction patterns, they remain outside the realm of the pragmatic perspective of human communication.

SEQUENTIAL INTERACTION PATTERNS. Watzlawick, Beavin, and Jackson's (1967, pp. 54–59) third "tentative axiom of communication" states: "The nature of a relationship is contingent upon the punctuation of the communicational sequences between the participants." (Emphasis deleted.) Punctuation refers simply to the grouping of elements, into a recognizable pattern. Without that grouping, the pattern or structure of the interaction is unrecognizable—only a continuous series of actions following and preceding other actions. Without the punctuational grouping of letters into words, words into sentences, and sentences into paragraphs, the printed page would be extraordinarily difficult to decipher.

For example, decipher the unpunctuated sentence, "idontknowabout-youbutiamratherthirsty." That sentence is much more easily read when punctuated with proper capitalization, spacing, and markings: "I don't know about you, but I am rather thirsty." Under any circumstances, the letters have a pattern recognizable as an English-language sentence. Punctuation, that is, grouping, makes the interpretation of meaning more easily accomplished. Moreover, punctuating the elements into the proper groupings is both natural and necessary in order to describe the appropriate relationship between the elements.

When one is punctuating a communication system, the principle of organizing behaviors into groupings is still applicable, even though spacing and punctuation marks are not as readily available. (On the other hand, remember Victor Borge's "phonetic punctuation"?) But if we take the lead from information theory, the punctuation of sequential behaviors is a function of their redundancy—recurrence or repeatability over time. Those sequences that recur with the most frequent regularity provide the appropriate punctuation, organization, or groupings of the interaction. Information theory's assumption of the equivalence of redundancy and pattern allows the observer to group the communicative behaviors into sequential patterns and thus define the nature of the communicative relationship.

CONTENT AND RELATIONSHIP DIMENSIONS. Watzlawick, Beavin, and Jackson's (1967, pp. 51–54) second tentative axiom of human communication specifies that two kinds of information exist in every communicative act—information pertaining to content and information pertaining to relationship. The content dimension of the communicative act provides the "data" aspect of the information. The relationship dimension provides the information as to how one is to interpret the data. The two dimensions are inseparable and always present in every communicative act. As Burke (1957) has suggested, providing data in a message absolutely requires that you "stylize" the message somehow. You have to say it "in some way"—wording, phrasing, inflection, nonverbal cues, and so on—and that "way" constitutes the relationship dimension and some clue to the definition of the interpersonal relationship—how the "data" are to be interpreted.

Though the content and relationship aspects of communication are considered "dimensions" and thus inseparably interdependent, they may be observed as analytically distinct qualities of the same act or interaction. Moreover, relationship aspects of communication, like content, are subject to the same interpretations of patterning, punctuation, and sequencing—principles from information theory. As dimensions of communication, content and relationship are similar to the task and social dimensions of group process—interdependent but separable only for purposes of analysis. Furthermore, one dimension undoubtedly affects and is affected by the other.

In summary, the applications of system theory to communication focus on individual behaviors that, through empirically observable patterns based on redundancy, serve to characterize the social system that is called *communication*. The pragmatic perspective of human communication is based on principal assumptions from system theory and information theory, but is not the only way in which system theory is applicable to human communication. (See, for example, the discussion of the HSM in Fisher and Hawes, 1971.) Nevertheless, the pragmatic perspective is an appropriate application of system theory to human communication and is a clearly discernible trend of scholarly inquiry among members of the scientific community of human communication.

IMPLICATIONS

The implications of the pragmatic perspective are broader and more far-reaching in terms of their departures from the conventional wisdom surrounding human communication. In many respects the pragmatic perspective is blasphemous to the cardinal principles of mechanism, psychology, and interactionism. In the true sense of multiple paradigms espoused by Feyerabend (1963, 1965, 1970), the pragmatic perspective offers a highly disparate alternative paradigm when compared with the other three perspectives. By no means does the pragmatic perspective reflect the mainstream of theory or inquiry within the scientific community of human communication. But the perspective does claim many adherents, whose numbers appear to be steadily increasing.

Externalization

As communication focuses on behavior, a virtual cliché associated with communication begins to assume new meaning. The cliché—"One cannot not communicate." If this double-negative sentence is not yet meaningful, substitute the word *behave* for *communicate*. Now try to *not behave*. That simply does not make any sense. There is no such thing as *not behaving*. Even remaining quiet and not moving is a form of behavior. Behavior has no opposite. Neither does communication.

But does this emphasis on behavior imply that all behavior is necessarily communicative? Is random foot tapping communicative? Of course not! But it does imply that all communication is behavioral and, therefore, sensorially accessible to the participants in a communicative situation. Clearly, then, a communicator's introspection of self, along with such internalized phenomena as perceptions, attitudes, images, and values, take on less significance in the pragmatic perspective. When the focus of analysis is from the level of the system, individuals serve to constrain the system, that is, the social interaction. An internalized attitude simply cannot affect the sequence of interpersonal behaviors. It may, however, affect the actions of one person and, as such, indirectly affect the interpersonal sequence. Although the effect is indirect, the attitude may be relevant to the interaction pattern. The pragmatic perspective does not deny the existence of internalized conceptual filters; it simply considers them a different form of analysis.

These internalized phenomena enter the communicative system as externalized behaviors, or they do not enter the system at all. Then, and only then, are internalizations part of the system. But even the individual's actions do not constitute the entire system. When we recall the principle of nonsummativity, the sequence of those actions, together with the actions of other individuals contributing to the sequence, comprises the communicative system; and the system is not the same as the sum total of the actions of the individuals. It is nonsummative—different from the individuals' actions summed together. Internalized phenomena are simply not very significant in the wholeness of the system, although they may be highly significant to the individual. The pragmatic perspective recognizes that fact and considers it a fruitful area of inquiry—but not a pragmatic inquiry—into phenomena of human communication.

If pragmatics sounds like a rejection of individually oriented approaches to communication, the impression is accurate. If the phenomenon of human communication is derivable from the properties or attributes of individuals, then communication is a summative "heap" that can be totally analyzed by observing the individual communicators in isolation. But orienting to individuals rejects the systemic nature of social interaction. If interaction or communication is truly a social system, then the behavioral sequences (which, by definition, include more than one person's behaviors) are interdependent and inseparable. The sequences, then, must be conceived and interpreted as a "whole" that exhibits structure, that is, a redundant pattern. Individually oriented approaches to human communication must inevitably be seen as contrasting with the pragmatic perspective with its emphasis on the social system.

Stochastic Probability

The typical analysis of research data in the social sciences has employed inferential statistics and, often, experimental designs. The nature of the pragmatic perspective causes some problems for scholars trained only in the traditional research methods. The principle of equifinality, which characterizes the open system, does not rule out the experimental method altogether, but it certainly decreases its significance. And the nature of the data—ongoing sequences of interactive behaviors—is not easily susceptible to analysis by traditional statistical techniques. Again the pragmatic perspective does not legislate against the use of inferential statistics, but they certainly won't be the typical analytical methods employed in pragmatic research. Clearly, more and different analytical techniques are called for.

Buckley (1968, p. 497) indicates that, in a system perspective, "the unit of dynamic analysis thus becomes the systemic *matrix* of interacting, goal-seeking, deciding individuals and subgroups. . . ." As a matrix, the data take the form of a series of events that occur in some sequential pattern reflected in redundancy of certain sequences in a given time interval. As Buckley (1968, p. 499) goes on to say, new analytical tools are available to treat such data. These analytical "processes include treatment of the interaction matrix over time as a succession of states described in terms of transition probabilities, Markoff [sic] chains, or stochastic processes in general."

In a nutshell, the new analytical tools stem from the statistics used for analysis within information theory. They are typically "stochastic" in the sense that they assess probabilities of occurrence of a subsequent state from an antecedent state. As such, a stochastic process differs substantially from a predictive process; that is, in the conditionally stated theorem, knowledge of the antecedent state allows one to be able to predict the occurrence of the consequent state. The if-then statement of conditionality is a linear or quasi-deterministic statement that is explicitly a statement of necessity and/or sufficiency regarding the relationship between the antecedent and the consequent states. In other words, the antecedent state is, at the very least, a sufficient (if not necessary) condition to bring about the existence of the consequent state.

Stochastic probability implies no such linear relationship between antecedent state and subsequent (rather than "consequent") state. A stochastic process includes determining the probability that a specific subsequent state (from among the range of probabilistic states) does follow a specific antecedent state. That level of probability (ranging from 0 to 1.0) is computed from analysis of past sequential patterning in the interaction matrix representing a sufficiently long time interval. The level of stochastic probability, then, is a measure of redundancy (that is, constraint) that is descriptively evident in the interaction sequence. It states implicitly that, given the history of past interaction, one can expect B to follow A 75 per cent of the time (by actual measurement).

A key difference between predictability and probability lies in the event that the second state (consequent or subsequent) does *not* follow the antecedent state. As a stochastic (probabilistic) process, the event of nonoccurrence of the subsequent is a statement about complexity (differentiation of the subsequent). The nonoccurrence of the subsequent state merely demonstrates that the system is not a simple system but includes a measurable level of complexity. (Nonoccurrence is as measurable as occurrence.) However, in the predictive statement (if-then conditionality), the nonoccurrence of the consequent is a statement of error. Either the conditional relationship between antecedent and consequent does not hold, or the observation itself was erroneous. The predictive model based on conditional logic does not account for the principle of complexity.

I hasten to point out that the pragmatic perspective does not rule out statements of prediction. To the contrary, the philosophical issue of the significance of predictability in a theory (see Part One) is not the point of this discussion. But the covering-law model of prediction, based on conditional (if-then) logical statements, is the issue; and though the pragmatic perspective does not eliminate such theoretical statements, they do become problematic and less significant—certainly not the typical mode of inquiry in this perspective.

The more pertinent point is that the nature of prediction changes from that of consequents made requisite by existence of initial conditions to one of shorter-range probabilistic statements based on redundant patterns reflected in the ongoing interaction over a given time interval. Furthermore, such predictions should not be considered inherent in the interaction but should reflect an expectation of future occurrence for that time period. As interaction continues over a greater span of time, these expectations (or predictions) can also change. (We shall return to this issue in Part Three, which includes a discussion of the impact of feedback processes on continuing interaction sequences.)

Qualitative Analysis

Lofland's (1971) guide to qualitative analysis, directed primarily to sociological research, tends to equate qualitative analysis with field settings and methods. Apparently, Lofland chose to contrast his kind of research with that of controlled laboratory experimentation. His depiction of qualitative analysis is, nonetheless, relevant to the pragmatic perspective, although the difference between the laboratory and field settings seems more significant to sociology than to communication.

Lofland (1971, pp. 13–14) suggests that inquiry into social phenomena is reducible to three basic questions seeking to discover the "characteristics," the "causes," or the "consequences" (that is, effects) of such phenomena. Qualitative analysis is most concerned with inquiry into the *characteristics* of social phenomena—their forms, their kinds, types, variations, interrelationships, and so forth. Research questions dealing with causes and effects are thus less important to the qualitative researcher and are either inapplicable, impractical, or premature.

Certainly, the mechanistic and psychological perspectives of human communication lead directly to scholarly inquiry into causes and effects. The openness of social systems, intrinsic to the pragmatic perspective, however, implies that causal inferences may be less vital to understanding the process of human communication, if not downright inappropriate. More important and relevant are qualitative issues regarding the characterization of communication systems. This section will attempt to delineate some of those qualitative issues most significant to the present status of communication study.

Rosen (1972, pp. 61) provides a starting point for the qualitative analysis of communication systems. He indicates that "the only way in which we know how to approach complex systems is to simplify or abstract from them in some way." He goes on to suggest that the system must be broken down into smaller systems (subsystems) that are manageable, that is, are "simple enough to be characterized in isolation." Qualitative analysis of a complex system, then, involves breaking apart the larger system into its component subsystems and then putting the system back together again on the basis of empirical observation of the functioning of the various subsystems.

To say that individuals, through their behavior, constrain and thus form the social system called communication is to suggest a functional differentiation among the various communicative actions; that is, every act is not the same as every other act. They are somehow different. On the other hand, some acts are sufficiently similar to each other so that they may be considered the same kind of act and are thus repeatable. This suggests that one important characteristic of human communication is the delineation of categories of communicative actions. Therefore, acts within the same category are considered similar whereas acts in different categories suggest differentiation. Consequently, the more categories of communicative actions, the more complex (that is, differentiated) the qualitative analysis. Characterizing communicative behaviors within a system of action categories is thus a first step in the qualitative analysis of human communication.

But analyzing human behaviors into categories creates another problem. What are the categories of human behavior that, taken together, comprise the social system of human communication? Rosen (1972, p. 54) suggests that the criterion for selecting the categories should be to preserve the functions of the system; that is, the categories of human communicative behavior should comprise a list of the functions that human communication can perform. Identifying those functions (and thus the categories of communicative behaviors) is the task of the communication investigator, and often the variation of interests among investigators leads to a variation in category systems used in communication research. These variations in category systems will be discussed later in this chapter in discussing the research conducted within the pragmatic perspective.

Once qualitative analysis of communication systems categorizes human behaviors into functional categories, the next issue is the analysis of the categorized behaviors. From the earlier discussion of information theory, we know that the behaviors occur as a continuous sequence of events that, because of the repeatability of behaviors (that is, behaviors included within the same functional category), can exhibit patterning or redundancy. But if acts are repeatable, so, too, are sequences of acts. In fact, sequences of acts, showing the constraints of acts upon each other, are fundamental to the qualitative analysis of communication systems. Hawes (1973, pp. 13–14) makes the same point and refers to it as his "postulate of concateneity."

This act-on-act constraint in a sequence of behaviors is a fundamental difference between *content analysis* and *interaction analysis*—two techniques used in qualitative research. Although content analysis may involve categorizing phenomena, the technique does not include the

temporal analysis of such categorizations as a series of events or occurrences. Interaction analysis inherently involves temporal analysis of
sequences of categorized actions, so that the single act is not the primary
unit of the qualitative analysis. Rather, the fundamental analytical unit
is the interact (a recurring sequence of two contiguous acts), the double
interact (a recurring sequence of three contiguous acts), a triple interact
(four acts), and so forth.

Any sequence of interaction, then, can be organized into acts, interacts,
double interacts, and so on. That is, every act is both an antecedent act
to the act that follows it and a subsequent act to the act that precedes
it. In other words, in an exchange of ten acts in a normal conversation,
there are nine interacts (1–2, 2–3, 3–4, 4–5, 5–6, . . . 9–10), eight double
interacts (1–2–3, 2–3–4, 3–4–5, 4–5–6, . . . 8–9–10), and seven triple
interacts (1–2–3–4, 2–3–4–5, 3–4–5–6, . . . 7–8–9–10). The various
lengths of the chains of acts comprise the level of interaction analysis.
Most interaction analysis involves interacts for what will soon be obvious
reasons.

The discussion of complexity has, up to this point, considered only
spatial complexity (differentiation among material or quasi-material objects). For example, a unit of four persons in a social system is more
complex than a three-person system; that is, in network analysis there are
only three channels possible to link the communicators: A–B, B–C, and
A–C. But in a four-person network, there are six channels available for
use: A–B, A–C, A–D, B–C, B–D, and C–D—in other words, greater differentiation among alternatives (in this case, channels) for selection. The
number of categories of human behavior is a further example of spatial
complexity; that is, for each act, an individual can select alternatives
(categories) for regulating his behavior in a communicative system. The
more categories available for selection, the more choices available and
thus the more complex the system—but only at the act level, a quasi-
spatial complexity.

Temporal complexity involves a sequence of choices that increase in
complexity over time. And as complexity increases, you will recall, the
probability of expected occurrences also decreases. For example, the
probability of flipping "heads" on a coin is one out of two possibilities
or .5 (assuming the coin is not biased, of course). The probability of
flipping two "heads" in succession, however, is significantly lower—.25
(one out of four possibilities). The longer the sequence of occurrences,
the less probable any given sequence under random circumstances, that
is, the greater complexity in time.

Figure 5 illustrates the phenomenon of temporal complexity in a communication system—a continuous sequence of acts or behaviors. If a
very simple category system is used—only two functions performed by

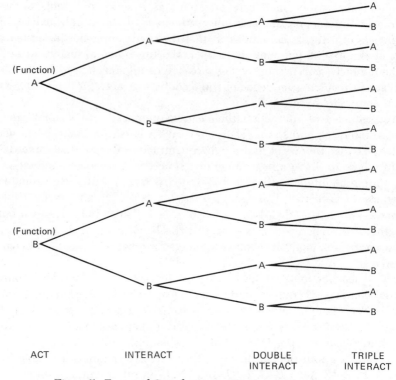

Figure 5. *Temporal Complexity in a Communication System.*

communicative behaviors (*A* and *B*)—the number of available choices increases remarkably over time. Though there are only two alternative choices available at the level of "act," the communicators have four available choices of interacts, eight choices of double interact sequences, and sixteen choices of triple interacts. If we ignore for the moment the constraint on the choices of acts due to prior interaction, the probability of occurrence of an *A–A* interact is .25 (that is, random probability), the probability of an *A–A–A* double interact is .125, and the probability of an *A–A–A–A* triple interact is only .0625. As complexity (differentiation) increases geometrically over time, the probability of random occurrence decreases geometrically over time.

Qualitative analysis of communication systems is clearly the principal research methodology emphasized within the pragmatic perspective. Qualitative analysis involves fractionation of all possible communicative acts into categories representing the functions performed by communicative behavior. Interaction analysis of those communicative functions involves issues of spatial and temporal complexity in terms of the number of communicative functions reflected in the analytical categories and the length of the sequences of acts analyzed. Because a characteristic of open systems stipulates that they tend to increase in complexity over time, the qualitative analysis of complexity is significant to communication inquiry within the pragmatic perspective.

Complexity of Time Concepts

It should be apparent at this point that the pragmatic perspective of human communication has expanded greatly the concept of time. Within the pragmatic perspective, time becomes much more complex and much more of an integral part of human communication. Though the mechanistic and psychological perspectives relied more on spatial concepts, the pragmatic perspective inherently includes a variety of time concepts that simply do not exist when time is considered as only a physical property based on the earth's physical rotation on its axis and revolution around the sun.

Conceptualizing time in other than a physical sense is rather difficult. We tend to restrict our thinking about time by the conceptualizations dictated by the "clock." Time is unidirectional and moves inexorably forward. (You can't turn the clock back—except, of course, when daylight saving time ends.) Time is also constant. It neither speeds up nor slows down. Every day is precisely the same length as every other day —24 hours. Every hour is sixty minutes long. Every minute is sixty seconds long. And, above all else, time endures. We measure age by the number of years lived, work by the eight-hour day, classes in school by the fifty-minute period, and distance by the minutes or hours it takes to get there. Physical time is certainly durational.

The pragmatic perspective of human communication includes the concept of physical time, of course. Physical time remains the standard against which all other dimensions of time are measured, but the pragmatic perspective also includes other concepts of time as well. One pragmatic aspect of time involves its alleged unidirectionality. In that an event or a behavior can recur in measurable redundancy, time can repeat itself. The same category-event, through recurrence (redundancy), thus occurs at different times.

Recurrence also leads to a reconceptualization of past, present, and future. Redundancy, in the sense of a constraint or a limitation on behavioral choices, suggests that the past affects the present and, in a sense, exists in the present. Likewise, the present affects the future and exists, therefore, in the future. Kolaja's (1969) concept of the "two-layered present" helps clarify the complex relationship between past, present, and future times.

Kolaja points out that all time, whether past or present or future, extends during the present time. For example, the past "layers onto" the present in the sense of a past action that is relevant or similar to the present or when an event recurs. Present action oriented to a future goal, as in the ability of a self-regulating system to compare its present state with some future goal state and to make appropriate modifications in the present, exemplifies the future-to-present orientation. Though any event always occurs in the present, that event often contains elements of the past or future, too—the two-layered present.

But what of the nature of the present? Clearly, the present is a highly complex concept. For example, in terms of duration the present may be very brief—an instant—or very long—hours, days, or even years. The sentence "I am leaving town right away" could imply that the person is in an automobile on his way out of town at that very instant, or it could suggest that he is taking the first flight out of town in the morning or that he is in the process of selling his home and will leave within a few months. In such a manner, the present can be of varying lengths depending upon the perspective used to manipulate time, much like the human manipulation of a linguistic symbol.

Human experience in time is not like human experience in space, however. We tend to think of "objective" observation as actual sensory impressions. It is "real," we say, if we can touch it, see it, hear it, smell it, or taste it. But sensory data are almost exclusively oriented to spatial concepts—material objects. Humans have no sense to be used for time data. Such kinds of data are more susceptible to one's perspective and, of course, memory.

More than the five senses, human memory is relevant to time concepts. We cannot experience time without the influence and assistance of memory. But as Kolaja (1969, p. 10) points out, memory is not identical with time but serves as an "operator-on-time." Besides the fact that memory is selective (that is, only some experiences and, even then, only parts of experiences are retained by the human memory), memory does not operate on the present in any consistent manner. Although time is chronological, humans don't always recollect experiences chronologically. (Or even if they do, the chronological order is often construed.) Moreover, the memory organizes some experiences in different chronological order from the order in which they originally occurred—not necessarily in error, but in terms of similarity and difference among past experiences.

Nor is memory necessarily associated exclusively with the past. In fact, the only "pure" past is the absence of any recurrence—a unique event that is never repeated. Many events are recollected by the memory without any data of their occurrence. They then impinge upon the present in a sense of timelessness. We say, for example, that you never forget how to ride a bike. It is an experience that stays with you. In a similar sense we guide our behavior by some timeless moral or ethical principle, for example. That recollection is a principle that has no date, no notion of even being an event in the past experience. It is true for all time.

One final point about the pragmatic perspective's reconceptualization of time as a concept of greater complexity concerns the physical constancy of time. To say that one minute equals a constant sixty seconds, regardless of when it occurs, is accurate only in terms of the clock. But in the pragmatic perspective of human communication, time speeds up and slows down. Have a fifteen-minute conversation with a good friend, and time "flies," but have a fifteen-minute conversation with a social boor, and time "drags." As a communication system approaches its goal (for example, a decision-making group nearing consensus), time shortens; that is, it goes faster. But when the same group seems to be haggling over trivial issues and seemingly is not accomplishing anything, the time seems to be abominably slower. See also Brodey's (1969) discussion of "time-driving" and "time-graining."

Clearly, some of the expansion of time conceptualizations is a matter of perception—specifically, human perceptions of time (see Ornstein, 1969). As time is related solely to human perception, the concept is more closely aligned with a psychological rather than a pragmatic perspective of communication. But the time conceptualizations are observable within the sequences of human behaviors. The point is that time concepts (for example, multilayered presents, memory, and information time) are reflected in observable behaviors and can be revealed within functional categories of communicative behavior. To the extent that the time concept remains merely a matter of human perception (and thus internalized within the individual), it is of course less relevant to the pragmatic perspective. As reflected in functional categories and patterns or sequences of interaction, however, it is significant to the pragmatic view of communication.

The complex nature of time is a significant element within the pragmatic perspective of human communication. Kolaja's (1969) concept of recurrent behavior as a time dimension of the social system clearly illustrates this increased complexity in terms of information theory and system theory. In the sense that a number of different ways to conceptualize time increases, it follows that time is one of the indications of an open system's tendency toward increased complexity (that is, differentiation) as it continues to exist.

The conceptualization of time is much more demanding on the attempt to explicate a theory of communication within the pragmatic perspective, perhaps more demanding than any other single factor. The full implications of the increased complexity of time are not yet fully comprehended in the performance of contemporary communication research.

Interpersonal-Mass Communication

One of the distinct advantages of general system theory is its high level of abstraction, thus allowing its application to a wide variety of phenomena. In a field as diverse as human communication, the applicability of a systems perspective to communicative phenomena could allow the pragmatic perspective to serve as a framework within which various approaches to different fields of communication could be unified. One problem in the scientific community of human communication is the tendency to view communication at one sociological level as substantially different from communication at another. Specifically, some communication students and scholars view interpersonal and mass communication as fundamentally different, even though they allegedly share one characteristic in common—the phenomenon called human communication.

The tendency to partition communication into sociological levels—for example, intrapersonal, interpersonal, group, organizational, societal, or mass—should suggest the unifying potential of system theory. The hierarchical organization of systems is inherent within any pragmatic perspective—subsystem, system, and suprasystem. Thus, the pragmatic perspective should be equally applicable to any level of the hierarchy —depending upon the sociological level of greatest interest to the investigator. The concept of behavioral sequences and redundancy is generalizable to any level of the systemic hierarchy. Although a behavior in a two-person system may be an individual's verbal comment, a behavior at the level of society (that is, mass communication) may be more abstract, but it is a "behavior" nonetheless.

For example, an investigator of television networks may perceive the subsystems to be composed of network executives, FCC commissioners, station executives, media consumers, advertisers, and so on. A single behavior may not be an individual's verbalized comment; it may be a programming decision, an FCC order, a Neilsen rating, or some other behavior of one of the subsystems. The principle of recurrent or redundant behaviors forming a pattern should remain relevant.

The following model of human communication is explicated in terms of the interpersonal or group level rather than that of mass communication. There are basically two reasons for this choice. First, my major interest is interpersonal and group communication. Therefore, I choose to write about phenomena that are of most interest and relevance to me and about which I have more knowledge and understanding. Second, and more important, nearly all the scholarly inquiry into communicative phenomena within the pragmatic perspective has been conducted at the interpersonal and the group level. Mass phenomena and variables have not yet been defined or sufficiently developed to provide any discussion that could be more than speculative. Nevertheless, the implications of the pragmatic perspective, with its roots in general system theory, for an equivalent treatment of interpersonal and mass communication are so strong as to warrant this brief mention of the potential.

A PRAGMATIC MODEL

The pragmatic perspective clearly indicates the absurdity of equating a pictorial description with a communication model. Knowing full well that complexity of time rather than space is most relevant to a pragmatic perspective of human communication, I have included Figure 6 as a pictorial representation of communicative phenomena viewed from a pragmatic perspective. But though the interactional perspective was not well adapted to spatial concepts exemplified in a drawing, the pragmatic perspective is even less so. As I suggested in Part One, some perspectives are simply more susceptible to pictorial models than others.

In all honesty, the only reason Figure 6 is included in this chapter is to provide some symmetry to the chapters comprising Part Two—each perspective includes a pictorial representation at the outset of the chapter in which that perspective is discussed. Another possible reason for including Figure 6 is to satisfy the demands of some readers who expect a model to take the form of a drawing.

It may be pertinent at this point to distinguish further between concepts of space and time in order to illustrate the shortcomings of Figure 6. The concept of space includes three dimensions: height, width, and depth. If anyone is old enough to recall 3–D (three-dimensional) movies (you had to wear special glasses to view the screen), you should be able to recall the novel impression of depth (the third dimension) in the projected motion picture. That dimension simply was not present in other movies. New camera and projection lenses, along with other technological advances in cinematography, have eliminated the need

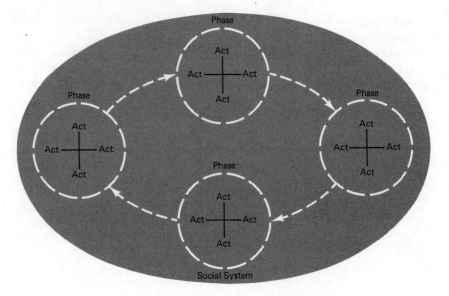

Figure 6. *A Pragmatic Model of Human Communication.*

for wearing special glasses for 3–D movies and suggest the visual perception of depth without them. Today the television picture remains "flat," that is, without perception of depth; and a sheet of paper or a page in a book on which a communication model would be represented is also "flat" (2–D) although depth can be suggested in a drawing.

Time, on the other hand, possesses only one dimension—sometimes called the "fourth dimension." And how can a 2–D drawing on a sheet of paper represent that fourth dimension of time? It simply cannot do so adequately. It can only suggest the time dimension. Figure 6, for example, includes dotted-line arrows connecting the dotted-circle phases. Those arrows are intended to suggest a progression of time moving from one phase to another. Moreover, the fact that, taken together, the dotted-line arrows connecting phases in time form a circle is meant to suggest that the chronological ordering of time is cyclical—the sequence of phases repeats itself.

These aspects of time included in Figure 6 are simply not readily apparent upon only observing the drawing. In fact, the drawing itself is rather meaningless until it is explained within a verbal format. Whoever first said, "A picture is worth a thousand words," was obviously referring exclusively to spatial concepts represented in a picture. When time concepts need to be comprehended, a few words are worth far more than a thousand pictures.

Typical Components

Communication in the pragmatic perspective begins with the behaviors of the persons involved in communication. The most fundamental unit of communication, then, is the *act*—a behavior or action performed verbally or nonverbally by a participant in the communicative event. Acts are then categorized into the various functions performed by communication. However, no single list of functional categories is widely accepted among members of the scientific community as *the* list of appropriate functions. Rather, a number of category systems exist that have typically reflected the investigator's unique interests and research purposes. Nonetheless, acts performed by communicants are classified into functional categories and are thus repeatable. Figure 6 illustrates four categories—an arbitrary number possessing no particular significance.

Because acts occur in a continuous chain of events, the sequentiality (Hawes' [1973] principle of "concateneity") of the acts becomes significant. Some act must precede every act, and some act follows every act; therefore, the more important analytical unit of a communication system is not the act but the *interact* or *double interact*. Every possible pair of acts by category (interacts) occurs at some level of probability; that is, given the occurrence of an instance of act-category #1, what is the probability of the occurrence of #2, #3, or #4? Perhaps investigation of past interaction indicates that #3 tended to follow #1 85 per cent of the time. Thus, the *transition probability* of the 1–3 interact is .85 —the expectation that #3 will occur, given the occurrence of #1.

Transition probabilities are determined for every possible interact or double interact in the period of interaction observed. The most redundant interacts and double interacts serve to characterize interaction as a "pattern." And the patterns (that is, redundancy or constraint) of the interaction that emerge from the observation make up the structure and function of the communication system. Understanding communication within the pragmatic perspective constitutes a search for interaction patterns.

Over time the pattern of interaction is susceptible to change. The communication system may modify the characteristic interaction patterns, and those changes are empirically recognizable through recording the changes in the redundant patterns of interacts and double interacts. Moving from one pattern of interaction to another characteristic pattern suggests that the communication system leaves one *phase* of interaction and enters another. (See Figure 6.) On a common-sense level, it should be reasonable that the ritualistic "small talk" of individuals during the beginning moments of a conversation is quite different from the kind of interaction among those same communicants some time later. The number of phases, of course, may vary considerably from one communicative situation to another. Figure 6 illustrates four phases for illustrative purposes—again an arbitrary number with no particular significance.

Some communication systems are ongoing systems that continue as a system for an extended period of time. Such systems include families, work groups, friends, and social clubs. Ongoing groups generally do not move continuously from one different phase to another, ad infinitum. More likely, they develop certain behavioral norms and patterns, including interaction patterns and phasic patterns, which tend to be reestablished over and over during the period of the system's history. In other words, the phases through which ongoing social systems evolve tend to repeat themselves in an ongoing *cycle*. Characteristic of ongoing communication systems, then, are interact patterns, phases, and cycles. Over a long period of time the specific characteristic pattern of the interaction and the phases may change, perhaps as a result of environmental changes or structural changes in the system as members enter and leave the system. But the conceptual distinctions of interacts, phases, and cycles (however they may be modified over a long period of evolutionary time) remain characteristic of ongoing communication systems. (See Fisher and Hawes [1971] and Lofland [1971].)

Figure 6 brackets the action patterns, phases, and cycles within the parameters of an identifiable social system; that is, a communication system is inherently a social system whose members serve to constrain and thereby define the system by their actions and subsequently patterns of interaction. It is in this sense of the social system and communication visualized as a sequence of events that Birdwhistell (1959, p. 104) says that an individual does not "do" communication. Rather, "he engages in or becomes part of communication"; that is, "he participates in it." Communication not only "takes place" in a social system; it serves to define the very nature and existence of the social system. The social system and the communication system are one and the same and may be used interchangeably. They are inseparable entities and should not be viewed as independent entities.

Naturally, all social systems are not alike. A family is not the same social system as a business work group. A jury is not the same social system as a neighborhood bridge club. But some social systems are very much alike, which suggests that scholarly inquiry into communicative phenomena would benefit from the development of a morphological classification of social systems, that is, communication systems. I (1975, p. 203) have previously called for the development of a morphology of social systems and have even participated in attempting to develop such a classificatory scheme (Werbel, Ellis, and Fisher, 1974) based on

Laszlo's (1972a, p. 47) suggestion that "the strategic level of the next higher suprasystem be chosen for clear conceptual grasp." Until further empirical investigation validates this or any other scheme for classifying social systems, however, any further discussion of the point would be only speculative. Under any circumstances, however, communication exists within the parameters of a social system and, through the interaction patterns of members of that system, serves to define the system—its structure, its function, and its evolution.

Locus—Sequential Behaviors

The next few paragraphs appear to be highly redundant. Even the most casual reader of this chapter should be aware by this time that the locus of communication in the pragmatic perspective is clearly the behaviors, the actions, performed by the individuals who are members of a communication system. We must be careful, however, not to conceptualize any communicative act in isolation. Without its place in the whole system, that is, in the redundant sequence or pattern of interaction, the act itself is relatively trivial and meaningless. Only when the sequence is reestablished by its level of probable recurrence (its pattern of repeated communicative functions) does the act become significant to the system and serve to constrain or define the system. A behavior in isolation is, within the pragmatic perspective, quite uninterpretable.

Recalling Birdwhistell's notion that communication is not something that someone "does" but an event or system in which one "participates" or "becomes a part of," the locus of communication in the sequence of behaviors should be rather clear. Information theory stipulates that redundancy is constraint (of choices), and constraint is structure. And structure is orderly organization—negentropy. The more redundancy or structure, the more stability is possessed by the system, and the more the system is capable of resisting deterioration or destruction. But that is true only up to a point.

I hasten to point out, however, that too much structure can be as harmful to the social system as too little. The more structured the system, the less capable is the system of adapting to environmental changes, for example, a bureaucratic organization. Another example is the stultifying redundancy of behavioral patterning of the assembly-line work group in a factory. Kolaja (1969, p. 76) points out that such an overwhelming amount of redundancy breeds monotony and tends to become "humanly meaningless." It "leads to the deterioration of the social relationship." Kolaja goes on to state the obvious—that the problem of how much redundancy or pattern is an optimal amount has never been solved, even theoretically. Indeed, the optimal amount of patterning may vary from one type of social system to another.

Remember, lest you be hypercritical prematurely, the pragmatic perspective is very new and has not yet answered all the questions. But a symptom of its vitality is the plethora of questions it has raised in true heuristic fashion; that is, the pragmatists within the scientific community of communication don't have answers for all their questions, but they do have a good idea of what questions should be asked.

SELECTED AREAS OF RESEARCH

Scholarly research from a pragmatic perspective is incredibly recent. Nearly all published research has appeared in the last decade, and the research has been performed almost exclusively in the interpersonal-group setting. Conducting such research is a rather tedious process of coding literally thousands of human behaviors or actions into categories and then analyzing the matricized data. Tom Scheidel emphasized the tedium of such research when he once remarked that interaction analysis is a valuable research technique, which is utilized by many communication investigators—once!

But the purpose of this section is not to point out the complexities and difficulties of research techniques. Nor is the purpose to summarize the findings of research conducted within the perspective. Rather, this section shall seek to organize areas of pragmatic investigation of communicative phenomena into major trends or areas in which members of this scientific community of human communication have conducted research. These trends reflect some selected areas or research purposes that investigators have utilized in conducting their inquiry.

Behavioral Categories

To repeat from an earlier discussion, a single list of categories documenting the functions performed by communicative behaviors does not characterize the research performed within the pragmatic perspective of human communication. Although the development of a communication theory of any generality would probably require more agreement on a list of behavioral functions, the analytical categories used thus far have tended to reflect the specific research purposes and interests of the investigators who use the categories.

But the proliferation of category systems does not necessarily imply that any of the lists of categories is irrelevant, insignificant or inappropriate. Beer (1966, p. 243) suggests that, in attempting to understand the internal workings of a system, "we select, from an infinite number of relations between things, a set which, because of coherence and pattern and purpose, permits an interpretation of what might otherwise be a meaningless cavalcade of arbitrary events." When the categories permit the investigator to interpret the operation of the communication system, they cannot be considered either insignificant, irrelevant, or inappropriate; but, of course, the interpretations will differ as a function of the categories used to classify behaviors. This variability among interpretations unfortunately restricts clear-cut comparisons and tends to limit their generalizability.

Though some communication research has proceeded from category systems developed outside the discipline of human communication and has utilized categories developed by Bales (1950) or Morris and Hackman (1969), the bulk of the category systems used have been developed by the investigator for specific purposes. Moreover, the bulk of communication research has attempted to analyze "content" functions, although "relationship" functions of communication are becoming more popular among members of the scientific community.

Analytical categories of content functions have emphasized many popular functions long attributed to communication. Such functions include those of feedback (for example, Leathers, 1971), idea development (for example, Scheidel and Crowell, 1964), systemic maintenance (for example, Hawes and Foley, 1973), decision making (for example, Fisher, 1970), theme development (for example, Berg, 1967), conflict management (for example, Ellis and Fisher, 1975), and social information processing (Fisher, Drecksel, and Werbel, 1978). The categories vary widely in the operational definition of a single behavioral unit as well as in the sophistication with which the data are analyzed. But they all proceed from the assumptions attributable to the pragmatic perspective of human communication.

Category systems analyzing the relationship functions of human communication typically define relationship functions according to the functions of relationship communication formulated by a psychiatrist (Bateson, 1958). Bateson visualizes the relationship dimension of communication as quasi-status functions of one-up (attempt to dominate), one-down (attempt to be submissive), and one-across (attempt to be equivalent). Thus, an interact may reflect a symmetrical relationship (for example, competitive or equivalent) or a complementary relationship (dominant-submissive) between interacting pairs of individuals (see Sluzki and Beavin, 1965). But though communication researchers conceptualize a common view of complementary and symmetrical relationship interaction, the operational definitions used to apply these functions to communicative behaviors vary widely. (See, for example, Rogers and Farace [1975] and Ellis [1976].)

Social Settings

Typical communication research conducted within the pragmatic perspective has observed the social systems of either dyads or groups. The nature of the dyads and groups also shows some variety in the selection of social systems. For example, Hawes (1972) observed communication within the social setting of a medical interview between physician and patient. Rogers (see, for example, Millar and Rogers, 1976) and her colleagues, studying relationship communication, have observed marital pairs—husband-wife dyads.

Group systems selected for observation exhibit an even greater variety. Because most scholarly research is conducted in academic settings, many groups selected for observation have been composed of ad hoc groups manufactured from classroom students (for example, Gouran and Baird [1972], Ellis and Fisher [1975], and Stech [1975]). Other groups observed have included decision-making groups in a variety of field settings (for example, Fisher [1970] and Larson [1971]) but have also included groups as diverse as two-generational family units (for example, Glover, 1974), health care delivery teams (for example, Thornton, 1976), juries, and so on.

Although some principles from general system theory have been widely applied to communication research in organizational settings, those principles have not clearly or consistently reflected the pragmatic perspective and its locus of communication in sequential behavioral patterns. The organizational setting, with its inherent hierarchy of subsystems, should be a veritable breeding ground for communication research guided by the principles of the pragmatic perspective. Much research of this kind will probably be produced by organizational communication scholars in the years ahead.

Phases of Group Development

The area of progressive group development has long been a popular and fruitful area of research within the field of social psychology. It should come as no surprise that communication scholars should also focus their efforts in this area. The typical difference between social psychological research into phases of group development and similar communication research is the analysis of data and characterization of the phases by interaction patterns. Although social psychologists, Bales and Strodtbeck (1951) being a notable exception, tend to characterize the phases of group development by tracing changes of cognitive and affective variables of group members, pragmatic communication research utilizes changing patterns of interactive behaviors as the fundamental basis for differentiating among the phases.

From Scheidel and Crowell's (1964) description of a "spiral process" of idea development during group interaction, communication research into group development has proceeded to the discovery of phases of decision making (Fisher, 1970) and conflict management (Ellis and Fisher, 1975). Mabry (1975) has recently attempted to explicate a model of group development with much greater generality. As research techniques and statistics for analyzing sequential interaction data become more refined and familiar, communication research into group development should yield even more fruitful results in programmatic research.

Miscellanea

The pragmatic perspective could well be applied to other areas within the discipline of human communication. But the very "newness" of the perspective would tend to suggest that developing trends of research are simply not yet well formulated. However, several recently published articles provide new and different directions for pragmatic communication research. Bloom (1975) proceeds to take a broader perspective of pragmatism as a general philosophical stance or a critical perspective for assessing communicative experiences as well as a perspective for performing disciplinary research. Though his essay is more of a "think piece" than a report of research, his viewpoint is provocative and applicable to a wide range of research in communication, including critical research methods.

Beale (1975) reflects a pragmatic perspective for viewing the internalized phenomenon of "intent." His perspective is blunted by numerous mechanistic assumptions within his communication "model" and his categories, and his implicit research techniques are relatively unsophisticated, but he does exhibit one way of relating internalized communicative phenomena to externalized communicative behaviors. Such research is undoubtedly a trend of the future and should serve to wed several of the principal perspectives currently employed in the study of human communication.

SUMMARY

The pragmatic perspective of human communication is, among the four perspectives described in Part Two, the most different in terms of its philosophical origins and fundamental underlying assumptions. It appears an alternative to, principally, the mechanistic and psychological perspectives with its focus on ongoing behavioral sequences within the philosophical and methodological environs of general system theory and information theory. Its emphasis on the ongoing sequences of interaction constraining and serving to define the social system is a departure from the interactional perspective's emphasis on internalized role taking. However, the emphasis on interactive behaviors, although the explanation for their occurrence differs, is a common emphasis of both the pragmatic and interactional perspectives.

Fundamental to any serious study of human communication within the pragmatic perspective is a list of categories that represent the functions performed by human communication and that allow a communicative action to be repeated at different points in time. A next step in understanding human communication is the organization of the ongoing sequence into characteristic groups so that the events "fit" together within an interpretable pattern. The sequences are punctuated by virtue of the constraints they place on interactive choices; that is, the more redundant the sequences, the more structure is exhibited by the interaction pattern (and thus the social system of communication).

Research within the pragmatic perspective is incredibly recent and, as yet, rather sparse. The bulk of the research concentrates on the interpersonal and group settings, although the perspective of different levels of generality of systems suggests that the perspective should be applicable to any systemic level, including organizational and mass communication. Pragmatic research into human communication reflects a proliferation of category systems for analyzing communicative functions and reflects the specific and unique interests of each investigator rather than a clear-cut paradigmatic inquiry into communicative phenomena performed by a substantial portion of the scientific community.

The pragmatic perspective of human communication is clearly in a growth pattern of continuing theoretical and empirical development. As a body, the perspective reflects the most recent trend in the study of human communication. Though mechanism and psychology probably represent the mainstream of popular thought among members of the scientific community, a thorough understanding of the phenomena of human communication requires an understanding of an appreciation for the interactional and pragmatic perspectives as well.

To conceptualize communication from the pragmatic perspective is to revise drastically one's original thought patterns about communication. For example, conceptualizing communication as "doing" something (such as sending or receiving a message, expressing an attitude, or perceiving an object) is rather familiar and quite consistent with our conventional thinking about the communication process. But to conceptualize communication as an act of "participation" or "entering" a communication system or relationship requires a "flip-flop" of our traditional modes of intellectualizing. However, the ability to reorganize our thinking and to utilize multiple perspectives is the mark of an educated person, and the ability to conceptualize, including the ability to re-conceptualize, is a symptom of increased understanding.

Part Two Miscellanea

After the discussion of the four major perspectives of human communication, several observations seem appropriate. At the outset, I suggested that the basis used to analyze scholarly inquiry into communication is somewhat arbitrary. One might choose perspectives, for example, on the basis of the structure or syntactical variations of theoretical perspectives, including such potential categories as axiomatic theory, rules-based theory, or taxonomic theory. The basis chosen for this volume is more epistemological, emerging from similarities among scholars in how they choose to explain and observe the actual phenomena of human communication.

The perspectives of mechanism, psychologism, interactionism, and pragmatism, thus represent only one approach to analyzing the field of human communication. Generally speaking, the various content-free structural variations of theory (for example, axioms or laws, rules, and even general system theory) could be applied within any or all of the four perspectives discussed in Part Two. Of course, the degree of appropriateness to any specific perspective might vary somewhat.

I cannot overemphasize the importance of interpreting these perspectives as unique to the field of communication. Although the philosophical assumptions underlying each perspective can be traced back to other disciplines, there is no implication intended that the principles of those assumptions directly govern the conducting of communication inquiry. Nor do communication scholars in a particular perspective have any specific or extensive background in the philosophical tradition. When I label a particular communication inquiry consistent with a mechanistic or interactional perspective, I do not mean to imply that the investigator is knowledgeable in either Laplacian physics or symbolic interactionism. Nor is the particular study absolutely consistent with a strict interpretation of its physical or its sociological origins. That is simply not the point.

Each perspective appears to be conceptually grounded in a philosophical tradition. But when communicologists have applied that tradition to inquiry into communicative phenomena, the perspective then becomes relatively independent of its philosophical basis. The perspectives should thus be interpreted as paradigms of communication and not as "pure" theories borrowed intact from other disciplines.

COMBINATIONS OF PERSPECTIVES

I suggested earlier that the four perspectives are clearly not mutually exclusive categories. Communication scholars frequently combine elements of several perspectives and utilize this combination to view the process of communication. The most frequently occurring combination is undoubtedly that of psychologism and mechanism. Indeed, the mechanistic-psychological perspective is clearly the most popular approach to communication overall. It could probably claim the allegiance of a considerable majority of scholars who would consider themselves to be within the scientific community of communication.

One clear-cut instance of combining the psychological and mechanistic perspectives of communication is the recently popular research into ethos—source/communicator credibility. In Part One we discussed the change in correspondence rules in applying the theoretical term to empirical observation, that is, a change in where to look for the phenomenon of credibility—as actual characteristics "possessed" by the source or as source characteristics that are "perceived" by the receiver. With the perspectives fresh in mind, that discussion can now be more explicit.

To conceptualize credibility as source characteristics perceived by the receiver is to view the concept psychologically in the receiver-as-active-interpreter effects paradigm. In a mechanistic conceptualization, credibility "originates" with the source and is "transmitted" to the receiver over a channel. But in a psychological perspective, credibility exists only when the active interpreter selects appropriate stimuli and organizes them into an image of credibility as assessed by the conceptual filters.

Mortensen (1972, p. 143) exemplifies the combined perspectives when he argues against conceptualizing credibility exclusively within any single one of the two perspectives. "Rather," he points out, "we should think of credibility as a result of the interaction between source-related attributes and perceived attributes that are held by receivers." Mortensen thus opts for a combination of mechanistic and psychological perspectives in viewing credibility.

The interactional and pragmatic perspectives have also been combined in communication inquiry. Some scholars (see, for example, Hawes, 1972) have advocated the desirability, if not the necessity, of using stimulated recall in order to develop and validate the pragmatic categories of communicative behavior. Stimulated recall is a technique used, in this context, to interview the subjects or social actors after having observed their behavior. Before pragmatically analyzing the behaviors, however, the investigator might play a video tape of the social actor's behavior, stop the tape, and ask the subject to describe her own behavior. The descriptive categories of the pragmatic analysis of communicative functions thus arise out of and are validated by these stimulated-recall interviews, that is, by the social actor herself.

The application of the categories to analyze communicative behaviors remains quite consistent with a pragmatic perspective, but the means and philosophy of validating and developing those categories is clearly within the interactional perspective. The emphasis is on the social actor as an individual role taker.

These are but two instances of the use of combined perspectives in human communication. Part Two has discussed each perspective as relatively isolated from the others, but this discussion should not be interpreted as implying that each perspective is unique. In fact, I suspect that most instances of scholarly inquiry into communication employ some combination of perspectives. I would also contend that the investigator, to be most productive, should be aware of using a combination of perspectives and consciously guard against inconsistent or incongruent combinations. Prerequisite to any theoretical development of communication is a profound awareness of the theoretical perspectives available and being employed.

OTHER MISCELLANEOUS "PERSPECTIVES"

The four perspectives of mechanism, psychologism, interactionism, and pragmatism are not the only perspectives that might have been included in this volume. I have consciously omitted other possible candidates for perspectives for several reasons. The minor perspectives may not be so pervasive or as visible as the four perspectives that were discussed. Only a small portion of the scientific community may be using those perspectives. Then, too, the minor perspectives are rarely as fully developed theoretically and consequently have not generated sufficient or significant empirical observations. The primary reason for omitting some of the minor perspectives is their restricted scope. Some minor perspectives deal with only a small portion of the communicative process and cannot be used to explain or take into account the bulk of communicative phenomena.

Ecology

An ecological or contextual perspective of human communication is consistent with a definition of communication as the process of an organism's adaptation to an environment. Such a perspective is evident in the studies of group ecology that hypothesize that contextual elements affect group interaction (for example, Sommer [1969] and Pendell [1976]). Such studies assume that interaction is maximized across a corner of a table, that leaders tend to choose the seat at the head of a rectangular table, that room design and decoration influence the communication process.

An ecological perspective may be more assumptive than actual. Some studies on territoriality or crowding (proxemic, that is, spatial, variables of context) conducted on nonhuman species have suggested an ecological impact on behavior. The results of similar studies on humans have failed to yield consistent results. Moreover, the alleged effects on communication are often superficial aspects of communication (for example, amount or number of transceived messages). For such reasons, an ecological perspective was not deemed as significant as the four major perspectives.

Dramatism

More influential and popular than an ecological view is the impact of dramatism on communication. In actuality, dramatism is more analogical than theoretical. The dramatistic model places individual and social behavior within a dramatic analogue characterizing social actors on a real-life "stage." One dramatist, Erving Goffman (1959, 1963, 1967), views expressive behavior as a presentation of self to public view in an attempt to portray a "role" or "character" as a manipulated self.

Nonpublic behavior is "behind the scenes" and quite different from that in public presentation.

The foremost exponent of dramatism, Kenneth Burke (1946, 1950, 1967), views social behavior as interactions or ratios between five dramatistic elements (act, scene, agent, agency, purpose) or the use of symbolic strategies in manipulating language. The emphases on strategies and on viewing the communicator as a social "actor" are remarkably similar in Goffman's and Burke's writings, even though one is a sociologist and the other a literary critic.

As a model or analogy of organizing communication, dramatism is extremely heuristic, rich in potential ideas generated. Burke's writings have often been used, however appropriately or innovatively, as a source for critical methodologies. However, as an overall conceptual and theoretical explanation of communicative behavior, a dramatistic perspective is too restricted. The model is intriguing but not highly explanatory.

McLuhanism

When I was told recently that today's generation of college students had probably not even heard of Marshall McLuhan, I was immediately skeptical. I confidently inquired in one of my classes about the students' familiarity with McLuhanism—either the person or the ideas. I am still astonished at their reaction. Although quite a few students were familiar with the catchphrase, "The medium is the message," only three members of the class admitted to any familiarity with the name Marshall McLuhan.

My surprise does not stem necessarily from the mandatory significance of McLuhan's ideas (for example, 1962, 1964), but because of the immense popularity (both academic and nonacademic) that McLuhan enjoyed only a single decade ago. Throughout the 1960s vast numbers of people were mouthing the clichés of what came to be known as McLuhanism: "The medium is the message" (Later "the massage"), "hot and cold media," the world as a "global village." McLuhan dealt innovatively, often ingeniously, with the covert effects and implications of the mass media on our mass society. On the societal level he visualized the new communication technologies as extensions of our five senses. Though not outwardly manipulative, the electronic mass media were characterized as image-provoking and image-producing subliminal agents.

Perhaps not so strangely, the immense popularity of McLuhan generated more how-about-that discussions than solid empirical inquiry. McLuhanism became known more for its pithy and jingoistic phrases than for any fresh insight into mass communication. The fact that contemporary students of communication are only vaguely conversant with McLuhan's ideas is testimony to the failure of McLuhanism to exert a significant impact upon communication as a field of scholarly inquiry. The contribution of McLuhanism remains unclear today and certainly insufficient to discuss comprehensively as a major perspective guiding communication inquiry.

Balance Theories/Models

A number of models to explain individual cognitions or behaviors through some balance principle have arisen in psychology over the past several decades. Such models include those of cognitive dissonance, congruity, equity, consistency, symmetry, among many others. Though differences among these models are discernible, they are also quite similar philosophically in that all are characterized by a closed-system assumption of a balance principle; that is, the model conceptualizes the existence of sets of opposing forces that create psychological discomfort when they are in a state of imbalance.

The typical mode of resolving this dilemma or feeling of discomfort caused by out-of-balance forces is to initiate a step toward restoring balance—either a maximization or equilibrium principle. A maximization principle would stress the positive and negative values (for example, costs and rewards) of the opposing forces within an economic model that strives to maximize the positively valued elements. A maximization principle is typical of such balance models as "social exchange" (See, for example, Thibaut and Kelley, 1959) or behavioral decision theory (see, for example, Edwards and Tversky, 1967).

An equilibrium principle, on the other hand, would stress the need to equalize the opposing forces. The latter principle would not conceptualize good-versus-bad forces necessarily but, rather, forces in opposition that need to be equilibrated. Such a principle is similar to the entropy-negentropy equilibrium of a closed system, which was discussed earlier in Part Two. The equilibrium principle strives to achieve a state of homeostasis (an equilibrium point of stability). Nonequilibrium is inherently unstable.

Newcomb's (1953) A–B–X model for studying communicative acts provides the most directly relevant example of a balance-model approach to communication. Newcomb suggests that two persons (A and B) have a positively or negatively valued orientation to each other as well as to a common object of reference (X). Newcomb goes on to suggest that his triangular orientation of A and B to each other and to X needs to be equilibrated to reflect a state of "symmetry" (for example, A and B positively oriented to each other and with equivalent orientation, either both positive or both negative, to X). A state of asymmetry might reflect a positive orientation to each other but differing orientations toward X. The state of asymmetry or disequilibrium would result in a feeling of discomfort and a "strain toward symmetry"—the equilibrium principle.

Balance models applied to communicative phenomena have typically been borrowed from psychology. They thus reflect a clearly psychological emphasis on internalized cognitions or assessments. Strictly speaking, they are of limited usefulness as a broad explanatory framework within which communication scholars could develop a comprehensive theoretical perspective of the process of communication. Their adaptation to communication has been fairly well restricted to communication research in persuasion, serving to explain attitude change or postdecision (that is, equilibrated conflict of opposing forces) behavior within a psychological perspective. As a candidate for a more complete perspective of human communication, any of the balance models (including Newcomb's A–B–X model) is of limited scope and theoretical utility.

THE INFLUENCE OF PERSPECTIVES

We have pointed out constantly throughout the preceding chapters that one's perspective clearly guides and virtually dictates the observation and understanding of communicative phenomena. It not only directs the investigator where to look for those phenomena significant to communication but restricts what will actually be observed and what won't be observed during the act of observing. Some may interpret the perspective as a methodology of inquiry. It clearly is not. Nor is a particular methodology unique to or even most appropriate for any perspective. In fact, any research methodology should be appropriate within any of the four perspectives, depending only upon the nature of the specific research question asked—not the philosophical perspective itself.

Lofland's (1971) distinction between quantitative and qualitative research may again be helpful in distinguishing the difference between research questions and perspectives. Quantitative research questions, you will recall, are directed at discerning the "causes" or the "consequences" of phenomena, that is, cause-effect relationships between phenomena; and qualitative research questions seek to discover the "characteristics" of phenomena. Both quantitative and qualitative research can be conducted within any and all of the four major perspectives.

Some specific methods, however, are not especially appropriate to one or another of the quantitative-qualitative research questions. On the other hand, some methods and techniques are equally applicable to both types of questions. For example, a critical method that applies justified criteria to observed phenomena in order to assess those phenomena along some dimension or combination of dimensions might appropriately be employed to discover cause-effect relationships or to describe phenomenal characteristics. However, an experimental method that controls or manipulates predesignated characteristics in order to assess the impact of one or a combination of characteristics (variables) on another or combination of other characteristics, is ill-adapted to qualitative research questions. The primary, if not sole, value of the experimental method lies with quantitative research issues.

Other techniques (for example, sociometry, interaction analysis, scalar techniques, participant observation, hermeneutics, ethnomethodology, conversation analysis, and context analysis) are appropriate to either quantitative or qualitative questions, depending upon their use in a specific study. The only valid question regarding which research method or technique to use in any study is its appropriateness to the question being asked at that particular time. Although some methods are often associated with one of the perspectives, the theoretical perspective guiding the study does not dictate which methodology can be employed.

The perspective does exert maximal influence on the potential accumulation of knowledge regarding the communicative process. Programmatic research that unites a series of studies in order to provide a richer and more comprehensive explanation of a broader range of communicative phenomena is possible only when oriented to conceptual issues broader than the study itself, that is, more comprehensive than merely those variables chosen to be included in the study. In other words, programmatic research must be conducted consistently within the same perspective or combination of perspectives. Skipping willy-nilly from one perspective to another while performing research will not generate a genuine accumulation of research findings. It will result, at best, in a mere multiplication of similar research findings.

But the principal influence of perspectives is that they define and thus direct one's understanding of the concepts of communication. One way of stating this influence is to say that different perspectives provide different interpretations of the concepts. But the influence is more significant and pervasive than that. A perspective constrains and defines the nature and even the very existence of any given concept. A perspective restricts one from interpreting the concept in any other way, and a perspective may not even account for the existence of a given concept. For example, what or where is the concept *channel* in either the interactional or pragmatic perspective? Any answer to that question is, at best, a rationalization. Nevertheless, channel is central and absolutely essential within a mechanistic perspective.

Consider the view of a table from a vantage point directly above the table. The vertical visual perspective does not simply interpret differently the table's characteristic of "height"; it does not even allow the observer to conceptualize the existence of such a characteristic. Only a horizontal visual perspective allows one to be able to interpret this physical concept. An identical analogical principle holds for philosophical or theoretical perspectives as well. Each perspective does not merely provide for a different interpretation of some concept. The use of a perspective actually "creates" each concept. Although a concept with the same label (for example, meaning, feedback, or message) may be present in several perspectives, the perspective creates that concept within it and defines it accordingly. It is in this sense that perspectives allow for different interpretations of the same concept as well as create different concepts relatively unique to that perspective, and it is in this sense that none of the interpretations of concepts can possibly be "wrong." They are all "correct," each within its own perspective. This influence of perspective on understanding communication is the subject of Part Three.

CONCEPTUAL IMPLICATIONS

Introduction to Part Three

Scheflen (1974, p. 197) said it all: "...the epistemology we employ in approaching any event will make a great difference in the kinds of answers and meanings we deduce." In a very real sense, the perspective used to view human communication is an epistemology—a scientific or theoretical or paradigmatic epistemology, but an epistemology nonetheless. To paraphrase Scheflen in order to relate specifically to our purposes, we can then make the following statement. The perspective we employ in approaching a communicative event will make a great difference in the kinds of answers and meanings we deduce. Part Three attempts to illustrate those differences directly attributable and naturally consequential to the epistemological choice of perspective.

Some historians have suggested that many contemporaries of Christopher Columbus considered him a failure because he failed to find a westerly trade route to the Far East. Certainly, Seward was considered to be committing a "folly" when he arranged the purchase of Alaska. Seward's critics looked for and found frozen desolate wastes in that forbidden territory. They were not looking for vast mineral deposits or a natural wildlife habitat, for example, and sure enough—they didn't find them.

I also recall one of my undergraduate instructors in a class about the American novel who explained to the class that a realistic novel we were assigned to read was written by the author intentionally and expressly to avoid any trace of symbolism—a characteristic of romanticism. But he blatantly instructed us to look for symbolism in that novel, and he lectured us that we should be able to discover it. And he was right!

The point is simply this. You bring to an event a certain way of looking at that event—a perspective. From the vantage point of your perspective, you will see that event as a certain kind of event with certain kinds of properties. These are the categories or the analytical tools that you use to observe the event. They are much like a pair of spectacles that direct your eyes to observe certain elements which, by definition, means that you ignore other elements and classifications.

Your perspective will prompt, even dictate, the kinds of questions you are able to ask, and your answers will be based on those questions. To say that the perspective used to view that event leads you to different answers is to state only part of the epistemology. Your perspective leads you to ask different questions. You will be likely to find answers only to questions that you ask. In other words, questions unasked are typically questions unanswered. Moreover, your perspective allows you to be aware of only what you know or can know. You won't even be aware of what you don't know.

If this is confusing thus far, consider how confused I was when I first read Walt Whitman's poem "When Lilacs Last in the Dooryard Bloomed." I read it "cold" as a high school student and, being something of an aesthetic "clod," I didn't care much for the rambling and apparently nonsensical poem about the deteriorating glory of nature. When the instructor told us to read the poem as a poetic reaction to the death of Abraham Lincoln, Whitman's verse suddenly took on new meaning as a lament for and praise for the dead American president. In my first reading I had simply skipped over the references to "coffin" and thought that a line such as "O how shall I warble myself for the dead one there I loved?" was some oblique reference to a dead relative—or maybe Mother Nature. And "O powerful western fallen star!" might have been initially some adolescent's overreaction to a meteor glimpsed in the night. The point should be obvious by now that the perspective that you bring to an experience guides your understanding of that event, and changing your perspective of that event inevitably modifies your understanding of that event.

It is important to note that your perspective always precedes your observation; that is, you can observe an event with the openest of minds, but you must inevitably observe that event *in some way*. When you view an optical illusion such as the familiar figures of two faces or a vase, the young girl or the old hag, the stairs that go up or down, and so on, you first see one interpretation or the other. You do not see both at once. You can study the figure, change your visual orientation, and eventually see the other image. With a little experience, you can change perspectives at will and watch the figure snap back and forth from one image to the other.

That visual experience of the optical illusion is analogous to viewing human communication. You can observe the same communicative event as an exchange of messages (mechanistic) or as a redundant pattern of interaction (pragmatic) and even go so far as to switch back and forth between the two perspectives. If you can master that feat, which amounts to changing your epistemological view of scholarly inquiry, you will have taken one giant step toward increased tolerance for multiple theoretical perspectives.

But that does not mean to imply that you have necessarily gained in understanding of the process of human communication merely because you can use more than one perspective. In fact, the student of human communication who flits back and forth between perspectives—between epistemologies—is probably either totally confused, undecided, or quite naïve. It is possible, of course, to maintain a perspective that combines elements of several perspectives and that constitutes a single perspective —hybrid though it may be. But the true student has a perspective because it maximizes his understanding—not merely because it happens to be convenient at a particular time. Furthermore, maintaining a perspective necessarily implies being consistent with that perspective, taking it where it leads, and understanding fully its heuristic implications—both good and bad.

This, then, is the purpose of Part Three. Given a perspective for viewing human communication, where does it lead? What are its implications for viewing communicative phenomena? Part Three is organized around specific concepts—concepts that typify and pervade the vast bulk of the literature in human communication. Some of these concepts are most relevant or significant to only a few of the perspectives. Most of the concepts are utilized in all the perspectives; but how they are used, how they are interpreted, how they function, and what they look like may vary significantly from one perspective to another. The purpose of Part Three is to illustrate those variations and understand each concept as it is applicable within a given perspective.

Interestingly enough, the concept itself typically retains the same theoretical term in each of the perspectives, but merely because the term is the same does not imply that the concept is theoretically similar in the different theoretical explanations. In other words, the variations in the concept across the boundaries of the perspectives are not simply the variations in correspondence rules used to operationalize the concept (although correspondence rules typically vary, too). The theoretical term itself, its conceptual definition, its place in the theory or the perspective varies significantly from one perspective to another.

Thus, for example, the operationalization of the concept of meaning may vary from one perspective to another. But more importantly, the meaning of the concept of meaning also varies. Furthermore, the meaning of the concept of "shared" meaning depends on the perspective's meaning of meaning. It, too, varies. Only the term itself (the word *meaning*) is constant across the four perspectives. What it means, conceptually and operationally, is variable and dependent upon the perspective used to view the entire process of human communication.

Lest anyone should get the wrong impression, Part Three provides no definitive answers as to which is the "proper" or the "true" utilization of any concept—for the simple reason that there are no definitive answers. Remember Scheflen's point that your epistemology leads you to the meanings and answers you deduce. Each perspective is "true" and "proper" as an epistemological approach to human communication. Therefore, the only question to ask is whether the concept is used appropriately or consistently or compatibly within that perspective.

Part Three, then, does not offer conclusions. It offers only the realization that the meaning, the significance, the relevance, and in some cases even the very existence of a concept are functions of the perspective within which it is defined and conceptualized.

– 8 –

The Concept of Meaning

One of my personal pet peeves is the statement that goes something like "Oh, it's just a problem of semantics." Use of such a statement is generally intended to suggest that the disagreement or confusion in the communicative situation is "merely" one of having different meanings—a matter of differing interpretations, just a simple case of misunderstanding. Furthermore, such a statement implies that the communicational problem is consequently quite trivial because it is based on just "semantics." That is why the hairs on the back of my neck stand on end whenever I hear such a statement—not because I disagree that the problem may be one of differing meanings, that is, misunderstanding, but because someone would be so naïve as to believe that the communicational problem of differing meanings is trivial!

More than forty years ago, I. A. Richards (1936, p. 3) wrote that the scope and purpose of rhetoric (that is, communication) should be "a study of misunderstanding and its remedies." A study of misunderstanding certainly does not imply necessarily a search to discover the communicational faults of the communicators and then to devise ways to correct those personal faults. Quite the contrary is the case; misunderstanding is a typical and quite normal phenomenon—perhaps even characteristic of all human communication. Misunderstanding is thus not a "fault" attributable to someone who is doing something "wrong" during a communicative event, but it is a typical problem that is extremely serious and that needs to be dealt with directly—managed by communicators within and during the process of human communication. In other words, misunderstanding is not a "failure" of one communicator to "understand" the "real" meaning, but a problem of differing meanings held by the participants in a communicative situation.

The concept of meaning is not limited to the field of communication. It is a "domain" of inquiry that slices across numerous academic disciplines and scientific communities—philosophy, linguistics, psychology, sociology, English, anthropology, among others. That is to say, the study of the concept of meaning does not necessarily involve a study of human communication, for meaning may exist with or without the existence of communication. But where there is communication, there is also meaning. Meaning is thus not unique to human communication, but it is inherent within the process of communication. To study meaning is not necessarily to study communication, but to study communication necessarily involves a study of meaning.

MEANINGS OF MEANING

Meaning is an abstract concept, which has fascinated philosophers and social theorists for the past 2,000 years. Since Plato conceptualized human meaning as a facsimile of an "ultrareality," great thinkers have plied the concept with a multitude of interpretations ranging from Locke's mental representations to Skinner's elicited responses. "But," as Jerold Katz (1973, p. 37) has pointed out, "every attempt to give a direct answer has failed. Some, such as the Platonic answer, proved too vague and speculative. Others gave the wrong answer." A direct definition of the concept of meaning is probably out of the question. We are left with differing interpretations of meaning, often in the form of correspondence rules or operational definitions, rather than a clear consensus on the nature of the concept of meaning.

Book titles such as *The Meaning of Meaning* and *Understanding Understanding* are rather provocative but tend to promise more than they deliver. Perhaps some reason for the conceptual confusion over meaning is the prevalent tendency to think of meaning as a unitary concept. Brodbeck (1963) suggests, for example, that there are actually three different notions of the concept of meaning. One type of meaning, according to Brodbeck's typology, is *referential* meaning; that is, the meaning of the term is the object, thought, idea, or concept to which the term "refers." This variety of meaning is similar to Morris's (1946) "semantic" aspect of language—symbol-to-referent relationship.

Brodbeck's second type of meaning implies the *significance* of the term. In other words, a symbol or term is "meaningful" to the extent that it is "lawfully connected" to other terms, other concepts. A term may have a referential meaning in the first sense that it has a referent, but because it is not related to numerous other concepts, it is not meaningful (the second type of meaning). Phlogiston, for example, "means" the concept of the substance possessed by flammable objects and serves to explain the process of combustion. However, since the discovery of oxygen, the concept of phlogiston is no longer "meaningful" within the current explanation of combustion; that is, the term is no longer related to many other terms in the theory of combustion.

Brodbeck's third type of meaning involves *intentional* meaning in the sense that the meaning of a term or a symbol is a function of what the user "intends" the symbol to mean. Unlike the first two types of meaning, which can be validated by referents or by empirical observation outside the person's head, the third type of meaning is inherently a characteristic of the mental act and is located exclusively within the mind of the individual person. Thus, two symbols may have the same referential meaning as persons in a communicative situation refer to the same specific object or person, and the term may have an identical "significance"—a product of empirical knowledge. But the intentional meaning of the term is inevitably a product of the individual (inside the head) and is, to some extent at least, unique to that individual. Strictly speaking, then, no two intentional meanings are ever identical, although they could be quite similar. According to Brodbeck, at least, one can infer that the concern over misunderstanding expressed by Richards is most relevant to intentional meanings and less important in terms of referential or significance varieties of meaning.

But Brodbeck's threefold meaning of meaning is only one approach to understanding the concept. Rubenstein (1973) suggests three quite different "formal theories of meaning," which include "referential theory," "ideational theory," and different subvarieties of "psychological theories." But Rubenstein attempts to discover the nature of meaning adapted to the study of languages. Brodbeck is primarily concerned with the meaning of terms within a scientific theory. Their purposes differ and, hence, so do their explanations of meaning. Nevertheless, these two examples illustrate the overwhelming conceptual confusion, both philosophical and empirical, surrounding the term *meaning*. The meaning of meaning, in other words, remains unclear.

But our purpose is not to discover the "true" nature of the concept of meaning. Nor is our purpose to take sides in this philosophical controversy regarding the concept. The foregoing discussion is intended to point out the inescapable fact that meaning is a highly ubiquitous and multifaceted concept. Furthermore, depending on one's purposes and perspective, the concept itself may be interpreted in a variety of ways.

However, our concern is not with the general concept of meaning but only with those uses of the concept directly relevant to human communication.

All philosophical confusion aside, each of us has an intuitive understanding of what meaning is. When we ask of another person, "What do you mean by that statement?" she generally responds with a further explication of what she "means" without indulging in a philosophical debate over what type of meaning was implied in the question. In other words, we may not be able to explicate a precise theoretical explanation of meaning, but we can cope with the concept of meaning in our everyday lives and conversations.

Therefore, though philosophers, theorists, and researchers continue to argue over the meaning of the concept *meaning*, we consistently use the concept as though we all know full well the meaning of meaning. The sense in which we actually utilize the concept of meaning in our communicative experiences, then, is the emphasis of this chapter. Furthermore, that sense of "meaning" is a function of our perspective used to view the communicative process and, of course, differs from one perspective to another.

MEANING IN COMMUNICATION

For years teachers of communication have pointed out to their students that the linguistic origin of the word *communication* is the Latin *communis,* meaning "common." Gode (1959, p. 5) even defined communication etymologically as "a process that makes common to two or several what was the monopoly of one or some." One clear characteristic of meaning which is relevant to human communication, then, is its "commonness"; that is, meaning as it relates to communication is inherently a social phenomenon. Meaning as a communicational concept includes more than the interpretation or understanding of a single individual. It inevitably includes multiple understandings—those aspects of understanding that are "common" to the communicators.

The aspect of commonness, however, does not necessarily suggest that all participants in the communicative process have identical understandings of the symbols or thoughts (or whatever), but that some understanding is common to them all. Without some degree of what Goyer (1970, p. 7) calls "commonality of 'meaning'"—that is, the "vicarious sharing of experiences"—communication could not exist. Shands (1967, p. 104) is more emphatic when he asserts: "The meaning of meaning is consensus, and the birth of meaning is in the social process allowing consensus to develop." The "social process" in Shands's "general theory of communication" is the process of communication itself.

Clearly, then, the fundamental aspect of meaning as it exists in human communication is its social nature—commonality or consensus or "shared-ness" of individual meanings. The notion of "shared meaning" pervades virtually every perspective of human communication. But this is not to say that the mechanistic view of "shared meaning" is the same, for example, as that of the interactional perspective. In fact, the concept of "sharedness" varies among perspectives as much as the concept of meaning.

What does meaning "mean" in communication? How and why do communicators "share" meaning in communication? Where is meaning in communication? In the symbol? In a person's head? In the pattern of interaction? All these questions are eminently answerable within each perspective. But the answer from one perspective is not the answer from another perspective. Although the answers vary, none of them is to be considered false. To the contrary, all the answers are "correct" and quite "true." To reiterate what must now be abundantly obvious, the answers to these questions must be sought within the perspective from which communication is viewed. Although a single answer may be considered "appropriate" to a given perspective and inappropriate to another, to ask whether any answer is "true" or "best" is simply irrelevant. "Truth" is never an issue. Theoretical utility, however, is.

Mechanistic Meaning

If you recall that the locus of communication viewed mechanistically is in the channel, it logically follows that a mechanistic treatment of meaning should also focus on the channel. Because the message flows along the channel, the meaning must somehow be relevant to the message as well. Meaning, then, resides in the message at each and every point on the channel. Now this does not necessarily imply that meaning is in the words or the symbols that comprise the message. (No one seriously believes that old saw.) It does imply, however, that the meaning of the message is a function of the channel, that is, the location of the message at some specific point on the channel.

The message at the point of transmission (for example, encoding a message from a thought) is as convenient a place as any to begin. A mechanistic view might then suggest that the message at the point on the channel as a thought may have one meaning and another meaning as the message is encoded and transmitted. Noise can, of course, attack the fidelity or clarity of the message at any point on the channel—both external and internal to the communicators. As the information is transformed from one form to another at points of encoding and decoding, the meaning of the message is very likely to be modified or somehow changed—probably resulting in some loss of information—and thus meaning—as an inevitable result of the transformation.

Because mechanism stems from the theoretical paradigm of classical physics, an analogy comparing physical and social phenomena may be in order. In physics, the force that provides the "go" for a physical system is energy, and a classical physical law regards the inevitable degradation of energy—Gibbs's "second law of thermodynamics." The universe possesses only so much energy. It cannot be created but can only be transformed from one form to another. Thus, we speak of energy existing in different forms. For example, energy in coal or petroleum is stored energy and thereby dormant. If we ignite these fossil fuels, we transform the dormant energy to an active form—kinetic energy—which we use to heat our homes, operate our automobiles, run our factories, generate electricity (another kind of energy), and so forth. Biologically, we eat food and transform that form of energy into kinetic energy—human action.

Relationships among social phenomena, on the other hand, are best explained with the concept of information rather than energy. (Information as a specific concept in human communication is the subject of a later chapter.) Information, then, is the social counterpart of energy. In a mechanistic view of physical phenomena, energy is the appropriate force. But information, rather than energy, provides the "go" for a social system. Moreover, like energy, information is transformed from one variety to another at points of encoding and decoding. At each point of transformation, one can expect some loss of information consistent with the thermodynamic law of degradation of energy. And the transmission of information across time-space will also result in some loss of information as well.

The modification and, hence, loss of information is the principle underlying the common classroom exercise in serial transmission of messages —sometimes called the "telephone game." Even elementary school children play a variation of the game in which the object is to relay a message to someone else who hasn't heard it, and that person relays the message to someone else, and so forth. After three or four relays, the final message bears little resemblance to the message originally transmitted. In television's yesteryear, when Jack Paar hosted the NBC "Tonight" show, one of his favorite ploys was to tell a joke (in English) to a German professor, who, in turn, retold the joke (in German) to a Spanish professor, who related the joke (in Spanish) to Jose Melis (the bandleader), who retold the joke (in English) to Jack Paar. The original joke simply lost its humor in the various transformations of the information. In fact, the joke became nonsensical. In other words, the "meaning" of the message changed considerably during the various repetitions of the encoding, transmitting, and decoding transformations.

What, then, is the concept of meaning viewed in the mechanistic perspective of human communication? Meaning is variable and subject to the communicative functions performed on the message at each point on the channel—both internal and external portions of the channel. To say that meaning resides in the message—or even in the information contained in the message—is an oversimplification of the mechanistic perspective. That information must be transformed—for example, decoded or interpreted. At each point on the channel that transformation or interpretation occurs, the meaning may be expected to be different. Furthermore, noise on the channel (both internal and external noise) will also result in a loss of message fidelity.

A mechanistic perspective of human communication would consider meaning to be highly variable to the extent that every mechanistic cycle of communication would include several different meanings of the same message. These multiple meanings would include at the very minimum (1) the meaning of the message prior to encoding, (2) the meaning of the message encoded and transmitted, (3) the meaning of the message received, (4) the message decoded, (5) the respondent (that is, feedback) message prior to encoding, (6) that message transmitted, (7) received, and (8) decoded. A mechanistic view of communication might then include principles for alleviating message distortion and potential misconceptions—for example, how to say what you mean, how to structure the message for maximum clarity, how to use visual aids or multimedia presentations, and how to encourage feedback responses to check on the accuracy of the received message.

In a word, the meaning of a message in the mechanistic perspective is a function of the transmission/reception of the message on the channel. Those transmissional problems of transforming information from one mode to another and the problem of noise (including the "noise" of misinterpretation) are problems that derive directly from the emphasis of the mechanistic perspective. Mechanistic meaning is variable and multiple. To ask what the meaning of a message is from a mechanistic perspective is to ask also where on the channel the message is located. Meaning inevitably varies from one point to another as the message flows along the channel—the locus of the mechanistic perspective of human communication.

Psychological Meaning

At the risk of appearing overly repetitious, I feel the need to make the disclaimer once again. The heading of this subsection is not intended to forecast a discussion of "psychological meaning" in the sense that the section will include a discussion of how meaning is conceptualized in the field of psychology. Indeed, there are as many variations in the psychological conceptualizations of meaning as there are variations in the theoretical perspectives employed by psychologists—actually, many more than exist in communication. Rather, the following discussion attempts to provide a general discussion of how the psychological perspective of human communication conceptualizes meaning. Any similarity between meaning in the psychological perspective of human communication and meaning in the field of psychology is certainly more than coincidental, but there are differences, too. These differences between psychologists and communicologists should not be tolerated; they should be expected.

The axiom of the psychological perspective is one of the clichés of communication: "Meanings are in people" or "Meaning is perception" or "People, not words, mean." Meanings, then, are the result of the individual's perceptions through internalized conceptual filters, and those internalized filters are the result of the individual's past experiences—the reinforcement pattern the individual has experienced, all the S–R associations of the past. Add the principle of commonality inherent in communication, and "shared meaning" becomes the extent to which the past experiences of the communicators are similar. Upton (1961) makes the point explicitly:

> Communication takes place insofar as the meaning of utterance corresponds to the meaning of interpretation. Since both are . . . conditioned responses, the success of the communication depends upon the extent to which the past experiences of the communication have been similar. . . .

Although Upton is not technically a member of the scientific community of human communication, other scholars who are definitely communicologists make the same point. Berlo (1960, p. 184), for example, writes, "People can have similar meanings only to the extent that they have had similar experiences, or can anticipate similar experiences." Hanneman's (1975, pp. 25–26) discussion of meaning is precisely the same as the psychological perspective in that he views meaning in communication as "based on experiences" and a direct function of the degree of "shared experiences of a common culture and upbringing" among the communicators.

The psychological perspective of the communicative process, you will recall, is based in large part on an S–O–R explanation. The locus of the perspective is the internalization of the conceptual filters of each communicator. Thus, communication involves the sensory intake of stimuli, filtered by the perceptual "sets" of the communicators, and the communicative response, also filtered by those same internalized "sets." Thus, the interpretation of stimuli and elicited responses of two or more communicators can be similar only to the extent that their sets (that is, conceptual filters) are similar. Moreover, because these sets are products of the S–O–R associations developed through past experiences, it logically follows that similarity of interpretations and similarity of elicited responses are directly attributable to the extent to which the past experiences of the communicators are similar.

Central to the conceptualization of meaning in the psychological perspective of human communication is the concept of "isomorphism." Isomorphism is a term borrowed from biology, referring to the similarity of biological organisms of different ancestry. Applied to communication, isomorphism refers to the similarity of meanings in two people as a function of their similarity of past experiences and hence similarity of perceptual sets. Sharedness of meaning, then, refers to the isomorphism of the internalized conceptual filters of the communicators.

All adherents to the psychological perspective will hasten to add that total ismorphism is an ideal state and will never exist in the "real world." In other words, the meanings of a given symbol held by any two people will never be absolutely identical. That is to say, the experiences of any two people—even identical twins—are never precisely the same. Some difference inevitably exists. Therefore, isomorphism is relative, so that sharedness of meaning is enhanced when communicators are from the same culture, the same socioeconomic status, the same educational level, the same geographical origins, the same ethnic group, the same political group—in short, when the communicators have a maximal number of experiences in common.

To say that meaning in communication is never totally the same for all communicators is not to say that communication is impossible or even difficult—only that it is imperfect. For the most part, communication occurs in contexts in which the similarities among the communicators are maximized and the differences are discounted. The communicative context that includes members from differing cultures is, of course, more problematic; hence the study of intercultural communication typically focuses upon the differences between the cultures themselves—differences among the past experiences—as a primary mode of inquiry. That emphasis, only indirectly associated with communicative phenomena, is quite consistent with the psychological perspective of human communication.

Isomorphism - sim. of meanings as a function of sim. of past experiences

As is true of the mechanistic perspective, meaning from the psychological perspective of human communication is variable. But where mechanism conceptualizes this variability as a function of a message's location on the channel, the variability of psychological meaning is a function of the similarity of conceptual filters and past experiences within the communicating individuals. The result (that is, variabiliy of meaning) may be the same, but the theoretical/philosophical explanation of that result differs substantially in the mechanistic and psychological perspectives. Of course, the two explanations do not necessarily contradict each other; they are only different. Therefore, it would not be difficult to combine both mechanistic and psychological explanations of meaning, and that combination is a typical practice.

Interactional Meaning

The term *shared meaning* probably originated in the interactional perspective but has become so ubiquitous that it pervades all the perspectives applied to human communication. But the notion of sharedness varies considerably from one perspective to another, as we have continued to emphasize throughout this chapter; that is, the mechanistic perspective views sharedness as an attempt to minimize the distortion and loss of information. Psychological sharedness implies a similarity of conceptual filters internalized within the communicators—and hence similarity of communicators' past experiences. In the interactional perspective, sharedness implies a more abstract concept—an active component of mutual role taking on the part of the communicators.

Though psychological meaning treats the uniqueness of the past experiences of the individual, interactional meaning emphasizes the commonality of social experiences. The distinction between the two is not one of contradiction but of different emphases. The psychological perspective emphasizes the significance of the internalized set—the uniqueness of the "black-box" self. The interactional perspective views self as a social creation achievable only through communication with others. Thus, psychological meaning is shared through similiarity of individual experiences. The individual is a rather passive "victim" of past experiences. But interactional meaning is shared by a process of mutual empathy through active role taking. The individual plays a more active role, seeking out the meaning of other and sharing it with other. The individual, in this way, transcends an internalized self by engaging in social role taking—particularly in role-taking the generalized other.

Meaning in the interactional perspective is a creation of the social situation, and the premise for any social relationship is a set of shared meanings—significant symbols, if you will. The meaning of any symbol —word or object—is a function of the social situation. The social situation includes only a limited number of meanings for any symbol. For example, an object that we call *pencil* has only a limited number of "meanings," all of which are socially created by people who function with that object. The pencil is thus a writing instrument not because of any inherent characteristic to be perceived but because people have used the object to write with. Secondarily, the pencil is also a pointer, an object for chewing, a table tapper, a head scratcher, even a fingernail cleaner. The point is that all the meanings are socially created by people functioning with the object, and any meaning arises only as a function of a particular social situation. For example, you probably wouldn't view the pencil as a fingernail cleaner if you were interviewing for a job.

Mead (1934, p. 81) placed an interactional meaning within what he called a "conversation of gestures," in which a gesture signified any potentially meaningful act. Thus, meaning occurs as a "triadic relation of a gesture of one individual, a response to that gesture by a second individual, and completion of the given social act initiated by the gesture of the first individual."

To illustrate Mead's point with a common example, a baby cries and the parent gives the baby a bottle of milk, which satisfies the baby. The meaning of the cry is a function of the act that follows and the closure of the initial act—in this case, cessation of crying. Both the parent and the child together create the meaning of the gesture—they designate the cry as a request for food. That is clear not because of any similarity of past experiences necessarily, but because of the acts that followed in the "triadic relation." The meaning of any gesture, then, lies in the symbolic behavior of interacting individuals in an already socialized situation. Because both parent and child behaved symbolically in a similar fashion, significant symbols were present in the interaction.

In this sense, the interactional perspective allows individuals to "carve out" their own environment. I recall a television movie a few years ago in which the members of a nineteenth- or early twentieth-century mining town lived in self-pity and disappointment over their misfortune—a worked-out silver mine. The mine contained tons of molybdenum—a useless object for them—but no more silver. In fact, in their despair over their own fate they pronounced the unwanted substance "molly-be-damned" and even symbolically named their town after it. Only later, when they discovered the mineral was quite valuable in the production of steel alloys, did they change their attitudes toward the mine and subsequently toward their previously useless shares of stock in the mining company. The social situation changed and hence the meanings of the symbols.

Conversational communication from an interactional perspective, according to Meerloo (1952), emphasizes "mutual understanding" and "mutual empathy" as the source of shared meaning. The process of role taking and maximum sharedness of meaning is made possible through what Meerloo calls "the natural wish for mutual identification, for psychological understanding, and a loving approach toward others." Though the abstract concepts included in Meerloo's approach mitigate against adequate operationalization, they do emphasize the point that interactional role taking transcends the individual's self and allows for each communicating individual to seek actively the standpoint of the other and attempt to adopt that standpoint—hence, shared meaning. The key words are *mutual* (each participant engages in role taking) and *identification* (taking on the other's frame of reference).

The concept of interactional identification remains an abstract concept in that it retains an individual self at the same time the self is taking on the self of other. Interactional identification or empathy is similar to Kenneth Burke's (1946) concept of "consubstantiality"—retaining at once elements of both self and other as the result of identification. Although Burke's dramatism is not always congruent with the interactional perspective, his "consubstantiality" concept and interactionism's "mutual identification" concept are quite similar.

Ruesch (1963, pp. 134–135) makes a similar point when he distinguishes between understanding and agreement as communicative processes. According to Ruesch, understanding occurs when communicators establish a "correspondence of information." But agreement implies the isolation of one aspect or topic of communication and "decision-making and commitment" relative to that aspect. Thus, communicators can understand each other during communication but may not necessarily agree.

The interactional perspective has been very popular among a group of psychotherapists and has been characterized in the field of communication under a variety of labels including "medical communication," "therapeutic transaction," and "growth-promoting communication." Principal proponents of interactionism and dialogical communication among psychoanalysts and psychotherapists include Erich Fromm, Carl Rogers, Joost Meerloo, and Jurgen Ruesch. They have highlighted their approach to shared meaning through mutual identification by elucidating techniques designed to maximize mutuality. These techniques include such common principles as reflective feedback (for example, "What I hear you saying is . . .) and nondirectiveness in psychotherapeutic treatment.

Unlike mechanism and psychologism, the interactional perspective deals directly with the sharedness or mutuality of meaning through active participation (through role taking) in the communicative process. To a much greater extent than either of the first two perspectives, interactionism locates meaning external to the individual in the behavior or gesture of the communicator. But the heavy reliance on such internalized concepts as "empathy," "identification," and "understanding" suggest that much of the communicative process regarding the concept of meaning remains resident within the individual. But even then the individual is a product as well as participant in the social situation—the dialogue of the communicative process.

Pragmatic Meaning

Albert Scheflen, a psychiatrist and consistent advocate of the pragmatic perspective of human communication (see, for example, Scheflen, 1969), captures the essence of pragmatic meaning when he emphasizes (1974, p. 183) "asking what behavior means rather than asking what people mean by their behavior. This is an issue of focus; does one focus on people or on behavior forms?" But isn't this statement blasphemous to the axiomatic wisdom that meanings are in people? Of course, it is. However, the alleged axiom actually begs the question by assuming that meanings must be either in words or in people. The pragmatic perspective suggests a third alternative—not merely words but patterns of behavior that constrain the choices of people.

Inimical to the axiomatized cliché that meanings are in people is the philosophical assumption that behaviors are principally a reflection of internalized feelings, emotions, personality, attitudes, and so on. Behaviors are thus significant only to the extent that they accurately represent these internalized concepts. To the degree that observable behaviors are not representative of internal constructs, they are considered "insincere" or "false" or "unintentional"—in short, less "meaningful." This assumption is consistent with a focus on the individual. But recall that the focus of the pragmatic perspective of human communication is on the social system—a holistic and nonsummative entity unexplainable by considering individuals separately. Thus, behaviors in and of themselves are significant and hence meaningful to the social system —more meaningful to the extent that they recur in redundant patterns. Whether they accurately reflect individual intentions is not meaningful. Behaviors affect the system and are affected by the system whether or not intentionality or sincerity is present.

Pragmatic meaning is thus a selective function performed on the range of choices available to the communicator (see McKay, 1969, pp. 24–25). The patterned sequence of actions punctuated by frequency of recurring patterns illustrates both how and why meaning accrues as a product of the social system developed during ongoing interaction. McHugh's (1968) interactional approach to communicative meaning during social interaction possesses pragmatic overtones in that he discovered that subjects often create order or meaningfulness in interaction even under alleged conditions of controlled anomie (that is, lack of order or meaninglessness). McHugh pragmatically searched for meaning as it occurred and developed during social interaction. He was guided by the principle (p. 132) "that nothing of interest to us is private and hence unobservable." That is, McHugh did not assume that behavior is primarily a reflection of some internalized and hence unobservable states or filters. Nor did he necessarily draw any inferences about internal states from the observation of behaviors. McHugh (p. 134) states explicitly:

> The public displays of rules and definitions are themselves rules and definitions, not surface effluences of private essences. Definitions are not owned, if by that we mean they are ineluctably private property, hidden away in the recesses of mind and self. They are *performances*, applied and validated, and thus public and observable. . . .

Interpretation of any symbol is, according to the tenets of information theory, choice(s) from among those interpretations available to be chosen. Moreover, because redundancy is equivalent to information and hence the reduction of available alternative choices, the actual performances or behaviors reflect the reduced choices in the pattern of interaction (that is, in the redundant sequences). Meaning, then, is equivalent to choosing from a repertoire of possible interpretations or meanings, and the choice process is a process of elimination—reducing available meanings to a manageable number, perhaps a single choice. The reduction is evident in the redundant frequency of patterned interaction and develops as an evolving or emergent process during ongoing social interaction among communicating individuals—a product of the social system. Meaning is then not in any person but in the social system, reflected by redundant patterns of interaction—performance "rules."

Liklider (1973, p. 205) describes the process of reduced choice and hence meaning as a social process of "modeling." He suggests that communication "is a joint activity of two or more people . . . modeling together—creating, exploring, comparing, modifying, adjusting, and evaluating models together." The meaning in communication, then, is the "model" that results from the social give-and-take of interaction, which allows and even requires individuals to adjust to each other and, in so doing, to the social system. For meaning (or modeling) as a concept of communication is not a product of or possessed by any individual but an inherent creation of the conjoined individuals only through interaction with other individuals. As such, meaning is a product of and possessed by the social system as a whole; and, furthermore, the meaning is reflected in and represented by the patterning of social interaction punctuated by recurring sequences of acts.

SUMMARY

Philosophers and theorists do not exhibit consensus on the meaning of meaning. Neither do the members of the scientific community of human communication. The meaning of meaning as a concept relevant to the process of communication depends upon the perspective used to view the communicative process. Mechanistic meaning focuses on the transformation of messages transmitted and received on the channel. Psychological meaning emphasizes the individual's conceptual filters or perceptual sets. Interactional meaning occurs from mutual identification of role-taking interactants, and pragmatic meaning observes meaning in the recurring patterns or sequences of interacts and double interacts.

Shared meaning is the province of communication's inherent emphasis on commonality. But the explanation of how individuals share the same or similar meaning also differs from one perspective to another. Mechanistically, shared meaning occurs to the degree to which the distortion or loss of information is minimized at points of transforming information. The psychological perspective of shared meaning is equivalent to the amount of sharedness of past experiences that exists within the communicators. Sharedness of meaning in the interactional perspective refers to the mutuality of empathy or identification—the abilities of the interactants to transcend self and assume the role of other. Pragmatic meaning is inherently shared in that meaning is represented by behavioral redundancy of all participants in the social system—a product of the holistic system and not the separate individuals.

Meaning is also variable in that mechanistic transformations of messages or information inevitably result in different meanings of the message at different points on the channel. Psychological variability of meaning is also inevitable in that the past experiences and hence conceptual filters of no two individuals are identical. Interactional identification is also never complete because the self always remains to some extent separate from other, even during states of extreme mutual empathy. Pragmatic variability of meaning is a function of the amount of redundancy reflected in the interaction patterns. The statistic from information theory that measures that redundancy is called "stereotypy" and ranges from 0.0 (random variability) to 1.0 (no variability). Remember that open systems evolve to states of increasing complexity, that is, greater variability. Furthermore, total structure or no variability is even undesirable (see Chapter 7).

What is the meaning of meaning in the process of human communication? That depends on the perspective used to view human communication. Are meanings in people? That, too, depends on the perspective—the emphasis on what behavior means or on what people mean by their behaviors. Certainly, the concept of meaning is an extraordinarily significant concept in human communication. It is always present in any discussion of the communicative process, regardless of the perspective used to guide the discussion. But the "true" meaning of meaning is the direct result of the perspective applied to human communication. Although each perspective views meaning quite differently, each meaning of meaning is as "true" as the other.

— 9 —

The Concept of Message

In 1968 the New Orleans Conference on Research and Instructional Development in communication (see Kibler and Barker, 1969, pp. 33–36) drafted five recommendations concerning research priorities in the field of communication. Those recommendations named as the central focus of communication research the concept of message. Although the conferees disagreed strongly over the locus of messages, the recommendations for and description of communication research clearly reflect an emphasis on the message. But like meaning and many other concepts conventionally associated with the communication process, the concept of message is variable, that is, signifying different things to different people.

The discussion of the four perspecives of human communication included in Part Two included message as a component in only one—mechanism. But because the mechanistic components are so familiar and "traditional" in discussing human communication, message could be and has been utilized in discussing psychological stimuli, interactional behaviors, and pragmatic acts. But this does not mean to imply necessarily that the concept of message is equally essential, significant, or even viable in all four perspectives. Though meaning is a concept inherently involved in communication, whatever perspective is employed to view the process, the concept of message varies considerably from one perspective to another in its signficance and relevance to the process of human communication.

THE VARIABILITY OF THE "MESSAGE" CONCEPT

As a component in a mechanistic model of human communication, the concept of message is certainly significant to a mechanistic perspective. Furthermore, because the traditional view of human communication is a blend of mechanistic and psychological perspectives, message remains a significant concept utilized in many theoretical, practical, and empirical discussions of human communication. Nevertheless, the concept itself varies considerably in these discussions—sometimes subtle but often drastic variations; that is, the blend of mechanism and psychologism as the most popular view of human communication encompasses and thus allows for considerable variations in its meaning.

The principal variations are the subject of the following pages. The ensuing discussion is intended to provide the "flavor" of conceptual variation rather than to provide a comprehensive and definitive review of conceptualizations leading to a discussion of the "true" nature of message in a single perspective. In all likelihood, persons holding a traditional view of communication could find all six variations acceptable; that is, the variations do not, strictly speaking, contradict each other so much as they reflect differing emphases or interests. The variations are thus not necessarily inconsistent with each other; they are merely different.

As Transmitted Signal

A cursory reading of Shannon and Weaver's (1949) mechanistic model of human communication would lead one to conceptualize message as a phenomenon that travels on its circular route on a channel connecting two or more source/receivers. (I have taken liberties with Shannon and Weaver's model because they do not include the response flow of messages to complete the circular flow on the channel.) Strictly speaking, such a reaction to a mechanistic flow of messages is at once true and false.

Recall that a message in a mechanistic model is transformed at points of encoding and decoding so that the message itself is a thought or an idea somewhere in the neurophysiological system of the source/receiver and, after encoding in a face-to-face situation, is transformed into a series of atmospheric vibrations (sound waves) and reflected rays of light (visual mode). The decoding apparatus of the source/receiver transforms those phenomena of physical energy back into words, paralinguistic cues, gestures, and thoughts. But in the form of physical energy *between* the source/receivers, the message is not a thought, nor is it words. Rather, it is a set of physical signals.

Colin Cherry (1964, p. 171) distinguishes between the concepts of message and signal on the basis of where each exists on the channel and, consequently, on the form in which the message-signal appears. As Cherry puts it, "A message might, for instance, be a thought, . . . but this thought is not physically transmitted." But when the physical form of the message (that is, the signal) is decoded, it becomes a thought once again and hence a message. According to Cherry, the message in its physical form of actual transmission over space (for example, sound waves, electrical impulses on a telephone line, radio or television signals in the atmosphere) is more appropriately called a signal. As the signals are encoded or decoded, the form is a message.

Clevenger and Matthews (1971, pp. 12–14, 93–94), like Cherry, distinguish between a message and a signal on the basis of physical form and location on the channel; that is, a signal is the "physical" event, and the message exists only on the channel internal to the source/receivers. But Clevenger and Matthews go one step farther and suggest that, in every communicative event, three potential messages exist. The message sent constitutes one message; the message received is a second message. They explicitly state that the two messages are not to be understood simply as different "versions" of the same message but are "entirely different events."

The two messages are different events because they occur at two different spatial locations (in the source and in the receiver) and at two different temporal "locations" (the message received always follows after the message sent). They then go on to discuss the principle of isomorphism as the "fidelity" of the communication obtained by observing the corresponding similarity of the two messages. A third message may also occur within an observer of the communicative situation—the "communication analyst," who is differentiated from the "communication participant."

The message, then, is conceived as the form and location of the thought, verbalization, and so on, within the individual. The "message" that exists on the channel external to the source/receiver is in the form of physical energy and is more accurately conceived as a signal. Thoughts are encoded into signals; signals are decoded into thoughts. Or, stated another way, messages are encoded into signals; signals are decoded into messages. The distinction between message and signal, you will note, is a purely mechanistic distinction—a distinction based exclusively on the physical form obtained from mechanistic transformation and on the spatial location of where the message or signal exists.

As Structural Form

Disregarding momentarily the distinction between message and signal, one might ask, "What does a message look like?" That is, what are the properties or attributes of a message that are susceptible to sensory observation? Miller (1972, pp. 76–77) uses the structural form of a message to distinguish its composition into "three principal factors": "verbal stimuli" (including the words or the linguistic symbols), "physical stimuli" (including gestures or movements, facial expressions, and so on, in a face-to-face interaction), and "vocal stimuli" (including the paralinguistic cues of speaking rate, loudness, inflection, emphasis, accent, and the like, in face-to-face interaction). In many respects, Miller's conceptualization of message is more an operational definition of the concept than a conceptual distinction; that is, the listing of the physically observable properties or attributes of the message reveal the appearance of the message as it is observed by the sensory apparatus. But the operational definition does not really attempt to describe the functioning of the concept within the communicative event.

Implicit in viewing the message as a structural form is a view of message as transmitted (that is, encoded). Miller operationally defines the message from the viewpoint of the decoder—the receiver or the third-person analyst of communication. This interpretation, of course, does not necessarily suggest that the message does not exist except at the point of transmission. Rather, the issue is one of emphasis, and Miller (pp. 15–17) believes that the message (that is, the structural form of the encoded message) has received far too much emphasis in formal instruction or education in human communication. Though one can argue whether the instructional emphasis on message encoding has been accentuated beyond its worth, his point is clear only when one considers message as an encoding process of verbal, physical, and vocal stimuli—the message as structural form.

But whether it is true that formal instruction in communication has emphasized structural forms of the message, it is certainly true that much of the communication research in the past three or four decades has placed considerable emphasis on the structural form of messages. Many of the studies emphasizing "effects" of communication have related them to structural variables of messages. In rhetorical criticism, the emphasis on assessing effects of rhetorical form has been dubbed "neo-Aristotelian" criticism (see Black, 1965). Then, too, the "textual criticism" of rhetorical messages clearly places a premium on the structural form of the message. The "effects" studies in persuasion and attitude change have emphasized behavioral effects of such structural variables of the message as sidedness, primacy-recency structure (or climax-anticlimax order), other factors of message organization, delivery, linguistic style, compressed speech, forms of argument, evidence, logical structure, and so on. Add to this list the plethora of mass-media effects studies related to message variables of depicted violence or sex, side of the screen, and different typefaces in newspapers. Emphasis on the structural form of messages clearly pervades both instruction and research in human communication. Whether that emphasis is exorbitant is a matter of opinionated conjecture.

As Social Influence

Closely aligned with the view of message as structural form is the view of communication as a means for social influence. Aristotle originally conceived of communication (that is, rhetoric) as persuasion. His historical and cultural environment during the classical age of Greece (see Chapter 1) certainly would lead him to such a belief. The culture of today would tend to support a similar view of communication such as that which the social psychologist, Schachter (1951), has explicitly stated: "the mechanism by which power is exerted." The view of Steve King (1975, p. 32), a communication scholar, is not nearly so blatant as that of Schachter. Nevertheless, King does perceive message as an encoded form with implicit social influencing. He writes, "The message, put simply, is the need-relevant behavior of the influencer."

Lest anyone misinterpret King's point of view or the concept of message as social influence, it is important to note that to see the concept message functioning in the process of social influence is not to endow the concept with any mystical power to "cloud men's minds." In fact, King's notion of communication as "informational social influence" is, contrary to Schachter's concept, explicitly nonmanipulative. (See King, 1975, p. 27.) In King's view, communication, virtually inevitably and inherently, has some social effect—not necessarily manipulative or intentional, but effectual nonetheless.

King also differs from Berlo's (1960, pp. 11–12) notion that "our basic purpose in communication is to become an affecting agent, to affect others, our physical environment, and ourselves. . . . we communicate to influence—to affect with intent." (Emphasis deleted.) But whether intentionality of influencing is implicit, explicit, or irrelevant, King and Berlo would probably agree on the fundamental principle that communication influences; messages do have an effect.

Probably a majority of communication scholars and students would agree that communication (messages) inherently influences or affects participants in some way and to some extent. Though widespread disagreement would surround the process of how or why that effect occurs

—whether directly or indirectly attributable to message variables—the fundamental principle of influencing or effecting potential of the message persists. Many would explain communicative effect as a "transaction" between receiver and message in the sense that "fear appeals" are not a property of the message alone but involve a transaction between the message and some fear already latent in the receiver, which is elicited by the message. The message as social influence, direct or indirect, is a widely accepted phenomenon among members of the scientific community of human communication.

As Interpretation

Most consistent with the psychological perspective of human communication is the view of message as an interpretation of symbols or stimuli. You will recall that the S–O–R model of communication located communication in the interpretative-perceptual process of encoding stimuli through conceptual filters. The locus thus renders less meaningful or less significant the distinction between encoding and decoding processes; that is, encoding and decoding become essentially the same process of interpreting or perceiving meaning in selected stimuli. Therefore, a message, whether encoded or decoded, is a matter of individual interpretation.

Borden (1971, pp. 74–76) relates message explicitly to symbolic behavior—behavior that can be symbolic only if interpretations of that behavior occur in the mind of a source or a receiver. Thus, isomorphism is a similarity of interpretations of the same behavior in the mind of source and in the mind of receiver. Clevenger and Matthews (1971, p. 94) are equally explicit: "a message is a symbolic event representing an interpretation of the physical occurrence" by either source or receiver. The process of interpretation (that is, the encoding-decoding process) endows stimuli with message value. Uninterpreted stimuli, in the sense that the interpreter does not select them or is not exposed to them, are not part of the message.

Mortensen's (1972, p. 19) definition of message includes two requirements that would appear to summarize the concept of message as interpretation. Those requirements include (1) that the behavioral stimuli "must be available for inspection" and (2) that "the behavior must be interpreted as significant by at least one of the parties." Mortensen's first requirement stipulates only the availability of the stimuli for sensory reception. As the sensory apparatus of the communicator takes in the stimuli, they are interpreted.

Mortensen goes on to state implicitly that the process of interpretation automatically endows the stimuli with significance, that is, with meaning. In this case, the intent of a communicator is not particularly relevant to whether the stimuli have message value or whether they are irrelevant. (The concept of intent will be discussed more specifically in the following section.) Furthermore, interpreted stimuli have message value regardless of their origin—a transmitting person, the environment, within the interpreter, and so on.

The message conceived as interpretation renders quite credible the conceptualization of different messages as they exist within different people, that is, different interpreters. A strictly mechanistic viewpoint might (but not necessarily) be used to conceive of different versions of the same message at different points on the channel—at the point of transmission and at the point of reception—owing to interference of noise on the channel affecting the message flow. But a strictly psychological perspective of communication would conceive of the message as "created" by the interpreter; that is, the transmissional property of message is not necessary to conceptualizing communication within psychologism. The intake and subsequent interpretation (that is, assignation of meaning) of stimuli are sufficient to create the message. In this sense, one looks at a painting or a sculpture and assigns meaning to it. The original interpretation of the artist is not particularly relevant to the observer's interpretation. Each of them can encode her own message —that is, interpret the stimuli—independent of the encoding of the other.

Conceptualizing message as a process of interpretation is quite susceptible to a psychological explanation of human communication. Under any circumstance, such a conceptualization of message is highly receiver-oriented in the sense that it places message within the individual—an intaker and perceiver of stimuli. Then, too, it breaks down the mechanistic distinction between encoding and decoding and thus renders less significant the phenomenon of transmission in explaining a message concept. Message as a process of interpretation is also a highly popular belief among members of the scientific community of human communication.

As Reflection of Self

Also consistent with a psychological perspective of human communication is the veritable axiom that the message reflects the internalized states of the individual; that is, behavior is, in some form or another, an outward manifestation of the black-box concepts of attitude, belief, perception, values, images, emotions, and so on. In fact, Berlo (1960, pp. 168–169) explicitly states that messages "are behavioral events that are related to the internal states of people."

To say that behavior accurately or adequately reflects internal states, however, is to engage once again in the tiresome attitude-behavior-discrepancy problem or, if we go back far enough philosophically, the mind-body-dualism controversy. But the controversy does not actually focus on whether, for example, behavior is a reflection of attitude in the same sense that behavior is related to internalized states. The controversy relates more specifically to how accurately or how adequately behavior determines attitude (or vice versa)—that is, how closely behavior and internalized states are related, whether deterministically, transactionally, or whatever.

Disregarding that controversy for the moment, one can conceptualize message as symbolic behavior that is related in some way and to some degree to some specifiable internal state. This assumption does not suggest that attitude precedes behavior (or vice versa). It assumes only that behavior and attitude are related somehow, so that observing behavior will allow the observer to draw some inference, with varying degrees of accuracy, as to the presence or character of an internalized state.

The internal state most often associated with message is that of intent. To what extent does the message reflect the intent of the communicator? Berlo (1960) is unequivocal—we communicate with intent! No ifs, ands, or buts! Borden (1971, p. 75) is more cautious. He suggests that intention is relative and ranges along a continuum from "no conscious desire" to "total dedication." To what extent the message reveals intentionality on the part of the communicator is a matter for some speculation, of course. The importance of intention as a variable in communication study, particularly in persuasion, was an issue of some significance a few decades ago. Much of that interest has dissipated in recent years, although there is some recent evidence of a resurgence of scientific interest in the variable of intentionality in communication research.

Nowhere is the belief in message as a reflection of self more evident than in the area of nonverbal behavior. Clevenger and Matthews (1971, p. 103), for example, are emphatic in their assertion that nonverbal communication is a direct indication of "attitude" and "emotions" as well as "feelings" and "moods." Zealots of nonverbal behavior are wont to suggest that one simply cannot "lie" in the nonverbal mode of encoding messages. Your nonverbal cues will "give you away." Many students and scholars of human communication subscribe to this belief in a direct link between internalized states and nonverbal messages.

Although the research to validate or support such a link between nonverbal behavior and internal states is extremely scarce, the belief in that link persists, and research beginning with an assumption in the existence of that link flourishes. Moreover, the claims for the internal-nonverbal link included in the growing number of popularized books written for mass consumption (for example, *Body Language, Body Talk, How to Read a Person Like a Book,* among others) are based primarily on zealously held convictions rather than on any scientific basis of empirical research. The more serious researchers in nonverbal behavior (including Mehrabian, Harrison, Knapp, and Ekman and Friesen) are more cautious in their claims while maintaining, with varying degrees of certainty, the assumption that nonverbal behavior is a relatively direct reflection of internalized states.

The concept of message as a reflection of self (that is, internal states) is also prevalent in the communication research dealing with persuasion and attitude change. For example, one message variable used in such research is "discrepancy," implying some measurable differentiation between the receiver's attitudinal position and that expressed in the message. The variable of "counterattitudinal advocacy" also implies a relationship between message and a communicator's internalized attitude, that is, the difference between the attitudinal position internalized by a source and the position expressed in his encoded message. King, you will recall, suggests message as emphasizing the "need-relevant behavior of the influencer," thereby relating behavior and internalized needs.

To what extent behavior adequately or accurately reflects (that is, is related to) some internalized state of an individual communicator is clearly a popular method for conceptualizing message in the study of human communication. The question is asked, in one form or another, in literally thousands of research studies relevant to human communication. Though students of communication will certainly differ on the extent to which a message reflects intent or attitude or feeling (in the sense that the behavior is consistent with the internalized state), the assumption that a behavioral message is somehow related to one or more internal states and that that relationship is a significant area for communication research provokes considerable inquiry and instruction in the area of human communication.

As Commonality

Many of the participants at the New Orleans Conference on Research and Instructional Development in communication (see Kibler and Barker, 1969, p. 34) expressed belief in the conceptualization of message directly relevant to the "commonality" implication inherent in human communication. (You will recall this implication from the discussion in the preceding chapter concerning the etymological derivation of the word *communication*.) More specifically, many of the New Orleans conferees agreed that the research focus on messages implies a research focus on the "*linkage* between people in the communicative act," that is, "on the way the communication act binds two or more people together"—communicated messages as a "'coupling system' which links source and receiver."

The recently popular trend to view communication as a "transaction" between communicators has encouraged the conceptualization of message as a function of interpersonally linking communicators with each other—that is, developing a social unit. (Like most "fads"—in the sense of immediate and extreme growth of popularity—the term *transaction* has been so overused and misused that the concept that underlies it has become muddled in the process. I have avoided using the term to denote any specific perspective toward communication—not because of the value of such a perspective but because of the ambiguity surrounding the term itself. Purists of transactionalism should find an affinity for the pragmatic or interactional perspective although any of the four perspectives can be conceptualized transactionally—depending upon how one defines the term.)

To return to the point at hand, message may be conceived as the link that binds people together in a communicative situation. Mortensen (1972, p. 19), for example, defines message as the performance of a coupling function—"whatever unit of behavior serves to link the parties of communication" (emphasis deleted). If communication serves "to make common" something like "meaning" between the communicators, the message seems to be a logical variable or concept in which to locate that making-common function. But precisely how messages serve to "link" communicators is rather problematic. Mortensen provides little conceptual assistance as to the "how" of linkage, particularly as he emphasizes individualized interpretations as a functional requisite of messages.

MacKay (1969, p. 109), an information theorist, provides one insight into how messages might serve to link participants in the communicative process. In discussing the concept of meaning in communication, MacKay utilizes the analogy of "a key in relation to a given lock" as the linking function of a message. The key has the effect of (that is, function of) opening the lock but is not equivalent to opening the lock. For example, one could inspect the lock mechanism and the key separately and consequently determine whether the key would open the lock if it were inserted, and that determination is possible without ever actually inserting the key into the lock. In the same sense, the message does not necessarily imply a common interpretation of meaning, but it "betokens" that meaning. To the extent that communicators operate with a similar set of rules, they will find that the message serves as a "key" to "unlock" the application of those rules.

MacKay's concept of message, then, implies that all participants in the communicative situation perform the same operation on the message whether that message is sent, received, or observed; that is, they have agreed on a set of rules that implicitly govern their communicative relationship. To the extent that the participants agree beforehand on the implicit set of rules, they will perform common or similar functions during the communicative act. The message, then, serves to activate those rules and thus link (that is, make common) the communicants. But the message itself does not link the participants; it activates the rules, which, in turn, link the participants. Therefore, the message "functions" to link the participants in the communicative situation. The linking function of the message is an inherent and functional relationship rather than a directly linear or causal relationship.

As an example in everyday conversation, the message "Hi. How are you?" does not directly link participants within a communicative event, but it may activate a set of rules within our American culture that we can call a "greeting ritual," so that the participant may respond with the message "Fine. How are you?" The participants are then in agreement (that is, linked or coupled) on the rule governing the communicative event. If the respondent is from a different culture (not familiar with the rule) or decides not to "play that silly game" (in other words, does not agree on the rules governing the American greeting ritual), she might respond as though the message represents an inquiry into her physical well being: "I feel rotten today. My asthma is really acting up!" The two participants are operating under different sets of rules. The message, then, does not as adequately function to link the participants (although they are still linked somewhat by agreement, for example, on the linguistic code of English)—not because of anything in the message, but because of the failure of all the participants to agree on a common set of rules to govern the communicative event.

MacKay's view of message functioning is not the only way, of course, to conceptualize a message as performing the linking or coupling function of communication. Nevertheless, it does provide one way in which message may be conceptualized as social commonality. This view of message is probably less adaptable to communication in a purely mechanistic or purely psychological perspective than in an interactional or pragmatic perspective. On the other hand, any of the four perspectives can be broadened conceptually to accommodate the commonality principle, particularly the message as a reflection of functioning commonality.

One can view the commonality of the message as mechanistic fidelity (relatively noisefree), as isomorphism of meaning (similarity of past experiences allowing a common interpretation of the message), as role taking (perhaps a generalized other), or as a redundant (and hence common) pattern of interaction. Commonality is simply too pervasive a principle of human communication to resist being accommodated within any or all the perspectives of human communication.

THE USEFULNESS OF THE "MESSAGE" CONCEPT

During the past two decades of scientific inquiry into human communication, the concept of message has received a steadily decreasing amount of emphasis. The recommendations of the New Orleans conferees notwithstanding, a growing number of communication scholars have concluded that the message is a relatively superfluous element in the communicative process; that is, the process of human communication can be explicated and understood quite comprehensively without employing the concept of message. Curiously enough, many of those same scholars would probably find themselves in perfect agreement with the New Orleans conferees, but they would not use the concept of message to verbalize or to conceptualize their agreement with those same research priorities.

The erosion of the conceptual significance of "message" has come from two different directions, which have resulted in quite disparate conclusions concerning the concept *message*. One of those trends in the devaluation of the message concept is to modify the concept to mean something quite different from that originally intended. One approach symptomatic of such a trend stems from the McLuhanistic syndrome, which endows the communicative mode with informational value—that is, the familiar cliché that the "medium is the message." Another indication of this trend emanates from advertising—specifically, the political image makers who have essentially degraded the message as informational in favor of the "gestalts" of the message; that is, the actual message is subordinate to the implicit "flavor" of the person, the style, the overall impression—in short, the "image." The trend in advertising is to sell, in Elmer Wheeler's terms, the "sizzle" rather than the "steak"—to sell the carefree life-style of youth rather than the particular brand of soft drink, to sell the freedom of the great outdoors rather then the specific brand of cigarettes, to sell the sexual allure of the model rather than the furniture.

This trend toward a changed character of the concept of message is intriguing but not directly of interest to us for several reasons. For one thing, the claims made to support the claims of medium and sizzle remain a source of considerable controversy. Subliminal forms of persuasion, for example, are more provocative than probable. For another thing, this trend has generated more conviction of belief than serious empirical inquiry into communicative phenomena of mass advertising. As a result, the changed character of message is of limited significance as a topic of value in any serious discussion regarding the scientific inquiry into human communication.

On the other hand, a second trend resulting in a devaluation of the conceptual significance of message stems directly from scholarly theorizing and inquiry. In this instance, the decreased significance of message is a direct result of viewing communication from nonmechanistic perspectives. Though the first approach attacks the significance of message directly by transplanting its value to other phenomena or variables, such as the medium or mode of communication, the second trend views the entire process of human communication from quite a different point of view and, consequently, discovers that the concept of message itself is superfluous or, at least, only a term that is substitutable for more descriptive or more appropriate conceptual terms.

The following pages discuss two specific approaches to human communication, which reflect a questionable significance of the message concept. Under no circumstances should these approaches be construed as arguing for eradication or abolition of the term *message*. In fact, one could easily explain these approaches fully and use the term *message* consistently. But the ensuing discussion would employ the term to imply something quite different from any of the six variations discussed earlier in this chapter. The result is to render the concept of message not so much harmful or a hindrance as it is superfluous and simply inessential.

Message "Bits"

A few years ago as a graduate student I heard Sam Becker (1968) discuss his experiences upon hearing of the assassination of Martin Luther King, Jr. Becker was attending a professional convention in Chicago at the time and acquired his information over a period of several days in small bits and pieces—from a cabdriver, a television newscaster, overheard conversations in a hotel lobby, newspaper articles, viewing rioting mobs in the streets outside his hotel, conversations with friends, and so on. A few short months following Becker's presentation, I experienced an incredibly similar experience in acquiring information surrounding Robert F. Kennedy's assassination. You will recall that the

1960s was a decade of political assassinations, and 1968 was the bloodiest year in that terrifying decade.

On the day that Robert Kennedy was assassinated, I had just passed my final Ph.D. oral examination, and my wife and I were celebrating my success in downtown Minneapolis. At the restaurant where we ate dinner, we overheard people discussing the apparent victory of Robert Kennedy in the California presidential primary. As the evening progressed and the days followed, the tragic events of the story came to us in small bits and pieces from a multitude of differing sources—newspaper headlines showing through the glass of a sidewalk vending machine; the offhand conversation-making comment of the hotel desk clerk; the incredible filmed footage of Rafer Johnson and Rosie Grier wrestling Sirhan to the floor (viewed on early morning television); the pictures in Life magazine a few days later; a memorial service on the university campus; conversations with my wife that evening and with my office mates the next day (my office mates included a liberal Democrat and a conservative Republican); my own thoughts about Robert Kennedy, John Kennedy, and Martin Luther King, Jr.—all victims of political assassins. In short, I was sensitized by my experience of having heard Sam Becker discuss his experiences, and I essentially relived that experience in an incredibly similar fashion. Becker's point about human communication was thus much more credible and realistic to me.

Becker developed what he called a "mosaic" model of human communication, which he felt more accurately reflects the current process of human communication in our modern society. We typically conceive of human communication in terms of a source delivering a message to a receiver, who then responds, directly or indirectly. This common conceptualization is even more prominent in mass communication, Becker's primary area of interest, in which a mass audience is conceived of as receivers of a single message through some mediated source, such as a television newscast or program or a newspaper article or column. But Becker's mosaic model suggests that this concept of a message as a unitary "whole" does not accurately represent mass communicative phenomena (or interpersonal communication, for that matter) at this stage of technological development in the twentieth century.

The explosion of information and the technological revolution in communication in recent years, which Berlo (1975) calls a "revolution" in communication, and particularly in terms of electronic or nonprint media, have fostered substantial changes in our conceptualization of messages. Today there is simply too much information from too many sources to be included easily within a simple model of single-message exchange. The more accurate depiction of information processing is probably the receiver who takes in and interprets numerous sets of messages in varying degrees of directness from numerous sources over an expanded and ongoing period of time and across many different situations. The identification of source(s) of the information is much more complex (that is, differentiated), and, consequently, the concept of message is much more complex. Becker thus refers not to "message" but to "message bits" (not to be confused with "binary digits" or choices in information theory, but in the sense of small, fragmented, and inherently incomplete "bits and pieces" of a larger whole).

Becker's resulting analogy of communication in contemporary society is that of a "mosaic"—a single picture composed of many small pieces of glass, metal, tile, and so on, which "fit together" to form a pattern of wholeness. Though each isolated piece in the mosaic is relatively meaningless, its place in the pattern, along with all the other little pieces, eventually provides an organized whole. Communication, then, is the exposure to many small pieces of information received from many different sources and in many different situations over a period of time. Moreover, the communicant, in responding to others, creates more message bits of his own, which also fit into the developing mosaic. The result is a final mosaic of information processing which is organized into a unitary whole but which is composed of numerous message bits. On the other hand, the mosaic is never "final" in the sense that the individual is constantly moving within the informational environment and constantly adding, deleting, strengthening, selecting, and substituting message bits comprising the mosaic.

To consider each message "bit" as a single message is to ignore the "mosaic" analogy. Furthermore, the message conceived as a unitary whole possesses certain relevant properties or variables such as organizational structure (for example, primacy or recency) or style (for example, linguistic phrasing or syntactic variations). But these properties or variables are simply not appropriate or relevant attributes of the mosaic of bits. Becker suggests three potential variables of message bits, which are equally inappropriate to the concept of a unitary message: frequency, gaps, and redundancy.

"Frequency" refers simply to the sheer number of relevant message bits—a measure of quantity ranging from a very few to an unprocessable "many." "Gaps" suggest the potential significance of the length of time intervening between exposures to various message bits. For example, are bits more significant or more relevant in the mosaic if they occur in "bunches" (that is, brief periods of time separating exposure to message bits) rather than widely dispersed over a period of time? Are bits more significant as the gaps approach some regularity (that is, approximately equal periods of time separating exposure)? "Redundancy," of course, suggests the variable of being exposed to the same or similar message bits more than once. Perhaps, as information theory might suggest, a repeated message bit possesses more informational value than a seldom heard bit. On the other hand, does novelty make a message bit more significant precisely because it is out of the ordinary—not redundant and hence not immediately familiar?

Unfortunately, Becker's mosaic model has not stimulated many communication scholars to generate much research into message bits. However, it has generated numerous serious discussions and rethinkings of communicative phenomena, particularly about mass communicative phenomena. Probably the principal reason for its failure to generate research is the overwhelming complexity of the communicative process depicted in the model. It is not easily adapted to laboratory research settings, nor is it easily designed for a naturalistic field setting. Nevertheless, the mosaic remains a highly provocative and eminently reasonable model, which can be used to view human communication, particularly mass communication, in our contemporary culture embodying the "communication revolution." Most significantly, for our purposes, the model unveils a new perspective on the concept of message and implies drastic conceptual revision of that concept within the "big picture" of expanded notions of time and social situations.

Nonmessages

Watzlawick, Beavin, and Jackson (1967, p. 50) define message as simply "a single communicational unit," which they also call "a communication." They go on to point out that a higher-level unit of human communication is "interaction" and a still higher-level unit is "patterns of interaction." Ruesch and Bateson (1968, p. 34) refer to message as "any action," and that action inherently "constitutes a message to ourselves as well as to others." In a similar view, Scheflen (1969) argues for viewing "relations" or "patterns" within the behavioral "program" of human communication, thereby de-emphasizing the single "behavioral unit," the message. The pragmatic perspective of human communication views message rather clearly. The term may be used to refer to a behavioral unit, but the behavioral unit (that is, the message itself) is relatively insignificant within the perspective's emphasis on patterns of interaction (that is, sequences of messages) rather than on messages per se.

The pragmatic perspective of human communication offers several implications for the concept of message. First of all, any of the preceding six variations of message are necessarily of questionable relevance or applicability within the pragmatic perspective. For example, the distinction between message and transmitted signal is clearly irrelevant with the pragmatic reliance on observable behaviors—no concept of channel, either internal or external to the individuals. For a similar reason the significance of message as a process of interpretation or as an indicator of internal states is also of questionable relevance. The pragmatic perspective emphasizes the social system rather than the individual and thus de-emphasizes internal states of the individual in favor of externalized behaviors. The pragmatic perspective is simply not easily adapted to accommodate all the six conceptual variations of message.

A second implication concerns the use of the term *message* in explaining the pragmatic perspective of human communication. A rather comprehensive understanding of the perspective is possible with or without ever actually employing the term *message*. When the term is employed, message refers to the smallest behavioral unit of communication—simply another term for act, action, behavior, or even behavioreme. When the term *message* is not used, a term such as *act* or *behavior* serves the purpose adequately and completely—perhaps more so. Consequently, the concept of message has no inherent significance except as a substitute for another term that is probably more descriptive. Thus, message exists only as a term—not an essential concept—and as a term, message is redundant and ultimately superfluous.

A third and probably more important implication of the pragmatic perspective's use of the message concept concerns the emphasis on interaction—the sequence of acts or the patterns of actions. Even if *message* is used as the term for the behavioral unit of communication, the implication is clear. The unit is simply not very significant in and of itself. Only in the pattern or in the sequence or in the behavioral program of ongoing human communication does the single act assume significance —and only then if it exhibits sufficient redundancy or constraint. Karl Weick (1969), a social psychologist who advocates a pragmatic perspective, is thus led to emphasize interacts (a patterned sequence of two acts) or double interacts (sequence of three concatenate acts) as the fundamental units of human interaction—not the act. The single act— that is, the message—continues to be a unit of human communication only as it forms interacts and double interacts. Because of the revised emphasis on the holistic social system and thus on the patterned sequence of acts, the single act-message is substantially less meaningful—less significant—to the process of human communication.

Most advocates of the pragmatic perspective of human communication continue to use the term *message*, if for no other reason, because it remains a convenient and easily recognizable term. But the term, nonetheless, is quite superfluous and typically denotes actions or behaviors. In the sense that act or behavior is a more descriptive term than message, the unit of human communication is really a "nonmessage." In the sense that interaction patterns provide the focus of the pragmatic perspective, the unit of communicative behavior is composed of multiple messages as interacts and double interacts—"nonmessages." The result is a consistent trend toward decreased significance of the concept of message in communication theory, at least outside the mechanistic and mechanistic/psychological perspectives of human communication.

SUMMARY

Message as a concept significant to an understanding of human communication exists as an inherent component only in the mechanistic perspective. But because the components of the mechanistic model pervade all the perspectives of human communication, the concept is broader than simply its position in the mechanistic model. Unlike the concept of meaning, however, which exists in all four perspectives although conceptualized differently, the concept of message is of variable significance in the four perspectives. Though highly meaningful in the mechanistic perspective and only slightly less significant in the psychological perspective, message in the interactional or pragmatic perspective possesses more of a take-it-or-leave-it significance.

As a meaningful concept in explicating the process of human communication, message is conceptualized in several subtly different variations of meaning. Those variations are probably most applicable to the traditional view of human communication as a blend of mechanism and psychologism. Moreover, the variations are not necessarily inconsistent with each other, so that one could easily hold all six variations to be true within such a perspective. Those variations include conceptualizing the meaning of message as possessing structural form, as differentiated from physically transmitted signals, as a means of social influence, as interpretations of receivers, as an indicator of internal states, and as performing a social linking or coupling function.

But the concept of message is also of questionable importance or significance in viewing human communication from a perspective that differs from mechanism or psychologism. Because of the information explosion and technological revolution of the mass media of communication, message conceived as a unitary whole may be less descriptive of human information processing than the concept of multiple fragments of messages—"bits"—received over a longer period of time and in a variety of situations from a variety of sources. The resulting view of communication is an everchanging and developing "mosaic" model of communication composed of the information-processing individual, who is exposed to many bits and who organizes them into some conceptual whole.

The pragmatic perspective of human communication severely restricts the significance and usefulness of the concept of message because of its emphasis on behavioral acts and sequential patterning of those acts. Though the term *message* will probably continue to be employed indefinitely in popular parlance, the significance of message as a concept of human communication continues to decline within a pragmatic view of the communicative process. More descriptive terms, such as information, transaction, behavior, act, pattern, sequence, interact or double interact, and program, more adequately and more accurately characterize the pragmatically viewed process of human communication. And the nonmessage terms are decidedly more prevalent in the literature of the pragmatic perspective than the term *message*. The result is that the concept message is more popular as a term than significant as a concept in the study of human communication.

— 10 —

The Concept of Feedback

The concept of feedback pervades virtually all discussions of human communication. Moreover, feedback is a term included in the vocabulary of virtually every person in our society beyond the age of puberty. The typical lay person (that is, one who is not a member of the scientific community) would hardly consider feedback a highly technical term and thereby uses the term with impunity. The very popularity of the term and its ubiquitous use in everyday conversation have undoubtedly contributed to the explosion of meanings and interpretations applied to the concept. Furthermore, the variety of definitional treatments of feedback in the scholarly literature of human communication reflects a similar expansion of the potential interpretations of the concept (see Clement and Frandsen, 1976).

Feedback probably originates from and is the central process of cybernetics, a mechanistic theory of self-regulation or control. It is always popular to define the term *cybernetics* by referring to its Greek origin (*kybernetes*) and, hence, referring to cybernetics as "steersmanship." The man given credit for laying the mathematical and philosophical groundwork for cybernetics (indeed, for inventing cybernetics) is Norbert Wiener, who wrote his first extended treatise on the subject in 1948, later revised, expanded, and edited as *The Human Use of Human Beings,* subtitled *Cybernetics and Society* (1954). Wiener considered communication and control as virtually synonymous terms, so that his discussion of cybernetic systems was inherently a discussion of the communication systems that govern or control the functions of the mechanistic system.

In the minds of many people cybernetics has unfortunately come to imply communication between people and machines or treating human beings as machines. This machine-people identification of cybernetics has been fostered by such novels as *Cyborg* (short for "cybernetic organism"), which has appeared as a television adventure series under the name "Six Million Dollar Man" and served indirectly as the inspiration of "The Bionic Woman." This popularized interpretation of cybernetics is essentially a "bum rap," prompted undoubtedly by Wiener's (1954, p. 38) insistence in drawing analogies between the cybernetic mechanisms in "some of the newer communication machines" (such as analogue computers) and those in living individuals. But the human-machine analogy is just that—an analogy—and the analogy implies that feedback processes in humans function similarly *in principle* to mechanistic feedback processes. But the analogy does not, as some have surmised, imply that humans are little more than sophisticated machines.

Cybernetics as a theory of control or mechanisms for control remains central to virtually all the various uses of the term *feedback* both within and without the scientific community. The elementary concept of feedback-as-control stipulates that the output of a system is "fed back" into the system as additional input, which serves to regulate further output. In Wiener's (1954, p. 84) terms, "feedback is a method of controlling a system by reinserting into it the results of its past performance." The nature of cybernetic control remains relatively consistent across all treatments of feedback in human communication that will be discussed in this chapter. However, the specific nature or function of that control has been expanded to include virtually anything during communication that might serve to regulate subsequent behavior.

Our purpose is not to unravel all the subtle nuances of how feedback is conceptualized and operationalized in communication inquiry. Indeed, any thorough discussion of feedback would be book-length in itself. Rather, the following discussion considers only four fundamental variations of how communication scholars have utilized the feedback concept. These four variations correspond loosely but not unequivocally to the four major perspectives of human communication depicted in Part Two. For the most part, this chapter ignores the popularized treatments embodied in the socially conventional "knowledge" of feedback except insofar as those treatments are similar or relevant to one or more of the variations evident in scientific discussions.

FEEDBACK AS RESPONSE

By far the most common lay conceptualization of feedback is the return message transmitted from receiver to source, that is, the response of the receiver to the source's original message. Feedback is allegedly the difference between one-way and two-way communication, a distinction that will continue to be regarded as insignificant to an understanding of the phenomenon of human communication. Most consistent with a mechanistic view of human communication, feedback as response focuses on the flow of messages from receiver to source in the return loop linking communicators on the channel.

As a response, feedback can be said to vary in amount, a variation that is nonsensical in other conceptualizations of feedback. Focusing on the flow of messages or feedback responses on a channel, one can easily conceive of the flows being heavier at some times as the channel carries more responses. Leavitt and Mueller's (1951) oft-cited study on feedback responses sought specifically to test the effects of varying amounts of responses on subsequent communication. They established four laboratory conditions ranging from "zero feedback," increasing in graduated amounts to unrestricted responses—the "free feedback" condition. Their fundamental comparison—and the conditions established in their second reported study—was between free-feedback and zero-feedback conditions. The difference between amounts of feedback, consistent with a mechanistic view of communicative transmission, was the difference in barriers placed on the channel to restrict the amount or the flow of messages.

As a variation in amount of responses received by the source, feedback varies also as to level and number of channels used. For example, if source and receiver are connected by a telephone channel only, the visual channel is restricted. If the channel is an exchange of typewritten messages, the paralinguistic cues of the vocal message (for example, emphasis, pitch, rate, and inflection) are restricted. In a face-to-face setting in which the receiver may ask only yes-or-no questions, the level of feedback is less than a situation in which any type of question or response is permitted.

Variations in amount of feedback may include, then, variations in the number of responses, the variety of those responses, and the number of channels available for responses, among many others. The variations thus suggest differing "levels" of feedback in the sense of maximum, moderate, of minimum feedback (see Mulac [1974] and Adams [1973]). Furthermore, conceptualizing a variation of feedback by amount or level of responses allows for a situation in which the channel is blocked completely, that is, zero feedback and essentially one-way communication. Nevertheless, such a situation is undoubtedly an ideal state in the sense that any situation of zero feedback could occur only under strictly controlled laboratory conditions and rarely, if ever, in a realistic or normal setting for human communication.

The more realistic treatment of feedback responses is to consider them as simultaneous in the interchange of responses and messages in the conveyor-belt model of a mechanistic perspective. Ackoff and Emery (1972, pp. 187) discuss interchange of feedback responses as indicative of "two-party, two-way communication" and, of course, communication between more than two parties. Gardiner (1971) also emphasizes the simultaneous interchange of feedback responses just as communication inherently involves the simultaneous interchange of transmitted and received messages.

This simultaneity of responses is the same principle that suggests that the distinction between source and receiver is an arbitrary one. Though each communicator is at once a source and receiver, he is as well an initiator of and a respondent to messages simultaneously; that is, each communicator both sends messages and receives responses to his messages at the same time, so that feedback in human communication involves simultaneous processes of encoding and decoding by all participants.

A further approach to viewing feedback responses other than by amount is to observe the specific characteristics of the responses themselves. Leathers (1971), for example, developed a multiscale instrument for judging nine properties of a feedback response—attributes such as effectiveness, relevance, flexibility, comprehensiveness, involvement, and so on. Rather than observe how many responses or varieties of responses are returned to the source, Leathers's approach focuses on single responses and describes those responses more specifically. The former (amount of feedback responses) is a macroscopic approach to interpreting feedback whereas the latter (attributes of each response) is a more miscroscopic approach to feedback.

Conceptualizing feedback as response, then, is most closely aligned with a mechanistic perspective of human communication and similarly is the most popular view of communicative feedback outside the scientific community (and perhaps among scholars of communication, too). Conceived as potential restrictions placed on the channel to impede the flow of message-responses, feedback as response considers variations in amount or level of feedback as well as the number of channels available and used to convey these feedback responses. Significant to feedback as response is the conceptualization of human communication via the conveyor-belt analogy, implying a simultaneity of responses in the interchange of messages in the realistic communicative situation. A more microscopic approach to studying feedback responses also looks at the attributes or properties of the responses themselves. Though feedback as response is undoubtedly the most popular conceptualization of feedback in informal interpretations of the concept, it has not generated necessarily the most significant research in recent years.

FEEDBACK AS REINFORCEMENT

The earlier discussion of the psychological perspective of human communication in Chapter 5 pointed out that some S–R psychologists have suggested that the stimulus-response paradigm was really a misnomer. Rather than serve to explain behavior with only stimulus-response bonds, a complete explanation actually needs to account for stimulus-organism-response-reinforcement relationships. If we think of response behavior as a message in communication, then the reinforcement that follows the response is simply another word for feedback. In fact, Berger and Lambert (1968, p. 97) specifically use the term *feedback* to refer to the response or reward that follows response in "S–O–R–feedback psychology."

In the conditioning paradigm, feedback is seen as the response to the response that serves either to encourage or discourage continuation of that behavior. Thus, reinforcement serves the control function of feedback by affecting subsequent repetitions of that behavior. Whether one uses the classical conditioning model of Pavlov or the operant conditioning model of Skinner, words or linguistic symbols substitute for the dogs' meat powder, the rats' food pellets, and so on. Moreover, words as feedback reinforcement can function to reward or punish the source through that reinforcing message; that is, words may signify approval (for example, "Uh-huh," "You're right," I agree," "Okay," and nonverbal signs such as smiling or nodding the head) or disapproval (for example, "No," "You're wrong," "I disagree," "Hunh-uh," and such nonverbal signs as frowning or shaking the head).

Feedback as reinforcement, then, may serve to reward or punish the source and thus serve as positive reinforcement or negative reinforcement. Feedback as positive or negative reinforcement may even prompt the terms *positive feedback* and *negative feedback*. These terms shall arise once again in a later discussion of feedback as social process. As social process, positive and negative feedback may have much the same appearance and may even lead to similar effects, but they are conceptually quite different. Therefore, it is necessary to distinguish clearly how feedback is conceptualized, whether as psychological reinforcement or as social process, when employing the terms *positive* or *negative feedback.*

Simply stated, feedback as reinforcement may be positive or negative, depending upon whether the feedback serves to reward or punish the source's communicative behavior. Mortensen (1972, p. 325) utilizes the feedback-reinforcement conceptualization to discuss the difference between positive and negative feedback as whether the feedback positively (that is, enhanced or continued) affected subsequent communicative behavior or whether the feedback negatively (that is, inhibited or reduced) affected subsequent communicative behavior. In other words, Mortensen maintains the notion of control inherent in feedback by emphasizing its effect on subsequent communicative behavior.

Communication research into positive and negative feedback-reinforcement tends to support several relatively clear and noncontroversial assumptions. First, feedback reinforcement is terribly pervasive. (See, for example, Stolz and Tannenbaum [1963], Weiss [1966], Matarazzo et al. [1963], Verplanck [1955], Shapiro [1964], and Scott [1957].) Virtually any type of feedback response from virtually anyone in virtually any interactional setting can affect the source's subsequent communicative behavior. Secondly, negative feedback reinforcement results in debilitation of subsequent communicative behavior, and (less well supported) positive feedback reinforcement serves to enhance subsequent communicative behavior (See, for example, Bavelas et al. [1965], Vlandis [1964], and Miller et al. [1961].)

The pervasive effects, particularly of negative feedback, on subsequent communicative behavior is rather well supported in the mainstream of communication inquiry. Nevertheless, some additional variables are notable. For one thing, negative feedback from multiple receivers, such as an audience's giving feedback responses to a speaker, appears to exert the strongest deleterious impact (see, for example, Blubaugh, 1969). On the other hand, some research evidence questions even the fundamental assumption of the significance of the effects of negative feedback reinforcement (see, for example, Karns, 1969).

Another important variable that reduces the effects of negative feedback reinforcement is the prior speaking experience of the communicator. Rhodes and Frandsen (1975), for example, discovered that experienced speakers suffer less from negative feedback. They attribute this result to the source's increased confidence and less cognitive uncertainty about her own ability.

One must be cautious, however, about accepting uncritically the assumption that positive or negative feedback as reinforcement always affects subsequent communicative behaviors. If we recall the obstinate-audience principle of the psychological perspective, it is eminently reasonable to expect the source to be no less obstinate in receiving feedback responses than the receiver is in receiving manipulative messages. One should not lose sight of the fact that feedback—whether viewed as mechanistic response or psychological reinforcement—is, nonetheless, a message and is interpreted no differently from any message. Thus, feedback is subject to human interpretation through the internalized conceptual filters of the individual. In this way, feedback in human communication differs from feedback in a machine (apologies, if necessary, to Norbert Wiener). A machine's interpretation of feedback is predetermined, consistent with a priori procedures. Human interpretation of feedback is subject to interpretation through conceptual filters and may be nonrational and even inconsistent.

The individual communicator possesses the capacity to select stimuli from the environment. Whether those stimuli are in the form of initial messages or subsequent feedback-reinforcing stimuli, that capacity is in no way diminished or modified. In fact, McDavid and Sistrunk (1957) illustrated that individuals can negatively interpret feedback intended to be positive and regard as praise the feedback stimuli intended to be negative. (See also Nokes, 1961.) Selectivity may also affect the choice of person from whom feedback reinforcement will be accepted or received (see, for example, Maccoby et al., 1961); that is, individuals can regulate the amount and type of feedback (negative or positive) that they receive by exercising selectivity over their choices of people with whom they communicate.

A final variable mitigating against the direct effect of negative or positive feedback reinforcement on subsequent verbal behavior concerns the timing of the feedback. As we note that feedback in most normal communicative situations is simultaneous with encoding messages, the issue is whether the feedback reinforcement is most effective if immediate or delayed. A reinforcing feedback message may be interpreted as delayed (and hence less effective) even though it follows the message by only a few seconds (see, for example, Kraus and Weinheimer [1966], Fairbanks and Guttman [1958], and Argyle and Kendon [1967]). In the ongoing process of day-to-day human communication, such as social conversation, the interchange of messages implies an interchange of feedback responses. Delays in feedback reinforcement could severely restrict the effectiveness of that feedback as positive or negative reinforcement in that the conversation simply passes it by when it is only a fraction of a second too late.

FEEDBACK AS INTERNAL SERVOMECHANISM

Berrien (1968, p. 35) points out the principle of the "servomechanism" within the system, whether that system is mechanical, biological, or social. Within the system exists an apparatus that responds to certain specified variations in the operation of the system. For example, the thermostat (a typical example of a servomechanism) responds to specified variations in temperature such that the thermostat corrects the functioning of the system in order to maintain the temperature at a "steady state"—that is, maintaining a stability in the system allowing only minimal variations or fluctuations in the temperature. The servomechanism, then, copes with variations or disturbances, correcting or compensating in response to those variations so that the system maintains a stability in its functioning —otherwise known as a "steady state."

The key to a servomechanism, as Berrien points out, is that responses to variations (feedback) are automatic and present. In other words, the timing and the pattern of the disturbances need not be predicted or known before those disturbances occur. It is only necessary that variations do occur in order for feedback to operate to regulate those disturbances. Of course, the range of possible disturbances and the limits of those disturbances must be known beforehand, but not specifically when they will occur nor how often they will occur. Feedback automatically detects the disturbance and sets the servomechanism into operation, which, in turn, compensates. The servomechanism is predesigned within the system, of course. The nature of stability and, thus, the allowable amplitude of variation are also foreknown. The result is maintenance—smooth functioning of the system—in the case of the thermostat, maintaining the room temperature at the present 68 degrees (plus or minus an allowable variation).

Mowrer (1954) suggests that learning creates a psychological servomechanism within the individual. Attitudes, for example, are acquired through learning (that is, past experiences) and are internalized (as conceptual filters). These attitudes, then, may be said to function as a psychological servomechanism. According to Mowrer, "intelligent *control* of behavior then becomes possible." These attitudes prevent us from behaving inappropriately in a given social situation; and were we to do so, these same attitudes would serve to control our behavior through such unpleasant feelings as embarrassment, fear, and the like.

Naturally, Mowrer's notion of potential psychological servomechanism is rather controversial. The old attitude-behavior-discrepancy problem once again rears its diabolical head. Mowrer suggests that attitudes or other internalized conceptual filters function to control behavior much as an internalized servomechanism. He argues from learning theory in that attitudes or meanings have been previously learned (that is, acquired from prior experiences) and are internalized as a stabilizing influence on behavior. He specifically discounts behaviors or actions as a possible controlling element in that "attitudes, not actions . . . are the most immediate outcomes of learning." But though the concept of attitude as a psychological servomechanism may be controversial, it does seem to exemplify another way to view the operation of feedback in the process of human communication.

On the other hand, one might view an internalized servomechanism quite differently. In a view more closely representing an interactional perspective, the individual might view her own actions as feedback to herself and might then use that observation to regulate her own subsequent behavior. Wiener (1954, p. 39) is emphatic that *"performed action"* and not merely *"intended action"* is the input to the servomechanism of feedback in both humans and machines. Berrien (1968, p. 72) describes this self-servomechanism in terms highly similar to an interactional concept of role taking; that is, the human steps outside self and, in the role of other, views and evaluates self's action in a rather objective fashion. In more precise terms, the individual assesses her own past behavior and utilizes that evaluation to regulate further behavior in that and in other social situations.

The servomechanism, then, may be psychologically some set of conceptual filters gained through learning from past experiences. These learned concepts are predesigned to regulate personal behavior consistent with parameters allowable within these concepts. Interactionally, however, the servomechanism lies within the evaluation of self by other (as self) made possible through the individual's capacity to observe self behavior through role taking. The individual evaluates past and present behavior from the viewpoint of other and regulates further behavior by means of that evaluation.

The interactional concept of feedback as servomechanism is more consistent with the cybernetic notion that variations or disturbances are regulated retrospectively after those variations actually occur. Occasionally, this interpretation of interactional feedback as servomechanism is discussed as intrapersonal communication—sending messages to oneself by self observation and assessment of self behavior. Whatever it is called, the basic principle underlying this role-taking phenomenon is control of behavior—the fundamental principle of feedback.

FEEDBACK AS SOCIAL PROCESS

Earlier discussions of other feedback notions in this chapter have included the principles of simultaneity of interaction and of positive and negative feedback. These same principles are also characteristic of the discussion of feedback that follows—but with one major difference. Unlike former conceptualizations of feedback, this final conceptualization views feedback from the perspective of the social system—the communicating individuals as a holistic and irreducible unit, a system—rather than from the perspective of the single individual. Viewed from the perspective of the entire system rather than the component individual, feedback becomes a social process affecting the functioning of the entire system and is either insignificant or indistinguishable from the level of the individual.

Hawes (1973, pp. 14–15) defines his "postulate of simultaneity" as embodying the notion of social process so that the perspective shifts from the individual to the entire system. "Communication," writes Hawes, "is not something we do but something in which we engage." This holistic notion of communicative process echoes the sentiment expressed by Birdwhistell (1959), discussed in Chapter 7. Hawes goes on to describe the social system comprising two or more individuals as an irreducible unit. Smith's (1973, p. 27) notion of systemic feedback leads him to a similar conclusion: "Feedback relationships transform the behavior of individuals into systems behavior." Simultaneity of interaction and hence feedback, then, shift the focus from the individual to the social system of human communication.

The consequence of viewing feedback in the simultaneous functioning of interaction as a social process is, according to Watzlawick, Beavin, and Jackson (1967, pp. 126–127), a conceptual shift from energy to information as the crucial variable in a social system. That shift has led to an antideterministic conceptual stance—linear causal chains including a conditioning model or teleological model—to a circular or mutual process of causality. Hawes (1973) makes the same point in discussing simultaneity. Thus, feedback is not so much a response or even a reinforcement of a response. It is a circular process—a series of events—which loops back to the beginning. As a loop, the feedback process is repeatable and can occur again and again with predictable or, at least, probable regularity.

Viewing feedback as a loop should point out the futility of trying to pinpoint one behavior even arbitrarily as a feedback comment. It is similar to isolating a point on a circle as the beginning of the circle. Remember that same point is also the end of the circle, and that same principle is true of any arbitrarily chosen point on the circle. The circularity of response, then, necessarily involves not a single behavior or even pair of behaviors. Rather, it requires a sequence of behaviors to constitute just one instance, a single occurrence of feedback (see Watzlawick, Beavin, and Jackson, 1967, p. 46).

Scheidel and Crowell (1966, p. 274) define feedback as a sequence of interaction involving a minimum of three successive acts (XYX)—a single occurrence of feedback. One member (X) makes an initial comment, another member (Y) responds to that comment, and X then reacts to Y's response. This, of course, is the classic instance of a double interact. (See also Weick, 1969, pp. 45–48). The point should be clear. Given the necessity of a loop for feedback, the feedback process in human communication requires a minimum of three acts in sequence (a double interact) in order to constitute a single instance of feedback.

According to this view (a view that, of course, emanates from a pragmatic perspective), interpreting feedback as a single response of any kind at any time misses the point of the feedback loop. Leathers's (1971) instrument for microscopic examination of feedback responses does just that. He focuses on Y's act in Scheidel and Crowell's XYX double interact. However, Leathers views feedback from the mechanistic concept of response. Scheidel and Crowell's view of feedback is the pragmatic concept of social process. In that latter view, according to Miller, Galanter, and Pribram (1960), the response or reflex is simply not the element of feedback behavior—"the unit should be the feedback loop itself."

The concept of positive and negative feedback in viewing feedback as social process also differs from positive and negative feedback viewed as reinforcement. Like the presence of a servomechanism, negative feedback counteracts deviation or disturbance in the system so that the system can continue to function "normally," that is, in a steady state— stability. This is not to be confused with negative feedback seen as punishment, although verbal "punishment" may be involved as one of the behaviors in the double-interact sequence or loop; that is, the "normal" functioning of the system involves the most patterned or most redundant sequences of interaction.

In that those patterns of double interacts occur with the most probable regularity, they constitute the "steady state" of the interaction system and can be said to constitute loops of negative feedback—stability or maintenance of the system in a "steady state." Feedback loops acquired through empirical observation can be visualized in diagrammatic form as probabilities of transitions from one type of act to another (see Hawes and Foley [1973] and Ellis and Fisher [1975]).

Positive feedback, on the other hand, is a departure from the servomechanism of cybernetic systems that are inherently comprised of negative feedback loops—deviation counteracting loops. Positive feedback loops are so called because of the way they function on deviations or disturbances in the system. If negative feedback counteracts or corrects deviation, then positive feedback serves to encourage or amplify or accelerate the deviations or the disturbances. Although negative feedback implies maintenance of the system in a stable state, positive feedback implies change—the opposite of maintenance. Positive feedback places the system in a state of flux.

At first glance, one is tempted to view negative feedback as inherently desirable and positive feedback as inherently disruptive, that is, undesirable. After all, maintenance keeps the system going, but change also keeps the system growing. In point of fact, neither negative feedback nor positive feedback is inherently or consistently desirable or undesirable. Of course, negative feedback loops are necessary to keep the system functioning under some control during normal day-to-day operation, but too much control can lead to stagnation and render a system incapable of responding to some threat, stress, or external disturbance. On the other hand, too much change can be equally desirable or undesirable. Although a system that is capable of growth and change is also capable of progress, too much growth or progress can destroy the system just as quickly as too little.

The environmentalist movement in the United States during the past decade or so can be conceived as an attempt to place control (that is, negative feedback loops) on runaway growth—of industry, cities, government, mining, and so on—which threatens to disrupt our biological environment as well as the quality of life enjoyed in the social environment. Watzlawick, Beavin, and Jackson (1967, p. 31) illustrate how stability itself is not necessarily desirable. They cite the case of a family with a schizophrenic member. That family may be so stable that they resist any attempt at change—including therapeutic treatment of the schizophrenic member. Clearly, this type of stability is not desirable.

Hardin (1963) expresses a more defensible notion of steady state (also called "homeostasis"). He illustrates the existence of homeostasis as a middle region between the influences of positive feedback loops and negative feedback loops. Too much of either extreme spells death for the system. Thus, survival of the system depends on the blend and the utilization of both positive and negative feedback loops. The steady state (that is, homeostasis), then, can fluctuate rather drastically in response to the push and pull of both positive and negative feedback loops. Hardin calls that desirable middle region of allowable steady-state fluctuation a "homeostatic plateau"—a not-too-steady state, but in the long run characteristic of a stable system (a system that survives).

Several implications are evident within this view of feedback as social process. Furthermore, these implications make sense only when feedback

is viewed conceptually from this pragmatic perspective. These implications are largely inconsistent with or quite irrelevant to any of the other
three concepts of feedback. Dennis Smith (1973, p. 26) suggests, for
example, that feedback does not exist in amount and, therefore, cannot
vary in amount. Like communication, feedback is a process in which one
engages rather than an activity that one does or a quantity that one
receives. To say that one did not get "enough" feedback is quite meaningless when feedback is viewed as a social process.

But feedback can vary in the amount of information (that is, the pattern or the redundancy of the double interacts) that it possesses. Therefore, the phrase *not enough feedback* needs to be restated or reinterpreted
to suggest that the feedback that was occurring did not occur with sufficient redundancy or with sufficient recognizable patterning—thus, the
information value of the feedback was apparently insufficient. The focus
then shifts from the sheer amount of feedback received to the utility of
the feedback in terms of its information value (as determined by pattern
or redundancy).

Watzlawick, Beavin, and Jackson (1967, p. 158) suggest another implication of feedback in terms of the qualitative or descriptive notion
of the interacts themselves. These psychiatrists suggest that symmetrical
interaction (that is, all acts in the sequence are of the same type or
variety) is suggestive of positive feedback; that is, the anything-you-can-
do-I-can-do-better syndrome can lead to runaway competition—a pattern
that cannot be sustained indefinitely. Complementary interaction (for
example, dominance-submission, command-compliance, initiation-accep-
tance, question-answer) may, according to Watzlawick, Beavin, and
Jackson, characterize negative feedback in the sense that such interaction
is relatively stable as a definition of social relationship.

Neither these authors nor I would wish to carry the analogy between
positive-negative feedback and symmetrical-complementary interaction
too far. The analogy emphasizing stability and competition would soon
fall apart. However, the analogy does suggest an ineresting conjecture.
Perhaps steady-state interaction (and thus negative feedback loops) is
evident within the nature of the interaction itself. The emphasis of the
pragmatic perspective on the qualitative or descriptive characteristics of
the interaction might lead to some patterned stability inherent to certain
combinations of categories of communicative behavior. Up to this point,
that implication remains speculative—more intriguing as an heuristic insight than valuable as an empirical discovery.

Feedback viewed as a social process is clearly the most different among
the four conceptualizations of feedback included in this chapter. It stems
directly from the pragmatic perspective and retains that emphasis on
the social system as a nonsummative whole. It treats feedback as a

circular process or loop requiring a minimum of three sequential acts (a double interact) as a single occurrence of feedback. Its view of positive and negative feedback loops is distinct from positive and negative feedback reinforcement. The fundamental assumptions differ and, consequently, so do the implications to be drawn from the various perspectives.

SUMMARY

Feedback stems from the field of cybernetics—a mechanistic theory of control—and is widely applicable to various phenomena, including physical, mechanical, biological and social systems. The term *feedback* is consistently related to human communication, however, and may be viewed as inherent within the communicative process, although not unique to it. Central to feedback is the principle of control in which some output or past performance is reinserted into the system as input, which then serves to control or otherwise affect future performance. The nature of control through past behaviors that are "fed back" as input characterizes all the variations of the concept.

By far, the most typical view of feedback in human communication is the rather mechanistic concept of response. In this sense, feedback is a message sent back from a receiver to a source, informing the source of the receiver's reaction and providing the basis for the source to determine his subsequent behavior. Feedback-as-response can vary according to the amount or level, as well as the number or variety of channels used in conveying the feedback message. Generally, however, the view of feedback-as-response recognizes the simultaneous interchange of messages in communication and, consequently, the simultaneity of feedback interchange. Such a view is consistent with a conveyor-belt model of human communication as explicated in a mechanistic perspective.

From a psychological perspective of human communication, feedback is typically viewed as verbalized reinforcement in a conditioning paradigm. The S–R psychological model, then, becomes completed as an S–O–R-*feedback* linear chain in which feedback serves to reinforce (that is, reward or punish) the organism's response (in this case, communicative behavior). Feedback is thus endowed with positive and negative aspects of reinforcement, so that verbal feedback can serve to praise or blame the response and hence encourage continuation of that response behavior (that is, a positive feedback reinforcement) or to discourage or exert a deleterious effect on that behavioral response (that is, a negative feedback reinforcement).

As in the receiving of any message, including feedback reinforcement, the individual is an active encoder of feedback reinforcements, so that he exerts selectivity on the feedback message itself. Unlike a machine, the human actively interprets feedback reinforcement and can go so far as to interpret positive feedback as negative and negative feedback as positive. Furthermore, the active recipient of feedback reinforcement can even choose to ignore feedback reinforcement from certain people and choose the communicators from whom he will accept or attend to feedback reinforcement. A further variable of feedback as reinforcement concerns the timing of feedback reinforcement with a distinct advantage in effectiveness attributable to immediate rather than delayed (even for a fraction of a second) feedback.

Feedback may also be viewed as an internalized servomechanism that serves to regulate behavior within narrowly prescribed limits. The conceptual filters of a psychological perspective (for example, attitudes) may function to control behavior within acceptable parameters in social situations, although such a view of the attitude-behavior relationship is controversial, to say the least.

An interactional perspective of human communication could, however, view the process of role taking as indicative of a servomechanism that regulates behavior by assessing past behavior. The self, from the role of other, could view the behavior of self retrospectively and evaluate it as to appropriateness or some other criterion. That evaluation could then be used to select subsequent behavior in future communicative situations. The servomechanism is thus the role-taking self as other, assessing past behavioral performances and regulating subsequent behavior.

A pragmatic perspective of human communication views feedback as a social process from the viewpoint of not an individual communicator, but the holistic system of interactants. Feedback is then discernible within the patterns of interaction as a minimal sequence of three acts (a double interact). The feedback process becomes not simply a response but a circular closed loop of interaction—in its minimal form an initial comment, a response to that comment, and reaction to the response. As a loop or sequence of acts, then, feedback can recur and be reaccomplished.

A feedback process or loop is positive or negative, depending upon how the loop affects deviation from "normal" interaction patterns. If the process counteracts or corrects deviation from a normal interaction pattern, it is deemed negative. If the feedback loop amplifies or accelerates deviation from a normal pattern, it is positive. To the extent that negative feedback loops dominate the system (for example, high redundancy or patterning), the system is functioning at a steady state, that is, maintaining stability. To the extent that the positive feedback loops function in the interaction patterns, the system is in a period of change, that is, growth, increasing complexity. Communication systems normally contain both positive and negative feedback loops whose relative strengths fluctuate over time.

Feedback is an important concept in understanding human communication, but, like any concept, it is subject to understanding by virtue of its application to the actual phenomena of human communication. Regardless of the perspective used to view human communication, feedback is consistently viewed as a significant and probably inherent element of the communicative process. But how it functions, what it looks like, and how it is to be conceptualized are functions of the theoretical perspective used to view the phenomena of human communication.

— 11 —

Still More Concepts

Previous chapters in Part Three have hardly exhausted the list of concepts used in the field of human communication. In fact, the number of concepts that could be discussed could conceivably require several hundred additional pages. But such a discussion would try your patience as well as my own. The alternative is to be rather selective and discuss briefly only a few of those remaining concepts that have been most popular in the theoretical and empirical literature of human communication.

This chapter includes a variety of concepts, six in number, which take on a variety of meanings, depending on the perspective used to define each concept. Some of the concepts are quite important to communication in each perspective. Some concepts are vital to one or more perspectives, but insignificant or irrelevant in others. This chapter is essentially a potpourri of additional concepts that require less discussion than those concepts of the preceding chapters.

THE CONCEPT OF PROCESS

Communication is a process. Everybody knows that! I know of no student or scholar of human communication, regardless of the level of sophistication of knowledge, who would seriously suggest that human communication is something other than a process. Indeed, the word *process* is a "God-term" in the field of human communication. Yet few terms create so much controversy. David Smith (1972), for example, provides an excellent discussion of some important issues surrounding process and suggests that much of the belief in process among communication scholars is suspect. He suggests that we pay lip service to the concept of process but perform communication research that is incongruent with the contemporary notion of the concept. In fact, the convention paper that served as the basis for Smith's article suggested in its title that everybody talks about process but nobody does anything about it in research. Dennis Alexander (1975) arrived at a conclusion similar to Smith's several years later in a more specific examination of contemporary communication research.

There are several approaches to a discussion of process. One approach is to take a view similar to those of Smith and Alexander; that is, provide a definition of process, and document the shortcomings of communication research or theory in failing to conform to that definition. If we were to take this approach, we would undoubtedly suggest that "one-way communication" and the "target model" of communication fall short of the definition of process. But no one seriously believes in the viability of either one-way communication or the target model. These are simply straw-man issues. The target model is simply false and fails to take into account all the elements of human communication. One-way communication, a purely mechanistic phenomenon, is better explained as a barrier or breakdown—that is, some malfunction on the channel—for example, an overly zealous gatekeeper or the receiver's unwillingness or inability to perceive the responding messages (the feedback).

Perhaps a more realistic approach is to view process as reflecting variable meaning based on the perspective used to view human communication. After all, if everyone believes that communication is a process, then why doesn't everyone view communication similarly (unless, of course, they view process differently)? And if Smith and Alexander are correct (and they certainly are, in this respect), then broad disparity characterizes the views of communication process in the conducting of empirical communication research. Therefore, communication as a process is apparently a function of the perspective used to view the phenomenon of human communication.

The Covering-Law View of Process

Brodbeck (1958) describes the nature of process in terms of "process laws"—a direct analysis of process from a positivistic philosophy of science. According to Brodbeck, a process law is characteristic of a theory with "perfect knowledge." Such a law implies that knowledge of the state of any variable at any time implies knowledge of its effect on all other variables at all other times. Thus, any two states of the system can be inferred from each other (that is, either direction) regardless of the points in time at which those states occur.

Such process laws are causal and determinate. They are precise in their predictions of one event from another in either temporal direction, and their predictions are precise as to specific points in time. Process laws of physics, for example, allow precise predictions of the position of a planet at any and every point in the future or in the past from knowing only its present position. Process laws allow precise predictions, for example of the exact instant of sunrise and sunset for every day of the year at any spot on the globe. Moreover, those predictions are possible for any and every year in the past or in the future. Process laws are precise in regard to instants in time and reversible in regard to prediction in either temporal direction.

A process theory—that is, a theory composed of process laws—allows for prediction of states of a system at all times from knowledge of the system's state at any given time. Brodbeck believes that such a theory is logically possible in the social sciences although she argues for the necessity of methodological individualism in order to allow for that possibility. She also seems to imply that though perfect knowledge in the social sciences is logically possible, it is quite unlikely.

Gustav Bergmann (1962), one of the leading contemporary spokesmen of the covering-law philosophy of sciences, asserts three prerequisites for process knowledge: complete closure of the system, a complete set of all relevant variables, and knowledge of process laws (that is, all the possible lawlike regularities of how each variable can interact with all other variables in all possible combinations). Bergmann also refers to process knowledge as "the ideal" and essentially "the ultimate goal of all science." From his positivistic view of science philosophy, that goal is the only goal worthy of being sought in any science—and even more specifically for social science.

Smith (1972) suggests that this view of process underlies much of communication research and reflects the Newtonian, mechanistic view of process, which he considers clearly outdated. Smith argues convincingly that many members of the scientific community of human communication cling tenaciously to this ideal of classical physics; that is, many scholars believe that if one knows enough about human communication, she would be able to predict how people would behave in any communicative act or respond to any message stimulus. In terms of persuasion, process knowledge would allow communicators to manipulate their appeals in order to achieve, consistently and certainly, the desired responses in the receiver. This ideal may suggest a view of 1984—a brave new world of mass manipulation through communication.

Smith doubts that such an ideal as process laws is possible. He also doubts that anyone really believes that such perfect knowledge is possible. His basic concern is that communication scholars define communication process quite differently from this covering-law view and then proceed to conduct research in a manner quite consistent with the ideal of process laws. His argument is not flawless, but it is convincing. His primary concern is not that many people view process erroneously but that research and theory (or, at least, philosophical perspectives) of human communication are incongruent, if not downright inconsistent.

Other Views of Process

In a previous discussion of process (1974, pp. 15–16), I resorted to the dictionary to provide the starting point for understanding communication as a process. The dictionary provides four elements inherent to a process: actions (or events), change in time, progress or advancement over time, and a goal or result. These elements provide the basis for the bulk of discussion about communication as a process. To be sure, some discussions slight the concept of process by suggesting only that the concept of process implies nothing more than the exchange of source and receiver roles—in short, process is another name for two-way communication (see, for example, Hanneman [1975, p. 25]). But for the most part, the modeling of communication as a process implies considerably more than merely two-way communication. It implies a greater emphasis on the "action" of communication and, consequently, the organization of communication in time as well as in spatial structure.

Barnlund (1968, pp. 25–26) traces a "major change" in the field of communication when theorists began viewing communication as a process. Barnlund considers process to emphasize "the actual operations involved in communicating." Process thus stresses the significance of communicative functions—that is, what goes on during communication —rather than simply visualizing the structural components of the phenomenon of human communication in relative isolation. Thus, process inherently refers to events or occurrences—actions, behaviors—fundamental to the process of human communication.

Like events that occur in time, a process also accounts for the sequencing of those events. Clevenger and Matthews (1971, p. 176) refer to this sequence as "an interconnected series of events" and thereby imply that each event influences an outcome (that is, the next event in the sequence). They suggest that this sequence is, to some extent, determinate ("predetermined or determinable").

Berlo (1960, p. 24) may disagree in his nearly eloquent statement of a process when he defines the sequence of events as not "fixed" so that the relationships between events, as well as the events themselves, are "dynamic, on-going, ever-changing, continuous." Watzlawick, Beavin, and Jackson (1967, p. 34) agree and believe that the sequence of communicative acts is definitely not deterministic but stochastic—probabilistic and susceptible to variations in those probabilities over time. The nature of the relationship between actions or events, then, is a matter of theoretical or philosophical disagreement, but the temporal sequence of events is, nonetheless, an integral part of the concept of process.

A further view of process suggests the importance of change in uncovering a process. Reusch and Bateson (1968, pp. 59–60, 140–144), for example, consider tracing the changes that take place in time to be the key role of empirical observation or process. To trace changes in time, of course, requires that the observer utilize some point or period of time as a reference point against which the variety of temporal sequencing can be compared. (Reusch and Bateson refer to this reference point in time as "static fixation" of data.) Because of the ongoing nature of time and, hence, process, the selection of the point or period used as a temporal referent is quite arbitrary and subject to the purposes or desires of the investigation. The purpose is then to "observe evolution in time" and requires a more longitudinal observation and multiple observations of the system of events we call human communication.

Tracing the evolution of events in a communication system is similar to Whitehead's (1929) notion of process—what Smith (1972) refers to as "process in the twentieth century sense." The basic difference between Whiteheadian process and the positivistic notion of process is the difference between determinism/perfect knowledge and indeterminism/evolution. Contrary to the covering-law view, to ask how communication evolves is equivalent to asking why an event occurs. In the oft-quoted notion of Whitehead, being is becoming.

Gerard (1957) views the operation of a system in much the same sense. Using biology as his starting point, Gerard suggests that the explanation of a system involves explanation of its being, its behaving, and its becoming (that is, structure, function, and evolution). In this sense of process, the goal or result or outcome is a natural outgrowth of the change or process in the sequence of events leading up to it. To understand one is to understand the other.

To view communication as a process, then, does not imply searching for the ultimate or ideal state of perfect knowledge or process laws. To the contrary, to hold such a belief in perfect knowledge as the ultimate goal of science (see, for example, Bowers, [1970, p. 8], and Miller [1972, p. 45]) obviates the use of a covering-law view of the nature of process—specifically, process laws, a set of variables, and their deterministic-reversible relationships, that is, complete closure of the system. The conclusion drawn from this discussion is, therefore, that the concept of process is variable and depends to a significant degree on how one views the nature of the relationships among processual phenomena. To say that communication is a process is to say little about communication unless the processual relationships among communicative phenomena have been specified, and specifying them is a matter of being consistent with the overall perspective used to view human communication.

Perspective Views of Process

To repeat once again one of the major assumptions underlying Part Three, a concept associated with the empirical study of human communication is a function of the perspective used to view human communication. The concept of process is certainly no exception. It has become fashionable in recent years to refer to "the process view" of communication, implying that process is a specific way to view communication, in and of itself. The assumption underlying this volume suggests quite a different approach to process. The concept of process is present in all perspectives. Even the most die-hard perspectivist, whether mechanistic or psychological or interactional or pragmatic, would agree that communication is most certainly a process. But the nature of process differs considerably.

From a mechanistic viewpoint, the process of human communication is movement—the message (encoded, transmitted, and decoded) flowing on the channel. The message is followed by another message in response, which is also encoded, transmitted, and decoded in a continuous, circular transmissional process. An empirical study of communication process from the transmissional point of view would trace changes in the message as it flows on the channel—both internal and external to the source/receiver. Of course, the process of communication would involve the simultaneous exchange of messages, simultaneous encoding and decoding of transmitted messages, and simultaneous role switching of source and receiver. Problems on the channel can disrupt this process, and those problems are attributable to noise, which reduces the fidelity of the message. A more serious disruption on the channel might be called a communication breakdown or barrier—clearly antiprocessual concepts and the subject of discussion later in this chapter.

A psychological process would focus on the stimulus perceiving and responding of the individual communicator. As the individual selects stimuli, perceives stimuli, filters stimuli through internalized sets, assigns meaning to those stimuli, and responds to stimuli behaviorally, the process of communication is taking place. A study of communication process would trace changes in the person during the process. Typically those changes are traced via a black-box model of inquiry, which would trace contextual conditions and available stimuli into the individual and observe changes in responses or outcomes of those inputs. Thus, a psychological term for persuasion is often called *attitude change*. Often the observed changes are indirect (inferential measures of attitudes through paper-and-pencil tests, for example), although behavioral responses are often observed as the outcomes of certain stimuli and certain stimulus-conditions.

A process from a mechanistic or psychological perspective is relatively linear in its treatment of time; that is, antecedent events lead to future events. Feedback responses follow messages, and responses and perceptions follow exposure to stimuli. This temporal linearity is a functional characteristic of the process concept of communication as viewed from these two perspectives. It is also a characteristic that renders such perspectives quite amenable to formal theorizing in the received view or covering-law model of science philosophy. Such relationships between temporal phenomena of communication are easily expressed within the format of conditional logic—if-then relationships. Though a conditional (if-then) relationship is not precisely causal, it is more deterministic than other relationships. But it is no less a process than other relationships. It is merely linear—a particular variety of the concept of process.

Process in the interactional or pragmatic perspective is considerably less determinate and is less susceptible to precise formalization within conditional statements. The close linear relationships between events in temporal sequence is missing in these latter two perspectives. Rather, the temporal relationship is stochastic, suggesting that events occur in habituation (that is, quite frequently in the past) and are likely to occur again in the future. One person role-taking a generalized other, for example, will perform actions similar to those of another person who role-takes a similar generalized other. This habituation underlies the phenomenon of self-alignment of actions, allowing for social behavior to occur. Moreover, the pattern of communicative behaviors is also stochastic in the sense that specific sequences of acts (interacts or double interacts) in the pragmatic perspective can be assigned a probability level of their occurrence based upon observation of those sequences over a period of time in the past.

The concept of process in the interactional or the pragmatic perspective is much more Whiteheadian in the sense that a more longitudinal concept of time is necessary. The process of social behavior, through either self-alignment of actions or patterned sequences of behaviors, is an evolutionary development that can be traced over time. Moreover, changes in those patterns can also be traced through time in an evolutionary manner.

The linear relationship between events is destroyed in this evolutionary view because events or actions are repeatable and reversible. Furthermore, to suggest that event B follows event A at probability level of .82 is also to say that the probability of some event other than B following event A is .18. The process is probabilistic and considerably less deterministic than the linear relationship expressed in the conditional statement. The if-then statement suggests that antecedent conditions are sufficient to require the existence of consequent conditions.

Process, then, is characteristic of communication regardless of which perspective is used to view human communication. Like any concept, process is subject to definition and correspondence rules laid down by each perspective. Though process always involves temporal sequencing of events and tracing changes over time, for example, the nature of that sequential relationship and the identification of what changes can occur is a function of the perspective used to view the entire process of human communication.

THE CONCEPT OF BREAKDOWN/BARRIER

The concept of communication breakdown has received in recent years a great deal of "bad press" among members of the scientific community. Dennis Smith (1970), for example, refers to the concept as a "fallacy." Although the term continues to be popularly employed in the everyday parlance of human communication, as a scientific concept its usage is quite restricted and typically subsumed under other concepts, such as communicative effectiveness. As a rule, the limitations of the term stem from its inherent assumptions of a mechanistic or a psychological perspective. As a concept in an interactional or pragmatic view of human communication, it is either grossly insignificant or nonexistent.

The concept of breakdown is often interchangeable with that of barrier, although the former enjoys much more popular usage. One must keep in mind that a breakdown of communication need not be total and thus signify a cessation of the entire process of human communication. Breakdown may be partial or total, but it is virtually always partial when we consider communication to be ongoing and continuous although fraught with barriers in the sense of a generation gap, a credibility gap, a failure to communicate, people talking without speaking, or people hearing without listening. Thus, communication breakdown (or barrier or gap or failure) is a matter of degree, which is measurable on a continuum.

Breakdown and barrier are most typically associated with a mechanistic view of human communication. The reason for that association should be obvious. The term *breakdown* is a term directly attributable to the machine analogy in the same sense that a machine "breaks down" and ceases to run. A barrier is equivalent to a dam on the channel that obstructs the flow of messages much as a dam on a river channel obstructs the flow of water. As mechanistic terms, their conceptual meaning or significance is clear. A breakdown may be said to exist when the flow of messages on the channel is restricted, obstructed, impeded, or in some way disrupted. The problem could be internal to the individual (a failure to interpret adequately) or a disruptive gatekeeper. In either case, a mechanistic breakdown of human communication can be attributed to excessive noise on the channel, and noise is a disruptive force that can even result in total breakdown if it exists in too great an amount.

A psychological breakdown is clearly internal and refers to a distortion of meaning on the part of one or more of the communicators. Stimulus-messages can be misinterpreted or, at least, interpreted differently owing to cultural biases, role conflicts, conflicting social systems, or from a variety of other factors (see Berlo, 1960, pp. 152–164). Essentially, communication breakdowns in a psychological perspective represent a mismatch of conceptual filters within the communicators (see, for example, MacKay, 1969, pp. 111–115). If meaning is perception, then meaning is shared to the extent that the "sets" used to perceive are isomorphic. To the extent that those internalized sets differ from one communicator to another—that is, a mismatch of perceptual sets—then communication breakdown can be said to exist. Breakdown is thus the psychological antithesis of shared meaning (isomorphism).

Although breakdown (or barrier or gap) is a convenient term used to describe problems of human communication, the term is of limited usefulness to a scientific inquiry of human communicative phenomena for a variety of reasons. Perhaps the most significant limitation is the restriction the term places on the perspectives that may be used to view human communication (that is, able to be conceptualized only in a mechanistic or psychological perspective). Another important limitation is the tendency to oversimplify the complexity of human communication by using a convenient label for any potential problem, difficulty, or misunderstanding that might occur. (For a discussion of this oversimplification, see Mortensen, 1972, pp. 7–8.) Because of its limited usefulness and the possibility of describing breakdowns by using other concepts, no further discussion of communication breakdowns seems necessary.

THE CONCEPT OF INFORMATION

Information is another concept that is quite typical of, though not unique to, discussions of human communication. But unlike some of the other concepts discussed in Part Three, information is not actually a concept whose meaning or significance is a function of the perspective used to view the entire process of communication. Rather, information is a term that is legitimately applied to several different phenomena. Thus, variations in the conceptual meaning do not precipitate much confusion in or between perspectives, but using the same term to refer to several different phenomena may result in some confusion over the concept.

It is important to emphasize that these variations are not necessarily reflections of different perspectives. In fact, the term *information* could be used to refer to any or all of the three variations discussed below within the same perspective. The discussion is thus more a discussion of three separate concepts, all of which have the same label.

Perhaps the most typical nonscholarly use of the term *information* is to refer to facts or data that can be acquired during an act of communication. Thus, we speak of seeking more information before we can make a decision, or we speak of a journalist's gathering information from the scene of a news event or a detective's gathering information (evidence) about a crime. Used in this manner, information is conceptualized as a physical quantity that can be transferred from one point to another, from one person to another. It is not an event as such, but a conceptually material entity by virtue of its being extended through time. Once you acquire information, you have it. You possess it and store it in a memory. Thus, a message can be said to contain information, or information can be sent and received along a channel, or information can be selected from the environment in the form of a set of stimuli.

A second use of the term *information* refers to the meaning of data. You might recall an earlier discussion of Thayer's (1968) distinction between information and data so that data take on meaning or significance as they are interpreted by the communicator. For example, if you heard someone speaking in a foreign language with which you were unfamiliar, you would have a great deal of data but little information, that is, little meaning or significance of the data. Information in this respect is a matter of interpretation—conferring meaning upon data.

A third use of the term *information* is a direct function of information theory (sometimes even called *communication theory*) developed originally by Shannon and Weaver (1949). Information theory considers information a measurable quantity of uncertainty—removing uncertainty from a finite number of available alternative choices by successively reducing the number of alternatives by half. Each 50 per cent reduction of alternatives constitutes one "bit" (abbreviation for *binary digit*) of information. Information in information theory is solely a measurable quantity of reduction of choices and is devoid of "meaning" as such. This sense of information is central to the pragmatic perspective of human communication and is expressed as the amount of pattern, redundancy, or constraint (interchangeable terms) that is reflected in the ongoing sequence of communicative behaviors. This use of the term was discussed extensively in Chapter 7 in terms of the interaction sequences.

Information, then, is not so much a concept whose meaning varies as a function of a perspective. Rather, information is a term that is used to refer to several different concepts that do not necessarily reflect any perspective. As such, information itself is not a single concept but is a term to denote any of three concepts, that is, a term used rather ambiguously to refer to at least three different concepts. The only caution is to be clear as to what the term information refers when it appears in discussions of human communication.

THE CONCEPT OF INTRAPERSONAL COMMUNICATION

In recent years the study of human communication has been organized under the following classifications: intrapersonal communication, interpersonal communication, group communication, organizational communication, and mass communication. Of course, this list is only one of many legitimate ways to organize communication, but it does provide one way to view communication in a manner analogous with the common sociological grouping of increasing complexity: individual, dyad, group, organization, and society. The question arises, however, as to whether this sociological grouping suggests different *settings* or different *levels* of communicative phenomena. The fact is that the groups could refer to either settings or levels of human communication or to both. As an earlier discussion has suggested, our viewpoint will argue for the latter, so that intrapersonal communication refers to communicative phenomena relative to the individual. Moreover, these phenomena function whenever communication occurs, regardless of the sociological setting of the communicative event.

It is certainly possible to view communication in an intrapersonal setting—that is, an individual alone who is communicating with self. Wilmot and Wenburg (1974, p. 11), for example, consider intrapersonal communication as both a level and a setting. As a setting, intrapersonal communication occurs when "you have a dream, meditate, scribble in your personal diary, or just think privately." Now whether dreaming or private thinking constitutes communication is an issue that might generate considerable argument. To engage in that argument, however, seems an incredibly trivial exercise. Thinking is thinking, to be sure. Whether thinking is also communication is an argument that I shall leave to others. The following discussion will consider intrapersonal communication only as a level of communication that exists as part of the process, whether that process occurs in a conversation between two friends, during jury deliberations, in labor-management negotiations, in an audience listening to a platform speaker, in watching television newscasts, or whatever.

Of all the four major perspectives discussed in Part Two, a psychological perspective of human communication stresses most the importance of the intrapersonal level. From the discussion of the concept of meaning, you will recall that a psychological perspective places meaning squarely within the purview of the intrapersonal level of communication. In fact, Upton (1967, p. 379) goes so far as to equate the term *semantics* (linguistic meaning) with intrapersonal communication, considering them the same concept. That terminological equivalence is a logical inference from the meaning-is-perception conceptualization.

In a psychological perspective the intrapersonal level of human communication is central to the communicative event. Intrapersonal communication "focuses on the information-processing characteristics (including language use) of individual participants in a communication event" [Hanneman, 1975, p. 33] "when a person assigns significance to messages apart from the presence of another person" [Mortensen, 1972, p. 19]. Processing information (that is, data or facts or stimuli) is inherently internal to the individual. And the significance of the meaning of messages (or any stimuli, for that matter) is also internal, that is, assigned by the individual who applies his conceptual filters or set.

From a psychological perspective the intrapersonal level of human communication is the most significant level of communication. Encoding, decoding of stimuli, messages, responses—all communicative activities from a psychological perspective take place within the individual. Such a perspective leads directly to the belief, expressed by Wilmot and Wenburg (1974, p. 11): "Ultimately, *all* communication can be labeled intrapersonal."

In an interactional perspective, the intrapersonal level of human communication is also significant—but not significant in the same manner or the same degree as a psychological perspective. Recall that interactional role taking allows for a self-regulating feedback loop within self; that is, the individual is able to assume the role of other and assess self-behavior. Intrapersonally, then, the individual is able to modify her own behavior by intrapersonally directing present behavior, assessing past behavior, and modifying future behavior. Though meaning is largely socially constructed by the individual through self-indication of actions, feedback is largely intrapersonally constructed by role-taking other and viewing self as object. Although significant to an interactional view of human communication, the intrapersonal level is not nearly so central nor so inclusive as the intrapersonal level of communication viewed psychologically.

Only in a pragmatic perspective is the intrapersonal level of human communication deemed insignificant. Recall that a pragmatic perspective shifts the focus from the individual to the social system and thus de-emphasizes the individual qua individual; that is, a pragmatic perspective may deny intrapersonal communication as a setting for communication, but it clearly does not deny intrapersonal communication as a level of communication. Nevertheless, such a perspective renders the internal processes quite insignificant and virtually ignores them in concentrating on the observable behaviors.

Weick (1969, pp. 36–50) traces the conceptual argument, which shifts the focus of a pragmatic perspective from the individual to the social system (what Weick terms "collective structure"). In the first place, the social focus de-emphasizes people in favor of the relationships among people as the key to collective structure. He (p. 37) indicates that individuals provide only the "medium" for relationships but are not the relationships themselves. Individuals are thus the source of behaviors but are not equivalent to the behaviors themselves; hence, the only "elements potentially available for a collective structure consist of the behaviors that can be produced" [p. 46] by the participants. Thus, "it is behaviors, not persons, that are interstructured."

You will note that Weick does not deny the existence of any intrapersonal level of social behavior, but he does stress the significance of the behaviors actually produced by the individual as providing all the information that is necessary to understand collective structure. He goes on to suggest that the behaviors themselves are relatively meaning-less, but their interstructuring (that is, the information contained in the pattern or the redundancy of the behavioral sequences) constitutes the relationship between people and, hence, the definition and the signifi-cance of the collective structure.

To a person committed to a psychological perspective of human com-munication, such conceptualization must appear blasphemous. Inciden-tally, Weick is also a social psychologist—not specifically a communica-tion specialist. The first response might be to ask, "But what about perception?" Weick (pp. 38–39) shifts his conceptual focus from per-ception also and emphasizes "attentional processes" consistent with the retrospective focus on interactive behaviors (that is, discovering pattern-ing in past sequences of behavior). Weick considers perception to be "reactive" and does not allow the individual to "create" his environment. Thus, Weick opts for the pragmatic here-and-now that "controls the nature of the attention he directs to his past experience." In this way, Weick emphasizes that a pattern of interactive behaviors possesses information (constraint) only as it is continually reaccomplished, that is, redundancy (p. 36).

In a pragmatic perspective of human communication, then, the intra-personal level provides no data that allow for any fuller understanding of human communication on the level of the social system. All the "meaning" of a social relationship is included in the information (pattern, constraint) reflected in the sequences of interstructured behaviors. In a way, one can conclude that what an individual thinks or feels internally cannot be relevant to the social relationship until or unless it is mani-fested in the behavior. And as behavior, it is included in a pragmatic perspective of human communication. The individual, then, is a medium (a carrier) for behaviors. But ultimately all communication is behavior.

The intrapersonal level of communication is thus a legitimate level of communication in virtually all the perspectives. But though a psychologi-cal perspective of human communication views the intrapersonal level as the central focus for any communicative event, a pragmatic perspective considers the intrapersonal level only a medium for behaviors. And an interactional perspective considers the intrapersonal level as embodying a significant controlling function for communication, but by no means is the intrapersonal level the *sine qua non* for all communication. The con-cept of intrapersonal communication is thus a function of the perspective from which communication is viewed and achieves its significance or meaning as it relates to other concepts within each perspective. Like nearly all communication concepts, it can be discussed with any under-standing only within a perspective and cannot be viewed as meaningful in and of itself or in isolation from a theoretical viewpoint.

THE CONCEPT OF COMPLEXITY

If nothing else, human communication is certainly complex. I know of no one who would doubt the truth of such a statement. To some, though, such a statement suggests that human communication is difficult to understand. But such a reaction misses the point of complexity. Complexity suggests, in a word, differentiation. The more one can differentiate among varieties of a phenomenon, the more complex that phenomenon. A skier, for example, can differentiate among many different kinds of snow on the slopes—powder snow, corn snow, soft snow, "cheat" snow, dry snow, and so on. A nonskier will make fewer differentiations, and for him the phenomenon of snow is relatively simple, that is, not very complex.

A student of communication finds the phenomenon of interest increasingly more complex as she is able to make increasingly more numerous differentiations among various communicative phenomena. The concept of complexity, then, is not so much a function of each perspective as it is a function of the purposes of the investigator. She can choose a simple purpose, ask a simple question, and get a simple answer. Or she can choose a more complex purpose, ask a complex question, and get a complex answer. The result is increased sophistication of understanding if the phenomenon being investigated is truly complex. With a more sophisticated understanding comes the realization that there are no simple answers available for complex questions—hence, the conclusion that human communication is highly complex.

Two distinctions of complexity are important for being able to utilize the concept effectively. Complexity is a function of time as well as space. We shall refer to the former as *temporal complexity* and to the latter as *structural complexity*. Keep in mind that complexity is a function of the purpose or sophistication of the inquiry—not the perspective used to view human communication. In other words, one perspective is no more complex than any other in its treatment of communication, and each perspective may include differing levels of both structural or temporal complexity—depending once again on the purposes of the investigator.

Structural complexity refers to the number of differentiations made among spatial components. The more spatial components, the more complex. For example, a four-person group is more complex than a three-person group, or so it seems. But the number of persons does not necessarily indicate the functioning of complexity in the investigation; that is, a mechanistic investigation of all-channel networks would find the four-person group twice as complex as the three-person group. Three possible channels connect the three positions in a three-person network: A–B, B–C, A–C. But the four-person group includes six possible channels —A–B, B–C, C–D, A–C, A–D, B–C. And because channels are conceptually spatial connections or spatial relationships between positions (also in space)—in this case, persons represent positions—the differentiation among channels exemplifies a form of structural complexity that increases geometrically from a three-person group to a four-person group.

Other examples of structural complexity might include the number of conceptual filters (attitudes, perceptions, and so on) in a psychological perspective of human communication. The more attitudes or values conceptualized within the individual, the more complex the information-processing operation of the individual. Then, too, complexity increases as the conceptual filters are conceptualized as possessing various degrees of valence or strength. Moreover, an attitude may have varying degrees of ego-involvement or intensity—increased differentiation among attitudes. The various dimensions of source credibility suggest that the phenomenon of perceived ethos is more complex than simply a unidimensional construct. The increasing emphasis in communication research on multivariate analysis, factor analysis, interaction effects, multivariable studies, and so on, in recent years reflects the desire of the scientific community to match the inherent structural complexity of the phenomenon of communication with analytical procedures that are also complex.

A pragmatic perspective might reflect structural complexity in the number of categories used to differentiate among types of communicative acts or behaviors. The greater the number of categories, the more structural complexity in the interaction sequence. But the sequence of interaction also reflects temporal complexity in the sense that the sequence of acts may suggest concatenate relationships of varying lengths of sequences. For example, Altmann (1965) found that a triple interact (sequence of four acts) was the typically maximal level of temporal complexity because it exhausted nearly all the available information in the sequence; that is, a four-act sequential patterning removed nearly all the uncertainty among behavioral choices.

Altmann studied behaviors of rhesus monkeys in coming to his empirical conclusion of the triple-interact sequence. Fisher, Glover, and Ellis (1977), in a comparative study of human interaction, found that the information level revealed in different levels of temporal complexity (act, interact, double interact, and triple interact) varied from one category system to another and was not directly related to structural complexity (number of categories in the analytical system). Apparently, then, variations in temporal complexity are not necessarily related directly to variations in structural complexity. The conclusion once again is that human communication is a highly complex phenomenon—in terms of both temporal complexity and structural complexity.

Complexity or differentiation is thus not directly related to the perspective used to view human communication. The concept is more clearly relative to the purposes and functions of the specific act of scientific investigation. Knowing that communication is a complex phenomenon implies that inquiry into communicative phenomena needs to utilize complex methodologies and purposes. Certainly, there is a point of diminishing returns at which the level of complexity of the methodology exceeds the value of the results or the ability of the investigator to interpret the results. But communication is so complex—both temporally and structurally—that that point has not yet been reached.

THE CONCEPT OF COMMUNICATIVE EFFECTIVENESS

For over 2,500 years teachers and theorists of human communication have grappled with the issues related to communicative effectiveness. After centuries of attempts to solve these issues, they remain unresolved. In fact, one wonders whether we have made any progress at all toward their resolution. Certainly, this purposely brief discussion will do little toward resolving any of the issues surrounding criteria for effective communication. Nor will it provide any directions or recommendations as to how communicative effectiveness should be viewed. Rather, the paragraphs below attempt only to trace a few general and popular approaches to human communication.

Throughout history the concept of effective communication has fluctuated both in terms of describing communicative effectiveness and in defining the criteria for judging communication as effective. Quintilian's classical approach considered effective communication a blend of acquired skill and high moral character: "The good man speaking well." Later periods of rhetorical history defined effectiveness, for example, in terms of the skill in the artistic use of language (the stylistic rhetorics) and the skillful delivery of communication (the elocutionary period), among others.

A century ago our society viewed communicative effectiveness in terms of eloquence—a concept almost totally absent from the contemporary criteria of effectiveness. Our changing society has clearly reflected a shift from viewing effectiveness of communication as public speaking ability to the present focus on informal social communication or mass mediated communication. In any case, what constitutes effective communication and what criteria identify effective communication when it does exist remain quite arbitrary and ultimately ill-defined.

The one approach to communicative effectiveness that has remained through the years is the measure of effectiveness in terms of accrued effects. This neo-Aristotelian (see Black, 1965) criterion asks the question, "Did it work?" If it does, then it is effective. In a very realistic sense, much of the evaluation of communication inevitably boils down to effects. An advertising agency will remain in business only so long as its advertising results in sales of the product. A television programmer will remain in her job only so long as people choose to watch those programs. A political candidate can be effective only if she is elected. If the effects criterion smacks of the "sophistic," that is unfortunate; but such is the nature of reality in the world of business, politics, and so on.

Perhaps the most unfortunate element of the effects criterion is the apparent incapacity to understand or explain how and why the effects accrue. For example, a poster in my office has a caption that was described by one of my colleagues as the slogan for television programming: "If it feels good, do it!" The effects criterion breeds imitation—copying the "formula" of the successful television program, the successful commercial, the successful political campaign. From an empirical point of view, the effects criterion short-circuits understanding in favor of success. It breeds the sophistic—making the worse appear the better. Especially in the case of electing men and women to public office, such a viewpoint is very dangerous.

Another problem in assessing effectiveness with a criterion of effects is the problem of when effects should be measured. As Black (1965) has pointed out, the effects criterion is nearly always applied on too short-term a basis. We often speak of a person who is "ahead of his time," implying that the person was ineffective in the short run but presaging a much higher assessment of his effectiveness when viewed over a longer term of time. History is filled with examples. Edgar Allan Poe is viewed historically as a far more significant literary figure than Bret Harte, although Harte was more successful during his own time. Ernie Kovacs exerted a far more significant impact on the trend of visual comedy on television after his death. When are effects to be judged? The answer to that question will remain forever mystical.

A second approach to communicative effectiveness is to emphasize the techniques of communication. Such an approach suggests the identification of some standard of "good" or "bad" communication. Communicative effectiveness then becomes a matter of acquiring the skills to mimic the "good" model. Academia has long included courses in skills of communicational encoding (for example, linguistic style, delivery, message variables) and of decoding (for example, listening). Often these classes have led students to believe that effective communication is simply a matter of learning what things to do and what things to avoid doing. Despite the insistence of instructors to the contrary, students tend to regard communication as a rather simple phenomenon and certainly not a difficult subject to master. After all, practice (in techniques) makes perfect.

Under no circumstances should any reader interpret this discussion as my suggesting that techniques of communication cannot or should not be learned. Nor am I suggesting that "skills" courses in academic curricula should be considered insignificant. To the contrary, I would most vehemently argue quite the opposite. The issue is not the value of techniques per se, but the belief that we typically hold (erroneously) that techniques by themselves constitute an understanding of the concept of communicative effectiveness. Students typically enter "skills" courses with that belief, and, despite the efforts of instructors to impress on them the complexities of effective communication, they often leave with the same impression.

Like the criterion of effects, techniques are often substituted for an adequate understanding of the process of human communication. No level of skill in using techniques can substitute for understanding. Relying solely on techniques as a criterion for communicative effectiveness drastically oversimplifies the complexity of the process and again short-circuits a realistic understanding of communicative effectiveness.

A few years ago I overheard one of my daughter's subteen-age friends relate an incident of interaction with her mother, who had apparently just completed some course in how to be a better parent. Apparently her mother had reacted to what her daughter had said by saying, "You are angry, aren't you?" The daughter's reaction cut through the simplistic nature of that technique: "Of course, I was angry? Any one could tell that!" Her mother's comment served only to amplify her anger and increase her frustration.

The recent popularity of such technique-laden phenomena as assertiveness training, parent effectiveness training, est, encounter groups, and so on, have fostered perhaps too much reliance on techniques of communication. And lest anyone misinterpret my intention, I hasten to add that I do not mean to indict any of these approaches to personal growth out of hand. I indict only the reactions of some devoted alumni of these movements, who confuse technical skill with conceptual understanding. As Budd (1972, pp. 92–95) so clearly points out in regard to the encounter-group movement, the acquired techniques provide only one limited and highly oversimplified way to deal with interpersonal relationships. Sometimes they are beneficial; often they are not. Those techniques should not be considered as "the right way" but only "a way." Too much reliance on any set of techniques will result in a severe confrontation with the reality of communication as highly complex. Techniques are oversimplifications, are intended as oversimplifications, and should be interpreted and utilized as oversimplifications.

Academic "skills" classes in communicative effectiveness tend to stress a third approach to the effectiveness concept: adaptation to the other person communicating; that is, a person's communication is effective to the extent that she adapts her behaviors, her perceptions, her "set" to those of other communicators. Highly consistent with the role-taking phenomenon of interactionism, adaptation is also consistent with the psychological perspective of avoiding communication failure—a mismatch of cognitions among communicators. Adaptation then involves identifying the other person's conceptual filters, along with their relative valences and intensities, and adapting the message to be congruent with the other person's internalizations.

Adaptation is central to the dramatistic approach to human communication. Both Burke (1946, 1950, 1957) and Goffman (1969) emphasize employing strategies as a normal phenomenon of human communication—"stylizing" the message in order to maximize the likelihood of achieving the desired outcome.

Such adaptation through strategic interaction requires a more longitudinal approach to communication in order to discover as much as possible about the other person and, in the give-and-take of communicational exchange, achieve some degree of identification with the other person. On the level of mass communication, that longitudinal perspective would involve a campaign of multiple strategies designed to produce increasing levels of identification. In any case, adaptation through identification is a prominent approach to communicative effectiveness and takes into account a greater degree of the complexity inherent in the communicational process.

A final approach to communicative effectiveness is to assess the effectiveness of the entire communication system rather than that of a single individual. This systemic approach has been widely used in the field of therapy (see, for example, Costello, 1972), so that the individual is not so much the object of therapy as is an entire social system, for example, a family rather than a single schizophrenic member, a marital pair rather than a philandering spouse, or an entire group rather than each person individually. The therapeutic implication is that an individual communicates effectively only to the extent that his behavior is appropriate to and matched or patterned with the behaviors of others in the social context.

In fields other than therapy, communicative effectiveness has also been assessed via holistic nonindividualized concepts. For example, an effectively communicating group-system can be assessed with such group concepts as consensus, cohesiveness, role stability or compatibility. The recent research in relational interaction, specifically, symmetrical and complementary interaction, assumes that the relationship itself is stable, so that the behaviors of individuals are effective only if they "match" or "fit" with the behaviors of others—hence, a measure of communicative effectiveness.

I have always felt frustrated whenever I have attempted to discuss the concept of effectiveness in human communication. I inevitably experience no small degree of dissatisfaction, fostered by my inability to achieve any closure, to come to any conclusions. Any attempt at understanding communicative effectiveness somehow fails to secure any firm grasp on the incredible complexity of communicative phenomena. The result is oversimplification and increasing frustration. But frustration does not necessarily imply despair. It means only that increased understanding requires renewed efforts to understand. In short, we cope! And perhaps coping is as good a measure of communicative effectiveness as we could want.

SUMMARY

Many concepts have been related to the broad popularity of human communication over the years. Only a few of those concepts are discussed in the preceding pages. Among the more notable concepts discussed in Part Three are the concepts of process, breakdown or barrier, information, intrapersonal level, complexity, and effectiveness. These concepts possess variable meanings and variable significance from one perspective to another and significantly affect one's understanding of human communication.

Everyone undoubtedly agrees that communication is a process, although the nature of process and what process implies vary from one perspective to another. Not everyone would agree that communication breakdowns or barriers adequately characterize problems or failures of human communication. Implicit in such a concept are assumptions that are not congruent with all the philosophical perspectives of human communication.

The intrapersonal level of human communication is significant in some perspectives and virtually irrelevant (although not denied) in another perspective. The meanings of the concept of information and complexity vary but not necessarily as a function of the perspective used to view the process of human communication. The concept of communicative effectiveness has plagued theorists, scholars, and practitioners of communication for centuries. Like the previous chapters, these concepts emphasize the significance of understanding concepts when and how they are used, and it provides an increased appreciation for the multiple paradigms that characterize the scientific community of human communication.

— 12 —

Conclusion

Brodbeck (1962) suggests that terms have both referential meaning and significance meaning. Because referential meaning is a matter of convention (that is, people agree on the meaning), we control the meaning of a concept. But because significance is a factual matter (that is, discovery of empirical regularity), we do not control the significance of a term. In terms of significance, "It either has it or it has not." Of course, Brodbeck is quite correct. One cannot observe what is not there to observe. But Brodbeck may lend too much credence to scientific "objectivity" of observation in discovering significance. She implies that seeing is believing. More important, perhaps, is the fact that we will see only what we are looking for where we look for it.

Scheflen (1974, p. 197) emphasizes the epistemological significance of meaning. To reiterate from a previous discussion, Scheflen writes, "the epistemology we employ in approaching any event will make a great difference in the kinds of answers and meanings we deduce." In a very real sense, the perspective one uses to approach human communication will contribute significantly to the "answers" and "meanings" we observe through empirical inquiry—no matter how objective we are. Indeed, the perspective guides not only the answers we find (that is, the observations we make) but also the questions we ask (that is, where we do the observation). Each perspective is certainly an epistemology that guides our theorizing, our inquiry, our thinking about the process of human communication.

Berlo (1960, p. 25) makes the same point when he notes that humans do not *discover* reality; they *create* it. In a discussion highly reminiscent

322

of Hanson's duality of interpretation and observation, Berlo suggests that we inevitably observe something "in one way or another." We inevitably organize our observations and our perceptions and cannot avoid organizing them. On the other hand, we may not be aware of the nature of that organization or of why we look for certain kinds of observations. In other words, one approaches any observation of communication with some perspective—an epistemology, if you will—of one sort or another. Whether the observer is aware of that perspective is not quite to the point. He must observe reality in one way or another and, in so doing, "creates" the reality of his observations. He may understand reality without being able to articulate or even be aware of the identity of his perspective. But the degree of his potentially full understanding of that reality is severely restricted in the absence of such awareness.

How then, is one to utilize the various perspectives of human communication? Should we attempt to use them all at the same time? Clearly not! That would be impossible—conceptually inconsistent. The most obvious use of the perspectives is to be consciously aware of the perspective being used, what its implications are, and where it is leading us. We need to be aware of what questions are askable and, hence, answerable within that perspective. We need to know what questions are unaskable and, hence, unanswerable as well. We need to know what we need to know and how to utilize the perspective that will be the most likely one to lead us to that knowledge.

Above all else, we need to exercise tolerance. Not tolerance in the sense that anyone can do his own thing, but tolerance in the sense of understanding what others are doing and thereby understanding what you yourself are doing—and why you are doing it. We need to avoid the inexcusable narrow-mindedness of believing that there is only one "right" way to do science or that our way is the "best" way. The covering-law model, for example, is only a way to construct a theory and perform inquiry. System theory is only a way to observe interaction phenomena. Experimentation is only a technique to perform research. The perceived reality of subjects is only a reality—perhaps no better or no worse than the reality of the observer. In short, to select a perspective is to choose to do things in one way, not another. It carries with it all the advantages and limitations of that perspective. But it does not give one license to deny the worth or to question the validity of another perspective. Such arguments from synonymy are inexcusable and represent intellectual bigotry at its worst.

I appear to be arguing for a Feyerabendian view of human communication characterized by multiple paradigms, and I guess that I am—not necessarily from any conviction that a multiparadigmatic science is superior to a uniparadigmatic science, but because that is the way things are! The field of human communication is simply not characterized by a single paradigm. The reality of the scientific community is that of a loosely connected band of scholars who disagree on far more issues than they agree on. Attending any convention of the International Communication Association or the Speech Communication Association would confirm that reality. Fractionation and splintering characterize the scientific community of human communication. As Knower (1970, p. 23) reiterates the obvious, "When one area of the field tries to force others to accept their set of categories they can but increase the fractionation and splintering of the field."

I do not intend to suggest that any scholar of communication should avoid selecting one perspective as superior to the others. To the contrary, such a selection is almost inevitable. I do suggest, however, that the choice of one perspective over another is largely arbitrary—a matter of preference and purpose. You cannot make the choice on the basis that one perspective is inherently superior but rather on whether it asks the questions you wish to ask. But that selection of perspective should be one of which you are aware and should not occur by default —being unaware of the alternative perspectives you did *not* choose. And once you are aware of your own perspective, you should be equally aware of what you have "bought into"—the limitations as well as the benefits of that perspective.

Of course, some perspectives are combinations of several of the "pure" forms discussed in Part Two. We have already pointed out that probably the most popular perspective among members of the scientific community of human communication is a combination of the mechanistic and psychological perspectives. Inevitably, some mugwump will attempt to pick and choose elements from all perspectives under the misguided impression that he will borrow all that is "good" from each perspective and avoid all that is limiting. Such a conglomeration of theoretical perspectives is patently impossible. The philosophical and theoretical assumptions of all perspectives are not always congruent and, in many cases, actually contradict each other. Being aware of perspectives implies being aware of all the philosophical and theoretical assumptions, and that awareness should render clear the truism that a combination of all four perspectives is absurd.

Still other students of human communication attempt to shift from one perspective to another and back again—typically when conducting research. They are aware of the inconsistencies of the perspectives, but they believe that using only one at a time avoids the problem of being inconsistent, or so it seems. When the student is in the process of deciding which perspective is for her, such "skipping around" is to be expected. But transition periods come to an end eventually. They should serve only as preludes to conclusions that culminate in a choice of perspective. To delay indefinitely that choice is to be an intellectual dilettante. Research is thus unprogrammatic, not cumulative, and, in the long run, unproductive.

Of course, evolutionary processes may lead you from a commitment to one perspective to a new commitment to another. I require little introspection to realize that my own perspective on communication has changed considerably from what it was only ten or twelve years ago. But that is the nature of evolution—increasing understanding, increasing specialization, and changing interests. The key element is consistency—conceptual consistency. And consistency implies awareness and understanding, not only of your own perspective, but of alternative perspectives as well. Anything less is intellectual naïveté—intellectual dishonesty at worst and intellectual confusion at best.

In writing this volume, I have desperately sought to avoid thrusting my biases regarding perspectives on the reader. I know that I have not always succeeded in avoiding my biases. In some cases, my lack of success was conscious and intentional. I am positive that I am unaware of all my failures to conceal my unique preferences. Those who know me are well aware of what my biases are—particularly concerning my overall perspective of human communication. I suspect that your reading these pages will also reveal that preference to you. But if any person reads this book and cannot positively identify the perspective that reflects my bias, then I will consider myself, to that extent, successful.

References

ABELSON, ROBERT, ELLIOT ARONSON, WILLIAM J. McGUIRE, THEODORE N. NEWCOMB, M. J. ROSENBERG, and PERCY TANNENBAUM, eds. (1968) *Theories of Cognitive Consistency.* Chicago: Rand McNally and Company.

ABRAHAMSON, MARK (1966) *Interpersonal Accommodation.* Princeton, N.J.: Van Nostrand Reinhold Company.

ACHINSTEIN, PETER (1965) "The Problem of Theoretical Terms." *American Philosophical Quarterly,* **2:** 193–203.

ACKOFF, RUSSELL L., and FRED E. EMERY (1972) *On Purposeful Systems.* Chicago: Aldine-Atherton, Inc.

ADAMS, DONALD K., et al., eds. (1954) *Learning Theory and Clinical Research.* New York: John Wiley & Sons, Inc.

ADAMS, W. CLIFTON (1973) "The Effect of Various Channels of Feedback on the Communication of Information." *Speech Monographs,* **40:** 147–150.

ALEXANDER, DENNIS C. (1975) "Our Transactional Perspective: But Our Interactional Research." A paper presented to Western Speech Communication Association, Seattle.

ALTMAN, IRWIN, and DALMAS A. TAYLOR (1973) *Social Penetration.* New York: Holt, Rinehart and Winston, Publishers.

ALTMANN, STUART A. (1965) "Sociobiology of Rhesus Monkeys. II: Stochastics of Social Communication." *Journal of Theoretical Biology,* **8:** 490–522.

ANDERSEN, KENNETH E., and THEODORE CLEVENGER, JR. (1963) "A Summary of Experimental Research in Ethos." *Speech Monographs,* **30:** 59–78.

APPLBAUM, RONALD L., and KARL W. E. ANATOL (1975) "The Role of Communication in Small Group Choice Shift," in Ronald L. Applbaum, Owen O. Jenson, and Richard Carroll, eds. *Speech Communication: A Basic Anthology.* New York: Macmillan Publishing Co., Inc., pp. 221–233.

————, Owen O. Jenson, and Richard Carroll, eds. (1975) *Speech Communication: A Basic Anthology.* New York: Macmillan Publishing Co., Inc.

Argyle, Michael (1967) *The Psychology of Interpersonal Behavior.* Baltimore: Penguin Books, Inc.

————, and A. Kendon (1967) "The Experimental Analysis of Social Performance," in Leonard Berkowitz, ed. *Advances in Experimental Social Psychology,* Vol. III. New York: Academic Press, pp. 55–98.

Attneave, Floyd (1959) *Applications of Information Theory to Psychology.* New York: Holt, Rinehart and Winston, Publishers.

Auerback, Alfred (1959) *Schizophrenia: An Integrated Approach.* New York: The Ronald Press Company.

Backman, Carl W., and Paul F. Secord (1966) *Problems in Social Psychology.* New York: McGraw-Hill Book Company.

Bales, Robert F. (1950) *Interaction Process Analysis: A Method for the Study of Small Groups.* Reading, Mass.: Addison-Wesley Publishing Co., Inc.

————, and Fred L. Strodtbeck. (1951) "Phases in Group Problem-Solving." *Journal of Abnormal and Social Psychology,* **46:** 485–495.

Barnlund, Dean C., ed. (1968) *Interpersonal Communication: Survey and Studies.* Boston: Houghton Mifflin Company.

Bartley, W. W., III. (1968) "Theories of Demarcation Between Science and Metaphysics," in Imre Lakatos and Alan Musgrave, eds. *Problems in the Philosophy of Science.* Amsterdam: North-Holland Publishing Co., pp. 40–64.

Bateson, Gregory (1958) *Naven,* 2nd ed. Stanford, California: Stanford University Press.

Bauer, Raymond A. (1964) "The Obstinate Audience: The Influence Process from the Point of View of Social Communication." *American Psychologist,* **19:** 319–328.

Bavelas, Alex, A. Hastorf, A. Gross, and W. Kite (1965) "Experiments on the Alteration of Group Structure." *Journal of Experimental Social Psychology,* **1:** 55–70.

Beale, John (1975 Preliminary Model for the Examination of Intention Through Content Analysis." *Communication Research,* **2:** 86–96.

Becker, Samuel L. (1968) "What Rhetoric-Communication Theory Is Relevant for Contemporary Speech Communication?" Presented to University of Minnesota Symposium in Speech Communication.

Beer, Stafford (1966) *Decision and Control.* New York: John Wiley & Sons, Inc.

Berelson, Bernard, and Gary Steiner (1964) *Human Behavior.* New York: Harcourt, Brace Jovanovich, Inc.

Berg, David M. (1967) "A Thematic Approach to the Analysis of the Task-Oriented Small Group." *Central States Speech Journal,* **18:** 285–291.

Berger, Charles R. (1975) "Proactive and Retroactive Attribution Processes in Interpersonal Communications." *Human Communication Research,* **2:** 33–50.

Berger, Seymour M., and William W. Lambert (1968) "Stimulus-Response

Theory in Contemporary Social Psychology," in Gardner Lindzey and Elliot Aronson, eds. *The Handbook of Social Psychology*, 2nd ed., Vol. I. Reading, Mass.: Addison-Wesley Publishing Co., Inc., pp. 81–178.

BERGMANN, GUSTAV (1962) "Purpose, Function, Scientific Explanation." *Acta Sociologica*, **5**: 225–238.

―――― (1957) *Philosophy of Science*. Madison: University of Wisconsin Press Publishing Co., Inc.

BERLO, DAVID K. (1975) "The Context for Communication." Gerhard J. Hanneman and William J. McEwen, eds. *Communication and Behavior*. Reading, Mass.: Addison-Wesley Publishing Co., Inc. pp 3–20.

―――― (1960) *The Process of Communication: An Introduction to Theory and Practice*. New York: Holt, Rinehart and Winston, Publishers.

BERRIEN, F. KENNETH (1968) *General and Social Systems*. New Brunswick, N.J.: Rutgers University Press.

BERTALANFFY, LUDWIG VON (1968) *General System Theory: Foundations, Development, Applications*. New York: George Braziller, Inc.

―――― (1967) *Robots, Men and Minds*. New York: George Braziller, Inc.

BIRDWHISTELL, RAY L. (1959) "Contribution of Linguistic-Kinesic Studies to the Understanding of Schizophrenia," in Alfred Auerback, ed. *Schizophrenia: An Integrated Approach*. New York: The Ronald Press Company, pp. 99–123.

BLACK, EDWIN (1965) *Rhetorical Criticism*. New York: Macmillan Publishing Co., Inc.

BLACK, MAX (1967) "The Justification of Induction," in Sidney Morgenbesser, ed., *Philosophy of Science Today*. New York: Basic Books, pp. 190–200.

―――― (1965) *Philosophy in America*. Ithaca, N.Y.: Cornell University Press.

BLALOCK, HUBERT M., JR. (1969) *Theory Construction: From Verbal to Mathematical Theories*. Englewood Cliffs, N.J.: Prentice-Hall, Inc.

BLOOM, VINCENT L. (1975) "Pragmatism: The Choice of a Critical Perspective for Communication Inquiry." *Western Speech*, **39**: 2–12.

BLUBAUGH, JON A. (1969) "Effects of Positive and Negative Audience Feedback on Selected Variables of Speech Behavior." *Speech Monographs*, **36**: 131–137.

BLUMER, HERBERT (1969) *Symbolic Interaction: Perspective and Method*. Englewood Cliffs, N.J.: Prentice-Hall, Inc.

BOHM, DAVID (1974) "Science as Perception-Communication," in Frederick Suppe, ed., *The Structure of Scientific Theories*. Urbana: University of Illinois Press, pp. 374–391.

BORDEN, GEORGE A. (1971) *An Introduction to Human-Communication Theory*. Dubuque, Iowa: William C. Brown Company, Publishers.

BORGER, ROBERT, and FRANK CIOFFI, eds. (1970) *Explanation in the Behavioral Sciences*. Cambridge: Cambridge University Press.

BOULDING, KENNETH E. (1965) "General Systems Theory—The Skeleton of Science." *Management Science*, **2**: 197–208.

BOWERS, JOHN WAITE (1970) *Designing the Communication Experiment*. New York: Random House, Inc.

———— (1968) "The Pre-Scientific Function of Rhetorical Criticism," in Thomas R. Nilsen, ed. *Essays on Rhetorical Criticism.* New York: Random House, Inc., pp. 126–145.

BRAITHWAITE, R. B. (1953) *Scientific Explanation.* Cambridge: Cambridge University Press.

BRAYBROOKE, DAVID (1968) "Taking Liberties with the Concept of Rules." *Monist,* **52**: 329–358.

BRODBECK, MAY, ed. (1968) *Readings in the Philosophy of the Social Sciences.* New York: Macmillan Publishing Co., Inc.

———— (1963) "Meaning and Action." *The Philosophy of Science,* **30**: 309–324.

———— (1962) "Explanation, Prediction, and 'Imperfect' Knowledge," in Herbert Feigl and Grover Maxwell, eds. *Minnesota Studies in the Philosophy of Science,* Vol. III. Minneapolis: University of Minnesota Press, pp. 231–272.

———— (1958) "Methodological Individualism: Definition and Reduction. *Philosophy of Science,* **25**: 1–22.

BRODEY, WARREN M. (1969) "Information Exchange in the Time Domain," in William Gray, Frederick J. Duhl, and Nicholas D. Rizzo, eds. *General Systems Theory and Psychiatry.* Boston: Little, Brown and Company, pp. 229–243.

BRODY, BARUCH A., ed. (1970) *Readings in the Philosophy of Science.* Englewood Cliffs, N.J.: Prentice-Hall, Inc.

BRUYN, SEVERYN T. (1966) *The Human Perspective in Sociology. The Methodology of Participant Observation.* Englewood Cliffs, N.J.: Prentice-Hall, Inc.

BUCKLEY, WALTER (1968) "Society as a Complex Adaptive System," in Walter Buckley, ed. *Modern Systems Research for the Behavioral Scientist.* Chicago: Aldine Publishing Company, pp. 490–513.

———— (1968) *Modern Systems Research for the Behavioral Scientist.* Chicago: Aldine Publishing Company.

BUDD, RICHARD W. (1972) "Encounter Groups: An Approach to Human Communication," in Richard W. Budd and Brent D. Ruben, eds. *Approaches to Human Communication.* New York: Spartan Books, Inc., pp. 75–96.

————, and BRENT D. RUBEN, eds. (1972) *Approaches to Human Communication.* New York: Spartan Books, Inc.

BUGENTAL, D. E., J. W. KASWAN, and L. R. LOVE (1970) "Perception of Contradictory Meanings Conveyed by Verbal and Nonverbal Channels." *Journal of Personality and Social Psychology,* **16**: 647–655.

BUNGE, MARIO (1967) *Scientific Research I: The Search for System.* New York: Springer-Verlag.

———— (1967) *Scientific Research II: The Search for Truth.* New York: Springer-Verlag.

BURGESS, IAN S. (1972) "Psychology and Kuhn's Concept of Paradigm." *Journal of Behavioral Science,* **1**: 193–200.

BURHANS, DAVID T., JR. (1971) "The Attitude-Behavior Discrepancy Problem: Revisited." *Quarterly Journal of Speech*, **57**: 418–428.

BURKE, KENNETH (1967) "Dramatism," in Lee Thayer, ed. *Communication: Concepts and Perspectives*. Washington: Spartan Books, Inc.

———— (1957) *Philosophy of Literary Form*. New York: Random House, Inc.

———— (1952) "A Dramatistic View of the Origins of Language: Part One." *Quarterly Journal of Speech*, **38**: 251–264.

———— (1950) *A Rhetoric of Motives*. Englewood Cliffs, N.J.: Prentice-Hall, Inc.

———— (1946) *A Grammar of Motives*. Englewood Cliffs, N.J.: Prentice-Hall, Inc.

BURTON, JOHN W. (1969) *Conflict and Communication: The Use of Controlled Communication in International Relations*. New York: The Free Press.

CAMPBELL, N. R. (1920) *Physics: The Elements*. New York: Cambridge University Press.

CAPPELLA, JOSEPH N. (1975) "An Introduction to the Literature of Causal Modeling." *Human Communication Research*, **1**: 362–377.

———— (1974) "A Cybernetic, Coorientation Model of Interpersonal Communication." Paper presented to International Communication Association, New Orleans.

CARNAP, RUDOLF (1955) "Logical Foundations of the Unity of Science," in Otto Neurath, ed., *International Encyclopedia of United Science*. Chicago: University of Chicago Press, pp. 42–62.

CHAPIN, F. STUART (1939) "Definition of Concepts." *Social Forces*, **18**: 153–160.

CHARTERS, W. W., JR., and THEODORE M. NEWCOMB (1958) "Some Attitudinal Effects of Experimentally Increased Salience of a Membership Group," in Eleanor E. Maccoby, T. M. Newcomb, and E. L. Hartley, eds. *Readings in Social Psychology*, 3rd ed. New York: Holt, Rinehart and Winston, Publishers, pp. 276–281.

CHERRY, COLIN (1964) *On Human Communication*. Cambridge, Mass.: M.I.T. Press.

CHURCHMAN, C. W. (1968) *The Systems Approach*. New York: Delacorte Press.

———— (1948) *Theory of Experimental Inference*. New York: Macmillan Publishing Co., Inc.

CISSNA, KENNETH N. (1976) "Interpersonal Confirmation: A Review of Recent Theory and Research." A paper presented to International Communication Association, Portland.

CLEMENT, DONALD A., and KENNETH D. FRANDSEN (1976) "On Conceptual and Empirical Treatments of Feedback in Human Communication." *Communication Monographs*, **43**: 11–28.

CLEVENGER, THEODORE, JR., and JACK MATTHEWS (1971) *The Speech Communication Process*. Glenview, Illinois: Scott, Foresman and Company.

COHEN, P. (1968) "The Very Idea of a Social Science," in Imre Lakatos and

Alan Musgrave, eds., *Problems in the Philosophy of Science.* Amsterdam: North-Holland Publishing Company, pp. 407–423.

COLLINS, BARRY E., and HAROLD GUETZKOW (1964) *A Social Psychology of Group Processes for Decision-making.* New York: John Wiley & Sons, Inc.

———, and BERTRAM H. RAVEN (1966) "Group Structure Attraction, Coalitions, Communication, and Power," in Gardner Lindzey and Elliot Aronson, eds. *The Handbook of Social Psychology.* 2nd ed. Vol. IV. Reading, Mass.: Addison-Wesley Publishing Co., Inc., pp. 102–204.

COMSTOCK, G. A., and E. A. RUBENSTEIN, eds. (1971) *Television and Social Behavior.* Vols. I–V. Washington, D.C.: U.S. Government Printing Office.

COSTELLO, DANIEL E. (1972) "Therapeutic Transactions: An Approach to Human Communication," in Richard W. Budd and Brent D. Ruben, eds. *Approaches to Human Communication.* New York: Spartan Books, Inc., pp. 420–435.

CUSHMAN, DONALD P. (1975) "Alternative Theoretical Bases for the Study of Human Communication: The Rules Perspective." A paper presented to Speech Communication Association, Houston.

———, and B. THOMAS FLORENCE (1974) "The Development of Interpersonal Communication Theory." *Today's Speech,* **22:** 11–16.

———, and GORDON C. WHITING (1972) "An Approach to Communication Theory: Toward Consensus on Rules." *Journal of Communication,* **22:** 17–238.

DANCE, FRANK E. X. (1970) "The Concept of Communication." *Journal of Communication,* **20:** 201–210.

——— (1967) "Toward a Theory of Human Communication," in Frank E. X. Dance, ed., *Human Communication Theory.* New York: Holt, Rinehart and Winston Publishers, pp. 289–309.

———, ed. (1967) *Human Communication Theory: Original Essays.* New York: Holt, Rinehart and Winston, Publishers.

DARNELL, DONALD K. (1972) "Information Theory: An Approach to Human Communication," in Richard W. Budd and Brent D. Ruben, eds. *Approaches to Human Communication.* New York: Spartan Books, Inc., pp. 156–169.

——— (1971) "Toward a Reconceptualization of Communication." *Journal of Communication,* **21:** 5–16.

DAY, DENNIS G. (1964) "Learning and Communication Theory." *Central States Speech Journal,* **15:** 84–89.

DEMERATH, J. J., III, and RICHARD A. PETERSON, eds. (1967) *System, Change, and Conflict.* New York: The Free Press.

DENZIN, NORMAN K. (1970) *The Research Act: A Theoretical Introduction to Sociological Methods.* Chicago: Aldine Publishing Company.

DE SOLA POOL, ITHIEL, et al., eds. (1973) *Handbook of Communication.* Chicago: Rand McNally & Company.

DIESING, PAUL (1971) *Patterns of Discovery in the Social Sciences.* Chicago: Aldine Publishing Company.

DORE, RONALD PHILIP (1961). "Function and Cause." *American Sociological Review*, **26**: 843–853.

DUBIN, ROBERT (1969) *Theory Building.* New York: The Free Press.

DuBois, RACHEL DAVIS, and MEW-SOONG LI (1971) *Reducing Social Tension and Conflict: Through the Group Conversation Method.* New York: Association Press.

DUNNETTE, MARVIN D. (1966) "Fads, Fashions, and Folderol in Psychology." *American Psychologist*, **21**: 343–352.

DURKHEIM, EMILE (1938) *The Rules of Sociological Method.* Chicago: University of Chicago Press.

EDWARDS, WARD, and AMOS TVERSKY, eds. (1967) *Decision Making: Selected Readings.* Baltimore: Penguin Books, Inc.

EKMAN, PAUL, and WALLACE V. FRIESEN (1974) Detecting Deception from the Body or Face." *Journal of Personality and Social Psychology*, **29**: 288–298.

——— (1969) "Nonverbal Leakage and Clues to Deception." *Psychiatry*, **32**: 88–106.

ELLIS, DONALD G. (1976) "An Analysis of Relational Communication in Ongoing Group Systems." Ph.D. Dissertation, University of Utah.

——— (1974) "The Attribution Process: A Comparative Test of Two Theories of Persuasion." A paper presented to Western Speech Communication Association, Newport Beach, Calif.

———, and B. AUBREY FISHER (1975) "Phases of Conflict in Small Group Development." *Human Communication Research*, **1**: 195–212.

ELSASSER, WALTER M. (1966) *Atom and Organism.* Princeton: Princeton University Press.

EMORY, E. E., ed. (1969) *Systems Thinking.* London: Penguin Books, Inc.

FAIRBANKS, G., and N. GUTTMAN (1958) "Effects of Delayed Auditory Feedback upon Articulation." *Journal of Speech and Hearing Research*, **1**: 12–22.

FAST, JULIUS (1971) *Body Language.* New York: M. Evans & Co., Inc.

FAULES, DON F. (1976) "The Impact of Values on Organizational Communication," in James L. Owen, Paul A. Page, and Gordon I. Zimmerman, eds. *Communication in Organizations.* San Francisco: West Publishing Co., pp. 66–83.

FEARING, FRANKLIN (1953) "Toward a Psychological Theory of Human Communication." *Journal of Personality*, **22**: 71–88.

FEIGL, HERBERT, and GROVER MAXWELL, eds. (1962) *Minnesota Studies in the Philosophy of Science*, Vol. III. Minneapolis: University of Minnesota Press.

———, and MICHAEL SCRIVEN, eds. (1956) *Minnesota Studies in the Philosophy of Science*, Vol. I. Minneapolis: University of Minnesota Press.

———, and WILFRID SELLERS, eds. (1949) *Readings in Philosophical Analysis.* New York: Appleton-Century-Crofts.

FEYERABEND, PAUL K. (1975) "'Science.' The Myth and Its Role in Society." *Inquiry*, **18**: 167–181.

———— (1970) "Consolations for the Specialist," Imre Lakatos and Alan Musgrave, eds. *Criticism and the Growth of Knowledge*. New York: Cambridge University Press, pp. 197–230.

———— (1965) "Problems of Empiricism," in R. Colodny, ed. *Beyond the Edge of Certainty*. Englewood Cliffs, N.J.: Prentice-Hall, Inc., pp. 145–260.

———— (1963) "How to Be a Good Empiricist—A Plea for Tolerance in Matters Epistemological," in B. Baumrin, ed., *Philosophy of Science. The Delaware Seminar*, Vol. I. New York: John Wiley & Sons, Inc., pp. 3–40.

FISHER, B. AUBREY (1975) "Communication Study in System Perspective," Brent D. Ruben and John Y. Kim, eds. *General Systems Theory and Human Communication*. Rochelle Park, N.J.: Hayden Publishing Company, Inc., pp. 191–206.

———— (1974) *Small Group Decision Making: Communication and the Group Process*. New York: McGraw-Hill Book Company.

———— (1974) "Paradigms of Communication," A paper presented to Western Speech Communication Association, Newport Beach, California.

———— (1971) "Communication Research and the Task-Oriented Group." *Journal of Communication*, 21: 136–149.

———— (1970) "Decision Emergence: Phases in Group Decision Making. *Speech Monographs*, 37: 53–66.

————, G. LLOYD DRECKSEL, and WAYNE S. WERBEL (1978) "Social Information Processing Analysis (SIPA): Coding Ongoing Human Communication." *Small Group Behavior*.

————, THOMAS W. GLOVER, and DONALD G. ELLIS (1977) "The Nature of Complex Communication Systems." *Communication Monographs*.

————, and LEONARD C. HAWES (1971) "An Interact System Model: Generating a Grounded Theory of Small Groups." *Quarterly Journal of Speech*, 57: 444–453.

FODOR, JERRY A. (1965) "Explanations in Psychology," in Max Black, ed. *Philosophy in America*. Ithaca, N.Y.: Cornell University Press, pp. 161–179.

FOTHERINGHAM, WALLACE C. (1966) *Perspectives on Persuasion*. Boston: Allyn & Bacon, Inc.

GARDINER, JAMES (1971) "Synthesis of Experimental Studies of Speech Communication Feedback." *Journal of Communication*, 21: 17–35.

GARFINKEL, HAROLD (1967) *Studies in Ethnomethodology*. Englewood Cliffs, N.J.: Prentice-Hall, Inc.

GEIER, JOHN G. 1967 "A Trait Approach to the Study of Leadership in Small Groups." *Journal of Communication*, 17: 316–323.

GELLNER, ERNEST (1956) "Explanations in History." *Proceedings of the Aristotelian Society*, 30: 157–176.

GERARD, R. W. (1957) "Units and Concepts of Biology." *Science*, 125: 429–433.

GILBERT, SHIRLEY J., and D. HORENSTEIN (1975) "A Study of Self-Disclosure: Level Versus Valence." *Human Communication Research* 1: 316–322.

GLASER, BARNEY G., and ANSELM L. STRAUSS (1967) *The Discovery of Grounded Theory: Strategies for Qualitative Research.* Chicago: Aldine Publishing Company.

GLOVER, THOMAS M. (1974) "Interpersonal Power in Family Groups: An Analysis of Complementary and Symmetrical Interaction." M.S. Thesis, University of Utah.

GODE, ALEXANDER (1969) "What Is Communication?" *Journal of Communication,* 9: 5.

GOFFMAN, ERVING (1969) *Strategic Interaction.* Philadelphia: University of Pennsylvania Press.

—————— (1967) *Interaction Ritual: Essays on Face-to-Face Behavior.* Garden City, N.Y.: Doubleday & Company, Inc.

—————— (1963) *Behavior in Public Places: Notes on the Social Organization of Gatherings.* New York: The Free Press.

—————— (1959) *The Presentation of Self in Everyday Life.* Garden City, N.Y.: Doubleday & Company, Inc.

GOLDHABER, GERALD M. (1974) *Organizational Communication.* Dubuque, Iowa: William C. Brown Company, Publishers.

GOURAN, DENNIS S. (1973) "Group Communication: Perspectives and Priorities for Future Research." *Quarterly Journal of Speech,* 59: 22–29.

——————, and JOHN E. BAIRD, JR. (1972). "An Analysis of Distributional and Sequential Structure in Problem-Solving and Informal Group Discussions." *Speech Monographs.* 39: 16–22.

GOYER, ROBERT S. (1970) "Communication, Communicative Process, Meaning: Toward a Unified Theory." *Journal of Communication.* 20: 4–16.

—————— (1964) "Cognitive Dissonance and Communication Theory." *Central States Speech Journal.* 15: 90–95.

GRAY, GILES W., and CLAUDE M. WISE (1959) *The Bases of Speech.* New York: Harper & Row, Publishers.

GRAY, WILLIAM, FREDERICK J. DUHL, and NICHOLAS D. RIZZO, eds. (1969) *General Systems Theory and Psychiatry.* Boston: Little, Brown and Company.

GROSSBERG, LAWRENCE, and DANIEL J. O'KEEFE (1975) "Presuppositions, Conceptual Foundations, and Communication Theory: On Hawes' Approach to Communication." *Quarterly Journal of Speech,* 61: 195–208.

GRUNBAUM, ADOLF (1962) "Temporally-Asymmetric Principles, Parity Between Explanation and Prediction, and Mechanism and Teleology." *Philosophy of Science,* 29: 162–170.

HALL, A. D., and R. E. FAGEN (1956) "Definition of System." *General Systems,* 1: 18–28.

HANCOCK, BRENDA R. (1977) "Interaction Analysis of Self-Disclosure Between Roommates." Ph.D. dissertation. University of Utah.

HANNEMAN, GERHARD J. (1975) "The Study of Human Communication," in Gerhard J. Hanneman and William J. McEwen, eds. *Communication and Behavior.* Reading, Mass.: Addison-Wesley Publishing Co., Inc. pp. 21–46.

————, and WILLIAM J. McEWEN, eds. (1975) *Communication and Behavior.* Reading, Mass.: Addison-Wesley Publishing Company, Inc.

HANSON, NORWOOD RUSSELL (1967) "Observation and Interpretation," in Sidney Morgenbesser, ed., *Philosophy of Science Today.* New York: Basic Books, pp. 89–99.

———— (1961) "Is There a Logic of Scientific Discovery?" in Herbert Feigl and Grover Maxwell, eds., *Current Issues in the Philosophy of Science.* New York: Holt, Rinehart and Winston, Publishers. pp. 20–35.

———— (1958) *Patterns of Discovery: An Inquiry into the Conceptual Foundations of Science.* New York: Cambridge University Press.

HARDIN, GARRETT (1963) "The Cybernetics of Competition: A Biologist's View of Society." *Perspectives in Biology and Medicine,* 7: 61–84.

HARNACK, R. VICTOR, and THORRELL FEST (1964) *Group Discussion.* New York: Appleton-Century-Crofts.

HARRÉ, ROM (1974) "Some Remarks on 'Rule' as a Scientific Concept," in Theodore Mischel, ed. *Understanding Other Persons.* Totowa, N.J.: Rowan and Littlefield, pp. 143–184.

HASTORF, ALBERT H., DAVID J. SCHNEIDER, and JUDITH POLEFKA (1970) *Person Perception.* Reading, Mass.: Addison-Wesley Publishing Co., Inc.

HAWES, LEONARD C. (1975) *Pragmatics of Analoguing: Theory and Model Construction in Communication.* Reading, Mass.: Addison-Wesley Publishing Co., Inc.

———— (1975) "A Response to Grossberg and O'Keefe: Building a Human Science of Communication." *Quarterly Journal of Speech,* 61: 209–219.

———— (1973) "Elements of a Model for Communication Processes." *Quarterly Journal of Speech,* 59: 11–21.

———— (1972) "The Effects of Interviewer Style on Patterns of Dyadic Communication." *Speech Monographs,* 39: 114–123.

———— (1972) "Development and Application of an Interview Coding System." *Central States Speech Journal,* 23: 92–99.

————, and JOSEPH M. FOLEY (1973) "A Markov Analysis of Interview Communication." *Speech Monographs,* 40: 208–219.

HEIDELBERGER, HEBERT (1969) "The Mental and the Physical," in Leonard I. Krimerman, ed., *The Nature and Scope of Social Science: A Critical Anthology.* New York: Appleton-Century-Crofts, pp. 409–415.

HEMPEL, CARL (1974) "Formulation and Formalization of Scientific Theories," in Frederick Suppe, ed. *The Structure of Scientific Theories.* Urbana: University of Illinois Press, pp. 244–254.

———— (1967) "Scientific Explanation," in Sidney Morgenbesser, ed., *Philosophy of Science Today.* New York: Basic Books, pp. 70–88.

———— (1965) *Aspects of Scientific Explanation and other Essays in the Philosophy of Science.* New York: The Free Press.

———— (1949) "Logical Analysis of Psychology," in Herbert Feigl and Wilfrid Sellers, eds. *Readings in Philosophical Analysis.* New York: Appleton-Century-Crofts, pp. 373–384.

HEWES, DEAN E. "Finite Stochastic Modeling of Communication Processes." *Human Communication Research,* 1: 271–282.

HOLTON, GERALD (1973) *Thematic Origins of Scientific Thought: Kepler to Einstein.* Cambridge, Mass.: Harvard University Press.

HOVLAND, CARL I. (1959) "Reconciling Conflicting Results Derived from Experimental and Survey Studies of Attitude Change." *American Psychologist,* 14: 8–17.

———, IRVING L. JANIS, and HAROLD H. KELLEY (1953) *Communication and Persuasion.* New Haven, Conn.: Yale University Press.

HULETT, J. EDWARD, JR. (1966) "A Symbolic Interactionist Model of Human Communication. Part One." *A–V Communication Review,* 14: 5–33.

——— (1966) "A Symbolic Interactionist Model of Human Communication. Part Two." *A–V Communication Review,* 14: 203–220.

HYMAN, HERBERT H., and ELEANOR SINGER, eds. (1968) *Readings in Reference Group Theory and Research.* New York: The Free Press

JANTSCH, ERICH (1975) *Design for Evolution: Self-organization and Planning in the Life of Human Systems.* New York: George Braziller, Inc.

JOHANNESEN, RICHARD C. (1971) "The Emerging Concept of Communication as Dialogue." *Quarterly Journal of Speech.* 57: 373–382.

KAPLAN, ABRAHAM (1964) *The Conduct of Inquiry: Methodology for Behavioral Science.* San Francisco: Chandler Publishing Co.

KARNS, C. FRANKLIN (1969) "Speaker Behavior to Nonverbal Aversive Stimuli from the Audience." *Speech Monographs,* 36: 126–130.

KATZ, ELIHU (1968) "On Reopening the Question of Selectivity in Exposure to Mass Communications," in Robert P. Abelson, Elliot Aronson, William J. McGuire, Theodore N. Newcomb, M. F. Rosenberg, and Percy Tannenbaum, eds. *Theories of Cognitive Consistency.* Chicago: Rand McNally & Company, pp. 788–796.

———, and PAUL F. LAZARSFELD (1955) *Personal Influence: The Part Played by People in the Flow of Mass Communications.* New York: The Free Press.

KATZ, JEROLD J. (1973) "The Realm of Meaning," in George A. Miller, ed. *Communication, Language, and Meaning.* New York: Basic Books, pp. 36–48.

KIBLER, ROBERT J., and LARRY L. BARKER (1969) *Conceptual Frontiers in Speech-Communication: Report of the New Orleans Conference on Research and Instructional Development.* New York: Speech Association of America.

KING, STEPHEN W. (1975) *Communication and Social Influence.* Reading, Mass.: Addison-Wesley Publishing Co., Inc.

KNOWER, FRANKLIN H. (1970) "What Do You Mean—Communication?" *Central States Speech Journal,* 21: 18–23.

KOLAJA, JIRI (1969) *Social System and Time and Space: An Introduction to the Theory of Recurrent Behavior.* Pittsburgh: Duquesne University Press.

KRAUS, R. M., and S. WEINHEIMER (1966) "Concurrent Feedback: Confirmation and the Encoding of Referents in Verbal Communication." *Journal of Personality and Social Psychology,* 4: 343–346.

KRIMERMAN, LEONARD I., ed. (1969) *The Nature and Scope of Social Science: A Critical Anthology.* New York: Appleton-Century-Crofts.

KRIPPENDORFF, KLAUS (1969) "Values, Modes and Domains of Inquiry into Communication." *Journal of Communication,* 19: 105–133.

KUHN, ALFRED (1974) *The Logic of Social Systems.* San Francisco: Jossey-Bass Publishers.

KUHN, MANFORD H. (1964) "Major Trends in Symbolic Interaction Theory in the Past Twenty-five Years." *Sociological Quarterly,* 5: 61–84.

KUHN, THOMAS S. (1974) "Second Thoughts on Paradigms," in Frederick Suppe, ed. *The Structure of Scientific Theories.* Urbana: University of Illinois Press, pp. 459–482. (Critical discussion pp. 500–517.)

——— (1970) *The Structure of Scientific Revolutions.* 2nd ed. Chicago: University of Chicago Press.

LAKATOS, IMRE, and ALAN MUSGRAVE, eds. (1970) *Criticism and the Growth of Knowledge.* New York: Cambridge University Press.

——— (1968) *Problems in the Philosophy of Science.* Amsterdam: North-Holland Publishing Company.

LANGE, DAVID L., ROBERT K. BAKER, and SANDRA J. BALL (1969) *Mass Media and Violence.* Vol. XI. Washington, D.C.: U.S. Government Printing Office.

LARSON, CHARLES U. (1971) "The Verbal Responses of Groups to the Absence or Presence of Leadership." *Speech Monographs,* 36: 452–455.

———, and ROBERT SANDERS (1977) "Faith, Mystery, and Data: An Analysis of 'Scientific' Studies of Persuasion." *Quarterly Journal of Speech,* 61: 178–194.

LASZLO, ERVIN (1972a) *Introduction to Systems Philosophy: Toward a New Paradigm of Contemporary Thought.* New York: Gordon and Breach, Science Publishers, Inc.

———, ed. (1972b) *The Relevance of General Systems Theory.* New York: George Braziller, Inc.

LAZARSFELD, PAUL F., BERNARD BEBELSON, and HAZEL GAUDET (1948) *The People's Choice.* New York: Columbia University Press.

LEATHERS, DALE G. (1971) "The Feedback Rating Instrument: A New Means of Evaluating Discussion." *Central States Speech Journal,* 22: 33–38.

LEAVITT, CLARK (1975) "Advertising, Marketing Communication, and Consumer Choice," in Gerhard J. Hanneman and William J. McEwen, eds. *Communication and Behavior.* Reading, Mass.: Addison-Wesley Publishing Co., Inc., pp. 285–303.

LEAVITT, HAROLD J., and RONALD A. H. MUELLER (1951) "Some Effects of Feedback on Communication." *Human Relations,* 4: 401–410.

LEWIN, KURT (1951) *Field Theory in Social Science.* New York: Harper and Row, Publishers.

LIKLIDER, J. C. E. (1973) "Communication and Computers," in George A. Miller, ed. *Communication, Language, and Meaning: Psychological Perspectives.* New York: Basic Books, pp. 196–207.

LINDZEY, GARDNER, and ELLIOTT ARONSON, eds. (1968) *The Handbook of Social Psychology*, 2nd ed., Vols. I–V. Reading, Mass.: Addison-Wesley Publishing Co., Inc.

LOFLAND, JOHN (1971) *Analyzing Social Settings: A Guide to Qualitative Observation and Analysis*. Belmont: Cal.: Wadsworth Publishing Co., Inc.

LOGAN, CHERYL A. (Undated) "The Kuhnian Notion of Shared Exemplars: Implications for Standardization in Psychology." Unpublished manuscript (mimeo).

MABRY, EDWARD A. (1975) "Exploratory Analysis of a Developmental Model for Task-Oriented Small Groups." *Human Communication Research*, **2:** 66–73.

MACCOBY, ELEANOR, NATHAN MACCOBY, A. ROMNEY, and J. ADAMS (1961) "Social Reinforcement in Attitude Change." *Journal of Abnormal and Social Psychology*, **63:** 109–115.

MACCOBY, ELEANOR, THEODORE M. NEWCOMB, and EUGENE L. HARTLEY, eds. (1958) *Readings in Social Psychology*. 3rd ed. New York: Holt, Rinehart and Winston, Publishers.

MACHLUP, FRITZ (1961) "Are The Social Sciences Really Inferior?" *Southern Economic Journal*, **27:** 173–184.

MACKAY, DONALD M. (1969) *Information, Mechanism and Meaning*. Cambridge, Mass.: M.I.T. Press.

MACLEAN, MALCOLM S., JR. (1969) "Communication Research: The Tie that Binds—But Loosely," in Robert J. Kibler and Larry L. Barker, eds. *Conceptual Frontiers in Speech Communication*. New York: Speech Association of America, pp. 204–206.

MALCOLM, NORMAN (1968) "The Conceivability of Mechanism." *The Philosophical Review*, **77:** 45–72.

MANDELBAUM, MAURICE (1957) "Societal Laws," *British Journal for the Philosophy of Science*, **8:** 211–224.

MANIS, JEROME G., and BERNARD N. MELTZER, eds. (1972) *Symbolic Interaction*, 2nd ed. Boston: Allyn & Bacon, Inc.

MARCEL, GABRIEL (1960) *The Mystery of Being*, Vol. I. Chicago: Henry Regnery Company.

MARK, ROBERT A. (1971) "Coding Communication at the Relationship Level." *Journal of Communication*, **21:** 221–232.

MARLER, P. (1961) "The Logical Analysis of Animal Communication." *Journal of Theoretical Biology*, **1:** 296–317.

MASTERMAN, MARGARET (1970) "The Nature of a Paradigm," in Lakatos, Imre, and Alan Musgrave, eds. *Criticism and the Growth of Knowledge*. New York: Cambridge University Press, pp. 59–90.

MATSON, FLOYD W., and ASHLEY MONTAGU, eds. (1967) *The Human Dialogue: Perspective on Communication*. New York: The Free Press.

MATARAZZO, J., M. WEITMAN, G. SASLOW, and A. WIENS (1963) "Interviewer Influence on Durations of Interviewee Speech." *Journal of Verbal Learning and Verbal Behavior*, **1:** 451–458.

MAXWELL, GROVER (1968) "Scientific Methodology and the Causal Theory of

Perception," in Imre Lakatos and Alan Musgrave, eds. *Problems in the Philosophy of Science.* Amsterdam: North-Holland Publishing Company, pp. 148–160.

McCROSKEY, JAMES C. (1969) "A Summary of Experimental Research on the Effects of Evidence in Persuasive Communication." *Quarterly Journal of Speech,* **55:** 169–176.

———, JOHN A. DALY, VIRGINIA P. RICHMOND, and BARBARA G. COX (1975) "The Effects of Communication Apprehension on Interpersonal Attraction." *Human Communication Research,* **2:** 51–65.

McDAVID, J. W., JR., and F. SISTRUNK (1957) "The Interpretation of Approval and Disapproval by Delinquent and Non-delinquent Adolescents." *Journal of Personality,* **25:** 420–435.

McGILL, WILLIAM J., and HENRY QUASTLER (1955) "Standardized Nomenclature: An Attempt," in Henry Quastler, ed. *Information Theory in Psychology.* New York: The Free Press, pp. 83–92.

McGUIRE, WILLIAM J. (1969) "The Nature of Attitudes and Attitude Change," in Gardner Lindzey and Elliot Aronson, eds. *Handbook of Social Psychology,* 2nd ed., Vol. III. Reading, Mass.: Addison-Wesley Publishing Co., Inc., pp. 163–314.

——— (1973) "The Yin and Yang of Progress in Social Psychology: "Seven Koan." *Journal of Personality and Social Psychology,* **26:** 446–456.

McHUGH, PETER (1968) *Defining the Situation: The Organization of Meaning in Social Interaction.* Indianapolis: The Bobbs-Merrill Co., Inc.

McLUHAN, MARSHALL (1964) *Understanding Media: The Extensions of Man.* New York: McGraw-Hill Book Company.

——— (1962) *The Gutenberg Galaxy: The Making of Typographic Man.* Toronto: University of Toronto Press.

MEAD, GEORGE HERBERT (1934) *Mind, Self and Society.* Chicago: University of Chicago Press.

——— (1922) "A Behavioristic Account of the Significant Symbol." *Journal of Philosophy,* **19:** 157–163.

——— (1913) "The Social Self." *Journal of Philosophy, Psychology and Scientific Methods,* **10:** 374–380.

MEEHAN, EUGENE J. (1969) *Value Judgment and Social Science: Structures and Processes.* Homewood, Ill.: Dorsey Press.

——— (1968) *Explanation in Social Science: A System Paradigm.* Homewood, Ill.: Dorsey Press.

MEERLOO, JOOST A. M. (1952) *Conversation and Communication.* New York: International Universities Press.

MELTZER, Bernard N. (1972) "Mead's Social Psychology," in Jerome G. Manis and Bernard N. Meltzer, eds. *Symbolic Interaction,* 2nd ed. Boston: Allyn & Bacon, Inc., pp. 4–22.

———, and JOHN W. PETRAS (1970) "The Chicago and Iowa Schools of Symbolic Interactionism," in Tamotsu Shibutani, ed. *Human Nature and Collective Behavior:* Englewood Cliffs, N.J.: Prentice-Hall, Inc., 3–17.

MELTZER, BERNARD N., et al. (1975) *Symbolic Interactionism.* London: Rout-ledge and Kegan Paul.

MERTON, ROBERT K. (1957) *Social Theory and Social Structure.* New York: The Free Press.

MESAROVIC, M. D. (1972) "Toward a General Theory for the Behavioral Sciences," in George J. Klir, ed. *Trends in General Systems Theory.* New York: John Wiley & Sons, Inc., pp. 251–269.

MILLAR, FRANK E., and L. EDNA ROGERS (1976) "A Relational Approach to Interpersonal Communication," in Gerald R. Miller, ed. *Explorations in Interpersonal Communication.* Beverly Hills, Calif.: Sage Publications, pp. 87–104.

MILLER, GEORGE A. (1973) "Psychology and Communication," in George A. Miller, ed. *Communication, Language, and Meaning.* New York: Basic Books, pp. 3–12.

———, ed. (1973) *Communication, Language, and Meaning: Psychological Perspectives.* New York: Basic Books.

——— (1967) *The Psychology of Communication: Seven Essays.* New York: Basic Books.

——— (1951) *Language and Communication.* New York: McGraw-Hill Book Company.

———, EUGENE GALANTER, and KARL H. PRIBRAM (1960) *Plans and the Structure of Behavior.* New York: Holt, Rinehart and Winston, Publishers.

MILLER, GERALD R. (1975) "Humanistic and Scientific Approaches to Speech Communication Inquiry: Rivalry, Redundancy, or Rapprochement." *Western Speech*, **39**: 230–239.

——— (1972) *An Introduction to Speech Communication.* 2nd ed. Indi-anapolis: The Bobbs-Merrill Co., Inc.

——— (1969) "Some Factors Influencing Judgments of the Logical Validity of Arguments: A Research Review." *Quarterly Journal of Speech,* **55**: 276–286.

——— (1963) "Studies on the Use of Fear Appeals: A Summary and Analy-sis." *Central States Speech Journal,* **14**: 117–125.

———, H. ZAVOS, and J. W. VLANDIS (1961) "The Effect of Differential Re-ward on Speech Patterns." *Speech Monographs,* **28**: 9–15.

MILLER, JAMES G. (1965) "Living Systems: Basic Concepts." *Behavioral Science,* **10**: 193–237.

——— (1965) "Living Systems: Structure and Process." *Behavioral Science,* **10**: 337–379.

——— (1965) "Living Systems: Cross-Level Hypotheses." *Behavioral Science,* **10**: 380–411.

MISCHEL, THEODORE, ed. (1974) *Understanding Other Persons.* Totowa, N.J.: Rowan and Littlefield.

——— (1969) "Epilogue," in Theodore Mischel, ed. *Human Action: Con-ceptual and Empirical Issues.* New York: Academic Press, Inc., pp. 261–277.

—— (1969) "Scientific and Philosophical Psychology: A Historical Introduction," in Theodore Mischel, ed. *Human Action: Conceptual and Empirical Issues*. New York: Academic Press, Inc., pp. 1–40.

—— (1969) *Human Action: Conceptual and Empirical Issues*. New York: Academic Press.

MONGE, PETER R. (1975) "Alternative Theoretical Bases for the Study of Human Communication: The Systems Perspective." A paper presented to Speech Communication Association, Houston.

MORGENBESSER, SIDNEY (1967) "Psychologism and Methodological Individualism," in Sidney Morgenbesser, ed. *Philosophy of Science Today*. New York: Basic Books, pp. 160–174.

——, ed. (1967) *Philosophy of Science Today*. New York: Basic Books.

MORRIS, CHARLES (1946) *Signs, Language and Behavior*. Englewood Cliffs, N.J.: Prentice-Hall, Inc.

MORRIS, C., and J. HACKMAN (1969) "Behavioral Correlates of Perceived Leadership." *Journal of Personality and Social Psychology*, **13**: 350–361.

MORTENSEN, C. DAVID (1972) *Communication: The Study of Human Interaction*. New York: McGraw-Hill Book Company.

MOWRER, O. H. (1954) "Ego Psychology, Cybernetics, and Learning Theory," in Donald K. Adams, et al., eds. *Learning Theory and Clinical Research*. New York: John Wiley & Sons, Inc., pp. 81–90.

MULAC, ANTHONY (1974) "Effects of Three Feedback Conditions Employing Videotape and Audiotape on Acquired Speech Skill." *Speech Monographs*, **41**: 205–214.

NAESS, ARNE (1975) "Why Not Science for Anarchists too? A Reply to Feyerabend." *Inquiry*, **18**: 183–194.

NAGEL, ERNEST (1967) "The Nature and Aim of Science," in Sidney Morgenbesser, ed., *Philosophy of Science Today*. New York: Basic Books, pp. 3–13.

—— (1961) *The Structure of Science*. New York: Harcourt Brace Jovanovich, Inc.

—— (1953) "On the Method of *Verstehen* as the Sole Method of Philosophy," *Journal of Philosophy*. **50**: 154–157.

——, PATRICK SUPPES, and ALFRED TARSKI, eds. (1962) *Logic, Methodology, and the Philosophy of Science*. Amsterdam: North-Holland Publishing Co.

NATANSON, MAURICE, ed. (1963) *Philosophy of the Social Sciences: A Reader*. New York: Random House, Inc.

NEURATH, OTTO, ed. (1955) *International Encyclopedia of United Science*. Chicago: University of Chicago Press.

NEWCOMB, THEODORE M. (1953) "An Approach to the Study of Communicative Acts." *Psychological Review*, **60**: 393–404.

—— (1948) "Autistic Hostility and Social Reality." *Human Relations*, **1**: 69–86.

NEWMAN, EDWIN, B. (1948) "Hearing." in Edwin G. Boring, Herbert S. Langfeld, and Harry A. Weld, eds. *Foundations of Psychology*. New York: John Wiley & Sons, Inc., pp. 313–350.

NILSEN, THOMAS R., ed. (1968) *Essays on Rhetorical Criticism*. New York: Random House, Inc.

NOKES, P. (1961) "Feedback as an Explanatory Device in the Study of Certain Interpersonal and Institutional Processes." *Human Relations*, 14: 381–387.

NWANKWO, ROBERT L. (1973) "Communication as Symbolic Interaction: A Synthesis." *Journal of Communication*, 23: 195–216.

O'KEEFE, DANIEL J. (1975) "Logical Empiricism and the Study of Human Communication." *Speech Monographs*, 42: 169–183.

ORCHARD, ROBERT A. (1972) "On an Approach to General Systems Theory," in George J. Klir, ed. *Trends in General Systems Theory*. New York: Wiley-Interscience, pp. 205–250.

ORNSTEIN, ROBERT E. (1969) *On the Experience of Time*. Baltimore: Penguin Books, Inc.

OWEN, JAMES L., PAUL A. PAGE, and GORDON I. ZIMMERMAN, eds. (1976) *Communication in Organizations*. San Francisco: West Publishing Co.

OZBEKHAN, HAZAN (1971) "Planning and Human Action," in Paul A. Weiss, ed. *Hierarchically Organized Systems in Theory and Practice*. New York: Hafner Publishing Co., Inc., pp. 123–230.

PATTEE, HOWARD H., ed. (1973) *Hierarchy Theory: The Challenge of Complex Systems*. New York: George Braziller, Inc.

PEARCE, W. BARNETT (1973) "Consensual Rules in Interpersonal Communication: A Reply to Cushman and Whiting." *Journal of Communication*, 23: 160–168.

PENDELL, SUE DAVIS (1976) "The Influence of Room Design on Small Group Communication." Ph.D. dissertation, University of Utah.

PEPINSKY, HAROLD B., ed. (1970) *People and Information*. New York: Pergamon Press, Inc.

PHILLIPS, GERALD M. (1968) "Reticence: Pathology of the Normal Speaker." *Speech Monographs*, 35: 39–49.

———, and NANCY J. METZGER (1976) *Intimate Communication*. Boston: Allyn and Bacon, Inc.

PLATT, J. R. (1964) "Strong Inference." *Science*, 145: 347–352.

POPPER, KARL R. (1968) "Remarks on the Problems of Demarcation of Rationality," in Imre Lakatos and Alan Musgrave, eds., *Problems in the Philosophy of Science*. Amsterdam: North-Holland Publishing Company, pp. 88–102.

——— (1959) *The Logic of Scientific Discovery*. New York: Basic Books.

PRINGLE, J. W. S. (1951) "On the Parallel between Learning and Evolution." *Behaviour*, 3: 174–215.

PUTMAN, HILARY (1962) "What Theories Are Not," in Ernest Nagel, Patrick Suppes, and Alfred Tarski, eds. *Logic Methodology, and the Philosophy of Science*. Amsterdam: North-Holland Publishing Co., pp. 240–251.

QUASTLER, HENRY, ed. (1955) *Information Theory in Psychology*. New York: The Free Press.

QUINE, W. V. O. (1953) *From a Logical Point of View*. Cambridge, Mass.: Harvard University Press.

RAPOPORT, ANATOL (1968) "Foreword," in Walter Buckley, ed. *Modern Systems Research for the Behavioral Scientist.* Chicago: Aldine Publishing Company, pp. viii–xxii.

――――― (1958) "Various Meanings of 'Theory.'" *American Political Science Review.* **52:** 972–988.

RAUSH, HAROLD L. (1972) "Process and Change—A Markov Model for Interaction." *Family Process.* **11:** 275–298.

REDDING, W. CHARLES (1972) *Communication Within the Organization.* New York: Industrial Communication Council.

ROGERS, STEVEN C., and KENNETH D. FRANDSEN (1975) "Some Effects of Instruction in Feedback Utilization on the Fluency of College Students' Speech." *Speech Monographs.* **42:** 83–89.

RICHARDS, I. A. (1936) *The Philosophy of Rhetoric.* New York: Oxford University Press.

ROBSON, R. A. H. (1968) "The Present State of Theory in Sociology," in Imre Lakatos and Alan Musgrave, eds. *Problems in the Philosophy of Science.* Amsterdam: North-Holland Publishing Company, pp. 349–370.

ROGERS, EVERETT M., and DILIP K. BHOWMIK (1971) "Homophily-Heterophily Relational Concepts for Communication Research." *Public Opinion Quarterly.* **34:** 523–538.

ROGERS, EVERETT M., and F. FLOYD SHOEMAKER (1971) *Communication of Innovations.* New York: The Free Press.

ROGERS, L. EDNA, and RICHARD V. FARACE (1975) "Analysis of Relational Communication in Dyads." *Human Communication Research,* **1:** 222–239.

ROSEN, ROBERT (1972) "Some Systems Theoretical Problems in Biology," in Ervin Laszlo, ed. *The Relevance of General Systems Theory.* New York: George Braziller Inc., pp. 45–66.

ROSENTHAL, PAUL I. (1972) "The Concept of the Paramessage in Persuasive Communication." *Quarterly Journal of Speech,* **58:** 15–30.

ROTHSTEIN, JEROME (1958) *Communication, Organization, and Science.* Indian Hills, Col.: Falcon's Wing Press.

RUBEN, BRENT D., and JOHN Y. KIM, eds. (1975) *General Systems Theory and Human Communication.* New York: Hayden Publishing Co., Inc.

RUBENSTEIN, HERBERT (1973) "Some Problems of Meaning in Natural Languages," in Ithiel de Sola Pool, et al., eds. *Handbook of Communication.* Chicago: Rand McNally & Company, pp. 27–48.

RUDNER, RICHARD (1966) *Philosophy of Social Science.* Englewood Cliffs, N.J.: Prentice-Hall, Inc.

――――― (1953) "The Scientist Qua Scientist Makes Value Judgments." *Philosophy of Science,* **20:** 1–6.

RUESCH, JURGEN (1963) "The Role of Communication in Therapeutic Transactions." *Journal of Communication,* **13:** 132–139.

―――――, and GREGORY BATESON (1968) *Communication: The Social Matrix of Psychiatry.* New York: W. W. Norton & Company, Inc.

RYAN, ALAN, ed. (1973) *The Philosophy of Social Explanation.* London: Oxford University Press.

RYLE, GILBERT (1956) *Dilemmas*. New York: Cambridge University Press.

SARBIN, THEODORE R., and VERNON L. ALLEN (1968) "Role Theory," in Gardner Lindzey and Elliot Aronson, eds. *Handbook of Social Psychology*, 2nd ed., Vol. I. Reading, Mass.: Addison-Wesley Publising Co., Inc., pp. 488–567.

SCHACHTER, STANLEY (1951) "Deviation, Rejection, and Communication." *Journal of Abnormal and Social Psychology*, **46**: 190–207.

SCHEFLEN, ALBERT E. (1974) *How Behavior Means*. Garden City, N.Y.: Doubleday & Company, Inc.

——— (1969) "Behavioral Programs in Human Communication," in William Gray, Frederick J. Duhl, and Nicholas D. Rizzo, eds. *General Systems Theory and Psychiatry*. Boston: Little, Brown and Company, pp. 209–228.

——— (1965) "Quasi-Courtship Behavior in Psychotherapy." *Psychiatry*, **28**: 245–255.

——— (1965) *Stream and Structure of Communicational Behavior. Context Analysis of a Psychotherapy Session*. Philadelphia: Eastern Pennsylvania Psychiatric Institute.

SCHEIDEL, THOMAS M., and LAURA CROWELL (1964) "Idea Development in Small Discussion Groups." *Quarterly Journal of Speech*, **50**: 140–145.

——— (1966) "Feedback in Small Group Communication." *Quarterly Journal of Speech*, **52**: 273–278.

SCHEIN, EDGAR H. (1969) *Process Consultation: Its Role in Organization Development*. Reading, Mass.: Addison-Wesley Publishing Co., Inc.

SCHILPP, P., ed. (1963) *The Philosophy of Rudolf Carnap*. LaSalle, Ill.: Open Court.

SCHRAMM, WILBUR, ed. (1963) *The Science of Human Communication*. New York: Basic Books.

SCHUTZ, ALFRED (1962) *Collected Papers I: The Problem of Social Reality*, ed. by Maurice Natanson. The Hague: Martinus Nihjoff, pp. 48–66.

SCOTT, W. (1957) "Attitude Change Through Reward of Verbal Behavior." *Journal of Abnormal and Social Psychology*, **55**: 72–75.

SCRIVEN, MICHAEL (1963) "The Temporal Asymmetry Between Explanations and Predictions," in B. Baumann, ed. *Philosophy of Science: The Delaware Seminar*. Vol. I. New York: John Wiley & Sons, Inc., pp. 97–105.

——— (1962) "Explanations, Predictions, and Laws," in Herbert Feigl and Grover Maxwell, eds. *Minnesota Studies in the Philosophy of Science*. Vol. III. Minneapolis: University of Minnesota Press, pp. 170–230.

——— (1959) "Explanation and Prediction in Evolutionary Theory." *Science*, **130**: 477–582.

——— (1956) "A Study of Radical Behaviorism," in Herbert Feigl and Michael Scriven, eds. *Minnesota Studies in the Philosophy of Science*, Vol. I. Minneapolis: University of Minnesota Press, pp. 105–130.

SEIBOLD, DAVID R. (1975) "Communication Research and the Attitude-Verbal Report-Overt Behavior Relationship: A Critique and Theoretic Reformulation." *Human Communication. Research*, **2**: 3–32.

SHANDS, HARLEY C. (1967) "Outline of a General Theory of Human Communication: Implications of Normal and Pathological Schizmogenesis," in Lee Thayer, ed. *Communication: Concepts and Perspectives*. Washington, D.C.: Spartan, pp. 97–131.

SHANNON, CLAUDE, and WARREN WEAVER (1949) *The Mathematical Theory of Communication*. Urbana: University of Illinois Press.

SHAPERE, DUDLEY (1974) "Scientific Theories and Their Domains," in Frederick Suppe, ed. *The Structure of Scientific Theories*. Urbana: University of Illinois Press, pp. 518–570.

SHAPIRO, D. (1964) "Group Learning of Speech Sequences Without Awareness." *Science*, **144**: 74–76.

SHERIF, CAROLYN W., and MUZAFER SHERIF (1967) *Attitude, Ego-Involvement, and Change*. New York: John Wiley & Sons, Inc.

———, and ROGER E. NEBERGALL (1965) *Attitude and Attitude Change*. Philadelphia: W. B. Saunders Company.

SHERIF, MUZAFER, and CARL I. HOVLAND (1961) *Social Judgment: Assimilation and Contrast Effects and Attitude Change*. New Haven, Conn.: Yale University Press.

SHIBUTANI, TAMOTSU (1970) *Human Nature and Collective Behavior*. Englewood Cliffs, N.J.: Prentice-Hall, Inc.

SKINNER, B. F. (1957) *Verbal Behavior*. New York: Appleton-Century-Crofts.

——— (1953) *Science and Human Behavior*. New York: Macmillan Publishing Co., Inc.

SLUZKI, CARLOS E., and JANET BEAVIN (1965) "Simetria y Complementaridad: Una Definicion Operacional y una Tipologia de Parejas." *Acta Psiquiatrica y Psicologica de America Latina*, **11**: 321–330.

SMART, HAROLD R. (1931) *The Logic of Science*. New York: Appleton-Century-Crofts.

SMART, J. J. C. (1968) *Between Science and Philosophy*. New York: Random House, Inc.

——— (1963) *Philosophy and Scientific Realism*. London: Routledge and Kegan Paul.

SMITH, DAVID H. (1972) "Communication Research and the Idea of Process." *Speech Monographs*, **39**: 174–182.

SMITH, DENNIS R. (1973) "Mechanical and Systemic Concepts of Feedback." *Today's Speech*, **21**: 23–28.

——— (1970) "The Fallacy of the Communication Breakdown." *Quarterly Journal of Speech*, **16**: 343–346.

SMITH, RAYMOND G. (1964) "Motivation and Communication Theory." *Central States Speech Journal*, **15**: 96–99.

SOMMER, ROBERT (1969) *Personal Space: The Behavioral Basis of Design*. Englewood Cliffs, N.J.: Prentice-Hall, Inc.

SPIELBERGER, C. D. (1965) "Theoretical and Epistemological Issues in Verbal Conditioning," in S. Rosenberg, ed. *Directions in Psycholinguistics*. New York: Macmillan Publishing Co., Inc., pp. 149–200.

STECH, ERNEST L. (1975) "A Sequential Structure in Human Social Communication." *Human Communication Research*, **1**: 168–179.

———— (1970) "An Analysis of Interaction Structure in the Discussion of a Ranking Task." *Speech Monographs*, **37**: 248–263.

STEIN, HERMAN D. (1968) *Social Theory and Social Invention*. Cleveland: Case Western Reserve University Press.

STEWART, JOHN, ed. (1973) *Bridges Not Walls*. Reading, Mass.: Addison-Wesley Publishing Co., Inc.

STOLZ, W., and PERCY H. TANNENBAUM (1963) "Effects of Feedback on Oral Encoding Behaviour." *Language and Speech*, **6**: 218–228.

STONE, VERNON A., and JAMES L. HOYT (1974) "The Emergence of Source-Message Orientation as a Communication Variable." *Communication Research*, **1**: 89–109.

SUPPE, FREDERICK, ed. (1974) *The Structure of Scientific Theories*. Urbana: University of Illinois Press.

SUPPES, PATRICK (1967) "What Is a Scientific Theory?" in Sidney Morgenbesser, ed., *Philosophy of Science Today*. New York: Basic Books, pp. 55–67.

SUSSMAN, LYLE (1975) "Communication in Organizational Hierarchies: The Fallacy of Perceptual Congruence." *Western Speech Communication*, **39**: 191–199.

SUTHERLAND, JOHN W. (1973) *A General Systems Philosophy for the Social and Behavioral Sciences*. New York: George Braziller, Inc.

TAYLOR, CHARLES (1970) "The Explanation of Purposive Behaviour," in Robert Borger and Frank Cioffi, eds., *Explanation in the Behavioural Sciences*. New York: Cambridge University Press, pp. 49–95 (including Comment by Robert Borger, pp. 80–88, and Reply by Taylor, pp. 89–95).

TAYLOR, DALMAS A., and IRWIN ALTMAN (1966) *Intimacy Scaled Stimuli for Use in Studies of Interpersonal Relationships*. Bethesda, Md.: Naval Medical Research Institute.

Television and Growing Up: The Impact of Televised Violence. (1972) Report to the Surgeon General. U.S. Department of Health, Education and Welfare (#HSM 72–9090).

THAYER, LEE, ed. (1968) *Communication and Communication Systems*. Homewood, Ill.: Richard D. Irwin, Inc.

———— (1967) *Communication: Concepts and Perspectives*. Washington, D.C.: Spartan Books, Inc.

THIBAUT, JAMES W., and HAROLD H. KELLEY (1959) *A Social Psychology of Small Groups*. New York: John Wiley & Sons, Inc.

THORNTON, BARBARA C. (1976) "Communication and Health Care Teams: A Multimethodological Approach." Ph.D. dissertation, University of Utah.

TOULMIN, STEPHEN (1974) "Rules and Their Relevance for Understanding Human Behavior," in Theodore Mischel, ed. *Understanding Other Persons*. Totowa, N.J.: Rowan and Littlefield, pp. 185–215.

———— (1970) "Reasons and Causes," in Robert Borger and Frank Cioffi, eds, *Explanation in the Behavioural Sciences*. New York: Cambridge University Press, pp. 1–48 (including comment by R. S. Peters, pp. 27–41, and Reply by Toulmin, pp. 42–48).

———— (1969) "Concepts and the Explanation of Human Behavior," in Theodore Mischel, ed., *Human Action: Conceptual and Empirical Issues.* New York: Academic Press, Inc., pp. 71–104.

———— (1953) *The Philosophy of Science.* London: Hutchinson & Co., Ltd.

UPTON, ALBERT (1967) "Communication and the Problem-Solving Process," in Lee Thayer, ed. *Communication: Concepts and Perspectives.* Washington, D.C.: Spartan, pp. 373–391.

———— (1961) *Design for Thinking.* Stanford, Cal.: Stanford University Press.

VERPLANCK, W. (1955) "The Control of the Content of Conversation: Reinforcement of Statements of Opinion." *Journal of Abnormal and Social Psychology,* **51**: 668–678.

VILLARD, KENNETH L., and LELAND J. WHIPPLE (1976) *Beginnings in Relational Communication.* New York: John Wiley & Sons, Inc.

VLANDIS, J. (1964) "Variation in the Verbal Behavior of a Speaker as the Function of Varied Reinforcing Conditions." *Speech Monographs,* **31**: 116–119.

WATKINS, J. W. N. (1957) "Historical Explanation in the Social Sciences." *British Journal for the Philosophy of Sciences,* **8**: 104–117.

WATZLAWICK, PAUL, JANET H. BEAVIN, and DON D. JACKSON (1967) *Pragmatics of Human Communication.* New York: W. W. Norton & Company, Inc.

WEAVER, RICHARD (1953) *The Ethics of Rhetoric.* Chicago: Henry Regnery Company.

WEBER, MAX (1949) *The Methodology of the Social Sciences.* New York: The Free Press.

WEICK, KARL E. (1970) "The Twigging of Overload," in Harold B. Pepinsky, ed. *People and Information.* New York: Pergamon Press, Inc., pp. 67–129.

———— (1969) *The Social Psychology of Organizing.* Reading, Mass.: Addison-Wesley Publishing Co., Inc.

WEISS, PAUL A. (1971) *Hierarchically Organized Systems in Theory and Practice.* New York: Hafner Publishing Co.

WEISS, R. (1966) "Some Determinants of Emitted Reinforcement Behavior: Listener Reinforcement and Birth Order." *Journal of Personality and Social Psychology,* **3**: 489–492.

WERBEL, WAYNE S., DONALD G. ELLIS, and B. AUBREY FISHER (1974) "A Comparative Morphology of Groups: A Systems Perspective." A paper presented to International Communication Association, New Orleans.

WESTLEY, BRUCE H. (1973) "Darnell Reconceptualized." *Journal of Communication,* **23**: 187–194.

————, and MALCOLM S. MACLEAN, JR. (1957) "A Conceptual Model for Communications Research." *Journalism Quarterly,* **34**: 31–38.

WHITEHEAD, ALFRED NORTH (1929) *Process Reality.* New York: Macmillan Publishing Co., Inc.

WICKER, A. (1969) "Attitudes Vs. Actions: The Relationship of Verbal and Overt Behavioral Responses to Attitude Objects." *Journal of Social Issues,* **25**: 41–78.

WIENER, NORBET (1954) *The Human Use of Human Beings: Cybernetics and Society*. Boston: Houghton Mifflin Company.

WILLIAMS, KENNETH R. (1973) "Reflections on a Human Science of Communication." *Journal of Communication*, 23: 239–250.

WILMOT, WILLIAM R., and JOHN R. WENBURG, eds. (1974) *Communication Involvement: Personal Perspectives*. New York: John Wiley & Sons, Inc.

WINCH, PETER (1950) *The Ideal of a Social Science and Its Relation to Philosophy*. London: Routledge and Kegan Paul.

WISDOM, J. O. (1968) "Anti-Dualist Outlook and Social Enquiry," in Imre Lakatos and Alan Musgrave, eds. *Problems in the Philosophy of Science*. Amsterdam: North-Holland Publishing Company, pp. 433–439.

WYMORE, A. W. (1972) "A Wattled Theory of Systems," in George J. Klir, ed. *Trends in General Systems Theory*. New York: Wiley-Interscience, pp. 270–300.

ZADEH, L. A. and E. POLAK (1969) *System Theory*. New York: McGraw-Hill Book Company.

ZNANIECKI, FLORIAN (1934) *The Method of Sociology*. New York: Farrar, Straus & Giroux, Inc.

Index

351